TROPICAL FAMILY VACATIONS

Also by Laura Sutherland

Great Caribbean Family Vacations
The Best Family Ski Vacations in North America

By Laura Sutherland and Valerie Wolf Deutsch

Innocents Abroad: Traveling with Kids in Europe
The Best Bargain Family Vacations in the U.S.A.

TROPICAL FAMILY VACATIONS

Laura Sutherland

St. Martin's Griffin
New York

All information included in this book was accurate at press time. However prices, accommodations, and schedules change over time and smart travelers should always verify information before making final plans.

TROPICAL FAMILY VACATIONS. Copyright © 1999 by Laura Sutherland. All rights reserved. Printed in the United States of America. No part of this book may be used or reproduced in any manner whatsoever without written permission except in the case of brief quotations embodied in critical articles or reviews. For information, address St. Martin's Press, 175 Fifth Avenue, New York, N.Y. 10010.

Library of Congress Cataloging-in-Publication Data

Sutherland, Laura.
     Tropical family vacations : in the Caribbean, Hawaii, South Florida, and Mexico / Laura Sutherland.
        p.   cm.
    ISBN 0-312-20451-5
    1. Caribbean Area Guidebooks. 2. Hawaii Guidebooks. 3. Florida Guidebooks. 4. Mexico Guidebooks. 5. Family recreation Guidebooks.
6. Children—Travel Guidebooks. I. Title.
F2165.S96   1999
910'.9113—dc21   99-32894
                                     CIP

Book design by Casey Hampton

10 9 8 7 6 5 4 3 2

To Lance, Madeleine, and Walker

CONTENTS

TROPICAL FAMILY VACATIONS

1.

Planning the TRIP

All I have to do is envision myself on a sugary white-sand beach lapped by translucent aquamarine waters and my heart rate slows and I feel like I've spent a couple of weeks at a yoga retreat. And once I'm actually on that beach, stretched out atop the sand in a lounge chair and resting in the sun, I reach a state of transcendental bliss that is . . . that is . . . that is quickly interrupted by my children as they run shouting up the beach, clamoring for my attention. Yet what might have been a petty irritation at home doesn't even begin to register when I'm on vacation in a warm spot with sun, sea, and sand.

There's nothing like the beach to keep all members of the family deliriously happy on vacation. Children can play uninhibited and run, splash, and scream without anyone trying to quiet or control them. The luxurious radiance of the tropical sun and the invigorating balmy saltwater refresh and renew even the most exhausted parent. Coral reefs close to shore teem with sea life and the entire family can go nose to nose with the creatures of the underwater world simply by donning mask, fins, and snorkel. As kids get older, windsurfing, sailing, and scuba diving challenge the most active of children. A tropical vacation is a place where fantasy and reality can meet, if you plan it right.

As you browse through the suggestions in this book, your family's ages, tastes, and personalities will help direct you to the right vacation choice. Linking all of the listings is the beach, but beyond that common bond you'll find great variety, from exclusive private hideaways to enormous palaces of nonstop action, along with simple and affordable beachfront rooms where you create your own fun in the sun.

There are glorious tropical retreats all over the globe—throughout Asia, the South Pacific, South America, and beyond. This book, however, covers those areas that are the most popular, convenient, and easy to get to for North American families: Hawaii, the Caribbean Islands, southern Florida, and Mexico.

WHEN TO GO

Families, more than any other group, travel to warm-weather destinations year-round. While winter has traditionally been the busiest season in the tropics, when people by the thousands head south to escape the snow and ice of home, families with school-age children often head south in the summer. Excellent bargains are available in summer months as many hotels and resorts offer low-priced packages and special programs to lure parents and kids to their properties. While summers can be hotter, especially the farther south you go, keep in mind that the islands of the Caribbean and Hawaii enjoy trade wind breezes that make their temperatures comfortable year-round.

The winter season, called the high season in the tourism industry (usually December 15 to early April), is the busiest time of year for tropical destinations. Hotels and resorts charge 25 to 50 percent more during this time, and reservations, especially over holiday periods, become harder to obtain. Many resorts add special family programs during the winter holiday and spring break, when the numbers of younger guests increase.

Fall and late spring, often referred to as shoulder season, can be delightfully quiet, with attractive prices and balmy weather. Late summer and fall is hurricane season in the Caribbean, Florida, and Mexico. If you find yourself traveling during this time, remember that sophisticated weather reports will keep you informed of developing storms and you can leave an area well before a hurricane threatens.

ON A BUDGET

Vacations create memories that our families savor for a lifetime: don't let money stop you from enjoying a tropical family paradise. Some clever planning and thoughtful shopping can buy you a vacation where you spend just a little but get a lot in return.

Saving on Transportation and Lodging

Be flexible: If your travel dates can be flexible, you may be able to pick up inexpensive tickets during airline airfare wars. Expedia.com offers e-mail updates of the latest bargain airfares.

Travel off-season: Most of the year—April through mid-December—is considered off-season for tropical destinations. Watch for special deals during this time, particularly in April, May, and October through early December, when prices drop even lower than their already discounted summer rates.

Do your research: The internet has an overwhelming amount of travel information; use it wisely and it can be a very helpful tool. Many sites advertise special deals at resorts with sunny weather and sandy beaches. A few, such as Travelocity.com and Fodors.com, also offer readers comments on resorts and destinations all over the globe. Use a specific lodging property's website to get information on details such as room configurations, recreational options, and prices, but keep in mind that its purpose is to entice you to visit. A number of family travel sites offer travel tips and unbiased opinions on family destinations. Try familytravelforum.com, familytraveltimes.com, miningco.com, parents.com, ivillage.com, or babycenter.com.

Avoid rack rates: The rack rate is the official published rate that a hotel charges for a room. It also tends to be the maximum rate a guest pays at any given time. Never pay rack rates, unless you are completely desperate! If you book a package, you will be paying much less than a rack rate, and if you're not traveling on a package, simply ask for the cheapest discounted rate. This book publishes rack rates as a standard of comparison, but if you're lucky, you'll never have to pay them.

Forget the ocean view: You'll pay top dollar for oceanfront or ocean view accommodations. Opt instead for a garden, mountain, or city view and save a bundle. The further from the beach you stay, the lower your nightly lodging bill. Often the older your children, the easier it is to stay a few blocks or more from the beach. When you're traveling with babies and toddlers, you'll have so much gear to transport between your hotel room and the sand, that you may want to spring for a room close to the water.

Phone more than one number: Call a hotel's direct line in addition to the 800 number to find out about any special rates and then compare which will give you the best deal.

Ask questions: It's easy to find luxury properties with oceanfront rooms on a gorgeous white sand beach with nightly prices that would cover a family's food bill for a month. You can find budget lodging oceanfront, too, but you can also be a victim of false advertising when looking in this price range. Ask specific questions about a property's location, especially in relationship to the beach; inquire about the size and exact location of the rooms; and ask what is and is not included in the price and how recently the place has been renovated. Find out if the beach is good for swimming at the time you'll be visiting. Always ask about AAA or family discounts.

Get a kitchen: Restaurant meals are real budget busters. Rent a room with a kitchenette, or a condominium with a full kitchen, where you can further save by doing your own cooking. Even if you just fix your own breakfast and lunch, you'll have extra change to pocket.

Get cozy: Most resorts and hotels, especially the larger ones, allow children up to age eighteen to sleep free in their parent's room in existing bedding. If you can stomach the lack of privacy, put the kids in with you. Or, get a one-bedroom suite or condo where the living room has a sofa bed.

Camping: Hawaii and Florida and some of the Caribbean Islands have campgrounds on or near the beach in areas of spectacular beauty. Prices are considerably lower than for resorts or hotels, and in some places you can even rent the camping gear. If your idea of a tropical vacation only requires a good beach and you're on a budget, look into camping, but carefully consider the time of year you plan to go: midsummer camping in the Florida Keys or the U.S. Virgin Islands with mosquitoes buzzing about is no fun. Fall, spring, and especially winter are perfect. You'll need to plan ahead during these times to obtain a reservation.

Packages: Sunday papers list amazing air and accommodations packages to sun-splashed destinations that often throw in a rental car or activities as well, especially in Hawaii and Florida. Packages can save a family hundreds of dollars on their vacation but should be scrutinized carefully. Consolidators offering these packages buy big blocks of tickets and rooms and can offer them at lower prices than when you buy à la carte. Be sure to purchase a package from a reputable company that has been in business for a long time, and ask about the operator's cancellation penalties. Study the fine print and find out exactly what is included—type of hotel, location, size of room, amenities (pool, watersports, etc.), and proximity to the beach. Some travelers recommend deciding where you want to stay first and then finding a package that features that property, keeping in mind that the savings aren't worth it unless you get to stay where you want. Stay away from shady-sounding deals; if a package is too low to be believed, it's probably risky.

Saving on Food and Recreation

Once you've settled on the two largest costs, accommodations and transportation, there's a lot you can do to whittle down the other two vacation budget breakers—food and activities.

BYOG: Bring your own gear. Consider buying your own snorkel equipment at a discount sporting goods store before you leave. Your child may get a better fit, adding to his or her enjoyment and saving you money and trouble in the long run. Inflatable rafts and floats are always cheaper at home and easy to pack.

Coolers: Some travelers carry a cooler and pick up simple breakfast and lunch foods on the go to cut down on meals eaten out. We often pack a collapsible cooler if our room doesn't have a refrigerator. We buy or bring cereal, and use the cooler to store milk and juice to make our own breakfast. The cooler can double as a picnic basket for day trips, allowing us to further save money by packing our own lunch. To avoid high bar tabs, mix your own cocktails and enjoy them on your balcony rather than paying resort bar prices for refreshments.

Eat dinner for lunch: If you're dying to try a fancy gourmet restaurant but your budget balks, try it at lunchtime. Prices are lower for many of the same special dishes. If you bring the kids with you, they are likely to behave better anyway, since they will be less tired than in the evening.

Coupons: When you request tourist information for the areas you'll be visiting, ask the operator if there are any pamphlets containing discount coupons or if special package deals for attractions are available. Once you arrive at your destination, cruise by the racks holding all the tourist brochures to see what kinds of discount coupons are included in their materials. Free tourist maps are often bordered by money-off coupons for all kinds of excursions and attractions.

Tipping: Read your bill carefully after eating a restaurant meal. Some establishments include a 15 percent tip on the bill while others do not. Make sure you don't tip twice.

WHERE TO STAY

Aristocratic retreat with gourmet dining or package resort with limbo contests and all you can eat? Villa in the hills or condo on the shore? Full-day kids program or full-time family togetherness? Before you pick up the phone to book your stay, take a minute to think about your family's interests, ages, and abilities, and flip through this book to get an idea of the hundreds of possibilities you have to choose from.

The proximity of your room to the beach may also greatly enhance or detract from your vacation experience. Stay too far away and the effort to schlepp the kids, gear, towels umbrellas, toys, etc. to the beach may exhaust you before you even get started. Add tired kids and everything coated in sand to the trip back to your room and you may need another vacation when you return home. Parents with little ones should especially consider spending extra money to get as close to the beach as they can possibly afford. Ask questions to make sure that your oceanfront accommodations are truly on a sandy beach, rather than a stretch of rocky shoreline, or across a busy a highway from the shore.

Hotels and Resorts

Resort hotels are expensive but worth the splurge if you can pony up the price. They offer especially abundant services and an extensive menu of activities and amenities all packaged in elegantly designed buildings. Most of the resort properties we list in this book are located right on the beach and have a variety of restaurants, a kids program, a ritzy swimming pool, and a dizzying number of activities. If you think your budget doesn't allow you to stay at one of these places, check summer package deals; you may be surprised.

Small hotels can be just as satisfying and a heck of a lot cheaper. What their rooms may lack in fancy bathroom amenities and plush comforters, they more than make up in price. You can still get a terrific location, clean and comfortable lodging, and daily maid service, and often enjoy a swimming pool, a restaurant, and other recreational extras. If you want to arrange special watersports not available on the property, most small hotels are affiliated with some kind of watersports center and can direct you where to go.

Some resorts contain condos and villas, offering fully equipped houses or apartments with the services of a resort. You won't have the privacy of your own secluded villa, but you may be able to get room service at odd hours, excursions arranged for you, windsurfing lessons, and other children for yours to play with.

Hotel Children's Programs

"I hope I make some new friends at this one, too," my seven-year-old said as we prepared to step through the doors of yet another Kids Club. She had come to realize that children's programs are really mixers where kids get to know each other while building sand castles, hunting for shells, and playing board games. The success of each program depends on who the other children are, as well as the quality of the program and personality of the staff.

You can expect to find children's programs in most large hotels and resorts during the summer and over holiday periods. Some resorts, like the Westin, the Hyatt, Four Seasons, or Ritz Carlton chains, offer day-long children's activities year-round. Most programs take children ages four or five to twelve. Parents of younger kids will need to find baby-sitters, usually available through the concierge. A few resorts, such as Club Med's family villages, have programs that take children starting at age two.

It's best to introduce your child to the kids program slowly, especially if he or she is younger and hasn't had much experience in day care or preschool. Start with an hour or two, or a morning or afternoon, rather than a full day. Parents who leave their young child in the kids program for a full day at the start of their vacation often find that the child refuses to return.

The best children's programs have:

- daily activities that incorporate an area's natural environment and culture
- a separate room with toys, books, games, and art materials
- outdoor activities equal in time to indoor activities
- only occasional use of the TV, VCR, and video games
- staff who have been trained in first aid and child development
- a low staff-to-child ratio, and a plan to add staff as the numbers of kids increases
- flexibility to appeal to all ages and interests, as young guests change daily

All-Inclusive Resorts

When you visit an inclusive, you pay one price that most typically includes accommodations, food, airport transfers, and activities. At first glance an inclusive resort may appear to cost more than a vacation of separate but equal parts. But if you take the time to add up what you get, you'll find they often cost less than an à la carte vacation, especially for families that want to sample a variety of activities. Most inclusives have a price adjustment for children, and some offer free accommodations and meals for kids when they stay in their parents' room, especially off-season.

All-inclusive means different things at different resorts. Always ask what is and what isn't included and read the fine print carefully. Some resorts offer complimentary watersports but charge for excursions, while others do the reverse. Some cover meals but not drinks, and a few include tips and taxes—which can be significant—in their price, while others do not.

Independent travelers who are looking for a quiet getaway should investigate carefully before booking this type of vacation. While some inclusives are elegant retreats or back-to-nature getaways, an equal number are three-ring circuses of shows, sing-alongs, pool games, and tournaments. Each family will have its own particular favorite.

Condominiums

A condo offers the atmosphere of a home away from home where you can eat breakfast in your bathrobe, or dinner in your swimsuit. Most rent by the week or more, and a rental car is usually a necessity so you can pick up groceries and get out of the house. Prices vary dramatically—some rentals are luxury properties, while others are quite economical, but most of them offer more space than you can buy in a hotel at the same price. Most of the condos recommended in this book have swimming pools, TVs, phones, and laundry facilities on the premises, and all have fully equipped kitchens stocked with dishes, pots, pans, and utensils.

The chief difference between a condominium and a hotel is service. Room service in a condo is a rarity, and you'll probably have to carry your own bags and wash your own dishes, although most condos have daily maid service or housekeeping every few days. A family of four can be accommodated quite comfortably in a one-bedroom unit and can really spread out in a second bedroom. Condos can be especially practical for families with babies who are napping, as the extra space allows baby to nap in privacy and other family members to amuse themselves in another room.

Vacation Villa Rentals

Staying in your own vacation villa affords you extra room, your own kitchen, and privacy when you want it. You can rent a place for just the family, or gather several families together and rent a big place, sharing the cooking and child care. Most privately owned villas rent by the week or more, and a rental car is usually a necessity to pick up groceries and take outings. Some villas come with their own staff of butlers, maids, and cooks, while others merely have daily maid service. Generally speaking, the larger the villa, the larger the staff.

Before you rent a villa, be nosy. Find out if the rental agency has personally visited all of the villas they represent. Mention that you have children, since kids are not allowed in some properties. Ask about extras such as washer and dryer, dishwasher, linens, and safety features if you have toddlers or preschool-age children. Ask to see a set of photographs and a floor plan so you'll know the sleeping arrangement possibilities. Find out how recently the property has been built and/or refurbished. Inquire about the types of furnishings; elegant villas with antiques and breakable collections are a nightmare with toddlers; and find out if baby-sitting is available.

Get a map before you commit to anything. In many places villas are tucked into the hills above the beach rather than right on the beach. Ask the tourist office for recommendations of the best areas to find villas for rent if you are not sure.

After you've made your decision, get information about the part of the island you'll be staying in, directions to the house, and a list of good restaurants and supermarkets. Try to plan your arrival for the afternoon rather than the evening so you can pick up supplies on your way to your villa.

Villa Leisure handles thousands of villas in Mexico, Hawaii, and the Caribbean; with over thirty-five years in business, they personally inspect all properties and arrange car rentals and airport greeters. Website: www.villaleisure.com, P.O. Box 30188, Palm Beach Gardens, FL 33420. 800-526-4244, 561-624-9000.

At Home Abroad handles villas throughout the Caribbean and Mexico. They personally inspect their properties. Website: http://members.aol.com/athomabrod/index.html, 405 East 56th Street 6H, New York, NY 10022-2466. 212-421-9165, fax 212-752-1591.

Hideaways International is a travel club dedicated to villa and condo vacations. Members pay a fee and receive the Hideaways Guide, a picture book directory published twice a year of vacation homes all over the world. Each listing has pictures and descriptions of locations, setting, accommodations, and rates. Members negotiate with the individual owners when they are ready to rent. Website: www.hideaways.com, 767 Islington Street, Portsmouth, NH 03801. 800-843-4433, 603-430-4433, fax 603-430-4444.

Rent A Home International rents villas, condos, and cottages all over the world. Website: www.rentavilla.com, 12600 SE 38th St., #202, Bellevue, WA 98006. 800-488-7368, 206-789-9377, 425-653-7733.

Special Family Tour Operators

Families who want a travel package with several other families should contact Rascals in Paradise, which specializes in this type of arrangement. Website: www.rascalsinparadise.com, 650 Fifth Street, Suite 505, San Francisco, CA 94107. 800-872-7225, (outside California) 415-978-9800, fax 415-442-0289.

Adventure Vacations

American Wilderness Experience offers adventures throughout North America and around the globe. If you're looking for an adventure farther out than the parts of the globe this book covers, they can hook you up with an adventure that will fit your style and your pocketbook. They personally check out each of the outfitters they do business with, and are reliable and high quality. They run trips to all areas that this book covers, and beyond. Website: www.awetrips.com P.O. Box 1486, Boulder CO 80306. 800-444-0099, 303-444-2622.

PACKING

The dress code is casual at most of the beach resorts mentioned in this book, so don't bother with much luggage; all you'll need are a few pairs of shorts, some T-shirts, sundresses, and a swimsuit. You may want to pack one dress-up outfit each as a few places require more formal wear in the evening. Because airplanes, airports, and restaurants can be over-air-conditioned, bring a lightweight sweater or fleece for everyone. Choose easy-care natural-fiber clothes that don't show dirt, and avoid nylon and synthetic shirts or dresses as they are too hot in the humid tropics. Be sure to pack sunblock and mosquito repellent.

It sounds like a petty chore, but before you leave home, itemize the contents of your suitcases and their value in case your bags are lost along the way. Keep your name and address and a copy of your itinerary inside all bags you check. And pack a swimsuit for each member of the family in your carry-on, just in case.

Let each child old enough carry his or her own backpack; even a toddler can manage a small knapsack. It can hold an extra set of clothes and small toys and games for the plane and later can double as a beach bag and carry home souvenirs. Best of all, it allows you to say, "take whatever you want, as long as it fits in your pack." Mom or Dad's carry-on should be crammed with snacks, drinks, and amusing distractions for the kids. That way you'll be well prepared for long days of traveling and inevitable airport delays.

Babies:
Our motto for packing light is tossed in the diaper pail for this age group since you'll need as much gear on the road as you do at home. Ask if cribs, high chairs, strollers, and laundry facilities are available where you are going. Many parents bring their own portable cribs when visiting Mexico or the Caribbean because the safety standards outside of the United States can be different from ours. You can always use it on the beach to corral a wanderer and let a tired baby nap. If you plan to rent a car, ask if car seats for children can be rented, too.

Pack a sun umbrella and wide-brimmed baby hat for the beach and the stroller. Cool cotton bodysuits help to keep the sun from burning a baby's delicate skin. Babies with sensitive skin may not be able to tolerate insect repellent; bring mosquito netting to protect them from uncomfortable bites. Disposable diapers can be expensive and difficult to find in certain parts of Mexico and some of the Caribbean islands so bring a complete supply unless you are sure you can find them.

Toddlers:
Even if your child is toilet trained, pack extra diapers since many young children revert back to wetting in an unfamiliar situation. Bringing along a plastic sheet will ensure that beds stay dry. A small roll of tape can cover electrical outlets if you have a very curious and busy toddler. Life jackets or arm floats are a must for the pool and ocean.

School-Age Kids:
Since your child will spend most of his or her time in a swimsuit, pack two suits, one to wear and one to dry to avoid any rashes from wearing damp suits. Check to see if your destination has child-size sporting equipment available such as fins, snorkels, and masks. If not, purchase or borrow your own before you go. Kids who wear glasses can get custom-made masks with prescription lenses so they can enjoy the spectacular underwater sights. A disposable underwater camera is a great gift for beginning snorkelers.

Teens:
Who can tell this age group what to pack? All you can do is make subtle suggestions and give them their own suitcase, thereby limiting what they can take. Small portable radios are a great gift for this age group so they can tune in to the local sounds—Latin or Cuban music in Florida; Hawaiian guitar in Hawaii; reggae, steel pan, zouk, or soca in the Caribbean, or banda in Mexico.

Indispensable Items
    sunscreen
    insect repellent
    hats for each member of the family
    sunglasses
    flashlight
    first aid kit
    plastic bags (for wet clothes and collections)
    waterproof sandals
    swimsuit!

HEALTH AND SAFETY

You're more likely to suffer a bad case of sunburn than any other problem on a trip to the tropics, so load up on the sunscreen before you leave home. To escape sun trouble, avoid midday exposure for at least your first few days (from 11 to 2)—even under a beach umbrella as the sun's rays bounce off the sand and water and can still burn you. Apply sun block religiously (SPF 30 or higher) and often, at least every two hours. Wear protective clothing, sunglasses, and a hat, and drink plenty of water and fruit juices. The best cure for sunburn is to cover up or head to the shade.

Other common sense guidelines for staying healthy:

• Bring a basic first aid kit containing bandages, disinfectant, antibiotic ointment, medicine for diarrhea and stomach upsets, decongestant, aspirin or Tylenol for adults and children, tweezers, and insect repellent.

• Bring prescription medicines in their original containers (to avoid problems with customs) and take enough to last your visit.

• Protect yourself from mosquito and other insect bites by covering up or conscientiously wearing insect repellent. The most effective on the market today contain DEET (diethylmetatoluamide), which should be applied to your skin or clothing. Adults can use a 20 to 35 percent concentration, but very young children should use a 6 to 10 percent concentration; read directions carefully. Make sure your accommodations are screened or air conditioned. Avoid wearing highly scented perfumes, soaps, or lotions, which can attract mosquitoes and other flying insects.

• Use bottled water for babies' formulas. Subtle changes in water can often upset a little one's delicate system.

• Avoid diarrhea: a change in diet or water or even the excitement of the trip can affect some children (and adults too). Ask your pediatrician for diarrhea medication for younger children. Pepto-Bismol or Imodium can help relieve symptoms in older children. Remember the BRAT Diet: Bananas, Rice, Applesauce, and Toast to counteract the effects of diarrhea, and drink plenty of liquids.

• Swim with caution. Ask questions about undertow and riptides if you're unsure. Get water shoes for the family before you go so as to avoid injury from sharp coral formations, broken shells, or sea urchin spines, and avoid jelly fish. Keep a careful watch on your little ones as few beaches or pools are protected by lifeguards. Don't ever swim or snorkel alone. Do not fly within twenty-four hours of scuba diving.

• In the rare situation that you or a family member is seriously ill and you need an air evacuation, contact Aeromedical Group at 800-854-2569 or 510-293-5968. Website: www.aeromedgrp.com.

Safety:
Use the same precautions you use at home when traveling in unfamiliar territory. Keep a close watch on your cameras, wallets, and purses, and don't bring expensive jewelry on your trip. Never leave valuables unattended on a beach while you swim; always use your in-room safe or the hotel's safe. Give your child a hotel business card to carry, or make sure he or she knows where you're staying.

ACTIVE FUN
Snorkeling
Nearly every age child enjoys snorkeling. When you head south for vacation it's easy to find coral reefs teeming with life just a few flips of your fins or a short boat ride from shore. You can bring your own equipment or rent it from a watersports facility. Look for waterproof plant and animal identification cards to take with you to the beach; they're often available at the watersports desk or tourist shops in the area.

Before attempting to snorkel in the ocean, test your child's mask, fins, and snorkel equipment in a pool or shallow water. Children will need to learn how to breathe through the snorkel, how to clear it, and how to defog their mask. If they don't wear fins, they should wear water shoes to protect their feet from fire coral and sea urchins. A T-shirt can be helpful protection against the sun, and don't forget to apply sunscreen to the backs of legs.

Younger children will last longer if you take them out on a raft or a boogie board with a "leash" that can be attached to a parent's arm. A few boogie boards have viewing windows in them, allowing very young children who can't manage a mask to enjoy observing the underwater world. Flotation devices should always be worn by children unless they are very accomplished swimmers.

A few rules for the road:

• never snorkel alone, and never snorkel at dusk or at night;

• snorkeling in rough seas is pointless and dangerous;

• never touch coral; it can damage an organism that takes many years to grow, and it can injure you;

• towing a dive flag is your best protection if you're in an area where there are boats;

• avoid sea urchins as their barbs can break off in your skin; remove as much of the barb as possible and soak the area in vinegar or ammonia;

• don't feed the fish: bread, cheese, peas, or other human foods are indigestible for fish; they will fill up on those foods but can't assimilate the nutrients and may become weakened and sick;

- and most important, take only photos and leave only bubbles.

Family Scuba Diving

The numbers of families diving together have increased ten times over the past decade. The pleasure of floating suspended in a crystal clear world of breathtaking beauty offers a common experience parents and teenagers can share. Neither age nor youth has an advantage; everyone is freed from the constraints of gravity and can glide from coral formation to sea sponge past graceful rays and sea horses.

Certification is available for youngsters age twelve and up, with a parent's approval, resulting in a Junior Diving Certification. The juniors need to be good swimmers and must be accompanied by certified adults in all of their dives. International standards with carefully thought-out guidelines govern the sport; consequently the safety record of scuba diving parallels that of skiing and bicycle riding.

Becoming certified involves classroom sessions, pool practice, and four to six actual ocean dives. If you're not sure that you'll like diving, take a resort course once you've arrived at your destination. Lasting from one to four hours, it gives you a bit of instruction that usually culminates in a boat dive in shallow water. You can't count it toward your certification, but you'll get a feel for the sport, which you can follow up on if you like.

People who know they want to learn the sport usually begin their full certification course at home, before they leave on vacation. That way they can get the classroom and pool work done and not waste time indoors on holiday.

Organizations that offer certification and information include:

PADI (Professional Association of Diving Instructors), Website: www.PADI. com, 1251 E. Dyer Road #100, Santa Ana, CA 92705; they will send you a free list of training facilities;

NAUI (National Association of Underwater Instructors); Website: www.naui. org, 9942 Currie Davis Drive, Suite H, Tampa, FL 33619-2667, 800-553-6284, 813-628-6284

CMAS (Confederation Mondiale des Activités Subaquatics) is a reputable name you are likely to see on the French-speaking Caribbean islands.

Snuba

If scuba diving is out of reach because of age or inclination, try snuba. It's a shallow-water dive system that allows participants ages eight and up to dive below the surface for a sustained amount of time without wearing heavy air tanks. After an orientation that discusses safety issues and a practice session in shallow water, participants head out on an inflatable raft that has two long air hoses connected to a supply of compressed air. The snuba divers are strapped into harnesses attached to the air hoses and can wander around in relatively shallow water (fifteen to twenty feet) while they explore the wonders of the underwater landscape. The raft lets you rest when you are tired and warns boats of your presence. It's an excellent way to test the waters if you're thinking of trying scuba diving. For more information: Website: www.snuba.com, 10035 Missile Way, Mather, CA 95655, 916-856-6500.

Windsurfing

Skimming the surface of the water with just a small board between you and the sea, and a sail between you and the brilliant blue sky, is an exhilarating experience. If you or your children are good swimmers and strong enough to hoist the lightweight sail without losing your balance, you are candidates for windsurfing. The U.S. Sailing Association suggests kids as young as six can learn to windsurf; other instructors recommend starting children at about age ten. Small children are taught on scaled-down boards; if your kids plan to windsurf, be sure to ask if children's sizes are available. Children should always wear life vests no matter how competent their swimming skills. Always wind-surf with someone around who can watch you and go for help if needed.

Sailing with Children

Children of any age can go on sailing trips, but if you wait until your children are six and up you won't have to keep your eye on them every minute. If you're not experienced sailors, start with a crewed yacht and request crews who like to be placed with children. The captain and crew (including a cook) are at your service and will go wherever you want to go, within reason. Everything is rolled into one fee that includes food, drinks, port fees, and fuel. Be sure to ask if there is special equipment aboard, such as safety harnesses and life jackets for children. Go through a broker who can help you make a selection based on your particular needs, your budget, the size and ages of your family, and your preferred destinations. The Caribbean is one of the world's best places to explore by sailboat: two of the biggest charter yacht brokers who know most of the charter yacht companies in the Caribbean are Sailing Vacations (Website: www.sailingvacations.com, 800-922-4880 or 407-454-4646), and Caribbean Sailing Charters (800-824-1331).

Bare boating is when you get the boat "bare," or without food, fuel, captain, and mates. You plan, equip, sail, and explore on your own. Costs are about a third less than crewed boats, and a further 20 percent less during the summer. Someone in your group must have skippering experience on a similar boat in comparable sailing conditions, and you'll be asked to fill out a sailing résumé. The charter company staff will review navigational charts, point out suggested routes, anchorages, and places to avoid, and wind strength and direction, so you know what to expect.

Be sure that your charter outfit has flotation devices small enough for your children. The law requires that a flotation device, or life jacket, be onboard for all passengers, and the law of common sense states that children should wear theirs at all times on deck. If your charter company does not carry sizes small enough to fit your children, purchase them before you go. Make sure the life jacket fits snugly so a child cannot slip out of it. It should have leg straps and a collar to keep the head out of water. Attach a whistle to each life jacket and instruct children to blow it if they fall overboard. Once older children become proficient swimmers they don't need to wear life jackets at all times. Sailing with toddlers and very young children requires the use of a safety harness whereby they are attached by a tether to the boat.

2.

FLORIDA

From the sharp Latin rhythms of Miami to the languid pace of the Florida Keys, southern Florida is a mélange of cultures, styles, and personalities. It's famous for its year-round sunshine—this is the sun belt, after all—with miles and miles of fine white sand, mangrove swamps, an intricate network of barrier islands, and coral reefs. Known for both its natural beauty and big city sophistication, southern Florida is one of America's most popular year-round destinations for families.

There's water everywhere, filled with abundant life and endless beauty and providing nonstop recreation twelve months of the year—swimming or kayaking both Atlantic and Gulf waters, sport fishing for big game, or scuba diving and snorkeling through exotic coral reefs teeming with colorful tropical fish. Miles of sandy beaches invite families to simply throw down their beach blankets and relax in the sun. Florida's wildlife is legendary; take a jaunt through the Everglades for glimpses of alligators, graceful birds, otters, and deer. If you're lucky, spot a giant sea turtle lumber ashore to lay her eggs, or watch the babies hatch and scramble to the sea. Florida has managed to protect miles of beaches and wilderness areas in national parks and seashores.

This book will cover Miami, north to Palm Beach, south to the Everglades and the Florida Keys, and west to Sanibel and Captiva islands. I've uncovered some terrific bargains and included some classic family favorites. As you thumb through, you'll find countless possibilities for a terrific vacation that will satisfy your family's interests and budget.

Visitor Information: Contact Florida Division of Tourism, Visitor Inquiry, 126 W. Van Buren Street, Tallahassee FL 32399-2000 (904-487-1462) with questions, or request their Florida Vacation Guide, a free publication that describes all the state's attractions.

WHEN TO GO

Families love southern Florida any time of year. Whether you go in winter or summer, you're likely to find sunny skies and warm water. The most popular time of year to travel to Florida is from mid-December to mid-April, called high season, when millions of people from cooler climates migrate south for

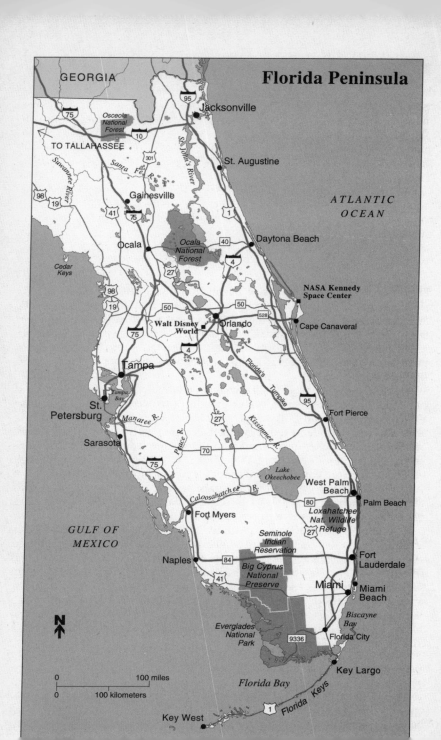

the warmth and sun of the sunshine state. In summer, when the temperatures rise, prices drop by as much as half of their winter season rates. In the summer and fall, the days are hot and humid, and frequent thunderstorms pop up in a hurry; carry an umbrella in case you're caught in a downpour, but keep in mind that the rain will usually be brief. Fall is also hurricane season, but the National Weather Service closely tracks storms and will give plenty of warning if storms are expected.

Baseball—Spring Training: During late February and March stadiums around the state fill up with major league baseball teams (and their fans) who come to prepare for the regular season by practicing and playing exhibition games. Tickets are a bargain, and most of the stadiums are small so you can get up close to your favorite players. Contact Major League Baseball, 350 Park Avenue, New York, NY 10022 (212-931-7800).

HEALTH AND SAFETY

The most dangerous condition a traveler is likely to endure in Florida is a bad case of sunburn, so slather on a high SPF sunscreen liberally and frequently and bring a hat for each member of your family.

Florida's mosquitoes bite, but they don't carry diseases. You'll find them along the coastal and marshy areas, especially during the wetter summer months. No-see-ums, or biting sand flies can also be a problem at dawn and dusk. Carry an insect repellent with you, or cover up to avoid bites.

If any family member has a medical condition such as diabetes, liver disease, or stomach ailments, they should avoid eating raw oysters. Those oysters harvested in Gulf of Mexico waters between April and October can carry a bacteria that can cause severe diarrhea, vomiting, and blood poisoning. Oyster lovers should order their bivalves steamed, broiled, or fried, as cooking kills the bacteria.

Always keep an eye on your possessions and lock your car doors and trunk. Never leave valuables on the beach while you swim; lock them in your hotel safe instead.

CAMPING

Contact the Florida Department of Natural Resources for a guide to Florida's state parks: Division of Recreation and Parks; Mail Station 535; 3900 Commonwealth Boulevard, Tallahassee, FL 32399-3000 (904-488-9872).

Miami

Nearly ten million tourists visited Miami last year and it's easy to see why. It's a region on the cutting edge of urban chic, with a healthy dose of palm-lined beaches and Latin American and Caribbean charm. Its unique blend of tropical and cosmopolitan sets it apart from other warm weather destinations, and it's one of the few areas where you can enjoy a big city vacation and a tropical beach getaway, all in the same place. When you plan your accommodations, place yourself near water to intersperse city attractions with carefree kid-pleasing fun.

Miami received some bad publicity a few years back when a rash of tourist attacks and murders caused international tourism to drop off. In response, the police increased their vigilance, especially in tourist areas, and have designated sections of highways marked by a bright orange sun that are patrolled and quite safe for tourists. As in any big city anywhere, be aware of your surroundings. Don't walk alone at night, and be extra careful in areas north or west of downtown and Little Haiti. If you fly into Miami and arrive after dark and are planning to rent a car, take a taxi to your hotel, and rent the car the following day when you have the advantages of daylight to familiarize yourself with a strange city.

Visitor Information: Greater Miami Convention and Visitors Bureau, website: www.tropicoolmiami.com, 701 Brickell Avenue, Miami, FL 33131 (800-283-2707, 305-539-3063).

Best Sweet Treat: Flan topped with fresh grated coconut is heavenly at Lario's in South Beach and at many other restaurants in the city. The key lime pie at Joe's Stone Crab is legendary.

WHERE TO STAY

Most hotels do not have their own private stretch of beach on Miami Beach, but share it with the other hotels and members of the public. Lounge chairs and watersports are managed by an on-beach concessionaire.

The price categories in this book show a full range of prices you'll encounter during the year, from low to high season. For the sake of comparison, it lists rack rates, but discounts and package deals may lower prices far below the published rate; be sure to ask. Compare what you're getting for your money: some places have kitchens, children's programs, and complimentary water-sport included in the price, while others do not. Prices are per night.

Expensive: over $225
Moderate: $125–$225
Budget: under $125

Expensive

Sonesta Beach Resort Key Biscayne

Address: 350 Ocean Drive Key, Biscayne, FL 33149-9990
Telephone: 800-766-3782, 305-361-2021, fax 305-361-3096
Website: www.sonesta.com

Key Biscayne, an island just south of the Miami Beach bustle, is half natural reserve and is separated from the mainland by a causeway that helps maintain its privacy ($1 fee). Families wanting to avoid the high-rise jungle of Miami Beach can stay here and have easy access to the glitz, glamour, and vacation sights while enjoying a more laid-back tropical island experience. The Sonesta isn't much to look at from the outside—sort of a concrete monolith—but as soon as you enter the modern and colorful lobby you feel as if you're on a tropical island far from the crowds. Walk through the lobby to take a peek at the back of the hotel for a glimpse of a spectacular beach and ample-sized pool and patio. The Sonesta is just a few minutes from the Seaquarium and not far from all of the sights of Miami . . . that is if you can tear yourself away from the beach. Outfitted with shady palapas and comfortable lounge chairs, its fluffy sands and balmy waters keep the kids busy for hours. Half of the guest rooms look out on the ocean with balconies that have two chairs and a table for a sunrise cup of coffee or an evening refreshment watching a storm and lightning at sea. The children's program specializes in field trips to Miami attractions in the morning, and stays on property for activities in the afternoon.

Accommodations: 296 spacious rooms are decorated in an art-deco-meets-the-tropics style and have two queen beds; connecting rooms, king-bedded rooms, and one- and two-bedroom suites are available.

For Kids: A complimentary program for kids from ages five to thirteen operates from 10 A.M. to 10 P.M. Every morning, kids go on a different "field trip" to places like the Miami Seaquarium, a bowling alley, Parrot Jungle, etc. In the afternoon kids stay on the grounds, enjoying arts and crafts, games and swimming. A fee is charged for excursions, and lunch is made available through room service.

Special Features: beach, swimming pool, water skiing, sailing, scuba, windsurfing, snorkeling, water cycle, fitness center, tennis, Ping-Pong, shuffle board, playground, restaurants, bar, car rental.

$$$: Children under eighteen are free in existing bedding in their parents' room. Daily rates, double occupancy: rooms $225–$405, suites $660–$1,375.

Casa Grande
Address: 834 Ocean Drive, Miami Beach, FL 33139
Telephone: 800-688-7678, 305-672-7003, fax 305-673-3669.
Website: www.islandoutpost.com

This sleek art deco hotel is one of the Island Outpost's (owned by Island Records mogul Chris Blackwell) hip Miami hotels, and offers "condominiums" with bedrooms and full kitchens in the center of South Beach's lively sidewalk scene. Parents with older kids can headquarter here, enjoy the beach just across the street (where umbrellas and beach towels can be rented from the concessionaire), partake of the South Beach action, and retreat to spacious and quiet guest quarters with full kitchens when they need a respite from Miami's fast pace. Each living room is outfitted with a CD player and a selection of Island Records' world-beat CDs—a fun touch. Guests can use the pool at the sister property, the Tides, not far away. Casa Grande's restaurant, Mezzaluna, offers indoor and outdoor dining, and room service is available during their business hours.

Accommodation: One- , two- , and three-bedroom units are quite spacious and are elegantly designed with a Balinese flair—dark teak furnishings, batik-print lamps shades, elegant Javanese-inspired artwork. Each comes with a completely outfitted kitchen and queen beds. The living room has a daybed, and roll-aways can be added to certain units.

Special Features: restaurant, bar, room service.

$$$: Daily rates, double occupancy: one-bedroom $225–$450, two-bedroom $350–$525, three-bedroom $750–$1500.

Moderate

Hilton Fontainebleau
Address: 4441 Collins Avenue, Miami Beach, FL, 33140
Telephone: 800-548-8886, 305-538-2000, fax 305-674-4607
Website: www.fontainebleau.hilton.com

A mega-resort best known for its sixties film role in *Goldfinger* and Jerry Lewis's *The Bellboy* (also *The Bodyguard*), the Fontainebleau has 1,200 rooms, a pool that looks like a star-shaped amoeba, and all the facilities any gargantuan resort worth its salt should have—shops, bars, restaurants, cafés, a game room, kid's program, watersports, spa, etc. Its conference and convention business is huge, and many attendees bring their families along. It's located on Miami Beach at about 41st Street, and its beach is broad and wide and dotted with umbrellas and beach chairs that you can arrange to rent from the concessionaire that handles most of the beach equipment on Miami's popular, sandy beach. Most of the guest rooms have been recently redone.

Accommodations: Most rooms have one king or two double beds. All are air-conditioned and some feature a minifridge, a cofeemaker, and a balcony. Connecting rooms are available upon request. There are a few one- and two-bedroom suites.

For Kids: The children's program (ages five to twelve), operating out of its own spacious room, is open 365 days a year from 9 A.M to 5 P.M. and has an especially lively and warm group of counselors. Days are loosely structured around themes, but playtime in the pool is the most popular with the kids. Special activities take place over holiday periods, and optional care is offered on Friday and Saturday evenings. Baby-sitting is available through two bonded outside agencies. The property is a "Hilton Vacation Station," which means kids are handed a complimentary gift (ours was a colorful lunchbox) and the opportunity to check out toys and games that range from activities centers for babies, large trucks and cars for toddlers, to board games for the entire family.

Special Features: two pools, fitness center/spa, game room, Ping-Pong, gift shops, evening entertainment, tennis courts, volleyball, watersports from beach concessionaire including boogie boards, small sailboats, banana boat rides, parasailing, rafts, and wave runners.

$$$: Kids under eighteen are free in their parents' rooms. Daily rates, double occupancy: $159–$305.

Silver Sands Oceanfront Motel
Address: 301 Ocean, Key Biscayne, FL 33149
Telephone: 305-361-5441

Just next door to the Sonesta, this pleasant one-story motel with a tropical garden offers an excellent buy on a beautiful beach on tranquil Key Biscayne. Guests can walk next door to enjoy the shops and restaurants. Everything about it is clean and fresh, and its rooms have extras such as microwaves and refrigerators so you can economize by doing some of your cooking. It's popular with both Latin American and European families, so you're likely to hear a variety of languages at the pool.

Accommodation: Minisuites have two double beds and cottages have one bedroom with living room sofa bed and one or two double beds. All have microwaves, refrigerators, and VCRs.

Special Features: Olympic-size swimming pool, baby-sitting, laundry facilities. Watersports available next door.

$$$: Daily rates, double occupancy minisuites: $129–189, cottages: $279–$349. Children under fourteen free in their parents' room.

The National
Address: 1677 Collins Avenue, Miami Beach, FL 33139
Telephone: 800-327-8370, 305-532-2311, fax 305-534-1426
Website: www.nationalhotel.com

The National is a short walk from the center of the South Beach action, directly on Miami Beach. Once one of the premier boutique hotels on the beach, it has recently been restored to its former forties classic art deco grandeur. Its lobby floors, concierge desk, bar, and many lobby furnishings are original and have been painstakingly revitalized. Guest rooms are a bit small, just as they were when the hotel was built, but the furnishings are all new and elegantly deco inspired. Its proximity to the beach and its stunning swimming pools make this hotel a good choice for families: one pool is a long narrow lap pool (the longest in Miami beach) flanked by lush tropical gardens; the other pool is smaller and flanked by a pool bar with the beach just a few steps beyond.

Accommodations: 154 rooms come in a variety of bed configurations: two twins, one king, one queen, or two queens. Connecting rooms are found on the ninth and tenth floors.

Special Features: two swimming pools, beach, restaurant, two bars, room service, car rental.

$$$: Daily rates, double occupancy $215–$300. Children under age fifteen free in their parents' room.

Budget

Brigham Gardens
Address: 1411 Collins Avenue, Miami Beach, FL 33139
Telephone: 305-531-1331, fax 305-538-9898
E Mail: wwwbrighamg.@interpoint.net

Many of these simple rooms have kitchens, making them an excellent bargain for families traveling on a budget. The Mediterranean-style hotel, right in the heart of the art deco district, is known for its lovely garden, which gives it the feeling of being a little farther out of the city than it really is. Dense with plants, the garden has tables, hammocks, lounge chairs, comical caged parrots that kids love to talk to, and lizards who sun themselves on large leaves. The garden is lit at night with candles—this is a real retreat at an excellent price. You're just four hundred yards from the beach. Its family run and one of the owners lives on the property.

Accommodations: Nineteen rooms and suites have air-conditioning; all are furnished differently, with a tropical theme. Rooms have either fully-outfitted kitchenettes or just a refrigerator, coffeemaker, and microwave. Standard rooms have one queen bed; large studios and one-bedroom suites have a queen bed and pull-out futon. Parking is available through a nearby hotel and costs $8 per day.

Special Features: coin-operated washer and dryer, beautiful gardens.

$$$: studios $85–$145: $5 per extra person; stay of seven days or longer, 10 percent discount on entire stay.

Compostela Motel

Address: 9040 Collins Avenue, Miami Beach, 33154
Telephone: 305-861-3083

The Bal Harbor section of Miami where this simple motel is situated has a beautiful and safe beach, and a ritzy shopping center, all within walking distance of your room. It's nothing fancy, but is an excellent place to headquarter if you want to do your own cooking and enjoy the sun, sand, and sights of Miami. Most of the rooms have full kitchens, and parking is free, an unusual extra bonus on Miami Beach. The beach is about a half block away.

Accommodations: Efficiencies/studios have two double beds and a tiny kitchen. The apartment has a kitchenette and living room and can sleep up to four people in its one bedroom. The suite has one bedroom with two double beds, a sofa bed in the living room, and a kitchenette.

Special Features: Coin-operated laundry.

$$$: Daily rate, double occupancy: efficiencies $55–$70 apartments $65–$80 suite $75–$90.

WHAT TO DO

Miami Seaquarium—Spend a lively day viewing shows of the ocean's most popular creatures: seals, dolphins (including TV's Flipper), and the perennial favorite, Lolita the Killer Whale. Schedule your visit to arrive at Lolita's show early so your kids can sit in the bottom four rows. That way, when Lolita performs great leaps that create an impressive amount of splash, they can be the lucky ones to get soaked (parents might want to sit farther back). In addition to the shows, there are scheduled shark feedings, sea turtle and manatee displays, aquariums full of fish, and a rain forest exhibit. The schedule is arranged so you can get a look at most of the shows in a long morning or afternoon. Scattered throughout the park are plastic sea life model-making machines that represent many of the characters you'll see up close: dolphins, seals, manatees—they make a great souvenir for a buck. 4400 Rickenbacker Causeway, Key Biscayne (305-361-5705) 9:30–6 P.M. daily.

Venetian Pool—The pool looks like a fantasy grotto out of nineteenth-century Venice . . . but with an American cinema sheen. I almost expect to see Esther Williams and her aquatic entourage perform a water ballet in lavish petal caps—she and Johnny Weismuller swam here decades ago. This spectacularly beautiful pool dates originally from 1924, and it is a fun place to cool off for an afternoon. It has a little café, lockers, a waterfall to swim under, and a special deep section reserved for older kids and good swimmers. The cave grotto is very popular with children, but make sure you accompany younger children inside, as it's out of view of the lifeguards and the horseplay can get a bit rough. Listed on the National Register of Historic Places, 2701 DeSoto Boulevard, Coral Gables (305-460-5356).

Parrot Jungle and Gardens—Much more than just rows of cages with exotic birds, Parrot Jungle tucks its wildlife into lavish jungle landscaping thick with vines and flowers and meandering pathways. Continuous shows at Parrot Bowl Theater star the cleverest and most trainable of their collection of parrots; you'll see macaws ride a bike along a high wire, cockatoos race each other in tiny cars, and more. Other animals are on display, such as alligators, tortoises, iguanas, and more birds. There's a monkey exhibit, a children's playground, and several other shows. 11000 SW 57th Avenue (Red Road), Miami (305-666-7834).

Miami Metrozoo—Sure, you could see a zoo in any big city, but this 290-acre complex is especially nice. Animals are not caged, but rather kept behind moats. Some of the zoos most famous residents include the lions upon which Disney's Mufasa and Simba of *Lion King* fame were modeled. There are rare white Bengal tigers, koala bears, a Komodo dragon, and a good petting zoo. Children can take an elephant ride, and the entire family can tour the zoo on its monorail system when their legs get tired. SW 152nd Street and SW 124th Avenue, south of Coral Gables (305-251-0403). Open daily 9:30 A.M. to 5:30 P.M.

Monkey Jungle—Visitors are the species protected at this sixty-year-old primate paradise. Humans explore the grounds from inside screened trails and watch the crazy antics of all kinds of monkeys overhead and alongside. There are daily shows and some beautiful and unusual creatures to view. Be prepared to hold your nose: the smell of the place can get a bit thick. 14805 SW 216th Street, Greater Miami South (305-235-1611). Open Tuesday–Saturday 10 A.M.–5 P.M., Sunday 12 P.M.–5 P.M., Thursday evenings until 9.

Miami Museum of Science and Space Transit Planetarium—Over 140 hands-on exhibits let kids play with everything from computers and robots to microscopes. Also on the premises is southern Florida's largest natural history collection and a wildlife center with more than 140 live animals, including a spectacular birds of prey exhibit. The planetarium provides another indoor break on a hot or rainy day, featuring multimedia astronomy and laser shows. 3280 S. Miami Avenue, Coconut Grove (305-854-4247).

Viscaya Museum and Garden—Older children especially will be impressed with this seventy-room Italian Renaissance-style mansion filled with fifteenth- to nineteenth-century furniture and art. The palacelike building took one thousand artisans five years to complete. When the kids have tired of admiring antiques and fine paintings, they can explore the formal gardens overlooking the bay. 3251 South Miami Avenue, Coconut Grove (305-579-2708). Open daily 9:30 A.M.–4:30 P.M.

The Everglades

Tourist Information: Website: www.everglades.national-park.com, Everglades National Park Headquarters, 4001 State Road, 9336, Homestead FL 33034 (305-242-7700).

Just one hour south of Miami, this spectacular primal wilderness is actually a very wide (40 miles across) shallow, slow-moving river. Its 1.5 million acres of vast saw-grass prairies, deep mangrove swamps, pinelands, and coastal islands are abutted by more wilderness, Big Cypress National Preserve, and Biscayne National Park. Rare and endangered animals make them their home, and on a lucky day you might spot any number of endangered species in their natural habitat, such as the leatherback turtle, American crocodile, Florida panther, or West Indian manatee. The farther south you go and the more off the beaten track you explore, the more wildlife you're apt to see.

There are two seasons in the Everglades. High season, from December to May (also called the dry season), is the best time to visit, when temperatures are cooler, mosquitoes less prevalent, and the lower water level attracts a larger variety of birds and animals. Wet season runs from June to November, and wildlife is much harder to spot as the migratory birds have moved on (although the mosquitoes haven't).

Hearty souls can try canoe camping to get a true insider's view of the Everglades. You can camp anywhere you want in designated campsites in the back country as long as you have obtained a permit, and you must register your itinerary before you leave at either the Flamingo or Everglade City ranger station. Many campsites are wooden platforms on stilts with a roof or cover, called chickees. Winter is the best time to camp in the Everglades, as the mosquitoes are fierce during the hotter, wetter season.

Hiking and biking trails begin in the gateways to the Everglades: Flamingo, Everglades City, and Shark Valley; or you can rent canoes in Flamingo or Everglade City to explore the grand watery wilderness; or you can join a guided boat tour.

There are campgrounds at both the Flamingo and Long Pine Key campgrounds that have tables and charcoal grills and cold showers. You may not build a campfire, but there are campfire programs conducted by the rangers during the winter season.

A few other motel and camping accommodations exist in Homestead and

Florida City and Shark Valley, but the following are the only lodgings inside the park.

FLAMINGO

Once a quiet fishing village surrounded by millions of acres of wilderness, Flamingo is still an outpost, but one meant today for travelers, rather than fishermen, exploring this region. The town provides lodging, food, and all kinds of boat rentals. You can canoe through saw-grass marshes, islands of mangroves, creeks, ponds, and small bays. Or you can hike a number of trails through tropical hardwood hammock, along coastal salt prairies, freshwater ponds, and old roads. If you want to leave it to the experts, excellent guided boat tours are available. Virtually all back country camping and canoeing trips begin here.

WHERE TO STAY

Flamingo Lodge and Marina
Address: 1 Flamingo Lodge Highway, Flamingo, FL 33034
Telephone: 800-600-3813, 941-695-3921, fax 941-695-3921
Website: www.amfac.com

Your options for accommodations include cottages, lodge rooms, and houseboats: *Houseboats* are certainly the most fun, but can be rented in the fall, winter, and spring only. Two different styles are available, a forty-foot pontoon-style boat that sleeps eight maximum, and a fancier thirty-seven-foot fiberglass model that sleeps up to 6 (although they are both much more comfortable with fewer). The forty-footer does not have air-conditioning but has everything else you might need for cruising the waterways in comfort and style—stove, oven, refrigerator, bathroom, full linens, life jackets, etc., all in one large room (except for the bathroom). The thirty-seven-foot boat is air-conditioned and has a rooftop sundeck, an electric two-burner stove, and a propane grill. All other necessities are provided except for food, which you can pick up in the marina store. Boats can cruise up to six miles an hour, and while boating experience is always a plus, they're very easy to use. *Cottages* have fully equipped kitchens, a separate bedroom, air-conditioning, and pool privileges, but no TV. *Lodge rooms* have two double beds, TV, phone, air-conditioning, and pool privileges.

Special Features: The Flamingo Marina has canoes, kayaks, motor boats, fishing equipment, bicycles, and even binoculars for rent, plus restaurant, naturalist-guided tours, a store, and a National Park Service information desk.

$$$: Houseboats have a 2 night minimum, 40-foot boats $340 for 2 nights, $455 for 3 nights, $570 for 4 nights, 37-foot boats $525 for 2 nights, $700 for 3 nights, $875 for 4 nights, cottages $89–$135, lodge rooms $65–$95. Children seventeen and under free in their parents' room in existing bedding.

The Florida Keys

This 100-mile chain of little islands called keys have the Atlantic Ocean on one side and the Gulf of Mexico on the other and is surrounded by the world's third largest barrier reef system. The islands are connected by the Overseas Highway, an engineering feat that leapfrogs from key to key in a series of giant arches of concrete and steel.

The keys are divided into three regions—upper keys, lower keys, and Key West. Key Largo, forty-two miles south west of Miami, is the longest island in the chain and is part of the upper keys. Here, John Pennecamp Coral Reef State Park, the first underwater preserves in the United States, and the adjacent Key Lag National Marine Sanctuary feature fifty-five varieties of delicate coral and almost five hundred different species of fish. Islamorada is the centerpiece of a group of islands, and it is known as the sport fishing capital of the world. Anglers can find sailfish, marlin, snapper, barracuda, and grouper in the ocean, and tarpon and bonefish in the shallow waters. Long Key is home to a number of dolphin facilities that have programs allowing guests to swim and play with these gentle creatures. Big Pine Key is noted for its miniature Key deer refuge and the Looe Key National Marine Sanctuary, which offers spectacular shallow-water dives. Key West is the final stop on the overseas highway. All these islands are linked by only one main road, U.S. Highway 1. Most addresses are noted by their mile marker (M), with Key West being mile marker one.

Note that the keys are not known for their beaches, and when beaches do exist, they tend to be man-made or quite small. Most properties have docks rather than sandy entries to get into the water. Recreational activities in the keys take place on boats or under the surface using scuba or snorkel gear. Families should definitely plan to take a snorkeling expedition and try ocean kayaking and boat excursions.

Many "Mom and Pop" motel establishments popped up in the 1940s, fell into disrepair during the last few decades, and have been remodeled or refurbished. Some excellent bargains exist throughout the keys (with the exception of Key West) and although they don't have much of a beach, they offer pedal boats, kayaks, and small sailboats for guests to use.

Visitor Information: Website: www.fla-keys.com Florida Keys and Key West Visitors Bureau, P.O. Box 1147, Key West, FL 33041 (800-FLA-KEYS, 305-296-1552).

Best Sweet Treat: key lime pie, of course!

WHERE TO STAY
Expensive

Westin Beach Resort, Key Largo
Address: 97000 S Overseas Highway, Key Largo, FL 33037
Telephone: 800-WESTIN-1, 305-852-5553

Website: www.westin.com

A tiny beach is tucked into the front of this pleasant property, which is a good place to headquarter if you plan to stay busy with boat trips and watersports such as windsurfing and parasailing, all conveniently available right at the resort. When it's low tide you can walk across to a tiny island not far away. Situated across the parking lot from the hotel and beach are two swimming pools separated by a waterfall; one is for families and the other is for adults only. The property is one long four-story building; restaurants and lounges are on the third floor and offer stunning views and good food but an expensive children's menu ($8 for a hamburger). A poolside grill serves snacks and lunch during the day.

Accommodations: Two hundred rooms on four floors all have a king bed or two double beds, a minibar, in-room safe, and coffeemaker. Rooms can accommodate a maximum of four people.

For Kids: The children's program, called the Fun Factory, operates from spacious rooms with plenty of appealing toys, games, and activities to draw in a reluctant child. Its many personal touches attest to the creativity of the staff. For children 4 to 11, it is fee based and includes lunch, a T-shirt, and all kinds of activities. The program operates seven days a week from 10:30 A.M. to 4:30 P.M..

Special Features: small beach, two pools, tennis courts, dive shop, catamaran, wind surfing, snorkeling, parasailing, wave runners, 24-hour room service, restaurants, bar, shop, baby-sitting.

$$$: Kids under seventeen free in their parents' room. Daily rates, double occupancy: $250–$350.

Cheeca Lodge

Address: Mile Marker 82, P.O. Box 527 Islamorada, Florida Keys, FL 33036
Telephone: 800-327-2888, 305-664-4651, fax 305-664-2893
Website: www.cheeca.com

A twenty-seven acre luxury resort with loads of elbow room, Cheeca is the top-rated property in the upper keys. It has vacation pleasures to appeal to everybody: a nine-hole golf course and night-lit tennis courts, both with resident pros; a saltwater lagoon and two freshwater swimming pools; and superlative sport fishing in the waters offshore. An artificial reef has been constructed at the end of the pier for snorkelers, where a sturdy ladder makes getting in and out of the water easy. Guest rooms are sprinkled throughout the landscaped gardens and along the shore and golf course. The oceanfront building has rooms only, all with a drop-dead ocean view, while some of the outer buildings have spacious family suites with full kitchens, and most rooms have screened porches. The resort takes pride in educating its guests about environmental responsibility and has won several awards for its efforts.

Accommodations: Guest rooms have ceiling fans, air-conditioning, and screened windows. Standard rooms have a king or two double beds and do not connect. One-bedroom suites have kitchenettes outfitted with small dishwashers, refrigerators, stoves, oven, cookware, and utensils. The living room has a sofa bed and there is a king bed in the bedroom. A connecting room with two double beds can be added.

For Kids: Camp Cheeca operates seven days a week in summer and during high season. In summer months each week has a theme and there are local children participating, so it may be a bit hard for your child to break in. The program operates during holiday periods as well. Baby-sitting is available twenty-four hours a day; sitters come from a list the hotel keeps.

Special Features: two freshwater pools, saltwater lagoon, six hot tubs, snorkeling, dive shop, beach area, parasailing, small sailboats, boat excursions, restaurants, par-3 nine-hole golf course, six lighted tennis courts, and classes for both adults and kids.

$$$: Children sixteen or under free in their parents' room. Daily rates, double occupancy: rooms $130–$500, one bedroom suites $320–$1,500.

Moderate

Hawk's Cay Resort

Address: 61 Hawk's Cay Boulevard, Duck Key, FL 33050
Telephone: 800-432-2242, fax 305-743-5215
Website: www.hawkscay.com

Hawk's Cay is expanding as fast as it can. It once consisted of a single resort built in 1959 that contained guest rooms, restaurants, and a lobby that has been renovated and improved over the years, but now family-style villas are being built and sold to individual owners throughout the sixty-acre property. Its central location in the keys, its marina and laundry list of activities maintains its popularity with families. Although there's not too much of a beach, there is an enormous artificial lagoon for swimming that is spacious enough for kids to paddle kayaks out in it or enjoy complimentary use of mats, tubes, and noodles. Hawk's Cay is one of the few resorts with its own dolphin program. It features three adolescent male dolphins who were originally used for research and are now used for three encounters per day. Children who want to swim with the dolphins must be four feet tall, and you should reserve the program when you book your stay.

Accommodations: 180 rooms, over 100 villas. Rooms have a king bed or two double beds, a minifridge and a coffeemaker; connecting rooms are available. Two-story villas all have two bedrooms and 1½ or 2½ baths, some with a den that can act as a third bedroom. All have porches and beautiful ocean views, washers, and dryers, TV and VCR. Many have pull-out couches in the living room. Villas have maid service every four days.

For Kids: Island Adventure Club provides activities for kids ages three to eleven, seven days a week throughout summer and over major holidays. Children ages three and four stay just for the morning. A schedule is posted the night before, and activities are scheduled throughout the day, such as sand-dollar painting, kayak tours, snorkeling, etc. A junior sailing club for seven to seventeen-year-olds consists of a 2-hour educational cruise.

Special Features: dolphin encounter, two swimming pools (one for adults only), one saltwater swimming lagoon, marina, reef fishing, game fish, sunset cruises, ecology tours, bike rental, eight tennis courts, croquet, game room with Ping-Pong, air hockey, video games, billiards, massage, library, fitness center, waterskiing, kayaks, scuba, snorkel, charter fishing, parasailing, glass-bottom boat rides, wave runner, catamaran rides, shops, restaurants, and bars.

$$$: Children under eighteen stay free in parents' room (up to five people per room). Daily rates, double occupancy: $160–$325, villas $325–$475.

Faro Blanco Marine Resort

Address: 1996 Overseas Highway, Marathon, FL 33050
Telephone: 800-759-3276, 305-743-9018, fax 305-743-2918

Although there are other unusual accommodations at this resort, your kids will never forgive you if you don't stay in the charming, working lighthouse that sits right at the water's edge. Situated on the dock, it has two separate apartments, each of which has a 360-degree view and can sleep up to four or five people. The top unit should be your first choice, as it's on the top three floors of the lighthouse. Your kids get to claim the highest room and its two twin beds. Just below is the parents' room with a king bed and bath, and below that is a kitchen/living area, a bath, and a fold-down bed. The lowest apartment, on the second level of the lighthouse, is all on one floor and includes a full kitchen. The rooms are rather cozy and rustic, but it's an experience your kids will never forget. Nearby are the resort's cottages and condominiums, and just down the road and across the street on the ocean side are houseboats for rent by the night or by the week.

Accommodations: In addition to the lighthouses described above, you can stay in a three-bedroom condominium that can sleep up to six people; garden cottages that sleep two to four people with a kitchenette (all one room, about 25-by-25 feet); and a double cottage that has a full kitchen. Houseboats are two-story buildings on floating barges that are permanently attached to the dock. Each one houses four separate units, two with a kitchen and two without, that offer connecting possibilities.

Special features: swimming pool, fishing, scuba, snorkeling, restaurants, full marina, powerboat rentals, playground, picnic areas.

$$$: Children under twelve stay free. Daily rates, double occupancy: lighthouse $145–$195, houseboats, $89–$195, cottages $79–$145, condominiums $215–$265.

Budget

Kona Kai Resort

Address: 97802 Overseas Highway, Key Largo, FL 33037
Telephone: 305-852-7200, fax 305-852-4629, 800-365-7829
Website: www.konakairesort.com

Take an old keys bungalow resort, redo it with contemporary tropical chic, and you get the Kona Kai. These charming one- and two-bedroom bungalows are situated back from the road and screened with a lavish tropical garden that ensures a minimum of car noise from the highway. The lobby is also an art gallery, and the owner's interest in modern art is reflected throughout this stylish resort. It's got just eleven rooms and the number of people on the property is kept purposely low. It's very fresh and pleasantly landscaped with resident squirrels scampering about the grounds hoping for a handout. There's a small but attractive pool and Jacuzzi near the beach. Complimentary beach towels are provided, which is rare for a property this reasonably priced. The beach has a few shade trees and a small dock. Another plus is a dive center, again rare in this small a property.

Accommodations: Eleven accommodations range in size from single guest rooms to one- and two-bedrooms suites. All are ground level with air-conditioning, TV, ceiling fans, and patios. No telephones or maid service; clean linens are available daily at the office. Some rooms have fully equipped kitchens, most have small refrigerators and coffeemakers.

Special Features: beach, dock, dive shops, pool, Jacuzzi, Ping-Pong, volleyball, tennis court, barbecue.

$$$: Daily rates, double occupancy: rooms $104–$172, one-bedroom suites $128–$290, two-bedroom suites $175–$425.

Breezy Palms
Address: Mile Marker 80, Oceanside, P.O. Box 767, Islamorada, FL 33036
Telephone: 305-664-2361, fax 305-664-2572
Website: www.breezypalms.com

This attractive property is one of my favorites in the budget range in the keys. The rooms have a fresher look than most in this price category, most have kitchens, and there are extra services you don't often find in economy lodging, such as fresh towels around the pool, a small shop with ice cream, sunblock and other sundries, movie rentals, and 320 feet of ocean footage with a dock that is lit for night fishing. There is a tiny beach area, and barbecues placed under the shade of the palm trees. Most rooms have views of the ocean from their screened porches.

Accommodations: one- and two-bedroom apartments, efficiencies, a beach cottage, and bungalows all have completely outfitted kitchens and air-conditioning. Most bedrooms have two queen beds.

Special Features: swimming pool, volleyball, coin-operated laundry, shop.

$$$: Daily rates, double occupancy: efficiencies $75–$85, one- and two-bedroom apartments $110–$200, beach cottages $140–$150, bungalows $70–$115.

Sunset Cove
Address: Mile Marker 99.5 Bayside, 99360 Overseas Highway, P.O. Box 99, Key Largo, FL 33037
Telephone: 305-451-0705, fax 305-451-5609
Website: www.digitalpark.com/suncove

Sunset Cove is easy to spot—its entrance is guarded by a gargantuan statue of a gleaming white swan. Head down the driveway, and the large animal statuary theme continues with a tyrannosaurus rex, zebra, deer, elves, a family of lions, and giraffes. This quirky budget resort doesn't allow anyone to climb on the animals (which may be frustrating for little kids), but the wildlife certainly adds charm and personality to this nicely kept property. The owners' pride in the place shows with thoughtful touches throughout—shady "chickee" huts (open air structures with cone-shaped straw roofs) hiding wicker swings are tucked throughout the property and along the water's edge, the use of nonmotorized boats is included in the price, plus there's a free continental breakfast. Twice a day guests can help feed the local pelicans, herons, and egrets. Units are plain but clean. You're in walking distance of many of Key Largo's restaurants, shops, and charter boat facilities and just two miles from beautiful John Pennicamp State Park.

Accommodations: Cottages vary considerably in bed arrangements and kitchen equipment, but all have refrigerators. Five cottages have queen beds and an extra double bed or futon, with a small kitchen. Best suited for bigger families are the "diver's dens," which allow for connecting possibilities. All rooms are air-conditioned, with cable TV. Many rooms without a full kitchen have a microwave. Avoid the units nearest the road as they're a bit noisy.

Special Features: barbecue pits, chickee huts for shade, free continental breakfast, sandy beach with a boat ramp and dockage, canoes, paddle boats, kayaks, rowboats, and swan pedal boat.

$$$: Double occupancy, per night: $75–$125; $15 per extra person.

Popp's Motel

Address: 95500 Overseas Highway, Key Largo, FL 33037
Telephone: 305-852-5201, fax 305-852-5200

One of the best buys in the Florida Keys, Popp's Motel has basic efficiencies and one-bedroom apartments that can accommodate up to four people. It's now run by the third and fourth generations of the Popp family. The motel opened nearly fifty years ago under the ownership of Alex and Bertha Popp. Much of the beach is shaded by 150 palm trees in the midst of which thoughtful touches have been placed—a simple children's play structure, tables, chairs, barbecues, and shady huts for lounging under. The beach is quite shallow and swimmers looking for deeper water start out at the end of the boat dock. The owners have supplied plenty of toys: foam noodles, hammocks, small peddle boats, and kayaks within easy reach of the guests. There are a total of ten cottages (really duplexes), a boat ramp, and a fishing pier. The motel is placed on a strip of land between the beach and Highway 1 that is narrower than in some other areas. Consequently, you can hear some car noise from most of the units.

Accommodations: The efficiencies usually have two queen beds and a tiny kitchenette; one-bedroom apartments have one queen bed plus a sleeper sofa in the living room. Efficiencies are "multi-purpose"—you use your bed as your couch or sitting area.

Special Features: barbecues grills, picnic tables, chickee huts, hammocks, boat ramp, fishing pier, kids playground.

$$$: Double occupancy: efficiencies $59–$79 per night, and $355–$500 per week; one-bedroom apartments $69–$89 per night, and $415–$550 per week. Each extra child $5, extra adult $10.

Bahia Honda State Park Cabins
Address: Mile Marker 37.5, 36850 Overseas Highway, Big Pine Key, Fl 33043
Telephone: 305-872-2353

These comfortable two-bedroom cabins with complete kitchens are a real find for families who love the out-of-doors. They sit right on the waterfront on the Gulf side, each with their own private fishing dock, picnic table, and grill. You've got the best beach in all of the keys just minutes from your door, plus all of the other natural attractions of Bahia Honda State Park (see below) on Big Pine Key.

Accommodations: Cabins have two bedrooms, each with a double bed, and one with two twins arranged bunk-style. They sleep up to six people. The efficiency kitchen is fully outfitted and there is a full bath and television but no phone.

$$$: Daily rates, for four people: $100–$125 per night with a two-night minimum. Reservations can be made up to eleven months in advance. Extra adult $6 per night. Key Deer Blvd., near Mile marker 30.5, Big Pine Key, 305-872-2239, 305-872-2353.

WHAT TO SEE AND DO
Swim with the Dolphins—A number of businesses are now offering the chance to swim with the dolphins. What you actually do with the dolphins in the water varies from place to place, but all are the same in that they require registration far in advance of your trip, and a minimum age for children. Most offer educational walking tours and opportunities for observing the dolphins even if you can't book a swim. All require that participants be good swimmers, and read, speak, and understand English. Proof of age is generally required, which must be a passport or birth certificate. No one under five may swim. Prices range from $95–$125 per session.

Dolphin Cove Research and Education Center is a relative newcomer in the swim-with-the-dolphins scene. Their two mother/son teams—Jeannie and Alphonse, and Spunky and Duke—along with Dreamer and Nicki swim under controlled situations with a few lucky people each day. Once guests have learned the commands, they request the dolphins to roll over for a pat, push them through the water, or take them for a ride as guests hang on to their dorsal fins. Website: www.dolphinscove.com, 101900 Overseas Highway, Key Largo, 305-451-4060.

Dolphins Plus offers a swim with the dolphins session that is combined with a special marine orientation program and a question-and-answer session. Children must be at least seven years old to participate in the swim. Dolphins Plus also offers a swim-with-the-dolphins therapy program for special needs children and their families who are dealing with developmental or physical disabilities, emotional challenges, and critical, chronic, or terminal illness. Website: www.dolphinsplus.com, 31 Corrine Place, Mile Marker 99, Key Largo, 305-451-1993.

Dolphin Research Center has a goal to educate the public and protect these bright animals that live in a 90,000-square-foot saltwater enclosure in the Gulf of Mexico. Kids must be twelve years old, and reservations can be made four to six weeks in advance of the date you wish to visit on the 1st or 15th of every month starting at 9 A.M. If you're not one of the lucky ones selected, you can still take a walking tour or take a class called Tips on Training where you see a training session up close and get to touch the dolphins. Mile Marker 59, Grassy Key, 305-289-1121.

Theater of the Seas (see below) offers guests a chance to swim with the dolphins. Called Dolphin Adventure it allows children ages thirteen and older to swim without a parent, but children under thirteen must have their parent or guardian swim with them. Those children between the ages of five and ten must rent the entire pool as a private session (all six slots). Fins are required and mask and snorkel are strongly recommended. Overseas Highway, Mile Marker 84.5, Islamorada, 305-664-2431.

Dolphin Research Center at *Hawk's Cay Resort* is open to the public for viewing but guests get first dibs to swim with the dolphins where half of the session is spent learning about the dolphins, the other half in the water. Children must be at least 4½ feet tall. A shorter program for younger children ages five and up, Dolphin Detectives, teaches children various training techniques that they get to practice on the dolphins. Research Center 305-289-1121.

Theater of the Seas—This vintage sea life zoo, established in 1946, shows its age. While there is still plenty of sea life to observe, both in their pools and on stage, the place is ready for a face-lift. In addition to the Swim with the Dolphin program (see above), there is a popular Swim with the Stingray program for children ages eight and older and a Trainer for a Day program where participants learn about the care and training of dolphins and sea lions. Throughout the park are saltwater aquariums, dolphin and sea lion shows, bottomless boat rides, a birds of prey exhibit, and shark-feeding times. Overseas Highway, Mile Marker 84.5, Islamorada, 305-664-2431.

John Pennecamp Coral Reef State Park is a wonderful place to stop and snorkel and explore the first undersea park in the United States. Take a boat out to the reef, where waters are so shallow that the coral and fish are particularly easy to view. Glass bottom boat, snorkeling, and scuba tours are conducted daily but be sure to reserve them in advance. The beach is lovely here too, and there are hiking trails through the mangroves and a tropical hardwood hammock. Canoeing is a popular pastime and you can rent canoes to explore the park's narrow mangrove channels and tidal creeks. Ranger- and naturalist-led canoe and hiking tours are conducted from November through April. Plus, there are forty-seven camping sites, a small aquarium and picnic areas, a gift shop and snack bar. Mile Marker 102.5, Key Largo, 305-451-1621.

National Key Deer Refuge is a 8,000-acre refuge for the tiny key deer, a 28-inch-tall miniature relation of the full-size animals that live in forests throughout the United States. Big Pine Key is the only key with a year-round freshwater supply, hence the deer made it their home. If you're driving on the Overseas Highway, you'll cut right through their habitat but you're not likely to see any. The best place to spot a deer is a rock quarry called Blue Hole that is filled with water. A marked foot trail, Watson Hammock Trail, about a third of a mile past Blue Hole may give you another chance to see the tiny creatures, especially in the early morning or late evening. Key Deer Boulevard, near Mile Marker 30.5, Big Pine Key, 305-872-2239.

Bahia Honda State Park has the best beach in all of the keys. In addition to lounging on the delectable stretches of white sand on both the bay and the ocean sides of the park, you can hike or canoe a variety of other ecosystems, such as beach dunes and tropical mangroves. The entire park is five hundred acres, big enough to disperse any crowds that come to enjoy all that it has to offer on a weekend. The waters offshore are perfect for snorkeling and scuba diving, and daily snorkel trips are operated to nearby Looe Key Coral Reef. You can rent snorkel equipment, boats, and windsurfers There are eighty campsites both with or without electricity, and six cabin units (described above). Mile Marker 37, 305-872-2353.

Key West

A strong preservation movement has kept old-town Key West looking like it did decades ago—gingerbread trimmed houses wrapped by Bahamian porches, lush tropical vegetation, white picket fences. Take a ninety-minute conch train or trolley tour (or use it to get from place to place) and relax while the driver points out highlights. The attractions—bars, restaurants, and shops—tend to be more adult than child-oriented but there are some fun exhibits that showcase the treasures collected offshore in the treacherous waters around the keys. There are a few family-friendly accommodations listed below, but since many of Key West's lodgings are bed-and-breakfasts, they are not as suitable for children as other places on the keys. Stay at the places discussed below, or in one of the other keys, visiting Key West for the day. Driving and parking are difficult on this tight island, so if you're staying in town, rent a bike, take the conch train (see below), or a hire cab.

WHERE TO STAY
Expensive

Sunset Key Guest Cottages
Address: 245 Front Street, Key West, FL 33040
Telephone: 800-HILTONS, 888-477-7SUN, 305-292-5300, fax 305-292-5395
Website: www.hilton.com

Sunset Key is a small private island just off the tip of Mallory Square in Key West, accessible by a launch from the pier at the Hilton marina. This exclusive island retreat has one of the best resort beaches in the keys, and a drop-dead gorgeous zero-entry swimming pool surrounded by comfortable lounge chairs. Guests check in at the Key West Hilton and then board the private launch for the ten-minute ride to Sunset Key. There are no cars on the key, and guests stay in attractively quaint cottages with big picture windows and sophisticated Keysian decor—blue doors, yellow walls, Italian coral tiles, and stylish furnishings. Many of the units are beachfront, and all have tiny kitchenettes. Your cottage pantry can be prestocked with your choice of groceries; a shopping list is sent out with a confirmation letter in advance of your stay. The clubhouse loans books and videos, and a small shop and deli has gourmet snacks and drinks, along with the more pedestrian fare preferred by children. A complimentary continental breakfast and newspaper are delivered to your cottage each morning. It is a very quiet and deluxe island getaway with the lively action of Key West just a short boat ride away—the best of both worlds.

Accommodations: Thirty-seven cottages come in one-, two-, and three-bedroom suites, all with kitchens, and living and dining areas. One-bedroom suites sleep up to three, two-bedroom suites up to five people, and three-bedroom suites up to seven people. All have ceiling fans, in-rooms safes, and air-conditioning.

Special Features: beach, swimming pool, two tennis courts, CD player, video, board game and literary library, restaurants, bar, spa, Jacuzzi, private charters, parasailing, wave runners, scuba, fishing, boat rentals, excursions, bicycle rental, room service.

$$$: Children eighteen and under free in their parents' room. Daily rates, double occupancy: one bedroom $295–$795, two bedroom $375–$1,195, three bedroom $595–$1,595.

Sheraton Suites Key West

Address: 2001 S. Roosevelt Boulevard, Key West, FL 33040
Telephone: 800-325-3535, 305-292-9800, fax 305-294-6009
Website: www.sheraton.com

This family-friendly property offers guests a home away from home and great spaciousness in its attractive two-room suites with kitchens. The living room has a comfortable sitting area backed by large picture windows and colorful tropical-print drapes. A table and four chairs double as a desk and seating area. A pleasant courtyard pool is lined with beach chairs, offering kids the opportunity to cut loose after touring the sites of Key West. The children's program is headquartered in a converted guest room that has been painted by local high school arts honors students to make kids feel like they're in the middle of a fish-filled tropical reef. Just out the door is a colorful playground with walkway, tube slides, and a sandy play area. The beach is across the rather busy street where you'll find parasailing, watersports, snorkeling, fishing, and sailing.

Accommodations: 180 suites. Two-room suites have kitchens with a tiny fridge, sink, and microwaves, but no utensils. A living-room couch folds out into a queen bed, the bedroom is separated from the living room by white louvered doors and has two double beds or one queen bed.

For Kids: Coral Reef Kid's Club for kids five to twelve usually starts each day with a treasure hunt for silver and gold doubloons that can be traded in for prizes at the end of the day. The Kids Adventure Camp operates from 10:30 A.M.–4 P.M. on Wednesdays through Sundays, and a movie night on Tuesdays from 6 P.M.–10:30 P.M. has games and prizes, a movie, and unlimited refreshments. A fee is charged and meals are included for both full-day and evening sessions.

Special Features: room service, restaurant, bar, gift shop, laundry, scooter and bicycle rentals, activities desk, free shuttle to old town, airport transportation, exercise room.

$$$: Daily rates, double occupancy: $219–$400; ask about promotional rates and special deals.

Moderate

Marriott Casa Marina
Address: 1500 Reynolds Street, Key West, FL 33040
Telephone: 800-228-9290, 305-296-3535, fax 305-296-9960
Website: www.marriott.com
Well located with a wide swath of ecru beach, and with two pools and its own fishing pier/boating dock, historic Casa Marina is a good place to enjoy the topical sun and waters while you explore Key West. You'll have to take a taxi into the old town as there's no shuttle, but it's a $4 ride or a short car trip. The rooms are spread about in several buildings and are spacious and fresh. Flagler built the resort in 1921 and situated it to take advantage of one of the best beaches on Key West.

Accommodations: Rooms have a king or two double beds, all are air-conditioned, and some have minibars. One-bedroom suites have a double sofa bed in the living room.

For Kids: A children's program for ages six and older, operates throughout the year with arts and crafts and lawn games. Parents must remain on the property.

Special Features: swimming pool, beach, scuba, sunset sails, kayaks, fishing, snorkeling, sailing, jet ski, bike rentals, three night-lit tennis courts, health club, shops, bars, restaurants, evening entertainment, room service.

$$$: Daily rates, double occupancy: rooms $189–$290; suites $199–$330. Children under 18 free in their parents' room. Ask about specials which can considerably lower room rates.

Budget

Travelers Palm
Address: 815 Catherine Street, Key West, FL 33040

Telephone: 800-294-9560, fax 305-293-913
Website: www.travelerspalm.com

This comfortable cozy resort in old town features cottages and apartments with full kitchens. It's located three blocks from Duvall Street and six blocks from the Atlantic Beach. You can walk or bike anywhere if you have older kids. The beautifully landscaped tropical gardens and pool are a shady retreat from the lively pace of Key West.

Accommodations: Seven one- and two-bedroom apartments have air-conditioning, complete kitchens, and their own private garden or patio area. The two bedroom has its own private pool.

Special Features: pool, jacuzzi, bbq grill, playground

$$$: Daily rates, double occupancy: $95–$350. Prices drop 10 percent if you stay a week.

WHAT TO SEE AND DO

Mallory Square at the southernmost tip of Key West is *the* place to watch the sunset, and as you wait for the spectacle, lively street performers provide rollicking fun that continues well after the flaming sun has dropped into the ocean. Our favorite was definitely the troupe of performing cats who jumped through hoops and performed for their quirky French ringmaster for little bits of tasty fish. Chairs are set up for the casual audience, and outdoor bars sell drinks of all kinds.

The Conch Train makes a circuit around Key West and stops at a variety of interesting places. Funny guides tell tales of Key West history and point out sites of interest. Trains leave from Mallory Square and many other places in the city (305-294-5161).

The Mel Fischer Treasure Museum is devoted to helping guests experience the twenty-year quest to find the sunken eighteenth-century Spanish treasure ship the *Atocha*. The museum tells the story of the search and displays a lot of the loot—emeralds, gold chains, silver bricks, and implements of daily life. A shop sells the actual treasures and some decent replicas. Fischer started his search in 1969 for the fleet of ships that were lost at sea in 1622 carrying a cargo of gold and precious gems. A trail of gold led him to one of the ships in 1980, but it wasn't until 1985 that he discovered the main cargo of the *Atocha*. The treasure is estimated to be worth 400 million dollars. 200 Greene Street, Key West (305-294-2633).

Shipwreck Historium uses live actors, displays, films and holograms to tell the story of one of Key West's most interesting industries—the shipwreckers. Treacherous reefs in the area caused many ships to founder and wreck. The cry "wreck ashore" would mobilize townspeople to head out to rescue passengers and precious cargo. Helpers got to keep a portion of what they saved. The exhibit covers several floors of a charming old building and culminates in a look out tower sixty-five feet above the town (305-292-8990).

The small but quaint **Key West Aquarium** was built in the depression by the CVC. An excellent touch tank holds horseshoe crabs, giant hermit crabs, conch, and sea slugs, and several larger "ponds" contain sharks and turtles.

Surrounding these indoor pools are walls lined with small aquariums filled with sea life. Outside, several large pools contain tarpon, various fish, sharks, and turtles. It's a good place to learn to identify creatures and fish you might see snorkeling. 1 Whitehead Street (305-296-2051).

Ernest Hemingway Home and Museum Literary teens may gain respect for their required reading when they see where Hemingway lived for the years he was in Key West. Younger kids can pat the fifty-six cats who live on the property. Many descended from cat-lover Hemingway's own beloved pets. Take the guided tour to learn more about the writer's habits and take a look at his writing study. A gift shop allows you to purchase his books along with other mementos. 907 Whitehead Street, Key West (305-294-1136). Open daily 9 A.M.–5 P.M.

Fort Zachary Taylor State Historic Site was built before the Civil War, and includes the largest collection of Civil War armaments in the country. Ranger-guided tours fill out the historical details. A small man-made beach makes it a good afternoon stop for swimming and picnicking. Southard Street on Truman Annex (305-292-6713).

Palm Beach and the Gold Coast

WHERE TO STAY
Expensive

The Breakers, Palm Beach
Address: 1 South County Road, Palm Beach, FL 33480
Telephone: 888-BREAKERS, 561-655-6611, fax 561-659-8403
Website: www.thebreakers.com
The Breakers is one of the North America's most beautiful hotels, combining old world elegance with new world comfort and service. Walk into the lobby with its soaring hand-painted ceilings and sixteenth-century Flemish tapestries and you're transported into the great room of a European castle. Walk outside and you're greeted by a luxurious pool and modern state-of-the-art spa complex on one side with the beach beyond, and two golf courses, twenty-one tennis courts, and a croquet green on the other side.

My kids were smitten with the resort's secret garden. Tucked into a corner next to the golf course is an enchanting piece of ground with a riot of flowers and a real hedgerow maze overseen by topiary monkeys and giraffes. Hidden in the maze's various twists and turns are special surprises that can change from year to year—a swing, a small fountain, a teeter-totter, or perhaps a tiny statue. The kids never tired of exploring it, nor did they tire of playing in the gentle rollers at the Breakers beach where one afternoon we saw a pod of dolphins frolicking in the surf a few feet offshore. The swimming pools and beach are edged by private cabanas; families can have their own shaded outdoor rooms where babies can rest out of the sun.

It's a resort with a rarefied air that makes families feel perfectly comfortable. There's an inviting children's program that runs every day of the year, and the staff will even childproof your hotel room if you bring a toddler, installing outlet covers and corner protectors and removing plastic liners from the garbage cans. During the winter holidays, the hotel welcomes little children at a diminutive reception desk staffed by an elf. Summer prices drop to very affordable if you've always wanted to sample this place.

Accommodations: Rooms and suites vary in size and location, but all are luxuriously appointed and have air-conditioning, electronic safes, and minibars.

For Kids: The kids program operates every day of the year from 10 A.M. to 3 P.M. for children ages six to twelve in a special room with books, a TV and VCR, magazines, toys, and a Nintendo that can be used after camp is over. A separate program for three-to-five-year-olds takes place in a special room with a large ball pit, books, and toys; segments of just two hours can be arranged for this age. There's a snorkel guide for kids right on the property, and fly fishing lessons for kids. Story time is often held at the secret garden. The summer program has kids participating from the community, while the rest of the year it's guests only. During the winter season there's a teen lounge staffed by an intern during the evening; it's very unstructured.

Special Features: beach, four pools, playground, bicycle rental, full-service spa, fitness center, jogging trail, lawn bowling, scuba, snorkeling, shuffleboard, game rooms, movies, two eighteen-hole golf courses, water aerobics, beach volleyball, croquet, horseshoes, twenty-one tennis courts, fly fishing lessons, restaurants, bars, 24-hour room service.

$$$: Daily rates, double occupancy: rooms $180–$570; suites $360–$2,300.

Boca Raton Resort and Club, Boca Raton

Address: 501 East Camino Real, Boca Raton, FL 33432
Telephone: 800-327-0101, 561-395-3000, fax 561-391-3183
Website: www.bocaresort.com
E-mail: reservations@bocaresort.com

A true destination resort you'll never have to leave, this Spanish Mediterranean-style hotel first opened in 1926. It has grown substantially over the years to a size of 350 acres straddling both sides of the intracoastal waterway. The Boca Raton Resort takes pride in having unique details such as an herb garden and cages of colorful and exotic birds scattered throughout the resort. Rooms in the historic Cloisters building contain architectural accents such as arched doorways, and high-beamed ceilings are pleasing to the eye, while finely carved writing desks and armoires, and Oriental rugs blanketing terra-cotta floors add comfort to the luxury. The beach club's rooms have a light and airy feel with marble floors, light colors, and sliding glass doors that open to salty ocean breezes. Rooms in the tower have a formal feel, with dark wood and rich colors. Golf lovers will enjoy the golf villas, which have patios overlooking the course. Half a mile of private beach laces the hotel with glistening sand and sparkling waters.

Accommodations: 936 rooms, 70 villa apartments, 37 suites all come with bathrobes, two phones, air-conditioning, minibars, TVs, full-length mirrors, and in-room safes.

For Kids: Year-round programs with experienced counselors supervising activities and outings.

Special Features: beach, nine restaurants, two lounges, two eighteen-hole golf courses, thirty-four tennis courts, five pools, racquet ball, fitness centers, marina, fishing, watersports, bicycle rentals, snorkeling and scuba lessons, croquet, volleyball, basketball, 24-hour room service, fitness classes, and a business center.

$$$: Kids under sixteen stay free, additional people are $30 per night. Daily rates, double occupancy: $130–$495; villas $125–$425; suites $230–$5,500.

Budget

Sheraton Yankee Clipper, Fort Lauderdale
Address: 1140 Seabreeze Boulevard, Fort Lauderdale, FL 33316
Telephone: 800-958-5551, 954-524-5551, fax 954-523-5376
Website: www.sheraton.com/yankeeclipper

The town of Fort Lauderdale is famous as a spring break destination for college students and it's a good idea to avoid the town that week. But the rest of the year it's an excellent place to visit to enjoy 23 miles of white sand beaches, sunny weather, and plenty to do. The Sheraton Yankee Clipper is directly on the beach right in the center of the action. It is a family oriented hotel with daily activities for all ages.

Accommodations: 501 rooms. Rooms have king-size beds or double beds, and all the basic amenities, plus safes and coffeemakers.

For Kids: Children four and up enjoy activities that vary throughout the week.

Special Features: The property has three swimming pools, several restaurants and lounges, a fitness center, tennis courts, shops, laundromat, deli, evening entertainment, watersports, car rental.

$$$: Rates range from $89–$249 per night during the high season.

Sheraton Yankee Trader, Fort Lauderdale
Address: 321 N. Atlantic Boulevard, Fort Lauderdale, FL 33304
Telephone: 800-958-5551, 954-467-1111, fax 954-462-2442
Website: www.sheraton.com/yankeetrader

The Sheraton Yankee Trader has many business guests, however it is an excellent deal and has significant amenities. The Trader is directly across from the beach and is close to the downtown club scene. Guest can walk across the street to the beach via the skywalk, a glassed-in corridor several stories above the street. An elevator takes guests back down to ground level where the sand is just steps away.

Accommodations: 460 rooms. Guests can choose from king or double beds; rooms come with the standard amenities, TV, telephones, and furnishings.

For Kids: Activities such as shell hunting, painting T-shirts, beach bingo, sand art, sports and games are offered throughout the day.

Special Features: pools, three tennis courts, a fitness center, live entertainment nightly, restaurants, shops.

$$$: Rates range from $89–$249 per night during the high season.

The Sea Breeze, Delray Beach
Address: 820 N. Ocean Boulevard, Delray Beach, FL 33483
Telephone: 561-276-7491, fax 561-276-7496

The Sea Breeze provides the essentials in hospitality, without luxury, making it perfect to pare down family vacation costs. The rooms have been recently renovated with comfortable furnishings such as chairs, sofas, tables, and armoires. If cooking is necessary, the studios and apartments have kitchenettes, and some even have full kitchens.

Accommodations: Rooms, studios, one-bedroom apartments, or two-bedroom apartments. All have large bathrooms, air-conditioning, TV, and telephones.

Special Features: There is a pool on the property, gas barbecue grills, and a laundry facility available.

$$$: Additional people are $15 dollars per night. Daily rates, double occupancy: rooms $49–$69, studios $52–$90, one-bedroom apartments $69–$119, and two-bedroom apartments from $85–$194.

The Southwestern Coast

Warm and gentle gulf waters await those who venture to Florida's west coast. It's especially suitable for families with young children as the water is always calm and stays quite shallow for many yards. Some of the world's best shelling and most beautiful sunsets are found on these beaches.

Visitor Information: Website: www.leeislandcoast.com, Lee County Visitor and Convention Bureau, P.O. Box 2445, Fort Myers, FL 33902, 800-237-6444, 941-338-3500, fax 941-334-1106.

MARCO ISLAND

WHERE TO STAY
Moderate

Radisson Suite Beach Resort
Address: 600 South Collier Boulevard, Marco Island, FL 34145
Telephone: 800-333-3333, 941-394-4100, fax 941-394-0262
Website: www.radisson.com

Marco Island is known for its powdery beaches, excellent for shelling, and seven golf courts within a 10-mile radius of each other. Suites with kitchenettes give the Radisson a nudge over some of the other resorts lining this section of exceptional beach that is filled with a row of high-rise hotels and condominiums. The flesh-colored hotel is built around a sparsely landscaped courtyard covered in white rock, but once you're inside your condominium, things pick up a bit, and the units are spacious and comfortable. As in most hotels, your view determines the price you pay; you might look out on gardens, a hotel next door, or the lovely gulf waters. A small freshwater pool lures some of the swimmers off the white-sugar sand beach that is topped with a layer of shells at the tide line. Guest quarters all have spacious screened porches. They offer an excellent value for families, especially off-season when summer family packages drop the price even further.

Accommodations: 268 units, most of which are one-bedroom suites with a king bed in the bedroom and a fold-out couch in the living room. All have fully equipped kitchens.

For Kids: Radisson Rascals for ages four to twelve operates occasionally throughout the year in its own special room. Activities include beach games, shell hunts, island bike tours, and crafts. Occasional parents nights out are offered with themes.

Special Features: beach, swimming pool, Jacuzzi, bicycle rentals, play rooms, wave runners, boogie boards, canoeing, trolley cars of Marco Island, aquacycle, parasailing, kayaks, banana boats, tennis court, shop, game room, Ping-Pong, fitness center, video game room, baby-sitting, shuffleboard, pizza takeout, two restaurants.

$$$: Daily rates, double occupancy: one-bedroom suites $159–$389; two-bedrooms, two baths $259–$529.

Marco Island Marriott Resort and Golf Club

Address: 400 South Collier Boulevard, Marco Island, FL 34145
Telephone: 800-438-4373, 941-394-2511, fax 941-642-2672
Website: www.marriott.com

This resort is an excellent option if you're looking for a full-service resort on Marco Island that welcomes families. The center of the action off the beach is in the two large pools, or in the wading pool. The resort's own mini–golf course has enough curves and sharp turns to keep a youngster occupied. Guests stay in two large nondescript towers connected by the lobby, restaurants, and a variety of shops. There are two pools, one between the tower wing and one off to the side. A series of "villas" fronted by the grassy mini–golf course and a wide lawn is on one side. There are two playgrounds for children and a kids program for five- to twelve-year-olds. A daily schedule of activities is published and includes tennis clinics, sailing excursions, tropical hair braiding, shelling excursions, and 18-hole miniature golf. "Dive-in" movies are offered on occasion—float in the pool on a mat while you watch a family-style movie being shown on the pool deck.

Accommodations: 732 rooms. All rooms have private balconies, air conditioning, minibar, safe, coffeemaker, and a king or two double beds.

For Kids: A Kids Klub program (fee) operates from 10 A.M. to 4 P.M. for children ages five to twelve. Activities include arts and crafts, sand-castle building, miniature golf, and more. A special nanny service is available through the hotel, with one nanny assigned to each family of up to three children. Teen activities, such as sailing camps, are scheduled on occasion.

Special Features: beach, two swimming pools, wading pool, two small playgrounds, sailing, kayaks, bike rentals, wave runner, eco-tours, basketball, board games, water trikes, beach stroller rentals, parasailing, jet skiing, sightseeing cruises, Sunfish, miniature golf, volleyball, shops, restaurants, bars, baby-sitting. Seven 18-hole golf courses are within ten miles of the resort.

$$$: Kids under eighteen free in their parents' room. Daily rates, double occupancy: $110–$389.

FORT MYERS AREA

WHERE TO STAY
Moderate

Pink Shell Beach Resort
Address: 275 Estrero Boulevard, Ft. Myers Beach, FL 33931
Telephone: 800-237-5786, 800-543-9816, 941-463-6181, fax 941-481-4947
Website: www.southseas.com

A quiet resort in a bustling beach town, the Pink Shell is geared to families who want the option to cook, as there are full kitchens or kitchenettes in every unit. The center of town with its lively restaurants and shops is about one mile away. Many rooms have views of the gulf and Sanibel Island off in the distance. A number of villas look out on an inland waterway and have their own docks or share a dock with one or two other units. The gulf beach is very shallow, making it safe for toddlers. The resort is spread along the northern end of Fort Meyers Beach on talcum-powder-soft white sand.

Accommodations: 208 guest rooms range from 1,000-square-foot two-bedroom condos with washer and dryer to simple efficiencies with kitchenette and two queen beds.

For Kids: Scooters Club House day camp entertains children three to twelve with activities such as supervised games, kite flying, pool bingo, shell art, and fishing. It operates for full or half days. Evening program features theme events such as Circus Night, Pirate Adventure, and movie and pizza parties.

Special Features: beach, three swimming pools, children's wading pool, two lit tennis courts, fishing pier, restaurant, shops, volleyball, water aerobics classes, pool bingo, country line dancing, fishing, boat excursions, catamaran trips, bicycle rentals.

$$$: Children under eighteen free in their parents' room. Daily rates double occupancy: rooms $119–$229, condos $135–$295.

Budget

Beach House Motel
Address: 26106 Hickory Boulevard, Bonita Beach, FL 34134
Telephone: 941-992-2644

Guests return year after year to this quiet getaway right on the beach that is an excellent value for waterfront accommodations. It's definitely no frills, but the cottages are clean and comfortable and have much more charm than most budget lodging. The lobby has books and magazines guests can borrow. Fresh white cottages are on the second floor with parking garages underneath; all have large screened porches on their beach side and some type of kitchen. There are thatched huts on the beach to provide shade, as well as lounge chairs, picnic tables, and barbecues for guests to use.

Accommodations: One- or two-bedroom units all have full kitchens; two-bedroom units have two baths. Efficiencies come in two sizes, including one that can sleep up to four on a queen bed and futon, with a hallway separating the sleeping from the living area.

Special Features: beach, barbecue, picnic tables.

$$$: Daily rates, double occupancy: efficiency $70–$105, one-bedroom $80–$125, two-bedroom unit for four people $125–$195. Extra person over age two, $8 per night.

SANIBEL AND CAPTIVA

Sanibel Island is a verdant relief from the oceans of high-rise hotels fronting Florida's coastline to the south. Half the island is a nature preserve and sanctuary. Resorts, time-shares, and hotels are found along the gulf side of this crescent-shaped island known for its spectacular shelling beaches, but none may be more than four stories high. Conservation groups work hard to keep the island undeveloped, by buying up land adjacent to the sanctuary as it becomes available. Residents are asked to turn out lights facing the gulf from May to November because that's when turtles lay their eggs and the hatchlings can mistake lights for the reflection of stars on the sea and head the wrong way when they emerge from the shell. Bike trails, completely separate from the roads, interlace the island, and most establishments rent bikes in adult sizes, kids sizes, tandems, and with kiddy seats. Jet skis and other motorized craft are not allowed.

WHERE TO STAY
Expensive

South Seas Plantation Resort and Yacht Harbour
Address: P.O. Box 194, Captiva Island, FL 33924

Telephone: 800-237-3102, 941-472-5111, fax 941-481-4947
Website: www.southseas.com

A veritable city on the sand, South Seas Plantation has every kind of accommodation you can imagine spread over 330 acres. The place is so big it has its own trolley system that takes guests back and forth between their rooms, the restaurants, pier, beach, and marina. Formerly a key lime and coconut plantation, the resort offer guests a fair amount of privacy in a setting that can keep you as busy . . . or as laid-back as you wish. A variety of family activities are planned each day, such as family bingo, alligator races, kayaking, fishing, and a perennial favorite—log rolling in the pool. Large families can rent a complete house while groups who don't want to cook can find elegant first-class hotel rooms and suites. A variety of condominiums are available in all parts of the property—near the tennis courts, on the beach, and next to the marina. Because it's like a small city, you'll find all kinds of dining options (reservations a must during high season) and a variety of shops. The resort's marina is home to Steve Colgate's Offshore Sailing School.

Accommodations: You name it, they've got it—six hundred accommodations in total, from private homes of all designs and sizes to elegant hotel rooms, one-bedrooms, efficiencies, suites, and condominiums with multiple bedrooms.

For Kids: Explorer Kids Club has both day and evening camps that include a kid-friendly meal and a variety of activities. Children are divided by age groups with programs tailored to their age. Programs vary daily and seasonally and offer themed activities. You'll also find preteen and teen activities including sea kayak trips, night volleyball, catamaran rides, and junior golf clinics.

Special Features: Beaches, twenty-one tennis courts (seven lit), two marinas, sailing school, eighteen swimming pools, nature center, parasailing, windsurfing, canoes, nature cruises, log rolling, boat rentals, scuba diving, rental bikes, shops, restaurants, nine-hole golf, fitness center, evening entertainment, sailing, parasailing, fishing.

$$$: Daily rates: rooms, $195–$340 one-bedroom suites and efficiencies $195–$395; two-bedroom condos $285–$535, two to four bedroom private home have a seven-night minimum $225–$850. Rates vary depending on view and season.

Moderate

Sundial Beach and Tennis Resort
Address: 1451 Middle Gulf Drive, Sanibel Island, FL 33957
Telephone: 800-237-4184, 941-472-4151, fax 941-472-8892
Website: www.southseas.com

This full-service resort with all the comforts of home makes for a family vacation as easy as you'll ever find. Situated on a breathtaking swath of powdery ecru sand, Sundial's condominiums are all just steps from the beach, and each comes with its own screened porch so indoor/outdoor living can continue into the evening hours (or when the kids are getting on your nerves!). All kinds of resort niceties, such as watersports, tennis, room service, fine dining, and full maid service are routine, so you get the space and amenities of your own private home with the benefits of first-class resort services. On-site bicycle rentals come in all sizes, and you can even rent a jogging stroller to explore the island's many trails at your own pace. A small Environmental Coastal Observatory Center has a 450-gallon touch tank, an aquarium, an endangered species exhibit, and a hermit crab petting zoo. A wide variety of activities for all guests, including children, is offered each day.

Accommodations: 270 condominiums. One-and two-bedroom, and two-bedroom with a den; each has a fully equipped kitchen, dining area; living room, in-room safe, and TV.

For Kids: On weekdays, the Explorer Kids Club conducts activities for three- to twelve-year-olds that might be hermit crab races, shell crafts, and tiny tots tennis classes. On weekend nights, and one other evening per week, Kids Night Out features themed activities such as Pirates Night and Jungle Adventure.

Special Features: beach, twelve tennis courts, five swimming pools, jogging trail, catamarans, boogie boards, kayaks, power boat rentals, sight-seeing and fishing cruises, three restaurants, shops, games area, bike and boat rentals, baby-sitting, room service.

$$$: Daily rates: one bedroom condo $151–$450, two-bedroom condo $231–$585, two-bedroom condo with den $281–$635.

Budget

Sunshine Island Inn
Address: 642 East Gulf, Sanibel, FL 33957
Telephone: 941-395-2500
Website: www.sunshineislandinn.com

Peter and Barbara Carlson have owned this small five-unit inn for four years and take pride in its presentation and decor. You get the impression that they enjoy fussing to constantly improve it. Its location across the street from a public-access trail to the beach keeps its price impressively low. Although it lacks the amenities and services of a large resort, rooms are beautifully decorated with modern and attractive furnishings, and it has a personal feel, making it one of the best deals on a rather pricey island. The center of the U-shaped property houses a large swimming pool. If you're looking for a family reunion site, this place is perfect to take over with one entire group. It backs onto a stretch of slow-moving river that receives visits from a local blue heron three or four times a day, and an osprey perches in one of the shady pine trees on the property. Several times a week a sea otter cruises the waterway, and a manatee has been spotted swimming past once or twice.

Accommodations: Five units. There are two-bedroom units that sleep up to six. Smaller studios can work for smaller families—they have two full-size beds, a table and chairs, and an efficiency kitchen. Another unit has two double beds and a living/kitchen area separated by a half-wall. All units have some sort of kitchen.

Special Features: swimming pool, resident wildlife, gas grills, outdoor tables, bicycles, laundry room.

$$$: Daily rates, double occupancy studios: $69–$139, two-bedroom units, $144–$239.

WHAT TO SEE AND DO

The Bailey-Matthews Shell Museum: Filled with shells from all the oceans around the globe, this attractive museum is the only museum in the United States entirely devoted to shells. An excellent video plays throughout the day, informing guests of the life cycle and idiosyncrasies of various shells, and an exhibition hall features displays of all kinds of shells and shelly things. Come here to learn the names of the many shells you'll pick up on Sanibel and the surrounding area. A charming exhibit of sailors' valentines—elaborate pictures made entirely of tiny shells—captivated my kids for many moments, and we vowed to try one of our own. There's a small shop with shell-related books, toys, and gifts. Open Tuesday–Sunday 10 A.M.–4 P.M.. 3075 Sanibel-Captiva Road, P.O. Box 1580, Sanibel, FL 33957, 941-395-2233, fax 941-395-6706, www.coconet.com.

NAPLES AREA

WHERE TO STAY
Moderate

Naples Beach Hotel and Golf Club
Address: 851 Gulf Shore Boulevard, Naples, FL 33940
Telephone: 800-237-7600, 941-261-2222
Website: www.naplesbeachhotel.com

Tucked into a rather residential section of Naples in an area thick with landscaped tropical gardens and no high-rises, Naples Beach Hotel has more character and interest than many of the towering hotels to its south on Marco Island or its north in Naples. It's spread out, with two original wings and several newer "towers," although the latter are not really that tall. It's got a small pool and a long beach that is a lovely beige color. The kids club house is at the back of an enormous grassy area where the children often play. Their eighteen-hole golf course is across the street. A well-stocked deli and shop sells pizza by the slice, fresh popcorn, ice cream, gourmet coffee, and pastry.

Accommodations: 315 rooms and suites vary slightly in size. Suites have kitchenettes with microwaves.

For Kids: Beach Klub 4 Kids is a complimentary program for children ages five to twelve that allows the kids to choose what they want to do for the day. Each day, (between the hours of 9 A.M. and 3 P.M.) the children present can select what they want to do. Choices include goofy Olympics, games on the broad lawn, swimming, and arts and crafts. Dinner and a movie are offered Friday and Saturday nights from 6:30 P.M. to 9 P.M.

Special Features: swimming pool, restaurants, golf course, tennis, bike rentals, afternoon tea, sailboats, bars.

$$$: Children under eighteen stay free in their parents' rooms. Daily rates, double occupancy: rooms $95–$170, suites $155–$305.

The Tides

Address: 1801 Gulf Shore Boulevard North, Naples, FL 34102
Telephone: 800-438-8763, 941-262-6196, fax 941-262-3055

A great find in a pricey neighborhood, the Tides has one- and two-bedroom units and efficiencies that let families further economize by doing their own cooking. It's right on a gorgeous strip of beach in a quiet and secluded section of Naples, with the most desirable units facing the gulf waters. There's a nice freshwater swimming pool and a continental breakfast included in the rates.

Accommodations: Efficiencies contain two double beds, a sitting area, a completely equipped kitchenette, and a screened porch. Suites have a living room with a king bed or two twins, a complete kitchen, and one or two bedrooms. One- and two-bedroom apartments have living room, dining area, twin or king beds, full kitchen, and private screened porch. All are air-conditioned.

Special Features: beach, two shuffleboard courts, swimming pool.

$$$: No charge for children under ten years. Daily rates, double occupancy: efficiencies $105–$170, one bedroom apartments $125–$260, two-bedroom apartments $225–$345.

3.

HAWAII

Hawaii is an easygoing family vacation: take a tropical island paradise with swaying palm trees, white sand, and aquamarine water, and plunk it down in the heart of Main Street, USA. You've got all the exotic sensibilities of a lush and lavish tropical vacation but without any of the fuss—pack your swimsuit, hop a plane, and you're there. No need to scramble for passports or birth certificates, schedule vaccinations, or brush up on your higher mathematical skills to negotiate foreign currency. It's a comfortable blend of domestic familiarity and exotic Polynesia with a distinctive culture that local Hawaiians enjoy sharing with visitors.

Where you go and where you stay are the two chief ingredients to consider when planning a trip to Hawaii and they are choices that will flavor your vacation experience. Each of the six Hawaiian islands that welcomes tourists—Oahu, Maui, Hawaii, Kauai, Lanai, and Molokai—are quite different from one another in weather, scenery, beaches, activities, and personality. There are islands that remain virtually untouched, offering secluded getaways where you can get a glimpse of the life of Hawaii as it used to be. Or you can pick an island with the fast pulse of urban excitement, nightlife, and nonstop activities. Most of the islands fit somewhere in the middle, with a balanced portion of upbeat action and quiet seclusion. There are very few places in Hawaii that don't allow children, but there are some establishments that put out the family welcome mat with particular warmth and enthusiasm. These are the places you'll find in this book.

Visitor Information Website: www.gohawaii.com. Hawaii Visitors and Convention Bureau (HVCB) Suite 801, Waikiki Business Plaza, 2270 Kalakaua Avenue, Honolulu, HI 96815, 800-GO-HAWAII, 808-923-1811, fax 808-924-0290; on the mainland 800-353-5846, 180 Montgomery Street, Suite 2360, San Francisco, CA 94104.

WHEN TO GO, CLIMATE

Hawaii has two seasons—summer and winter—and both are ideal for travel because temperatures vary little and you'll find balmy warm weather twelve months of the year. Winter is the rainiest season, but it is still the most popular

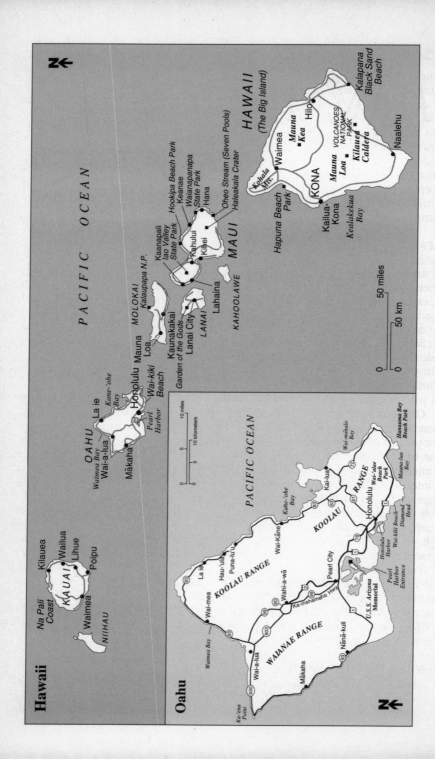

time to travel to the islands since many tourist visit to escape the cold of home. Summer, spring, and fall are the driest months, but you can find dry stretches of coast in the winter, too. Bring an umbrella during the rainy season or if you'll be staying on the rainy side of an island, such as Kauai. Temperatures can dip at the higher elevations, so bring a wrap or a quick-drying fleece if you're planning to explore the "upcountry" areas or volcanic peaks.

Summer is second in popularity, when families like to travel, and special programs are added at hotels and resorts to make their stay more inviting. The deepest discounts apply in the spring and fall, followed by summer. The Christmas season is the very busiest time of year; if you're planning to travel during this time, make plans far in advance.

HEALTH AND SAFETY

Sunburn: The worst problem you're likely to encounter in Hawaii is a bad case of sunburn, and since that is completely preventable, apply high SPF sunscreen liberally and regularly. Avoid direct sun exposure between the hours of 11 and 3, especially your first few days. Wear a hat and take an umbrella with you to the beach. Protect a young baby's skin with a lightweight cotton cover-up if he or she is too young for sunscreen.

Safety: Keep an eye on your wallet, camera, and purse, and never leave valuables unattended on a beach. Don't leave anything valuable in your rental car. On some highly touristy drives, thieves have been known to pop open a trunk to lift anything stored inside. Leave your prized possessions at home or in your hotel safe.

Ocean swimming: During the summer months, the islands' north-facing beaches are very calm and quite safe for swimming, but in winter, the north shores get pummeled by rough waters and big waves. On the southern side of the islands, the situation is reversed and the beaches are a bit rougher in summer (although not as bad as the northern shores in winter) and calmer in winter. In addition, the currents and undertow can be quite strong and un-expected; pay attention to posted signs and flags before entering the water. If you plan to visit a deserted beach where there are no lifeguards, ask the local people or your concierge about water-safety conditions. If there's no one to ask, stay out of the water. Never turn your back on the ocean; swells can appear out of nowhere and you should keep your eye on the waves at all times.

Varmints: There are no biting sand flies, snakes, fire ants, or malaria-carrying mosquitoes in the Hawaiian islands. There *are* just plain mosquitoes, however, and they love to bite fresh *haole* (foreigner) skin. Apply insect repellent during the early morning and early evening hours to avoid getting bitten. Once in awhile, weather patterns may draw a Portuguese man-of-war near a beach. Their sting can hurt; if you're stung, rinse the area with fresh- or saltwater and apply ice. Jellyfish are difficult to see in the water; if you are stung, apply vinegar to the sting to stop the burning, and apply ice for pain.

Driving: Hawaiian law requires that children up to age two be in car seats. If you plan to rent a car, reserve a car seat when you make a reservation with a car rental agency or be prepared to bring your own.

ON A BUDGET

Hawaii tends to be more expensive for the basics—any island is because of the added shipping costs that are thrown in to any product that comes from outside the island. If you're planning to do your own cooking, add about 25 percent on to what you'd expect to spend back home. Some families we know bring a cooler on the airplane stocked with their favorite foods to save on island food prices.

Activities Warehouse is a licensed travel agency that sells all kinds of island activities at a discount. One call allows you to book everything from a submarine or helicopter ride to a bicycle or snorkel-set rental, at 10 to 30 percent off. You should book more popular activities during peak season before you leave or immediately upon arriving in the islands. Website: www. travelhawaii.com, 800-923-4004.

PACKAGE TOURS

A package tour binds together airfare, accommodations, and often a rental car or activities into one low price. It's not a guided tour where you'll be with the same group of tourists escorted by a guide from place to place. Hawaii is famous for its bargain packages. The best deals at the nicest places are offered from May to early December, although you can get a package any time of year.

Many package-savvy shoppers decide where they want to stay before they buy a package, and look for a package that includes their accommodations. If you do it the other way around, make sure you do some sleuthing on where you'll be staying to make sure you'll be close to a sandy beach or in a hotel of the quality you wish. Read the fine print carefully and ask questions. Find out cancellation policies. To find packages, check the travel section of your local newspaper or ads in the back of travel magazines.

CULTURE AND FOOD

Hawaii's rich cultural heritage developed in isolation: the island chain is the most remote of any island group in the world, with the closest mainland more than 2,500 miles away. In recent years, Hawaiian culture has experienced a healthy revival throughout the islands, and programs that teach guests different aspects of the arts and culture have become popular offerings at resorts and hotels.

The Hula

Hula performances are the mainstay of nearly every hotel's evening entertainment, and hula classes are taught in virtually every children's program throughout the islands. The story behind this ancient art form is fascinating. In the absence of a written language, ancient Hawaiians used chants and dances to record their history and noteworthy events. Hula dancers left their families at a young age to live in a hula *halau* where they were taught both the physical and the spiritual aspects of the dance. Through the hula, the stories of the people were passed from generation to generation, and the dance was accompanied by instruments made from gourds, bamboo, feathers, shark skins, and ocean pebbles.

When Christian missionaries arrived in the early nineteenth century and were scandalized by the scant dress and suggestive movements, hula went underground. It was practiced and passed on in secret until 1874 when King David Kalakaua ascended the throne and reintroduced the hula at his inauguration. The dance began to incorporate modern instruments such as the ukulele, guitar, bass, and steel guitar, and hula songs later began using English words. Today, both the ancient and more modern form of hula is celebrated throughout the islands in a number of festivals and competitions.

The Lei

Get off the plane or arrive at your hotel check-in desk and you're greeted by aromatic stands of tropical flowers that are placed around your neck. Why? The Hawaiians created their jewelry and ornamentation from the land and the sea—garlands of flowers, ferns, shells, feathers, seeds, and leaves. They were once given to mark every important occasion in a person's life—birthdays, wedding, and funeral, as well as arrivals and departures, just as they still are today.

Native Hawaiian Language

Once spoken throughout the island chain, the Hawaiian language is now used mostly in songs, dances, and for ceremonial purposes. Many Hawaiian words, such as *mahalo* (thank you), *keiki* (children), *mana* (spirit), *lanai* (porch), and *ono* (delicious), have survived and are used in everyday conversation in Hawaii. Other words such as *alii* (Hawaiian royalty), *hale* (house or building), *pali* (cliff), and *heiau* (Hawaiian temple or place of worship), appear frequently in towns or on street signs thoroughout the islands. Today many Hawaiian children are taught the Hawaiian language and its alphabet of only twelve letters— a, e, i, o, u, h, k, l, m, n, p, w—in school.

Hawaiian Food

Hawaii is a true melting pot, as evidenced by its cuisine. Luaus offer a taste of the most traditional Hawaiian food, usually roast pig; *poi* (a starchy paste made from crushed taro root); and a pork, chicken, or fish wrapped in *ti* leaves and steamed along with a variety of other dishes. *Pupus* are hors d'oeuvres. Expect to find lots of fresh fish prepared in many different ways, and fresh tropical fruit sauces.

One dish you'll see served throughout the islands is the plate lunch, usually a main dish that is often a local specialty, with two scoops of rice, a scoop of macaroni salad, and some gravy. The plate lunches are an inexpensive way to taste the local food. Don't miss the chance to sample the Hawaiian version of the snow cone, Shave Ice, flavored with traditional flavors and exotic tropical fruit syrups.

WHERE TO STAY
Camping and Cabins

Year-round warm weather makes Hawaii an ideal place to pitch a tent, and there is a good selection of campgrounds throughout the islands. Simple camper cabins where you have a shelter and a few basic pieces of equipment are available as well. Both are found in county, state, or federally managed campsites, and because they are so affordable, families need to plan ahead and reserve as far in advance as possible. Each island has a section on camping. Contact the Division of Parks, 54 S High Street, Room 101, Wailuku, Hawaii 96793, 808-984-8109, fax 808-984-8111 for a brochure describing state-run campsites throughout the islands.

Oahu

Oahu, the third biggest and most populous Hawaiian island, draws more visitors than any other island. Most of them flock to sun-kissed Waikiki Beach, which sports the majority of hotels, but there are a few family-friendly resorts scattered around the island's other lovely beaches. Oahu is known for its legendary surfing beaches, and the tall waves on the north shore at places such as Sunset Beach and the Banzai Pipeline are some of the most dramatic anywhere in the world; try to plan a half-day trip to one of these beaches to watch master surfers take on these monolithic waves, but don't let your kids try surfing here. Instead, let your beginners learn to surf on the gentle waves of Waikiki—lessons are offered at nearly every resort.

To get an accurate picture of Oahu, venture out beyond Waikiki into the rest of Honolulu or other parts of the island. A scenic coastal highway wraps around much of the it, and there are fascinating side trips such as the Polynesian Cultural Center and the world's largest maze on the Dole Pineapple Planatation. Rent a car if you want the freedom to tour on your own time, or take advantage of the island's superb public transportation system called TheBus.

Visitor Information: Website: www.visit-oahu.com or www.gohonolulu. com The Oahu Visitors Bureau, 1001 Bishop Street, Pauahi Tower, Suite 47, Honolulu, HI 96813, 888-GO-HONOLULU, 808-524-0722.

Best Sweet Treat: chocolate macadamia nut pie or hula pie, macadamia nut ice cream in an oreo cookie crust topped with whipped cream and nuts.

On a Budget

Take your own island tour using the island's mass transit system, TheBus. Hop on bus #52 or #54 at the Ala Moana Shopping Center (808-848-444, for itineraries). The full Circle Island Tour costs $1 for adults and 50¢ for students through high school age.

The free Kodak Hula Show is an excellent budget alternative to the pricey luau shows of the big resorts, although you'll have to bring your own food—there's no roast pig or poi here. The show features Hawaiian musicians and dancers, some of whom are the sons and daughters of the original cast, as the show has been running since 1937. The performance takes place on the lawn adjacent to the Waikiki Band Shell on the Waikiki side of Kapiolani Park.

WAIKIKI

In the 1920s and 1930s Waikiki was *the* place to vacation for Hollywood celebrities and well-heeled sophisticates. Now it attracts people who crave urban excitement, night life, unlimited shopping, and a lively, boisterous (and sometimes crowded) beach scene. This famous stretch of sand is home to dozens of family-friendly resort hotels and high-rises in all price ranges. Its fame is deserved—good weather, calm ocean, and gorgeous golden sands. Many people plan a Hawaiaan vacation that includes a high-energy stop-over in Waikiki before they head out to one of the other islands for a more tranquil holiday experience.

You'll find infinite choices of restaurants, from fast and cheap to offbeat ethnic and superluxurious. Shopping is a serious pastime in the hundreds of shops and shopping centers, and if you can drag yourselves off the beach, there are fascinating field trips and activities that can keep a family busy for a week.

WHERE TO STAY

Because the number of hotel rooms on Waikiki Beach soars into the stratosphere, many properties offer special deals to fill their beds. Published here are rack rates, but be sure to inquire about discounts and packages before you book your stay. Don't eliminate properties in a price category that seems over your budget until you've investigated bargains that might drop the rack rate by as much as 50 percent. Many Waikiki properties charge a daily parking fee of around $10, so consider carefully whether you will need a rental car. Categories are per night:

Expensive: Over $225
Moderate: $125–$225
Budget: under $125

Expensive

Halekulani
Address: 2199 Kalia Road, Honolulu, HI, 96815-1988
Telephone: 800-367-2343, 808-923-2311, fax 808-926-8004
Website: www.halekulani.com

A soothing beachfront respite in a fast-lane neighborhood, Halekulani is in the heart of the Waikiki action, shoulder to shoulder with the rest of the concrete high-rises that flank the beach, yet miles away in attitude. I guess it's the gracious let-me-attend-to-your-every-need service and the sheer elegance of the place that sets such a tranquil mood, but it's not the kind of peace and quiet that makes parents grit their teeth. Families have come to the resort ever since it first opened its doors in 1917, and you're made welcome to this day with special touches like a welcome fruit basket and box of chocolates delivered to your room as you arrive. A children's program operates during the summer months and school holidays.

The resort has all the key elements of a quintessential Hawaiian vacation—a gorgeous sandy beach with views of Diamond Head in the background, a magnificent pool with a bottom mosaic of a Hawaiian orchid (made of 1.25 million tiny pieces of translucent glass), and a friendly concierge desk that can arrange all kinds of watersports and excursions. But it also has something no other resort can claim—the best restaurant in all of Hawaii. La Mer, open just for dinner, is the only AAA five-diamond restaurant anywhere on the islands. If you don't think your kids can polish off an entire order of bouillabaisse, featuring morsels of fresh island fish and lobster served with broth in a puff pastry, you can order them a half portion or try one of the resort's other more casual restaurants.

Accommodations: 456 rooms and suites have in-room fridge, luxurious bathrobes, three telephones, marble baths, and all kinds of other amenities.

For Kids: Complimentary children's activities program operates during Easter, summer, and winter school holidays. Children five to twelve can participate Monday through Friday from 8:30 A.M. to 3:30 P.M. in activities such as learning the hula, lei making, making a bookmark out of seaweed, etc.

Special Features: swimming pool, beach, three restaurants, two bars, fitness center with trainer, shops, hair stylist, 24-hour room service, full concierge service, car rentals, evening entertainment.

$$$: One child seventeen and under is free in parents' room utilizing existing bedding. Extra beds $30. During the summer, a second room can be reserved at a discounted rate. Daily rates, double occupancy: $295–$1,920.

Hilton Hawaiian Village

Address: 2005 Kalia Road, Honolulu, HI 96815
Telephone: 800-HILTONS, 808-949-4321, fax 808-951-5458
Website: www.hilton.com

One of the most complete resorts on the beach in Waikiki, Hilton Hawaiian Village boasts its own miniature golf course and a nonstop selection of flashy Hawaiian shows. It's the largest hotel in all of Hawaii with more than 2,500 rooms, four high-rise towers, and its own shopping mall. It even has its own bus depot, it's so big. Every day of the week a different selection of free activities is available for guests (as well as another list of those you must pay for), and the weekends are filled with free entertainment and a fireworks show. If you've got the bucks, stay in the Ali'i Tower, which has ultradeluxe guest rooms and suites and is like a luxury hotel within a hotel. The tower has its own concierge service, a private pool, and other special amenities. Options for both casual and more formal dining are plentiful; you can even take a dinner cruise aboard the hotel's own catamaran. Toddlers have a special shallow pool to themselves, and the resort's gigantic swimming pool is great fun for all ages. There's exotic wildlife, such as flamingos and penguins, wandering abut the resort's lavishly landscaped twenty acres, and somehow the beach doesn't feel too crowded— unusual for a place this size in Waikiki.

Accommodations: 2,545 rooms over twenty acres. Best for families are those closest to the beach in the Rainbow Tower or in the deluxe Ali'i Tower. Rooms have one king or two double beds, safe, and minibar.

Special Features: beach, restaurants, three pools, concierge tower, shops, beauty shop, minigolf, shows, children's program, family crafts demonstrations, penguin and fish feeding, exercise classes, yoga, and evening entertainment.

$$$: Daily rates, double occupancy: $200–$570. Children under eighteen free in their parents room.

Royal Hawaiian Hotel
Address: 2259 Kalakaua Avenue, Honolulu, HI 96815-2578
Telephone: 800-325-3535, 808-923-7311, fax 808-924-7098
Website: www.sheraton.com

Originally dubbed the Pink Palace of the Pacific, the Royal Hawaiian first opened in 1927 to the accolades of stylish travelers who journeyed to Waikiki's shore on luxury ocean liners. Designed in the Spanish Moorish style that was popular then, its first guests hauled their steamer trunks and servants along with them and stayed for months at a time. Early luminaries included Mary Pickford, Douglas Fairbanks, the Rockefellers, and the Roosevelts, and for many years it remained the epitome of Hawaiian luxury. The original building, still beautiful, is five stories high with a lobby that boasts massive crystal chandeliers, polished floors, and sumptuous furnishings. Guest rooms in this older, more formal wing have period furnishings, too. Newer buildings have less charm but their guest rooms are larger and more modern. Guests have access to the Honolulu Health Club nearby. It's a legendary and romantic hotel that still spells out Hawaii to many longtime guests.

Accommodations: 526 rooms, all have one king bed or two double beds, ocean views, air-conditioning, and small refrigerators.

For Kids: The hotel's Children's Center has a program for ages five to twelve that includes boogie boarding, lei making, shell collecting, swimming, fishing, snorkeling, and best of all, free ice cream.

Special Features: beach, swimming pool, dinner shows, restaurant, bars, beauty shop, health club, 24-hour room service, car rental desk.

$$$: Children under eighteen free in parents' room. Daily rates, double occupancy: $279–$535. Ask about promotional deals when you book your stay that can significantly lower your cost.

Sheraton Moana
Address: 2365 Kalakaua Avenue, Honolulu, HI 96815
Telephone: 800-325-3535, 808-923-3111, 808-923-0308
Website: www.moana-surfrider.com

When the Moana Hotel opened in 1901 as Waikiki's very first hotel (called the First Lady of Waikiki Beach), it featured novelties such as bathrooms and telephones in every room. The original building, looking a bit like a grand co-lonial/Victorian hotel with tropical features, is still lovely since a major restora-tion in 1989 brought it back to its original grandeur. Several modern additions over the years have added hundreds of rooms. All services offered at one of the Waikiki Sheratons can be enjoyed by guests of any of the other Sheratons.

Accommodations: Eight hundred rooms and suites; all have either a king bed or two double beds, air-conditioning, coffeemaker.

For Kids: A kids program called Keiki Aloha for children five to twelve offers indoor and outdoor fun such as boogie boarding, snorkeling, kite flying, sand-castle building, lei making, Hawaiian crafts, and field trips. The program operates during the summer (from 9 A.M. to 9 P.M.) and over vacation periods.

Special Features: beach, swimming pool, surfing, catamaran sails, restau-rants, bars, 24-hour room service, car rental desk.

$$$: Kids under eighteen stay free in their parents' room. Ask about the hotel's Suresaver rates, which are offered seasonally. Daily rates, double oc-cupancy: rooms $233–$495.

Moderate

Sheraton Waikiki

Address: 2255 Kalakaua Avenue, Honolulu, HI 96815
Telephone: 800-325-3535, 808-922-4422, fax 808-922-7708
Website: www.sheraton.com

One of Waikiki's tallest hotels at thirty-one towering stories, the Sheraton has an elegant dining room right at the top with spectacular panoramic views of the ocean and the lights of Waikiki. If your children are old enough, be sure to treat your family to a special meal here—even the glass elevator ride is a thrill. If your young ones are still at the milk-spilling, fork-flinging stage, place them in the kids program or hire a baby-sitter so you can enjoy the most romantic repast of your vacation. As you might imagine in such a large hotel, space at the beach can get tight in peak season, but many guests spill over onto the Royal Hawaiian's stretch of sand next door. There are two waterfront swimming pools lined with lounge chairs that help pick up the overflow. This Sheraton attracts a great deal of convention trade, and rooms are typical of those in many convention hotels, but independent travelers like it for its great location just a few steps from the Royal Hawaiian Shopping Center, and for its lively atmosphere.

Accommodations: 1,852 rooms, all have a king bed or two double beds, air-conditionning and coffeemakers.

For Kids: Children's program, the Keiki Aloha, operates daily for a fee during the summer from 9 A.M. to 9 P.M. and over certain holiday periods. For ages five to twelve, it includes boogie boarding in the ocean, snorkeling, Ha-waiian crafts, and games such as lei making, kite flying, and field trips.

Special Features: beach, two pools, five restaurants, bars, watersports nearby.

$$$: Daily rate, double occupancy: $215–$445. Children under eighteen stay free with a paying adult in existing bedding.

Hyatt Regency Waikiki
Address: 2424 Kalakaua Avenue, Honolulu, HI 96815
Telephone: 800-233-1234, 808-923-1234, fax 808-923-7839
Website: www.hyatt.com

This enormous hotel pulses with energy and excitement. Two forty-story twin octagonal towers are connected by a ten-story atrium that features a dramatic two-story waterfall, dozens of shops, a bar, and Hawaiian music. It's one of the liveliest places on bustling Waikiki to check in, but once you're tucked away in your room, the busy scene fades and quiet pervades. As you might imagine, views from the oceanfront rooms are spectacular, especially from Regency Club rooms on the highest floor, which offer a higher level of service and amenities along with a private concierge. The beach is across the street, and the pool is smaller than many other Hyatt resorts, but a long list of activities and events throughout the day will keep you happy and busy when you're not in the water or exploring the neighborhood. Parents of young children will appreciate the lifeguard on duty throughout the day.

Accommodations: 1,230 rooms and suites all feature a minibar, refrigerator, and air-conditioning.

For Kids: Camp Hyatt, for ages three to twelve operates daily from 9 A.M. to 4 P.M. and on Friday and Saturday evenings from 6 P.M. to 10 P.M. Kids might learn to do the hula, or participate in Hawaiian crafts, sports, and cookie decorating, or watch movies. Reservations are required and a fee is charged.

Special Features: beach, swimming pool, surfing lessons, restaurants, bars, evening entertainment, shops, room service.

$$$: Children under eighteen are free in their parents' room. Daily rates, double occupancy: rooms $190–$400, suites $750–$1,600.

Budget

Outrigger Reef Towers
Address: 227 Lewers Street, Honolulu, HI 96815
Telephone: 800-688-7444, 808-943-0202, fax 808-946-8777
Website: www.outrigger.com

Families on a tight budget looking for a place to cook their own meals should unpack their bags at this Outrigger. The location can't be beat, just a half block from the beach, and guests can use the facilities of any Outrigger Hotel in the area, including the Outrigger Reef on the beach that has a watersports center and children's program. The Reef Towers is a large property that has a swimming pool and four different dining options, including a pool grill and deli when you tire of cooking. Don't bother to rent a car; you're in walking distance of anything you might need. The Hawaiian Shopping Center is next door and the International Marketplace is one block down the road.

Accommodations: Standard rooms have a king bed or two double beds, a minifridge, an in-room safe, and a coffeemaker. Studio kitchenettes have a microwave or a stove and oven, a small refrigerator, a sink, cooking utensils, and a king bed and a twin or a queen sofa sleeper. One-bedroom units can accommodate up to five, with a king bed, a queen bed, and a queen sofa.

For Kids: The Outrigger Reef Hotel does not have its own children's program on the property, but guests can sign up for kids program (small fee) at sister hotel, Outrigger Reef on the Beach. Full-day (9 A.M.–5 P.M.) or half-day sessions are available year-round for ages five to twelve, and activities include body boarding, Hawaiian Olympics, fishing, crafts of Polynesia, and field trips to the Kodak Hula show.

Special Features: swimming pool, four restaurants, showroom that features Las Vegas–style shows, shop.

$$$: Daily rates, double occupancy: rooms $105–$120, studios $135; one-bedroom suite $145. The hotel has year-round rates that don't change season to season, but ask about discounts when you call to book; depending on availability, you can save 20–25 percent.

The Breakers
Address: 250 Beach Walk, Honolulu, HI 96815
Telephone: 808-923-3181, fax 809-923-7174
Website: www.breakers-hawaii.com

One of Waikiki's best values, this comfortable low-rise hotel is just a short block to the beach. Half the rooms are situated around an attractive swimming pool and tropical garden, and all rooms feature kitchenettes that are well-equipped and allow families to further economize by cooking their own meals. A 24-hour desk is handy to provide assistance to guests for almost anything they might want or need. The two-story hotel is a pleasant find with a personal atmosphere in a pricey neighborhood.

Accommodations: Forty-nine rooms and fifteen suites, all with air-conditioning, louvered windows, TVs, phones, safes, and fully equipped kitchenettes. Garden suites have one room with a queen-size bed and a sitting area with twin beds.

Special Features: swimming pool, Laundromat, snack bar.

$$$: Daily rates, double occupancy rooms: $91–$97, suites $130–$146.

WHERE TO STAY—AROUND THE ISLAND
Expensive

Kahala Mandarin Oriental Hotel
Address: 5000 Kahala Avenue, Honolulu, HI 96816
Telephone: 800-367-2525, 808-739-8888, fax 808-739-8800
Website: www.mandarin-oriental.com

Ten minutes east of Waikiki in a quiet and elegant neighborhood is this resort hotel that offers families several big pluses: it's on a quiet stretch of golden sand far away from the high-octane scene in Waikiki, yet close enough to partake of it when you need a jolt; and it's got a dolphin encounter program and a year-round kids program to keep your youngsters happily engaged in Hawaiian fun. A complimentary shuttle takes you into Waikiki when you're in the mood, but there's enough to do on the property to stay put for several days at a time. Most popular with kids is the Dolphin Encounter Program, an exclusive for hotel guests. Children need to be at least age seven or four feet tall, and adults can participate, too. During a 30- to 45-minute session, you'll help feed these intelligent marine mammals, pat them, and learn about their fascinating habits. Be sure to investigate packages at this resort: you can get real luxury living at an excellent value during certain times of the year.

Accommodations: 371 rooms in ten stories. Rooms are five hundred square feet with one king bed or two double beds, a sitting area, and a small refrigerator. Half the rooms have balconies, and connecting rooms are available as are suites.

For Kids: The year-round program for children ages five to twelve features Hawaiian crafts, fishing, volcano making, and visits to watch the dolphins. The program operates from 9 A.M to 4 P.M. and charges a fee.

Special Features: beach, swimming pool, paddleboats, rafts, tennis, game room during holiday periods, two restaurants, shops, fitness center.

$$$: Daily rates, double occupancy: $295–$450. No additional charge for children seventeen years and under when staying in same room with parent.

Ihilani Resort and Spa
Address: 92-1001 Olani Street, Kapolei, Oahu, HI 96707
Telephone: 800-626-4446, 808-679-0079, fax 808-679-0080
Website: www.ihilani.com

Guests at the Ihilani resort can't help but feel relaxed. They're a half-hour away from the hustle and bustle of Honolulu and the airport, and across the city from the frenzied action on Waikiki beach. Of course when guests are ready for some big excitement, they can make the short commute to see the nightlife, shops, and attractions nearby. The resort has a daily shuttle, and a car rental on the premises. Ihilani's beaches are on four man-made lagoons that are separated from the ocean by a rock wall making the water very calm and particularly enjoyable and safe for little ones. The interior lobby has an extravagant fifteen-story atrium, and a bridge over a pond leads you to the oceanfront wing. Frazzled nerves will be soothed by the soft music of a piano as guests check in.

The eighteen-hole golf course on the resort's property is a work of art in landscaping, with waterfalls, rock gardens, and a two-tiered lake. The Ihilani offers excellent food prepared with fresh local ingredients, and its complete spa features almost any treatment imaginable, from massages to body wraps. Rooms all have large lanais, furnished with teak patio sets, overlooking the ocean. Dining at the Ihilani can be as casual as a poolside barbecue, or as fancy as a French restaurant.

Accommodations: 387 rooms, with ceiling fans and air-conditioning, and a high-tech TV.

For Kids: The Keiki Beachcomber Club keeps children ages four to twelve entertained with a Computer Learning Center and an outdoor stage where kids can put on plays and puppet shows. The program operates year-round from 9 A.M. to 3 P.M. for a fee.

Special Features: beach, pool, lap pool, eighteen-hole golf course, complete spa, fitness center, six tennis courts, restaurants, bars, room service, car rentals.

$$$: Children under fourteen are free in their parents' room. Rooms range from $275–$550, suites from $700–$5,000.

Moderate

Turtle Bay Hilton Golf and Tennis Resort
Address: P.O. Box 187, Kahuka, Oahu, HI 96731
Telephone: 800-HILTONS, 808-293-8811, fax 808-293-9147
Website: www.hilton.com

Turtle Bay's beach is kind of an anomaly along the fierce and dramatic north coast. Built along a cove that is protected from the crashing surf by a reef, it is on one of the safest stretches of beaches for swimming you'll find on this section of the island. Venture just a few miles away to see the dramatic big waves of legendary Banzai Pipeline. The resort juts out into the Pacific on Kuilima peninsula. The rocky west coast of the property is lit at night, adding visual drama to the deafening crash of the waves, while the eastern side hosts the tranquil curve of beach. Swimming pools are found on either side of the resort. A beach activities center can outfit guests for surfing, kayaking, boogie boarding, windsurfing, scuba diving, or simply sunning in comfort. Not far away are ten tennis courts, some lit for night play, managed by the Nick Bollertieri Tennis Academy; the resort is one of Tennis Magazine's top fifty. The original nine-hole golf course has been joined by an eighteen-hole championship golf course that winds its way around a marsh, across sand dunes and ocean vistas, offering golfers twenty-seven holes of play. Horseback riding along the beach or through the forest is another popular pastime. Turtle Bay is the only complete resort on this side of the island.

Accommodations: 485 rooms and suites, all with an ocean view. Most of the rooms are in a six-story structure. Low-rise buildings called cabanas, next to the main building, offer greater space but less desirable views. Rooms have one king or two double beds, fridge, air-conditioning, and many have balconies.

For Kids: Kids age five to twelve who participate in the Turtle Keiki Program might find themselves painting coconuts, learning to hula, or snorkeling in the warm Pacific waters. Each day features different programs and activities, and a fee is charged that varies depending on what the kids do. Lunch and a T-shirt are included in the price; reservations are required. Special drop-by activities at no charge are offered each day at 3:30 P.M.; parents must accompany their children for these. It's a good way to introduce your children to a group situation.

Special Features: beach restaurants, snack shop, bars, golf, tennis, horseback riding, two swimming pools, kayaking, boogie boarding, surfing, scuba, windsurfing, guided nature walks, volleyball, horseshoes, shuffleboard, exercise room, shops, tours, glider rides, fishing, boating and sailing, helicopter tours, whale-watching cruises (in season), aerobics classes, par course, business services.

$$$: Children up to eighteen free in their parents' rooms. Daily rates, double occupancy: $165–$295.

Camping
For general information on camping on Oahu, contact the Division of State Parks at P.O. Box 621, Honolulu, HI 96809, 808-587-0300.

Several state parks near a beach offer camping; the most popular of these is the Malaekahana State Resort Area off Kamehameha Highway at Kalani point. It features a wooded beach park with swimming and bodysurfing, and camping at both the Kalanai Park section and the Kahuku section just north of Laie town. For reservations call Friends of Malaekahana at 808-293-1736. Kahana Valley State Park and Sand Island State Resort Area also offer ocean access and simple campgrounds. Contact the Division of State Parks, above, for information.

WHAT TO SEE AND DO
Hiking Diamond Head: Even young children can walk to the top of spectacular Diamond Head, Hawaii's most famous mountain. It's an easy 45-minute hike each way and once you're at the top you'll be rewarded by breathtaking 360-degree views. Bring water, binoculars, a camera, and a flashlight for the section of the hike that is actually inside the mountain! Most of the trail is marked by guardrails, and the only difficult section is a climb up one hundred steep cement stairs.

Submarine Rides: *Atlantis* submarine descends more than one hundred feet below the surface in air-conditioned comfort to view the riches of Oahu's underwater world. Each trip is accompanied by a staff member well versed in the flora and fauna you are likely to see. Children must be at least three feet tall. 800-548-6262 or 808-973-9800. *Voyager* submarines leave from Kewalo Basin between Waikiki and downtown Honolulu and offer a shuttle to pick you up at your hotel. You'll voyage out to the sub on a ninety-foot catamaran, then board the submarine for your underwater tour. 808-592-7850.

Nautilus Boat Tours: These consist of semisubmersible boats with enormous underwater viewing windows. They offer more space and are a less expensive and more successful option for younger children than the submarines. Kids can move around the underwater portion of the boat when they get tired of looking. 808-591-9199.

Surfing Lessons: Surfing lessons on Waikiki Beach are a must for any child who is a capable swimmer; after all, Oahu is where the sport was invented. The predictably gentle waves and warm water make it an excellent place to learn. There are "beachboys" offering surfing lessons throughout Waikiki at the various watersports stands on the beach and through certain resorts. Most of them are experienced both at surfing and at teaching and can get a beginner standing up within a short time.

If your family consists of true surf fanatics, stop in at the free North Shore Surf and Cultural Museum to see surf memorabilia such as vintage long boards and beach movie posters starring Frankie Avalon and Annette Funicello. In Haleiwa at the North Shore Marketplace, 66-250 Kamehameha Highway. 808-637-8888.

IMAX Theater: When you've had too much sun or the weather turns bad, stroll to the IMAX theater on Seaside Avenue in the center of Waikiki to view films such as *Hidden Hawaii,* or *Ring of Fire* with their life-size lava flows on a seventy-foot, five-story screen. 325 Seaside Avenue. 808-923-4629.

Kodak Hula Show has been around for decades, and is a great deal of free fun. It takes place outside in Kapiolani Park at the Waikiki Bandshell. Bleacher-type seating accommodates two thousand guests—get there by 9:15 A.M. for the 10 A.M. show to get the best seats, but no matter where you sit you'll have a decent view. Performances at 10 A.M. Tuesdays, Wednesdays, and Thursdays. 2875 Monsarrat Avenue. 808-627-3379.

Iolani Palace, built in 1882, is the only royal palace in the United States and was once home to the last monarchs of Hawaii. King David Kalakaua and his sister, Queen Liliuokalani, lived in the palace from 1882 to 1893, when the monarchy was deposed. Now a national historic site, children under five are not permitted because of the quantity of priceless, breakable treasures, but older children may enjoy the 45-minute guided tour. At S. King and Richards Streets. 808-522-0832. Tours offered Wednesday through Saturday.

Bishop Museum has an excellent collection of natural and cultural artifacts from Hawaii and around the Pacific. Highlights include feathered capes belonging to kings, the last grass shack in Hawaii, and artifacts from and information about Stone Age cultures. Kids enjoy the Hawaiian crafts demonstrations of quilting, lei making, and feather working, and there are hula shows daily at 11 A.M. and 2 P.M. An adjacent planetarium features three shows a day. 1525 Bernice Street. 800-847-3511.

USS *Arizona* Memorial at Pearl Harbor: This is a tribute to the sailors and marines killed in the 1941 attack on Pearl Harbor. After you view an impressive and emotional short documentary about World War II on shore, a navy shuttle boat takes you to the memorial itself, which spans the sunken hull of the Battleship *Arizona.* 1 Arizona Memorial Place, Honolulu. 808-422-0561, fax 808-541-3168.

USS *Bowfin* Submarine Museum: This museum pays a tribute to the intrepid sub that sank forty-four enemy ships during World War II. Visitors can go below deck, imagining the tight spaces lived in by brave sailors for weeks at a time. A museum explores the history of submarines from the first attempt to use a submersible in 1776 to the present day. 11 Arizona Memorial Drive, Honolulu. 808-423-1341, fax 808-422-5201.

Honolulu Zoo: This zoo features more than one thousand mammals, amphibians, birds, and reptiles and a quaint little petting zoo that is especially popular with tiny tots. The African savannah is one of the best exhibits in the zoo, as animals wander throughout a habitat free of fences and barriers. Be sure to pause at the enormous banyan tree out front that is the home to thousands of white pigeons. You can buy birdseed at nearby convenience stores to feed these very tame birds—they may even eat out of your hands. 151 Kapahula Avenue, Honolulu. 808-971-7171.

Waikiki Aquarium: Across the street from the zoo, this aquarium, founded in 1904, is the third oldest public aquarium in the United States. It offers visitors an excellent chance to learn about the underwater creatures of Hawaii before heading out on a snorkel trip or a glass-bottom boat ride. Favorite exhibits include the Hawaiian monk seal exhibit (monk seals have enormous soulful eyes) and an exhibit of living coral. 2777 Kalakaua Avenue, Honolulu. 808-923-9741, fax 808-923-1771.

Sea Life Park: The dolphins, sea lions, and penguins here perform for visitors. Top billing goes to the Wholphin, the world's only half false-killer-whale, half dolphin. A 300,000 gallon reef tank allows your kids to see the fish and marine life of Hawaii. A novel program, Splash U, lets guests work with professional dolphin trainers (minimum age is ten). 41-202 Kalanianaole Highway, Makapuku Point, Waimanalo. 800-548-6262, 808-259-7933.

Makap'u Beach: Just across the street from Sea Life Park, this is the best bodysurfing spot in all of Hawaii. In winter, giant swells and pounding waves thrill the experts, who maneuver through the water with grace and ease. Watch from a safe place on the golden sand at this time of year and enjoy the show. You can swim in the summer when surf conditions have calmed down enough to make it safe.

Waimea Valley and Adventure Park: This park offers tours of its gardens, which are overflowing with the world's largest collection of tropical gingers, hibiscus, and heliconias, but will your kids care? You're better off taking a downhill mountain bike tour, horseback riding tour, or kayaking and snor-keling expedition in this spectacular nature park. A reconstructed Hawaiian village lets kids try various games of native warriors, teaches Hawaiian crafts, and showcases "talk story," a Hawaiian storytelling form. Older kids may enjoy a special full-moon tour of the Waimea Valley and Adventure Park, and every-one will like the Butterfly Encounter that features hundreds of beautiful Ha-waiian butterflies and the Keiki Jungle Trek interactive family play area. 59-864 Kamehameha Highway, Haleiwa. 800-548-6262, 808-638-8511, fax 808-638-7900.

Hanauma Bay State Underwater Park: Even though it can get crowded in the middle of the day, a snorkel stop at this natural inlet surrounded by coral reefs will be a highlight for your children. The clear, warm waters of this underwater park are home to friendly tropical fish that are so used to people they'll nibble your fingers and swim up to your mask. Although concession stands sell "fish food," you really shouldn't feed the fish—it's not good for the fish and fills them up on unhealthy food. You can rent snorkel gear at the park or bring your own. Arrive early, especially on a weekend, to get a parking space—once the lot is full, visitors are turned away. 808-396-4229. Open Sunday–Monday and Wednesday–Saturday 6 A.M.–7 P.M. In Koko Head Regional Park off a well-marked exit of Kamehameha Highway.

The Dole Pineapple Garden Maze: Recognized in the *Guiness Book of World Records* as the world's largest maze, the Dole Pineapple Plantation's delightful garden maze, created in a pineapple shape, comprises nearly two acres with a total path length of 1.7 miles. It's made up of 11,400 colorful Hawaiian plants, such as hibiscus, plumeria, and heliconia. There are six secret stations along the way and if you get lost, you can look at a map. There's more than one way to get out. Open daily 9–5:30. 6401550 Kamehameha Highway. 808-621-8408.

Luaus and Shows: Several luaus are offered on the island, and guests are picked up on Waikiki and ride in air-conditioned buses: Germain's Too Good to Miss Luau (808-946-3111) and Paradise Cove Luau (808-945-3571). The Polynesian Cultural Center offers a package ticket combining admission and a luau with evening entertainment. 808-923-1861.

Polynesian Cultural Center: What some cultural purists complain about is what will make your kids adore this place—it's all done up like a Polynesian theme park, but in quite an authentic way. The center offers an inside view into the lifestyles and culture of seven different Polynesian groups—Fijian, Hawaiian, New Zealander, Tahitian, Samoan, Marquesan, and Tongan. Each group has a "village" that is inhabited (for the day, anyway) by students from Hawaii's Bright Young University who dress in authentic attire and answer questions. There are stage shows throughout the park, an Imax theater, and a nightly luau with entertainment. Visitors explore the center along waterways in canoes, or by walking. It's a must-stop for a family and one your children will certainly enjoy. Get there when it opens to have enough time to explore all of the park. Open Monday through Saturday 12:30–9:30. Reserve in advance if you want to attend the luau. 55-370 Kamehameha Highway, Laie. 808-923-1861.

Maui

Maui is the second most popular island for visitors, and one that offers more miles of swimmable beaches and incessantly sunny coasts than any other island. Maui is for families with interests as simple as lounging on the beach for their entire stay (and these are beaches that have made top ten lists for years) or as active as bicycling down the largest dormant volcano in the world. Its shoreline is filled with coral and diverse marine life, making it one of the best islands for snorkeling. Windsurfing is near legendary at Ho'okipa Beach with its perfect waves and brisk onshore breezes.

Four separate resort areas offer a wide selection of family resorts and the sunniest beaches on the island—Kaanapali, Hawaii's first planned resort area;

Kapalua on the northwest coast; Kihei and its bargain condos on the sunny south shore; and ritzy Wailea, just down the road from Kihei.

Visitor Information: Website: www.visitmaui.com. Maui Visitors Bureau, W1727 Wili Pa Loop, Wailuku 96793. 808-244-3530, fax 808-244-1337.

Best Sweet Treat: Look for *haupia*, a creamy coconut pudding usually cut into squares, at the restaurants that serve more traditional Hawaiian fare.

WHERE TO STAY
Expensive

Grand Wailea Resort Hotel and Spa, Maui, Hawaii

Address: 3850 Wailea Alanui Drive, Wailea, HI
Telephone: 800-888-6100, 808-875-1234, fax 808-879-4077
Website: www.grandwailea.com

One of the liveliest resorts under the Hawaiian sun, this posh family play-land is part elegant country-club-style resort and part high-energy water park. Its sprawling swimming pool complex is so big it's mind-boggling, and your children will happily take on the challenge of exploring its every corner. You may want to linger over its world-class art collection that includes stunning regional Hawaiian artwork alongside pieces by Picasso, Leger, and Warhol, but just try to drag your kids out of the 2,000-foot-long river pool and its water slides, waterfalls, caves, rope swings, rapids, and grottos. Although the beach is widely used, it's never too crowded because of the drawing power of the pools. A lavish full-service spa pampers guests with all kinds of exotic treat-ments, and luxury and opulence are everywhere at this veritable city of a resort.

Of the resorts more than 750 guest rooms, families will be most comfortable in those in the Lagoon Wing facing the Wailea Canyon Activity Pool; choose a room or suite on the ground floor and you'll be just steps from water park action central. The Volcano Bar by the pool complex's rope swing has delicious American grill fare and is casual enough that you can grab a bite in your swimsuit before heading back to the water fun.

Accommodations: 761 rooms and suites. All have air-conditioning, bal-conies, minibars, and safe. Rooms have one king or two double beds and are 640 square feet.

For Kids: The kids program is centered in a 20,000-foot indoor and out-door facility that includes a whale-shaped wading pool, a playground, its own restaurant, a game room, a movie theater, and a computer room. Called Camp Grande, it offers full-day, half-day, and evening camp for three- to twelve-year-olds for a fee. A variety of special classes for kids, in subjects like lei making, hula dancing, and pottery, are also offered, though not connected to the chil-dren's program.

Special Features: beach, megapools, scuba diving, sailing, windsurfing, boogie boarding, fitness classes, island excursions, full-service spa, three eighteen-hole golf courses, fourteen tennis courts, twenty-one restaurants, bars, and night clubs.

$$$: Children under eighteen free in their parents' room. Daily rates, double occupancy: rooms $342–$600; suites $1100–$10,000.

Westin Maui

Address: 2365 Kaanapali Parkway, Lahaina, Maui, HI 96761
Telephone: 800-228-3000, 808-667-2525, fax 808-661-5831
Website: www.westin.com

The Westin is one deluxe package, child friendly yet swank, with excellent restaurants, posh decor, an exquisite art collection, and the requisite fine white-sand beach. But once your kids have spotted the water slide, the rest of the place may fade. It's a 150-foot-long twister that empties out into a pool; just one of many at the resort. The centerpiece of the water playground is a 25,000-square-foot swimming pool, and several others cluster on a variety of levels around a central island bar and sundeck. Three of the pools are joined by water slides, and another is connected with a swim-through grotto concealing a Jacuzzi. The gardens and pools contain at least fifteen waterfalls, and landscaping is lavish and lush. Golf is just out the front door, as is tennis, and there are many other activities besides fresh- and saltwater swimming, including a children's program that operates every day of the year. Complimentary shuttles take guests to the Lahaina shopping area a few minutes away.

Accommodations: 761 rooms and suites have either a king bed or two double beds, air-conditioning, safes, minibars, balconies.

For Kids: Westin Kids Club is complimentary throughout the year and has a program for five- to twelve-year-olds and for ages thirteen and up. Daily activities such as arts and crafts, games, and wildlife tours are offered.

Special Features: beach, five pools, four kiddy pools, Jacuzzi, fitness center, eight restaurants, three bars, beauty salon, twelve tennis courts, water sports, two golf courses

$$$: Daily rates, double occupancy: $199–$600.

Hyatt Regency Maui

Address: 200 Nohea Kai Drive, Lahaina, Maui, HI 96761-1985
Telephone: 808-661-1234, 708-667-6030, fax 808-667-4499
Website: www.hyatt.com

Hyatt's garden fantasyland is the centerpiece of this attractive hotel that dazzles with an enormous half-acre free-form swimming pool bordered at one end by a rocky cliff covered in plunging waterfalls. Swim under one of the falls through a grotto that leads to another pool that features a 150-foot lava-tube water slide. Elaborate gardens filled with exotic animals, colorful Hawaiian flowers, and koi-filled ponds create a unique atmosphere wherever you wander. The pool is edged with beach chairs and separated from the beach by verdant lawns and shady palms. Three connecting buildings of guest rooms create a half circle around the extravagant garden and waterscape.

An unusual Tour of the Stars astronomy program allows guests to view the heavens through a high-powered telescope known as Big Blue on the roof of the ninth-floor tower. The telescope is programmed to identify and locate one thousand objects such as planets, star clusters, galaxies, and nebulae. Led by the hotel's director of astronomy, the show begins with a brief explanation of the constellation system followed by the chance to gaze at these objects. Shows are held nightly. Several other unusual tours are offered at the resort: the garden tour consists of a two-mile walk past nine waterfalls, rock formations, and a fascinating variety of Hawaiian plants. Art aficionados can take guided tours of the $2 million Asian-Pacific art collection.

More than fifty birds and hundreds of fish live on the grounds of the forty-acre resort. Most popular with children are the African black-footed penguins, who live in a special penguin pond off the lobby, and the parrots, who perch and play throughout the resort—guests are encouraged to talk to them. Three types of swans make their home in the swan court pond in the Japanese gardens, along with a variety of ducks and flamingos.

Every night begins with a traditional Hawaiian torchlighting ceremony, and special shows feature Polynesian and Hawaiian drum dances during the week.

Accommodations: 815 rooms (including 32 luxury suites), all have either a king bed or two double beds, air-conditioning, safes, minibars.

For Kids: Camp Hyatt, a daily, supervised program for children age three to twelve, operates year-round. Day camp, from 9 A.M. to 3 P.M., includes sports and games, snorkeling, arts and crafts, sand-castle building, excursions, and Hawaiian cultural activities such as lei making and hula dancing. Night camp, from 6 P.M. to 10 P.M. consists of table games, movies, video games, and snacks. A fee is charged for both programs.

Special Features: beach, pools, kayaking, snorkeling, scuba diving, windsurfing, sailing, dinner cruises, jet skiing, sportfishing, massages, whale watching, shops, restaurants, bars, fitness center, tennis, outdoor dinner theater, room service.

$$$: Children eighteen and under stay free in their parents' room. Daily rate, double occupancy: rooms cost $275–$495; and suites $600–$3,000.

Ritz Carlton Kapalua

Address: 1 Ritz Carlton Drive, Kapalua, Maui, HI 96761
Telephone: 800-262-8440, 808-669-6200, fax 808-665-0026
Website: www.ritzcarlton.com

Ritz Carlton's classy, sumptuous, Hawaiian plantation-style hotel overlooks a series of cascading pools with the ocean beyond. Very private, it's at the end of a road, and it's got everything right there so you never have to leave the spectacular grounds. The beach, although a bit on the small side, is a gorgeous stretch of sand, and there are loads of activities to keep even the busiest teens involved from dawn to dusk. Just around the point from the resort is an underwater preserve with excellent snorkeling that guests can reach via a complimentary shuttle.

Poolside cabanas can be rented to keep the sun off tiny babies, and the children's program Ritz Kids lives up to the resort's high standards. There's a full spa facility with steam, sauna, massage, and all kinds of treatments, plus a fitness center, and beauty salon. Rooms are spacious and elegant.

Three championship golf courses surround the resort, and guests can use them all at a reduced rate. A complimentary putting green and croquet is on the property.

Accommodations: 548 rooms have one king bed or two double beds, all with air-conditioning, oversize marble bathrooms, and a lanai overlooking the pool.

For Kids: Ritz Kids offers a complimentary daily program for children ages 5 to 12 that operates year-round. Children can participate for a full- or half-day and enjoy games, arts and crafts, nature walks, and such.

Special Features: beach, three swimming pools, ten tennis courts, health club, shops, beauty salon, restaurants, five bars, two hot tubs, nine-hole putting green, a full spa facility with steam and sauna, massage, fitness center, beauty salon, 24-hour room service, baby-sitting.

$$$: Daily rates, double occupancy: $255–$335.

Four Seasons Resort Wailea

Address: 3900 Wailea Alanui, Wailea, Maui, HI 96753
Telephone: 800-332-3442, 808-874-8000, fax 808-874-6449
Website: www.fourseasonsresorts.com

Four Seasons resorts offer upscale families a sophisticated blend of vacation elegance and warm family friendliness. This resort was the first in their chain of resort properties, and they've certainly set a high standard and stuck to it. Known for their superlative service, here the sand is cooled by sprinklers so that you won't burn your feet as you walk to the water. It's a "your wish is my command" kind of place done with great subtlety. Cabanas are thoughtfully placed along the beach—especially nice for families with babies and toddlers who need to stay out of the sun. There are children's menus in every restaurant, even the most deluxe, and a superb complimentary children's program that is one of the best resort programs anywhere.

Accommodations: 380 rooms and suites. Rooms have lanai, ceiling fans, air-conditioning, minibar; adjoining rooms are available, sometimes at a discounted rate.

For Kids: The Four Season's signature kids program, Kids for All Seasons, entertains children ages five to twelve with complimentary activities that feature the culture and crafts of the Hawaiian islands. Headquartered in its own appealing playroom, kids enjoy sand-castle building, hula classes, toys and games, and such.

Special Features: beach, swimming pool, tennis, croquet, health club, three restaurants, bars, 24-hour room service, beauty salon, exercise classes, concierge floors.

$$$: Daily rates, double occupancy: $305–$585. Children seventeen and under stay free in their parents' room.

Kea Lani Hotel

Address: 4100 Wailea Alanui, Wailea, Maui, HI 96753
Telephone: 800-882-4100, 808-875-4100, fax 808-875-1200
Website: www.kealani.com

The Kea Lani Hotel's unique architecture is only one aspect that makes it stand out from other resorts. The domes, arches, and bright white exterior all give the Kea Lani a Moorish feel, unusual in Maui. The Kea Lani offers privacy to those who want it, with two-bedroom oceanfront villas that have their own pools. Guests in the oceanfront villas have access to a Cadillac or a convertible for their visit, and the kitchen comes stocked with groceries. For those who want luxury at a relatively reasonable price, the one-bedroom suites are small but luxurious and less expensive than comparable accommodations on the islands. Even suites in the main hotel can offer a bit of seclusion with a spacious lanai, and they are also stocked with plenty of amenities.

The resort's 22,000-square-foot pool has two levels connected by a water slide, and the sandy beach is great for simply lounging in the sun or snorkeling and windsurfing just offshore.

Accommodations: 413 suites, 37 villas. The suites come with a lanai, mini-kitchen (microwave, minirefrigerator, coffeemaker, and dishes), living area, and entertainment center (TV, VCR, stereo). The living room also comes with a sofa bed. The villas have everything the suites do, plus a second bathroom and bedroom, a washer and dryer, a full kitchen, and a pool.

For Kids: The Keiki Lani program offers year-round activities for children ages five to sixteen, seven days a week from 9 A.M. to 3 P.M. Kids enjoy arts and crafts, swimming in the pool, and a lunchtime movie daily. Other activities might include sand-castle building, hunting for geckos, and feeding the koi.

Special Features: Three eighteen-hole golf courses a short distance away, beach, pools, spa, beauty salon, fitness center, snorkeling, scuba diving, windsurfing, sailing, three restaurants, two lounges, and a deli serving both American and Pacific food.

$$$: Kids under eighteen are free in their parents' room. Suites range from $255–$585, villas from $895–$1,195.

Moderate

Kaanapoli Beach Hotel

Address: 2525 Kaanapali Parkway, Lahaina, Maui, HI 96761-1987
Telephone: 800-262-8450, 808-661-0011, fax 808-667-5978
Website: www.kaanapalibeachhotel.com

It's a good thing that members of the staff chorus who entertain guests with traditional Hawaiian songs every Monday, Wednesday, and Friday have loud, resonant voices. If they didn't, you wouldn't be able to hear them over the distracting clatter of cameras as proud parents capture their kids dancing the hula to the melodic strains of these award-winning singers. The kids wear hula skirts and leis that they've made in the summertime Kalo Patch 'Ohana children's program, where they've been taught this ancient Hawaiian dance. Parents can participate in the kids program too, to learn Hawaiian crafts and games, or to learn to hula themselves. The resort is so committed to preserving and passing on the culture and heritage of old Hawaii that employees are required to take classes in subjects such as Hawaiian mythology, games, and language, which they in turn pass on to guests of all ages on a daily basis throughout the year.

The resort stretches out along one of the sunniest sections of coastline in Maui, in the Kaanapoli resort area. Because it was the first tourist hotel to stake its claim along this balmy cove, it has the best location and most beautiful beach in all of Kaanapoli. Just out the back door are two different golf courses that are available to the hotel's guests. A beach shack rents all kinds of water playthings, and free scuba lessons take place in the whimsical whale-shaped swimming pool. Kaanapoli's accolades range far and wide—Hawaii's most Hawaiian Hotel, Travel and Leisure's #1 Best Value in the State of Hawaii, and member of the *Condé Nast* Gold List.

Accommodations: 430 rooms and suites, all with in-room safes, refrigerators, coffeemakers, private lanais, and air-conditioning. Connecting rooms are available.

For Kids: Kalo Patch 'Ohna Program is a family-oriented program for children, or parents and kids together. Operating during summer months and over the winter holiday school break, its age limit ranges from four to ninety. A fee is charged for kids; parents and grandparents are free. Field trips to the Whale Museum and to ride the Sugar Cane Train are part of the weekly offerings along with beach treasure hunts, swimming, Hawaiian crafts, and an Aloha Friday performance. The program runs Tuesday through Saturday from 9 A.M. to 3 P.M.

Special Features: beach, swimming pool, scuba, snorkeling, boogie boards, sunset sails on a catamaran, seasonal whale-watching cruises, Ping-Pong, giant checkerboard, baby-sitting, beauty salon, Hawaiian library, shops, restaurant, bar, coin-operated laundry.

$$$: Children seventeen and under stay free in parents' room using existing bedding. Children five and younger eat free. Daily rates, double occupancy: rooms $160–$250; suites $210–$585.

Hale Pau Hana Resort

Address: 2480 South Kihei Road, Kihei, Maui, HI 96753
Telephone: 800-367-6036, 808-879-2715, fax 808-875-2038
Website: www.hphresort.com

As you approach these condos from the strip along Kihei Road, they certainly don't look impressive. But once you enter your comfortable oceanfront apartment, you'll be delighted by your location—just steps from the sand. This small and unpretentious resort has drawn a steady clientele of loyal families over the years. Families with younger children should get a ground-floor unit in the two-story low-rise section of the resort. They all have small patios that lead to a grassy green lawn just a few steps from the sandy beach.

Ground floor units have just one bedroom, but their convenient location means absolutely no schlepping of gear and toys. A small pool on the premises is always popular with the kids, especially in the afternoon. The uncrowded beach has excellent snorkeling just offshore. In the evening, you can barbecue and eat on your lanai, watching the sunset over the water. Anything you might need is a short walk away in the many shops and restaurants of Kihei Road. Note, there are ceiling fans rather than air-conditioning in this resort.

Accommodations: All units are oceanfront and have fully equipped kitchens. Most have one bedroom and one bath or one bedroom and two baths that sleep up to four in a sofa bed, and a queen or king bed in the bedroom. Two units have two bedrooms. All are individually owned so furnishings vary but are kept to a standard.

Special feature: beach, swimming pool, laundry facilities.

$$$: Daily rates, double occupancy: one bedroom units $130–$190. Two bedroom units $170–$210. Children six and under stay free; seven- to-ten-year-olds $10 per night, eleven and over $20 per night.

Budget

Punahoa Beach Apartments
Address: 2142 Illili Road, Kihei, Maui, HI 96753
Telephone: 800-564-4380, 808-879-2720, fax 808-875-3147
E-mail: www.pb6110@aol.com

These bargain apartments are a block from busy Kihei Road, making them quieter than most of the other condo clusters that line the Kihei strip. Everything you could ever need is still within walking distance—dive shops, restaurants, cafés, and shops—and the water is just steps from your door. From the ground-floor units you can walk out onto a patio, down to the grass, and then out to the water, where the shore is a bit rocky but leads out to an excellent snorkeling area with sea turtles and tropical fish. A glorious stretch of sandy Kamaole beach is about a 1½-minute walk away. The four-story building is about one hundred feet from a popular surf spot, so you've got many recreational options right out the front door. Many guests rent cars, but it's not necessary. If you don't rent a car at the airport, there's an Avis car rental about one block away.

Accommodations: Fifteen units of which twelve are available in the rental pool. All units have lanais looking out over the water, full kitchen, private phone, cable TV, and other extras. Studios have a queen bed plus a single bed. One-bedroom units have a queen sleeper sofa plus the king or queen bed in the bedroom; two-bedroom units have a king or queen bed in the master bedroom, two twins in the second bedroom, and a queen sleeper sofa in the living room.

Special Features: Laundromat, barbecue.

$$$: Daily rates, double occupancy, studios $69–$93, one-bedroom units $85–$127, and two-bedroom units $94–$130. Extra person charge, regardless of age, $12 per night. Reserve early.

Napili Bay
Address: 33 Hui Drive, Napili, Maui, HI 96761
Telephone: 888-661-7200 or 808-661-3500, fax 808-661-5210
Website: www.mauibeachfront.com

This quaint two-story property next to a glorious beach is an excellent place to headquarter for families watching their pocketbooks. Each studio is individually owned, and at 435 square feet, it's best for families who plan to be out most of the day and don't mind some real togetherness. But for low price and location, the Napili Bay simply can't be beat. Every unit is oceanfront with a private lanai looking out onto the sands of picturesque Napili Bay, known for its excellent swimming and snorkeling. While your lanai is beachfront, it's protected by a windscreen and you'll need to walk around the building to get to the beach. The hotel is in walking distance of Kapalua and the resorts of Napili, but most guests get a rental car for at least part of their stay.

Accommodations: Twenty-four units, all oceanfront, all have lanais, ceiling fans rather than air-conditioning, and complete kitchenettes with stove, refrigerator, and microwave. Most units have a sofa bed and a queen or double bed, but a few have twin daybeds and a sofa bed.

Special Features: Laundromat facility.

$$$: Daily rates, double occupancy: $89–$125, five night minimum. At these rates, you'll need to reserve in advance!

Kihei Beach Resort

Address: 36 South Kihei Road, Kihei, Maui, HI 96753
Telephone: 800-367-6034, 808-879-2744, fax 808-875-0306
Website: www.kbr.com
E-mail: kbr@maui.net

Behind the Kihei Beach Resort loom the vibrant, green West Maui Mountains, and in the distance rest the islands of Kahoolawe and Lanai. Every condominium in the resort is oceanfront with a private lanai. Malalaea Bay, known as "the playground of the whales," and the miles of white-sand beaches that typify the Maui experience are just out your front door. If relaxing on a white-sand beach or around the lagoon-shaped pool is more important to your family than a fancy hotel room, this Polynesian paradise is the essence of simplicity and tranquillity.

Accommodations: A choice of one-bedroom or two-bedroom/two-bathroom condos, each with a full kitchen including microwaves and dishwashers, cable TV, telephone, ceiling fans, air-conditioning, and daily maid service. There is a laundry facility on site, however the two-bedroom units have their own washer and dryer.

Special Features: A lagoon-shaped pool and barbecue area; the Concierge Connection will help plan golfing and island tour excursions, recommend restaurants, and provide maps and shopping guides.

$$$: One-bedroom condos range from $105–$130 per night, and two-bedroom condos go from $130–$165 per night, depending on the season and length of stay.

Waianapanapa Cabins

Address: Division of State Parks, P.O. Box 1049, Wailuku, Maui, HI 96793
Telephone: 808-587-0300

Waianapanapa is one of Hawaii's most beautiful state parks, lying along a craggy black-lava coast about three miles from Hana. Here, twelve simple cabins, all with ocean views, offer very affordable accommodations. They're not on the beach but are in one of Maui's most beautiful regions. You'll need to book early—at least six months in advance—unless you're one of the lucky few to sneak in on a cancellation.

Accommodations: Twelve wooden cabins are comfortable but basic, with a living room and bedroom. The bedroom has two double bunkbeds, and there are sleeping facilities in the living room; linens are provided. Kitchens come fully equipped with stove, refrigerator, and utensils.

$$$: Daily rate: $45 for up to four people, extra person $5 each per night.

Camping

Maui State Park features two sites for camping, one of which is suitable for families: Waianapanapa State (see cabin listing above) Park, off the Hana Highway, offers a true getaway into a wild volcanic coastline. You can hike an ancient Hawaiian coast trail into Hana, study seabird colonies, and visit a small black-sand beach. Contact the state park office at 54 S. High Street #101, Wailuku, HI 96793 (808-984-8109).

The national park campgrounds are found throughout the island: contact 808-572-4400 for information. Two of the campgrounds at Haleakala National Park are found within the crater's wilderness. Another campsite, Hosmer Grove, is at the 6,800-foot level of the volcano. Kipahulu offers oceanfront camping in a gorgeous part of the island.

WHAT TO SEE AND DO

Maui Ocean Center is a brand new aquarium that features the animal life that inhabits Hawaii's oceans. Plan to visit whether you snorkel or not, but if your family likes peering into the underwater world with mask and snorkel, a visit to the aquarium will reveal just exactly who and what you're apt to see underwater. The centerpiece of the aquarium is the 100-foot-long, 600,000-gallon tank that features sharks, tuna, triggerfish, and other large fish. Walk through an underwater tunnel and you'll see these enormous creatures of the tropical reefs swimming overhead. Young children love the touch pool with starfish and urchins. Website: www.coralworld.com/moc. At Maalaea Harbor Village, 192 Ma'alaea Road, Ma'alaea (808-875-1962). Open daily 9 A.M.–5 P.M.

Sugar Cane Train is a fully restored nineteenth-century locomotive that once carried sugar and now carries passengers between Lahaina and Kaanapali. You'll chug through plantation fields, past old homes, across a trestle, and along a golf course. Music and panoramic views add to the fun (808-661-0098 or 808-661-0800).

Luaus and Shows—Old Lahaina Luau is one of the best in the islands as they strive to be as authentically Hawaiian as possible, with a delicious luau feast and traditional music, chants, and hulas. Offered daily at 6 P.M. (808-667-1998). Front Street, Lahaina.

The Napili Kai Beach Club has an enchanting Keiki Hula Show performed by thirty children, who perform dances of the Polynesian islands. The children have made their own leis and skirts, which they pass out at the end of the show. Friday evenings. 5900 Honoapi'ilani Highway, Napili (808-669-6721).

Other hotels and resorts have good luaus too, such as the Maui Marriott in Kaanapali (808-661-LUAU) and the Aston Wailea in Wailea (808-879-1922). The Hyatt puts on a Polynesian review called Drums of the Pacific featuring a buffet dinner and traditional dances and chants from the islands (808-661-1234 ext. 4420).

Haleakala National Park's centerpiece is a 10,023-foot-high dormant volcano. Your family, along with the 1.3 million other people who have gone before you, can head to the top and take a peek inside the crater: the hole is 3,000 feet deep, 2½ miles wide and 7½ miles long, encompassing 19 square miles—big enough to hold the city of Manhattan. Views from the top are outstanding, and you don't need to worry about getting burned—the volcano hasn't erupted or even grumbled since 1790.

Dress warmly if you plan to hike here, as temperatures range between 40 and 65 degrees. The Visitors Center about eleven miles from the park entrance and the Summit Building at the peak of the mountain offer free naturalist talks by park rangers. Various hikes, such as a rain forest hike and a crater hike, head out from the Visitor Center Overlook.

The **Road to Hana** is legendary and many people consider it one of the highlights of their trip to Maui. I'll bet those people weren't traveling with children, or certainly with toddlers. The road is indeed spectacularly beautiful, but it is also a long and winding fifty-five miles riddled with hairpin turns and one-lane bridges. If your children are older and you plan to stop every few miles, do attempt it it as this is the Hawaii of fantasy and myth—rain forests with dramatic waterfalls plunging into idyllic pools bordered with lush tropical flowers and plants. You can stop and explore short trails that lead to small waterfalls and tranquil pools to swim in, and you can picnic at various wayside parks along the road.

Once you reach Hana, plan to visit the Hana Cultural Center, which has an excellent collection of Hawaiian quilts as well as a collection of stone implements, tapa cloths, and ancient Hawaiian household items. Stop at Waianapanapa State Park for a swim at its black-sand beach (make sure the water is calm).

About ten miles past Hana town are the pools at 'Ohe'o Gulch, also called the Seven Sacred Pools (although there are really more than seven). Many of these dazzling pools are fed by waterfalls, but be careful swimming and check with a park ranger before you do. Avoid swimming after a rain or during the winter months when the the waters can rise suddenly, as much as four feet in less than ten minutes.

If you do make the drive to Hana, plan to leave very early and make a day of it, or spend a night or two. The drive itself, without many stops, will take you 3 hours, but any car containing children will need to stop frequently.

Bicycling—The most spectacular bike ride on Maui starts at the top of

Haleakala (you're transported there in a van) and heads through flower farms and small towns to the beach at Paia. You won't be huffing and puffing like you would in the other direction, but note that this ride demands some skill in handling a bike and does have some uphill climbs. Other spectacular bike rides exist on the island, which is very committed to bikeways and has designated hundreds of miles of bikeways on Maui's roads. West Maui Cycles can set you up (808-669-0027).

Snorkeling—Molokini Crater, a crescent-shaped islet formed by the top of a volcano, is a popular and rewarding place to snorkel. It's a marine preserve teeming with fragile corals and colorful tropical fish. Because it's relatively shallow, introductory scuba dives take place here. Many commercial boat-tour operators offer half-day trips to Molokini; pick an early morning time for the clearest and calmest waters.

Maui Surfing School may be just the stop for youngsters wanting to learn to ride the waves. They operate from the Lahaina Harbor, which has predictably gentle waves. The school guarantees that it will take just one two-hour lesson to learn to stand up on a surfboard and ride a wave into shore (808-875-0625).

Whale Watching excursions head out between November and April when waters teem with these majestic giants. More than half the North Pacific's population of humpbacks winter in Hawaii to bear their young in warm and safe waters. You can see them breaching and blowing from the shore, or you can take boat tours that will take you even closer. There are many boat operators who can take you out, but the oldest, and one of the best, is the Pacific Whale Foundation (808-879-8811). They offer excursions aboard both power- and sailboats.

Located in Iao Valley, **The Hawaii Nature Center** is a fun and educational experience for children of all ages, with activities and hikes designed to teach children respect for nature. The Interactive Science Arcade on Maui tells the story of Hawaii's natural history with the help of more than thirty hands-on exhibits. The exhibits allow children and adults alike to experience the beauty of nature with live stream displays, including insects and animals. Children have only to step outside to witness the real thing, in Iao State Park. The park showcases the Iao Needle, an impressive 1,200 foot volcanic rock configuration, and the Iao Stream, both pristine examples of Hawaii's natural splendor.

*H*awaii

"The big island" is Hawaii's largest land mass—and it's still growing. It's got more microclimates than anyplace else in the state, from the hot dry west coast (as in beautiful beaches) to the verdant wet and lush east (Hilo has more rain than any city in the United States), with a firey volcano thrown in for contrast. When you first touch down at the big island's Kona Keahole Airport, the scene can come as a surprise—instead of palm trees swaying in the wind and a tangle of lush tropical vegetation you're greeted by a stark moonscape of lava flows, proof that the big island is still a work in progress. As you drive out of the airport, whimsical signs have been created along the road, "written" with white rock on top of the deep black lava fields.

Hawaii contains the only active volcano and tropical rain forest in the U.S. national park system. Hawaii Volcanoes National Park, on the island's eastern side, is a fascinating place to explore for a day or two, but if you're in a big rush, a helicopter excursion will take you up close to the red-hot center of the cone to see some red-hot lava rock spewing onto the slopes of the cone. On the always sunny western coast, the island's best beaches are host to some of Hawaii's most attractive family-friendly resorts. The island's northwestern side is largely ranch land, with rolling hills and spectacular views afforded those who venture upon it on horseback.

The Kona Kohala coast, north of the airport, has the best places to stay if you're feeling flush. They offer ritzy accommodations, children's programs, fine dining, a full selection of watersports and activities, and a spectacular location on a swath of warm sand. Less expensive options south of the airport tend to require a drive to get to the beach. There are several delightful possibilities near the volcano; stay on the beach for part of your stay, and explore Volcano National Park by headquartering in the vicinity.

Best Sweet Treat: Stop in at Mrs. Barry's Kona Cookies in the Kona Inn Shopping Village, 75-5744 Ali'i Drive, in Kona, to sample her award-winning macadamia nut cookies, or one of ten other delicious varieties.

Tourist Information: Big Island Hawaii Visitors and Conventions Bureau 808-961-5797, 250 Keawe Street, Hilo HI 96720, or 808-329-7787, 75-5719 W. Alii Drive, Kailua-Kona HI 96740, or the Kona-Kohala Coast Resort Association 69-275 Waikoloa Beach Dr., Kamuela, HI 96743 (800-318-3637, 808-885-4915, fax 808-885-1044).

On a Budget

If you're trying to save money, and like to rough it, there are a number of campgrounds along the shore or in several mountain parks, including Hawaiian Volcanoes National Park. Contact the State Parks Division at 808-974-6200, the Hawaii Volcano National Park at 808-985-6000, or the County Department of Parks and Recreation at 808-961-8311. See below for more information.

WHERE TO STAY
Expensive

Four Seasons Resort Hualalai

Address: P.O. Box 1269, Kailua-Kona, HI 96745
Telephone: 800-332-3442, 808-325-8000, fax 808-325-8100
Website: www.fourseasons.com

A spectacular swimming and snorkeling lagoon blasted out of black volcanic lava, rivals the beach for guests' recreation time at this dream of a first-class resort. The lagoon has its own marine biologist who oversees the thousands of fish comprising fifty different species. Scuba diving classes are held here, and it's a perfect place to teach children to snorkel and to explore the vivid underwater world in completely safe conditions.

The resort likes to teach its guests abut Hawaiian culture, and like everything else at the Four Seasons, it's done in a very classy way. The Ka'upulehu Cultural Center on the grounds has a vast collection of archival Hawaiian maps and books, ancient tools, textiles, paintings, and recorded music along with an assortment of classes in subjects such as Hawaiian language, the hula, the ukulele, and sea voyaging by the Hawaiian stars. Even the center's floor exudes Hawaiian artfulness: it's an exquisitely wrought inlaid koa wood map of a bird's-eye view of the globe with the Hawaiian islands at its center. Children learn about Hawaiian culture through the complimentary Kids for All Seasons Program housed in its own spacious, sunny, and colorful facility. The Four Seasons children's facilities are consistently some of the most well planned and enticing of any resort in the world.

Recreational opportunities abound. The eighteen-hole golf course, designed by Jack Nicklaus, is an official PGA Tour Resort. It wraps around gently sloping lava flows overlooking the Pacific, with the finishing holes actually touching the ocean.

Guest rooms are in beachfront bungalows that are arranged in four discrete crescents connected by paths fringed with poinciana trees, ginger, and orchids. Each crescent has its own pool or pond, including a toddlers' wading pool with a sandy beach and giant turtle sculptures. Families are made to feel welcome in many ways: children find plush animals on their pillows and a personal invitation to the kids program as soon as they arrive; there are children's menus in every restaurant, plus cribs, car seats, high chairs, strollers, and poolside playpens made available to guests.

Accommodations: 243 guest rooms are in thirty-six low-rise bungalows, most of which have ocean views. Over 600-square-feet in size, rooms have minibar, in-room safe, patios, walk-in closets, air-conditioning, and complimentary washers and dryers in each crescent.

For Kids: Kids for All Seasons offers daily child care for ages five to twelve. Housed in a pleasant room of its own, children enjoy both indoor and outdoor activities such as swimming, arts and crafts, and games.

Special Features: beach, eighteen-hole golf course, pools, tennis, watersports, scuba, snorkeling, sailing, a 10,000-square-foot spa, three restaurants, bars.

$$$: Children under eighteen free in guest room, three guests in each room, maximum. Daily rates, double occupancy: $450–$575. From May to December the 5th night is free.

Kona Village Resort
Address: P.O. Box 1299, Kailua-Kona, HI 96745
Telephone: 800-367-5290, 808-325-5555, fax 808-325-7450
Website: www.konavillage.com

I half expect to see Mitzi Gaynor coming from behind the palm trees serenading me with a tune from *South Pacific* when I visit Kona Village. But don't get me wrong. The place isn't corny. It's lush, beautiful, and ultrasophisticated in a Polynesian back-to-nature style. And you're not really on a remote Bali-Hai-like tropical island paradise far from any kind of civilization, but it sure feels that way. Kona's elegantly simple accommodations have no phones or TVs and are tucked under a forest of swaying palm trees in thatched-roof "hales" facing ancient fish ponds, lagoons, and the beach. Guests are lulled to sleep by the sound of the waves on the sand and wake up to the singing of birds. An 1801 lava flow surrounds much of the the resort, giving visitors a glimpse of the island's dramatic volcanic past.

A private dinner with your spouse can be a nightly affair, as all youngsters over age five are invited to a special children's early seating for dinner and then whisked away until 8:30 P.M. to make Hawaiian toys and play games. Three lavish buffet meals are included in the rates that have everything from oysters on the half shell and classic burgers and fries to island specialties such as macadamia nut pancakes, coconut cake with island fruit, and tropical scallops in lime and coconut milk. Daily activities for both kids and adults are a staple—hula classes, fishing contests, tide-pool explorations, glass-bottom boat tours, plus a luau and Polynesian revue (considered the most authentic on the islands) every Friday evening. Teens and adults are turned loose to try snorkeling, sunfish sailing, tennis, and kayaking, all complimentary. While there's plenty of action if you want it, it's the undisturbed tranquillity of the place that will win you over—definitely no plastic fantastic aloha here.

Accommodations: All hales have first-class furnishings, lanais, coffeemakers, ceiling fans, and a minifridge that is stocked daily with soft drinks and juices. A variety of room and bed configurations is available, and many rooms and suites can be connected for family reunions or especially large families.

For Kids: Kona Village was one of the first resorts to develop a children's program and it remains one of the best of its kind anywhere. Offered on a complimentary drop-in basis, it accommodates children ages six to twelve (younger ones are welcome accompanied by a parent), who enjoy a wide range of activities that emphasize Hawaiian culture along with old-fashioned fun; kids might create flower crowns and ti-leaf hula skirts for the luau show, explore tide pools, or fish in the lagoons. Teenagers have a program of their own.

Special Features: beach, two pools, kayaks, small sailboats, snorkel trips, glass-bottom boat rides, tide pool explorations, petroglyph tours, tennis, a fitness center with a masseuse, and a changing schedule of daily activities.

$$$: Daily rate, double occupancy includes all meals and activities: adults $440–$770, children ages six to ten are $130 per night, children under six are free. A third adult ages thirteen and over is $180 per night.

Mauna Kea Beach Hotel

Address: 62-100 Kauna'oa Drive, Kohala Coast, Hawaii HI 96743
Telephone: 800-228-3000, 808-882-7222, fax 808-882-5700
Website: www.maunakeabeachhotel.com

This Hawaiian classic, first opened by Laurance Rockefeller in the 1960s, has one of the most astonishing art collections in all the islands. More than 1,600 pieces of Asian and Pacific art are found throughout the rooms, halls, and grounds of the resort. Collected long before it became trendy to grace the walls of a tourist establishment with indigenous art, Rockefeller sent his collectors all over the world to obtain these now priceless treasures.

Since the resort was one of the first on the Kohala coast, it claimed one of the best beaches around. As you enter the open-air lobby, the floor seems to extend to the sky, as its deep blue tiles blend with the saphire ocean beyond, and finally to the open air. The exterior of the resort is still painted the precise color of the sand on the beach, just as Rockefeller had wanted it. The resort has been added onto since its beginnings, and guest rooms can vary in size from the older to the new sections.

The Maua Kea offers the most authentic luau on the big island, complete with a traditional luau menu and a show. The fun starts at 6 P.M. led by a conch blower. The food is delicious and an excellent hula school troop provides the entertainment. Be sure to reserve in advance.

Sister resort Hapuna Prince, a five-minute shuttle away, has more dining options, and guests enjoy reciprocal privileges at each resort. They also share the Mauna Kea Golf Course designed by Robert Trent Jones Sr., and the Hapuna Golf Course designed by Arnold Palmer and Ed Seay. A special golf program is offered for children during the summer months. The resort has its own stables in Waimea, twelve miles from the hotel.

Accommodations: 310 guest rooms all have a private lanai, air-conditioning, and either a king bed or two double beds.

For Kids: Full- and half-day sessions run seven days a week for children ages five to twelve. Activities include pole fishing, beachcombing, and Hawaiian culture, music, arts and crafts.

Special Features: beach, swimming pool, two golf courses, snorkeling, scuba diving, sailing, windsurfing, kayaking, catamaran rides, deep-sea fishing, whale watching (in season), thirteen tennis courts, fitness center, shops, beauty salon, guided art tours, Hawaiian arts and crafts classes, aerobics classes, restaurants, bars.

$$$: Daily rates, double occupancy: $292–$520

Mauna Lani Bay Hotel and Bungalows

Address: 68-1400 Mauna Lani Drive, Kohala Coast, HI 96743-9796
Telephone: 800-367-2323, 808-885-6622, fax 808-885-1484
Website: www.maunalani.com

When Kevin Costner's *Waterworld* was being filmed, he and the other stars stayed at the posh and secluded Mauna Lani Bunglows, each with their own private pool and round-the-clock butler. The bungalows are set apart in their own section of this first-class resort, insuring celebrities and dignitaries complete privacy; yet they can enjoy all the services and activities the resort has to offer. Most guests unpack their bags in the main resort, also very lovely.

The Mauna Lani is located next to an ancient sixteenth-century lava flow dotted with fifteen acres of spring-fed Hawaiian fishponds. There are acres of fascinating sites to explore—historic petroglyphs, shelter caves, and part of the restored King's Trail "Ala Loa." Ten beautifully landscaped man-made ponds contain tropical fish and green sea turtles. Be sure to walk along the beach and ponds to the The House, once lived in by one of Hawaii's legendary families and now filled with fascinating historical memorabilia.

Accommodations: 350 rooms, most with ocean views, air-conditioning, private lanais, honor bar, in-room safe, and refrigerator; most typically have a king bed or two double beds; many have connecting doors. Luxurious bungalows are 2,800 square feet with two-bedrooms, pools, whirlpools, and many amenities.

For Kids: Camp Mauna Lani is conducted by licensed and accredited child care providers and is offered year-round from 9 A.M. to 3 P.M. Children spend their time learning as well as playing, visiting tide pools and ancient Hawaiian caves, trying shoreline fishing and Hawaiian games and crafts. Evening camp is offered during spring, summer, Thanksgiving, and Christmas from 5:30 P.M. to 10 P.M. Seasonal programs are offered for teens thirteen to seventeen.

Special Features: beach, pool, golf, snorkeling, scuba diving, windsurfing, boogie boarding, deep sea fishing, catamaran cruises, glass-bottom boat tours, surfing, whale watching, health club, beauty salon, volleyball, softball, tennis, shops, restaurants, bars, aerobics classes, Hawaiian crafts classes, 24-hour room service, baby-sitting.

$$$: Daily rates, double occupancy: rooms $300–$570, bungalows $3,625–$4,550

The Orchid at Mauna Lani

Address: 1 N. Kaniku Drive, Kohala Coast, Hawaii, HI 96743
Telephone: 800-845-9905, 808-885-2000, fax 808-885-5778
Website: www.orchid-maunalani.com

This drop-dead-gorgeous and rather formal resort has extensive sports facilities, including two golf courses, and a spectacular setting on thirty-two beachfront acres. It's repeatedly ranked in the top tier by the readers of *Condé Nast Traveler* magazine for activities, facilities, location, and atmosphere. Step through the broad elegant lobby toward the back of the resort and you're rewarded with a sweeping view of a lavishly landscaped tropical terrace with the ocean beyond. Wide steps, almost out of a movie set, lead down to the courtyard, the 10,000-square-foot swimming pool, pretty cafés, and a Jacuzzi hidden in a natural rock grotto surrounded by dense tropical foliage. Past all that is the broad sandy beach, which has hammocks strung between towering palm trees and plenty of lounge chairs.

A vast array of activities are available. The popular golf courses sport water hazards, rolling fairways interrupted by rough lava forms, and several ocean holes. A full-service spa and fitness center, The Orchid Center for Well Being, has every imaginable beauty treatment, including massages on the beach; beach boys offer Hawaiian activities for adults, such as coconut husking and tasting, outrigger canoe paddling and adventures, and exploration of historic preservation sites.

The rooms, in two large parallel wings surrounding the gardens, are spacious and comfortable. Even the interior hallways of the resort are sumptuously decorated and inviting.

Accommodations: 485 guest rooms and 54 suites. Rooms have either two double or one king bed, air-conditioning.

For Kids: Keiki Aloha program for children ages five to twelve offers a daily activities schedule of Hawaiian storytelling, hula lessons, canoe paddling, coconut leaf weaving, and other islands arts and crafts along with outdoor activities. Full day, half day, and Saturday evening programs are available for a fee.

Special Features: beach, swimming pool, two golf courses, Jacuzzi, kayaking, ten tennis courts, fitness center, spa, beauty salon, 24-hour room service, restaurants, expeditions, deep-sea fishing, sunset sails, canoeing, shops.

$$$: Daily rates, double occupancy: $350–$625, suites $550–$3,500. Children free in their parents' room.

Hilton Waikola Village

Address: 425 Waikoloa Beach Drive, Waikoloa, HI 96738
Telephone: 800-221-2424, 808-886-1234, fax 808-886-2900
Website: www.hilton.com/hawaii/waikoloa

This sprawling playland at the beach is like a small city. It's spread out across sixty-two elaborately landscaped acres, with Swiss-made trams and Disney-engineered canal boats to help get you from place to place. The massive and bustling art-filled lobby is a bit reminiscent of Grand Central Station, but if you walk through the lobby and out the back, you'll eventually get to three separate guest "towers," various swimming pools, lagoons, shops, and restaurants.

Families should request rooms in the Lagoon Tower situated next to the resort's kid-pleasing pool with a 175-foot twisting water slide tucked into tropical vegetation. An adjacent four-acre saltwater swimming lagoon (marked off by a rope and buoys before it heads out to the rather rough sea) with its own small man-made sandy beach is a terrific place to learn to scuba or snorkel without any waves to obscure your view of tropical fish and a resident green sea turtle.

You can have a "Dolphin Quest" encounter with one of the resort's six Atlantic bottle-nosed dolphins who reside in a neighboring lagoon, if you or your offspring are lucky enough to get a reservation. You'll learn about their history and habits and swim with them in the dolphin lagoon. Teens can benefit from the teen encounter program, where thirteen- to nineteen-year-olds learn about dolphins and careers in marine science and veterinary medicine while they interact with these gentle creatures. Young people age sixteen and up can be dolphin doubles assisting the Dolphin Quest staff in training during a half-hour shallow-water encounter. It is essential that you reserve space for your kids (who get first dibs over adults) in these programs at the time you book your lodging, as they go very quickly.

A 25,000-square-foot full-service spa has a workout room, and fitness classes and Tai Chi are offered daily. In the spa is a complete beauty salon and spa treatment center. Plus, there's an eighteen-hole golf course, tennis, and other sports. The only time you'll ever need to leave is if you're looking for the wide boulevard of Hawaiian sun-warmed sand; the Waikoloa Village doesn't have a real beach and you'll need to go to the neighboring Outrigger Waikoloa Resort to spread your towels along the shore.

Accommodations: 1,240 rooms, including 57 suites, are air-conditioned with private lanais, minibar, in-room safe, coffeemaker.

For Kids: The Camp Menehune kids program (ages five to twelve) features daily themed activities and plenty of outdoor pool and play time. A special drop-by activity is planned each day at 3:30 P.M. so new guests can sample the program with their parents. Reservations are required by 6:00 P.M. the day before. The camp also offers an evening program on Friday and Saturday nights from 6 P.M.to 10 P.M. Activities include dinner, crafts, games, and movies.

Special Features: beach, three pools, water slides, croquet, Jacuzzi, volleyball, kick boards, two eighteen-hole golf courses, eight tennis courts, full-service European-style spa, six restaurants, dinner show, shops, car rental, baby-sitting, business center, Laundromat, night club.

$$$: Children under eighteen stay free in their parents' rooms. Daily rates, double occupancy: rooms $270–$450.

Moderate

The Outrigger Waikoloa Resort
Address: 69-275 Waikoloa Beach Road, Waikoloa, HI 96738
Telephone: 800-462-6262, 808-886-6789, fax 808-886-7852
Website: www.outrigger.com

Finally, a less expensive option on the glamorous Kona Kohala coast. The Outrigger is the plain sibling to the other fancier neighbors, but it enjoys a glorious beach, the full menu of activities, and a sizable free-form swimming pool. Rooms are smaller and more motellike than in the other, glitzier properties described above, but the Waikoloan offers very good value and a great deal of fun. The hotel surrounds a patio and pool; as you stroll to the beach, you pass historic fishponds edged by beautiful tropical plants, and children adore feeding the tropical fish. Part of the Outrigger chain, this place has packages galore; be sure to nose around before you buy to see just how low you can go. All-inclusive rates offer all meals and all watersports except scuba. Nightly rates are available as well.

Accommodations: 543 rooms, have either a king bed or two double beds, air-conditioning, coffeemaker, personal safes, and lanais.

For Kids: A variety of scheduled daily activities are planned throughout the day.

Special Features: beach, swimming pool, Jacuzzi, six tennis courts, volleyball, Ping-Pong, lawn bowling, bicycles, snorkeling, boogie boards, floats, kayaks, hydrobikes, catamaran rides, whale watching sails (seasonal), glass-bottom boat cruise, pedal boats, Sunfish, Laundromat, windsurfing, snorkeling, sailing, fitness center, restaurants, bars, Polynesian show, Hawaiian luau, massage, room service.

$$$: Kids seventeen and under stay free in their parents' room on the nightly rate. Daily rates, double occupancy: $175–$275.

Camping

Hapuna Beach State Resort Area Cabins, on Queen Kaahumanu Highway, 2.3 miles south of Kawaihae, is an upscale camping experience. Each four-person cabin consists of a single room with wooden sleeping platforms and a picnic table outside. Cold showers and rest rooms are shared, as is a cooking pavilion with a range, refrigerator, and tables. Contact the state park office for reservations. It's best to stay here during calm-weather months when the swimming, bodysurfing, and sunbathing are superb. During times of high waves, dangerous rip currents can occur and its best to stay out of the water. The park has a snack concession, picnic areas, a historic-coast hiking trail, and lifeguards. For state park cabin rentals, write or call the Department of Land and Natural Resources, Division of State Parks, P.O. Box 936, Hilo Hawaii, 96720 (808-933-4200).

Samuel M. Spencer County Beach Park is a popular spot for camping. Its reef-protected beach is safe for swimming year-round, and there are tennis courts and shade trees. Camping permits are required for country parks: contact them at 808-882-7094.

WHAT TO SEE AND DO

Whale Watching: Captain Dan McSweeney's Whale Watching Adventure takes several trips each day during the humpback season (usually December to April) and one morning trip daily during the rest of the year to look for pilot, sperm, false killer, pygmy killer, and beached whales. He's been a whale researcher for more than twenty years and guarantees a sighting or you get another trip, on him. There are no cruises offered in May and June because Dan heads to Alaska to whale watch there (888-942-5376, 808-322-0028).

Atlantis Submarines takes you deep below the surface of the water in airconditioned high-tech comfort. You'll cruise past colorful tropical fish, coral reefs, and all sorts of sea creatures, while listening to educated commentary about what you are seeing. It's an excellent way to observe the life of the deep, but make sure your children are old enough to appreciate sitting and observing before you pop for it. Leaves from the Kona Pier at 75-5669 Alii Drive (800-548-6262).

Snuba allows you to flit below the surface of the ocean attached to an oxygen tank that floats on the surface instead of being strapped to your back. You'll go out with an instructor after a short introduction and practice sessions. Big Island Snuba can set you up (808-326-7446).

Luau: The best luau on the island is at the Kona Village on Friday nights. It's advisable to book it before you leave home.

Kayak Irrigation Ditch Cruise sounds bizarre but it's actually a delightfully unusual excurison well worth a half day. After driving to your "put-in" point, you'll climb into inflatable kayaks (great for stability) and make your way along an irrigation ditch once used to irrigate sugar plantations. Built in 1905, it's filled with atmosphere, as you cruise along through narrow tunnels, past scenic waterfalls, ravines, and a Hawaiian rain forest. (808-889-6922, website www.Kohala.net/kayak).

Horseback Riding Adventure: Kohala Na'alapa Trail rides take you onto a 12,000-acre working cattle and sheep ranch where you ride through majestic rolling hills and lush pastures past cinder cones and ancient Hawaiian ruins partaking of panoramic views of the coastline and ocean beyond. The rides are tailored to your ability, and they aren't really trail rides, but rather open range rides where you can canter if you are an experienced rider. We saw a baby calf being born and struggling to stand on its wobbly feet on our way to the uppermost part of the ride, which looked like something out of Tolkien's *The Hobbit*, with groves of trees and swirling clouds atop grassy pastures that spilled down to the sea. Kohala Ranch: Call for directions to the stable. Rides offered daily; reservations required (808-889-0022).

Kauai

Your family has probably already visited Kauai and you didn't even know it. Its thick jungles and sharp-cliffed dramatic landscape shaped by the forces of water and fire have been regularly featured in the movies: *Jurassic Park, Blue Hawaii, Raiders of the Lost Ark*, and *King Kong* are just a few of the movies that have been filmed on the "garden isle." You can even visit a set and recreate a scene from the classic musical *South Pacific* at the gorgeous pool and waterfall where Mitzi Gaynor sang, "I'm Gonna Wash That Man Right Out of My Hair." Mitzi just stood there and sang while she sudsed, but you and your children can slide off the waterfall into the pool and enjoy a swim.

If you pick Kauai to visit, definitely linger on the island's winsome beaches, but plan some time to explore the natural grandeur of the landscape away from the sea. You'll view eroded peaks that plunge into deep mysterious valleys, rocky spires and volcanic grottos, and waterfalls and rain forests thick with a tangle of blooms and greenery. Kauai is the wettest of the Hawaiian islands and that's one reason it's so lush: five hundred inches of rain fall a year.

Kauai has a four-story limit on buildings, and while that eliminates any concrete skyscrapers crowding the shores, it still has a few pockets of tourist development, especially on the dry section of the island where the best beaches are. Most visitors to Kauai rent a car for their entire stay.

Visitor Information: Website: www.kauai-hawaii.com

Kauai Visitor Information Hotline 800-AH-KAUAI or 800-262-1400; Poipu

Beach Resort Association, P.O. Box 730, Koloa, HI 96756 (800-744-0888 or 808-742-7444) (website: www.poipu-beach.org).

Best Sweet Treat: Look for passion fruit chiffon pie, also called *Liliko'i*. The Hamura Saimin Restaurant at 2956 Kress Street, Lihu'e, serves a mean version of it. Look for fresh sugarcane stalks, often sold at fruit and vegetable markets.

WHERE TO STAY
Expensive: over $225
Moderate: $125–$225
Budget: under $125

Expensive

Hyatt Regency Kauai
Address: 1571 Poipu Road, Koloa, Kauai, HI 96756
Telephone: 800-233-1234, 808-742-1234, fax 808-742-1557
Website: www.hyatt.com

Your kids will adore the one-acre free-form swimming pool with a 150-foot water slide as much as they like the beach that fronts the Hyatt for five hundred yards. The pool is fed by waterfalls, and has a river-style section you can float along, a volleyball court in the water, and a special shallow area for tiny tots. Situtated on fifty oceanfront acres in sunny Poipu, the four-story resort also features a five-acre saltwater lagoon built at the edge of the Pacific Ocean for kayaks, snorkelers, and scuba diving enthusiasts. One of the special luxuries offered by the full-service spa is an outdoor massage.

Accommodations: Six hundred guest rooms and suites. Rooms have coffeemakers, minibars, ceiling fans, and air-conditioning, balconies, and a king bed or two double beds. Suites have a living room, bedroom, and dining area for four plus a wet bar.

For Kids: The Hyatt kids program is available for children ages three to twelve for a fee. Unusual activities, such as guided walks through the resort's archaeology sites, nature treks in the dunes, visits with the wildlife manager, lei making, and hula lessons, take place seven days a week, 9 A.M.–4 P.M. A night camp is available from 4 P.M.–10 P.M. (24-hour notice required).

Special Features: beach, swimming pool, tennis, spa, fitness center, bike rentals, horseback riding, nature walks, luau, four tennis courts, riding stable, windsurfing, snorkeling, diving, spa, fitness center, five restaurants, five cocktail lounges, evening entertainment.

$$$: Daily rates, double occupancy: rooms $295–$495, suites $785–$1,500.

Embassy Vacation Resort Poipu Point
Address: 1613 Pe'e Road, Koloa, Kauai, HI 96756
Telephone: 800-426-3350, 808-742-1888, fax 808-742-1924
Website: www.marcresorts.com

This resort is perfect for families looking for both the conveniences of home and the luxury of a resort. While the shore directly in front of the hotel is a bit rocky, a beautiful white-sand beach lies right next door. The staff is friendly and helpful, there is daily maid service, the front desk is attended twenty-four hours and a concierge is available. The one-bedroom condos can sleep up to four, while the two-bedroom condos sleep six. The interior is furnished with granite countertops and thick carpeting. The property is spread over twenty-two acres and is landscaped with lily ponds and tropical foilage. A continental breakfast and nightly cocktail party is included in your stay. Corner suites have the best views, although most of the units are oceanfront.

Accommodations: Each unit is air-conditioned and contains a big-screen TV, full kitchen, washer and dryer, and a lanai.

For Kids: Poipu Beach Park is nearby and provides a playground and picnic area for a fun family outing.

Special Features: swimming pool, two hot tubs, a steam sauna, and a health club.

$$$: Daily rates, double occupancy: one-bedroom condos $285–$440 per night, two-bedroom condos $340–$1,000 per night.

Moderate

Sheraton Kauai

Address: 2440 Ho'onani Road, Koloa, Kauai, HI 96756
Telephone: 800-325-3535, 808-742-1661, fax 808-742-4055
Website: www.sheraton.com

Situated right on one of beautiful Poipu Beach's five sandy crescents, the Sheraton Kauai sports $40 million worth of renovation spit and polish. Each one of Poipu Beach's crescents is known for something slightly different, and this particular slice of sugar sand is fronted by a reef that offers excellent snorkeling. The crescent adjacent to the Sheraton is a particularly calm and tranquil beach, just right for toddlers, while a section of beach preferred by surfers is yet another crescent over—there's something for all ages.

Guest rooms are clustered in several areas, with some over-looking koi-filled freshwater lagoons and lush gardens, and others looking out over the brilliant blue Pacific Ocean. Both of the resort's two pool areas have toddler wading pools; the beachfront pool features a popular slide, and the tropical garden pool is surrounded by waterfalls. During much of the off-season, kids twelve and under eat free in the main dining room, usually a buffet, when accompanied by a full-paying adult. Golf courses and horseback riding are within 2 miles.

Accommodations: 399 guest rooms and 14 suites. Rooms in four-story buildings contain a king bed or two double beds; all are equipped with mini-refrigerators and Sony play stations, in addition to more standard resort amenities. A number of oceanfront rooms have a love seat that opens into a hide-a-bed. More than 50 percent of the rooms connect. Cribs are complimentary, and roll-aways cost extra.

For Kids: Keiki Aloha Program for children five to twelve operates throughout the summer. Parents can book mornings, afternoons, or full days. Each day has a different schedule, such as bamboo-pole fishing, fish printing, hula lessons, lei making, ukulele lessons, and scavenger hunts. Free scuba lessons are available to teens.

Special Features: fitness center, two swimming pools, two children's pools, scuba, snorkeling, boogie boards, tennis, shops, restaurants, bar, coin laundry, baby-sitting.

$$$: Children eighteen and under stay free in parents' room using existing bedding. Daily rates, double occupancy: $195–$650.

Lae Nani Resort
Address: 410 Papaloa Road, Kapa'a, HI 96746
Telephone: 877-LAENAN, 808-822-4938, fax 808-822-1022
Website: www.lae-nani.com

The tranquility and peaceful ambience of the Lae Nani condominiums on Kauai's sunny eastern "coconut coast" is one of the pluses of this reasonably priced condo resort. Guests hear only the gentle lapping of waves on golden sand, despite the resort's close proximity to the Coconut Marketplace. For those who enjoy a little action, the Marketplace, in walking distance, has plenty of shops, restaurants, and nightclubs for the restless. From the king-sized lanai the view encompasses the manicured grounds, the large pool, and the beach. An eighteen-hole golf course is one mile away.

Accommodations: Each of the seventy units has a full kitchen, separate living and dining rooms, private lanai, and ceiling fans. Two-bedroom condos also have two bathrooms.

Special Features: Lae Nani's facilities include a pool, tennis courts, barbecue grill, and laundry room.

$$$: One-bedroom condos sleep four and range from $165 to $225, two-bedroom condos sleep six and go from $220 to $295.

Budget

Holiday Inn Sunspree Resort
Address: 3-5920 Kuhio Highway, Kapa'a, Kaua'i, HI 96746
Telephone: 888-823-5111, 808-823-6000, fax 808-823-6666
Website: www.holidayinn-kauai.com

The Sunspree is in a convenient location: Adjacent to this hotel is the Lydgate Beach Park, which has a covered pavilion, picnic areas, protected swimming, and a great snorkeling beach with a lifeguard and a playground. Across the street from the hotel is Smith's Tropical Paradise, which has lush botanical gardens and offers an evening luau. Also across the street is the Wailua marina from which boat tours leave for the famous Fern Grotto. The property has several ponds and beautiful gardens with picnic tables available. There are two swimming pools, and four options for meals and snacks: a restaurant, a lounge, a deli, and a pool-side snack bar.

Accommodations: 216 rooms including 13 cottages. Rooms have air-conditioning, in-room coffee, refrigerator, free local calls.

For Kids: The Kid Spree Vacation Club is a complimentary supervised children's program offered during the peak seasons. Kids under twelve eat free in the hotel restaurant when ordering from the kid's menu and dining with parents.

Special Features: two swimming pools, Jacuzzi, fitness room, tennis court, volleyball, shuffleboard, restaurant, lounge, deli, pool-side snack bar, room service.

$$$: Daily rates, double occupancy: $120–$160. Children nineteen and under stay free in their parents' room; there is also a package available that includes a rental car.

Camping

Koke'e State Park, fifteen miles north of Kekaha on Highway 550 adjoins Waimea Canyon State Park and offers tent camping and simple lodging. You can hike in a native rain forest and along the rim of Waimea Canyon and into neighboring forest reserves. There's a small museum and snack bar and seasonal plum picking and trout fishing.

Polihale State Park, at the end of a five-mile dirt road off Kaumuali'i Highway, past the Pacific Missile Range Facility, offers tent camping along a spectacular stretch of coastline with a large sandy beach backed by dunes. Plan to camp here during the summer months when the waters are calmer and safe for swimming. Sites are available with picnic tables, water, and a fire ring.

For further information and reservations, contact the Office of State Parks, Kauai District, 3060 Elwa Street #306, Lihue, HI 96766-1875 (808-274-3444).

WHAT TO SEE AND DO

The Hawaii Movie Tours are a hoot for anyone who remembers the lush tropical scenes in *South Pacific, Raiders of the Lost Ark, Jurassic Park,* or even *Honeymoon in Vegas.* The five-hour land tour takes you out in a fifteen-passenger van to many spectacularly beautiful movie locations. Meanwhile, back in the van, you can listen to pertinent commentary and view video clips of the movies themselves. Lunch on the beach is included in the price. The tours travel from the south to the north shore. This is a great way to tour the island and be amused by movie trivia at the same time. A more extensive (and expensive) tour is similar to the land tour but adds a hidden Hawaiian village, a visit to a location from the Harrison Ford movie *Six Days, Seven Nights,* a helicopter ride, and a two-hour sunset trimaran sail. Book in advance (800-628-8432 or 808-822-1192, www.hawaiimovietour.com). Leaves from the Kinipopo Shopping Village, 356 Kuhio Highway, Kapaa.

Fern Grotto—One of Kauai's most popular tourist attractions and one your young kids are sure to love, a trip to the fern grotto takes you in a flat-bottom boat up the Wailua River to the accompaniment of Hawaiian singing and dancing (and plenty of guest participation). The grotto itself is a pretty, natural amphitheater filled with ferns and full of legends. A variety of boat operators offer the ninety-minute tour and leave from the Wailua Marina.

Captain Zodiac Raft Expeditions takes you out in twenty-three foot inflatable rubber boats, called zodiacs, that ride low and fast over the waves. Several different tours are offered, but the best for kids is one of the snorkel tours rather than the sightseeing tours. Four-hour, and full-day snorkel tours are available. The full-day trip puts you on inaccessible Nualolo Kai beach for a day of snorkeling and hiking and a complementary lunch. Waters are calmer in summer months; in winter when the water is rough the tours can occasionally be canceled. Not advisable for very young children; reserve the full-day trip in advance (800-422-7824, 808-826-9371). Ching Young Village, Kuhio Highway, Hanalei.

Dolphin Watching Tours: This tour is actually a combination Na Pali coast tour, snorkel expedition, and dolphin- and whale- (in season) watching boat ride aboard a comfortable 38-foot cabin cruiser. You'll cruise past waterfalls, white-sand beaches, deep green valleys and sea caves. Trips are narrated by crew well versed in the natural and cultural wonders of the island.

Lanai

The last of Hawaii's main islands to be settled, Lanai was once known as the pineapple isle, as it was home to the world's largest pineapple plantation. Now the home of two spectacular luxury resorts, it's the island to head to to get away from the over stimulation of too much sightseeing, shopping, and touring because when it comes to seclusion, Lanai knows how to isolate its guests in grand style. Of the two ultrasophisticated hotels that comprise the bulk of the resort business, the most suitable for families is perched above the island's prettiest beach. Both have children's centers. There's also a very affordable campground right on the beach.

Most residents live in the old plantation town, Lanai'i City, and the entire island has a population of just 2,800. The island has historical sites, fishing villages, and outback adventures such as jeep trips, deep sea fishing, whale watching expeditions and mountain biking. Miles and miles of unpaved roads through pineapple fields and mountain trails lead to back-country beaches—you'll need a four-wheel-drive vehicle to explore this rugged terrain. Two airlines offer daily flights to Lanai from other islands. Boat access to Lanai is available from the Lahaina Harbor in Maui where ferries make the 45-minute round-trip five times a day (808-661-3756).

Visitor Information: Destination Lanai, P.O. Box 700, Lanai City, Hawaii 96763 (800-947-4774, 808-565-7600, fax 808-565-9316).

Best Sweet Treat: Lanai's fresh pineapple is possibly the sweetest in the world.

WHERE TO STAY
Expensive

Manele Bay Hotel
Address: P.O. Box 310, Lanai City, Lanai, HI 96763
Telephone: 800-321-4666, 808-565-7700, fax 808-565-3868
Website: www.lanai-resorts.com

This hotel exhibits a stylish blend of Hawaii's many cultures—Polynesian, Oriental, European, and Mediterranean—both in its architecture and its landscaping, where five different ethnic gardens overflow with tropical plants and water elements such as streams, ponds, and waterfalls. It is on one of the islands most beautiful and safe beaches, and it offers excellent tide pool explorations and the chance to observe spinner dolphins playing in the waves offshore.

Its art collection could fill a small museum, it is so extensive and carefully selected. The golf course is ranked in the top five by *Condé Nast* readers for best golf resort, and every hole on the Jack Nicklaus–designed eighteen-hole course boasts an ocean view.

Special excursions and lessons are available for kids. You'll find tennis, golf, and horseback riding lessons as well as trail rides and snorkel and sailing trips.

Accommodations: 250 luxury guest rooms and suites have air-conditioning, terraces, minibar.

Kid's Program: With a philosophy that emphasizes sharing the cultural and environmental riches of Lanai, the Pilialoha kids program folds in some secret learning about Hawaii with plenty of fun. For example, kids build their own volcano while they learn how the Hawaiian islands were formed. Other activities include crafts and games, hunting for artifacts, horseback riding, snorkeling, golf, and tennis. The program is headquartered in an activities center that all children may use when accompanied by a parent or guardian and when there is an activities attendant present. Pilialoha children's program is available for children and teens ages five to seventeen. The program operates in full- (9 A.M.–3 P.M.) or half- (9 A.M. to 12:30 P.M. or 11:30 A.M. to 3 P.M.) day sessions, and a fee is charged. An evening program is available Fridays and Saturdays year-round, and nightly during holiday periods. Children three to five may join the program when appropriate and when accompanied by a parent or attendant. Advance registration is required.

Special Features: beach, golf, tennis, swimming pool, fishing, snorkeling, scuba, bicycling, aerobics, horseback riding, jeep tours, Hawaiian crafts, archaeological walks, sailing, whale-watching excursions, boat trips, spa facilities, baby-sitting.

$$$: Daily rates, double occupancy: $275–$2,000

Camping

Just a five-minute walk from the ferry landing are six county-operated campsites. Tent sites for out-of-town guests are on a grassy area just across from the beach; the local people can camp on the sand. The camp area has bathroom facilities with toilets and wash basins, while showers are in the beach area. Winter is the best time for families to camp, since the beach is on the calmer south side of the island, about twenty-five minutes from Lanai City. Small children should be cautious swimming during the summer when bugs are more prevalent. Call to make reservations, and book in advance: It costs $5 for a permit and $5 per person per night for up to seven days. Checks must be received in time to send out a camping permit (808-565-3978 or 808-565-3982).

Molokai

The fifth largest and least developed of the Hawaiian islands, Molokai boasts the highest concentration of native Hawaiians anywhere in the world except Niihau, a private preserve that forbids visitors. Its ancient name is Moloka'i Puleo'o, or Moloka'i of the Powerful Prayer, and vacationers who travel here find a peaceful sanctuary from the hectic pace of their urban lives. It's still a wild place, untouched by any building taller than a palm tree, without any fast food joints, flashy souvenir emporiums, or crowds. It is an island of natural wonders, containing Hawaii's highest waterfall and largest white-sand beach, and the world's highest sea cliffs. People come here to create their own fun, playing on deserted beaches, hiking to visit sacred ruins, and mountain biking through miles of untouched forests.

The island is often remembered for its leper colony, Kalaupapa, an isolated peninsula that is now a national historic park. It was here that Father Damien ministered to Hansen's disease suffers in the late nineteenth century.

There are very few accommodations on the island—a couple of bed-and-breakfasts, a few simple condominium resorts, and an unusual set of luxury campgrounds. The island is just twenty minutes by air from Oahu and Maui, and frequent daily flights are available. A ferry transport, the Maui Princess, operates a ninety-minute trip between Molokai and Lahaina, Maui, on Tuesdays, Thursdays, and Saturdays (808-677-6165).

Visitor Information: Website: www.molokai-hawaii.com, e-mail: mva@-molokai-hawaii.com, Moloka'i Visitors Association: P.O. Box 90, Kaunakakai, HI 96748 (800-800-6367 or 808-553-3876)

WHERE TO STAY
Expensive

Molokai Ranch
Address: P.O. Box 259, Maunaloa, HI 96770
Telephone: 877-PANIOLO, 808-552-2741, 808-534-1606
Website: www.molokai-ranch.com

Molokai Ranch is a tough place to kick back on a lounge chair, although there are plenty of chaises along the beach. There's simply so much for families to do at this upscale camping resort, where adventures are personalized to match your family's interests, that baking in the sun slathered in cocoa butter takes a second seat. If you like to ride, whether it's on a mountain bike or a fast horse, there are trails lacing the ranch from top to bottom. Watersports? Try outrigger canoe sailing, shoreline fishing, or ocean kayaking. You'll even find climbing at the ranch's high and low ropes course and rock wall.

The 54,000-acre ranch was originally devoted to cattle, but now it features three different ritzy camp headquarters. If you're horsey, choose Paniolo Camp (*paniolo* is Hawaiian for cowboy) on a hillside next to the rodeo arena and the pens of baby calves that you can help bottle-feed. If beautiful beach is synonymous with Hawaii in your language, unpack your bags at Kapoa Camp on a double crescent of white sand with watersports and swimming, just steps from your door. The third camp is for adults only, but the entire family can enjoy all that it has to offer—hiking trails, the high and low ropes course, and a rock climbing wall. Meals are served buffet style and it's hearty ranch eating, with everything from Molokai-grown beef and prawns, to fish with rice.

Accommodations: Both Paniolo Camp and Kapoa Camp have canvas-covered cabins, called "tentalows" that feature solar-powered ceiling fans, lights, hot water, private bathrooms, queen or twin beds, and furnished decks; families up to five people can be accommodated in side-by-side double tentalows. Rooms come with daily maid service and a beverage cooler stocked with water and sodas.

For Kids: A children's program for ages four to twelve operates year-round. Each day features a different activity such as feeding the calves and horses, learning to rope a cow, nature walks, bug hunts, or tidal pool exploration. Children under age four can attend if they're accompanied by a parent.

Special Features: Guests can use all the facilities in the three camps. Kapua: beach, hammocks, canoes, fishing, beach volleyball, snorkeling, croquet, bocce ball, kayaks, mountain bikes and guided mountain biking tours, cultural hikes. Paniolo: swimming tank, horseshoe pits, nature walk, horseback riding, calf pens. Adults-only camp: ropes course (ages four and up) with twenty-three stations with both low elements and high elements, rock wall for climbing (minimum age four), mountain biking.

$$$: All meals, airport transportation, gratuities, taxes, and activities except for horseback riding and whale watching are included in the price: Daily rates, double occupancy: children 4–12, $75, adults $185–245; under 4 free.

Moderate

Paniolo Hale Condominiums
Address: P.O. Box 190, Lio Place, Maunaloa, Molokai, HI 96770
Telephone: 800-367-2984
Website: www.lava.net/paniolo

All the comforts of home are yours in these attractive condominiums next to the Kaluakoki Hotel and Golf Club along the ocean. Every unit has a large screened porch that wraps around the living room, allowing guests to dine on their verandah enjoying the fresh tropical air. You'll want a rental car to see the sites and pick up supplies; keep an eye out for the car rental packages that are offered several times during the year. Condo guests enjoy playing privileges on the eighteen-hole golf course and tennis courts next door. The ocean can have strong surf and currents during certain times of the year, so exercise caution when swimming.

Accommodations: Seventy-seven studios, one- and two-bedroom condominiums. Full kitchens, TVs, washers and dryers, and maid service every five days. Cribs and high chairs are available on request.

Special Features: beach, swimming pool, barbecue grills, picnic tables, paddle tennis court.

$$$: Daily rates, double occupancy: studios $95–$135, one bedroom $115–180, two bedrooms $145–$215.

Camping
Ten-acre Papohaku Beach park offers overnight camping and picnic facilities on the shore of the three-mile-long beach.

WHAT TO SEE AND DO
Kalaupapa is the island community that was once the site of a leper colony. The peninsula it sits upon juts out into the sea and is cut off from the rest of the island by a high cliff. Unfortunately visitors must be age sixteen or over to visit the community, either hiking the three-mile trail or taking a sure-footed mule down the cliffside trail to this fascinating historical site. The trail was first cut into the face of the north coast cliff in 1886, and visitors still traverse the same twenty-six switchbacks on the trail to Kalaupapa. Half-day, narrated ground tours of the settlement and park feature tours of Father Damien's church and a picnic lunch overlooking the north coast and the world's highest sea cliffs.

Moloka'i Horse and Wagon Ride takes visitors on horseback or in a wagon through Hawaii's largest mango grove to the Illiliopae Heiau, an ancient Hawaiian temple in Mapulehyu Valley. During the hour-long journey, guides regale you with local legends and songs. Tours culminate in a Moloka'i-style barbecue picnic lunch on the beach (800-670-6965).

Horseback Rides and Mountain Biking can be arranged at Molokai Ranch where riders on two wheels or four legs can explore the ranch's seventy thousand acres (808-552-2681).

4.

The
CARIBBEAN

While the islands of the Caribbean are made up of many different individual countries, each with their own customs and monetary systems, they all have in common a glorious tropical climate with a soothingly warm sun, cooling trade wind breezes, balmy turquoise waters, and spectacular beaches—all perfect ingredients for a fabulous family vacation. The island you choose to visit and the resort you decide to call home can vary from a tranquil private island retreat where you won't see anyone else for a week to a bustling full-service resort on an action-packed stretch of beach where you fill your days with golf, tennis, and planned activities. High rollers can brush shoulders with jet-setters at glamorous and exclusive resorts, and laid-back types need never change out of their swimsuits at condos where they can cook their own meals. There are fascinating cultures to delve into, or you can relax at an all-inclusive resort where you never leave the property.

The islands sweep down in a great arc from south of Florida to the coast of Venezuela. Closest to the United States are the Bahamas, Turks and Caicos, the Caymans, Jamaica, Cuba, Haiti, the Dominican Republic, and Puerto Rico. Most of the islands are accessible via flights through Miami or San Juan, Puerto Rico, or directly from American and Canadian cities to the larger and more populated islands.

Remember that tourism is the main economic force in most of these islands. While quite a number of island residents are employed in the hospitality industry, others create their own jobs selling crafts, snacks, and other merchandise to tourists. You're likely to encounter vendors selling jewelry, hair braiding, soft drinks, toys, etc., on beaches throughout the Caribbean.

Visitor Information: Request general information on the entire region from the Caribbean Tourism Organization:

North America: 20 East 46th Street, New York, NY 10017 (212-682-0435, fax 212-697-4258).

Caribbean: Second Floor, Sir Frank Wolcott Building, Culloden Farm Complex, St. Michel, Barbados, West Indies (809-427-5242, fax 809-429-3065).

If you want more island-specific information, see the addresses at the be-

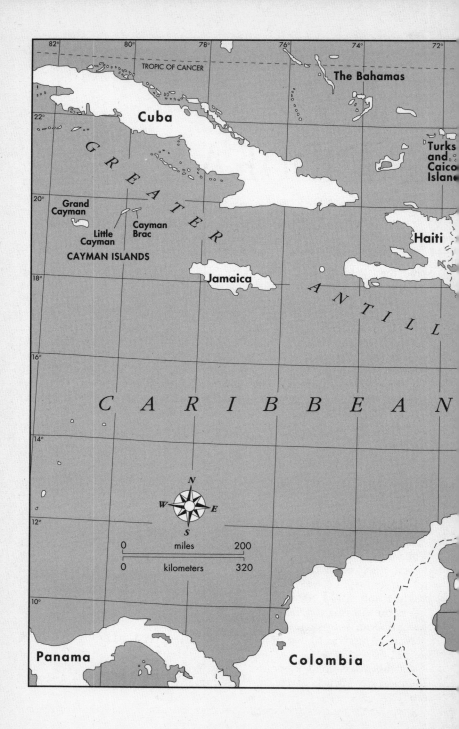

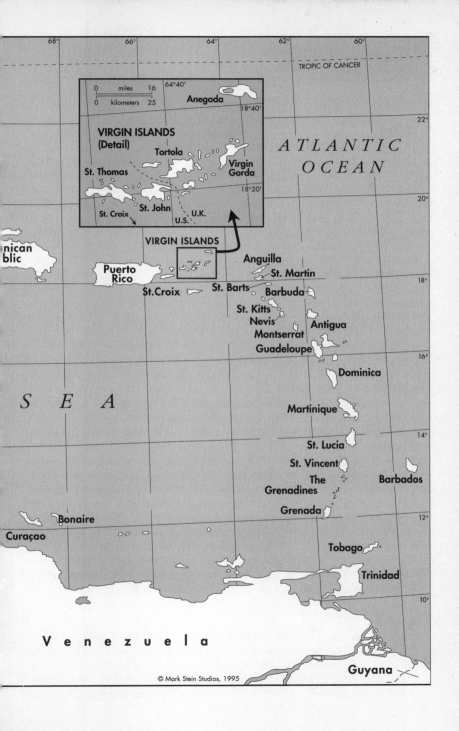

68° 66° 64° 62° 60°

TROPIC OF CANCER

64°40'

0   miles   16
0 kilometers 25

18°40'

Anegada

VIRGIN ISLANDS
(Detail)

Tortola

St. Thomas

Virgin
Gorda

18°20'

St. Croix

St. John

U.K.
U.S.

*ATLANTIC
OCEAN*

22°

20°

VIRGIN ISLANDS

Anguilla

St. Martin

**Puerto
Rico**

St.Croix

St. Barts

Barbuda

18°

St. Kitts
Nevis
Montserrat
Guadeloupe

Antigua

*nican
blic*

16°

Dominica

S E A

Martinique

14°

St. Lucia

St. Vincent

The
Grenadines

Barbados

Grenada

12°

Bonaire

Curaçao

Tobago

Trinidad

10°

V e n e z u e l a

© Mark Stein Studios, 1995

Guyana

ginning of individual island listings. If your children are stamp collectors, write to the tourist office on the island; the tiny island nations of the Caribbean have some of the most beautiful stamps in the world. Allow several weeks for a response, since mail service can be slow.

ENTRY AND EXIT REQUIREMENTS AND CUSTOMS

American Citizens: All islands except the U.S. Virgin Islands and Puerto Rico require visitors to carry proof of citizenship. Passports, one for each member of the family (even infants), can be obtained through the Department of State Office of Passport Services at 1425 "K" Street, Washington, D.C. 20522. The office's "Information Line" is 202-647-0518.

Some islands allow you to use an original birth certificate or voter registration card, accompanied by an official photo ID. A driver's license alone is not always sufficient as the photo ID, but you should bring it along in case you plan to rent a car. Note that the demand for passports is highest January through August because of summer vacations. Allow as much as eight weeks for application to be processed.

Canadian Citizens: Children under age sixteen may be included on a parent's passport, but they must have their own passport if they plan to travel alone. The passport office can give you information on where to obtain forms at 514-283-2152.

DEPARTURE TAX AND DUTY

Many Caribbean islands levy a departure tax (usually between $5 and $20) at the airport. Remember to save enough currency (try to have the exact change) to pay it before you go. Children under twelve are exempt from the tax on certain islands.

When you return to the United States or Canada, you must declare everything you have purchased. American families traveling together may make a joint declaration and are allowed $600 worth of goods per person duty free from most Caribbean countries as long as you've been gone for more than forty-eight hours and fewer than thirty days. Keep your sales receipts. For more information, contact the U.S. Customs service at 202-927-6724. Do not purchase any tortoise-shell jewelry or turtle products as they are not allowed. Canadians can bring in $300 worth of goods duty free once a year if they've been out of the country for at least seven days. For more information contact the Revenue Canada Customs and Excise Department at 613-957-0275.

WHEN TO GO

Hurricane season, usually early fall, is a slower time in the Caribbean since that region ranks third worldwide in number of hurricanes per year. However, some islands such as Bonaire, Aruba, and Curaçao are out of the hurricane belt. If you find yourself traveling or cruising during this time, remember that our sophisticated weather trackers will keep you informed and you can leave an island well before a storm has developed.

HEALTH AND SAFETY

In the Caribbean, a bad case of sunburn or a few mosquito bites are the most common problems you're likely to encounter. Many resorts have a doctor or nurse on staff, and medical personnel have often been trained in the United States or Europe. Children or adults with chronic health problems should consider a Caribbean cruise. Virtually all of the larger cruise ships have medical staff and facilities on board and some are outfitted for special medical needs.

The U.S. Public Health Service recommends diphtheria and tetanus shots for people traveling in the Caribbean, and all children should be inoculated against measles, mumps, rubella, and polio no matter where you live. In a few areas of the Caribbean (usually far away from any tourist areas), dengue fever, malaria, and yellow fever have been reported; to find out about specific disease risks for your itinerary, call the Center for Disease Control's International Health Requirements and Recommendations hotline at 404-332-4559 or find it on the internet at www.cdc.gov.

Here are some common sense guidelines for staying healthy in the Caribbean:

• Protect yourself from mosquito bites by conscientiously wearing insect repellent. Make sure your accommodations are screened or air-conditioned.

• Use bottled water for babies' formulas. Most islands have perfectly safe water, but subtle changes in water can often upset a little one's delicate system. Boxed unrefrigerated milk is common throughout the Caribbean and is safe to drink. It must be refrigerated once it's been opened.

• Swim with caution. Atlantic Ocean waters are generally much rougher than the Caribbean waters. Purchase waterproof shoes or sandals for the family before you go, to avoid injury from sharp coral, shell fragments, and sea urchin spines. Keep a vigilant watch on your little ones, as few beaches or pools are protected by lifeguards.

• Stay away from the highly poisonous manchineel tree found edging the beach on some islands. It's small, with a short trunk and numerous branches with shiny green leaves and tempting green applelike fruits. Once used by the Arawak and Carib Indians as arrow poison, just touching the leaves or standing under the tree in a rainstorm can give you a rash. Most trees on or near hotels and resorts have warning signs posted, and in more remote areas the trunks may be painted red.

• No-see-ums are pesky little biting gnats found on beaches and in swampy areas that gather on human ankles at dusk and after a heavy rain. They're so tiny you won't even know they're there until you feel an itchy tingle. A hearty dose of bug repellent should be part of your late afternoon wardrobe at all times.

MONEY MATTERS

Local currencies are used throughout most of the Caribbean. U.S. dollars are the official currency in the U.S. Virgin Islands, British Virgin Islands, and Puerto Rico, and they are accepted on many other islands alongside the local currency. Travelers checks and credit cards are readily accepted almost everywhere. ATMs are becoming more and more common, but check with your bank to find out whether your network is used in this part of the world; not all are.

Find out about tipping customs before you get to your island destination. Some islands dictate the 15 to 20 percent tip that is typical of the United States, while on the other islands, 10 percent is a standard tip. Tipping policies at different hotels and resorts vary as well. Some charge a service fee to cover tips for all staff; others expect guests to tip at the time services are rendered. Certain islands have a nightly room tax, and sometimes the room tax and service charges can add more than 20 percent to your bill. Always ask if service charges are included at a restaurant before you pay your bill, so you don't tip twice.

ON A BUDGET

The smaller islands that are farthest from the U.S. mainland can be less convenient to get to (which in some cases translates into more expensive airline tickets) but can offer much less expensive accommodations. St. Vincent and the Grenadines and Grenada offer some very low-priced hotel rooms. Tortola, in the British Virgin Islands also has some well-priced small and simple hotels. While the smaller budget properties won't have all the services of a glamorous resort, they'll offer you access to a beautiful beach and often your own kitchen.

MUSIC

Each island in the Caribbean seems to have evolved its own special get-up-and-dance sound, taking bits and pieces from all the different cultures that settled on and around it. African and Latin rhythms; European folk and court music; and American blues, jazz, and rock and roll get shaken up in spicy island stews, but come out with different flavors in different places; there's reggae from Jamaica, calypso and soca from Trinidad, merengue in the Dominican Republic, zouk from the French islands of Martinique and Guadeloupe, and rumba from Cuba—the list goes on and on. If you and your children like to listen to music, bring a small radio with you and explore the islands' many radio stations. In addition to hearing toe-tapping Caribbean popular music, you'll hear birthday and anniversary wishes, school updates, and all the news of a small island.

"Jump-ups" are popular throughout the islands and involve all kinds of catchy Caribbean music. They're simple: when you hear the music, jump up and begin to dance. Many jump-ups wind through the streets during holidays, festivals, and, of course, Carnival time.

For many tourists, steel band music is synonymous with Caribbean island music. The steel "pans" as the drums are known, are made from large oil drums. The music originated in Trinidad whose oil industry supplied the cast-off drums and whose poverty inspired the use of found objects for musical instruments. From these humble origins, steel band music has grown to be the mainstay of the tourist industry's evening entertainment. If you want to hear real "cutting edge" steel band music that's far from the tourist sounds, head to Trinidad for their steel pan festival.

Calypso music, popularized in the United States by Harry Belafonte in the 1940s, is all about the lyrics—listen carefully and you'll hear biting political content, witty social commentary, and gossipy rhyming rants. Calypso is like a musical newspaper with an Afro-Spanish rhythm; if you want to find out what's been bothering the residents of a particular island, attend a calypso competition. The best calypso can be seen at carnival and festival time when competitions showcase dueling calypso kings and queens.

In the 1950s, American urban blues, and rhythm and blues, were picked up over the radio by many Jamaicans. Riding the nationalistic spirit that came with Jamaica's independence from Great Britain, the R-and-B sound was re-shaped by Jamaican musicians and ska and rock steady were born. They were in turn transformed into reggae whose loping bass and African-based back beat have become recognizable around the world. Bob Marley is still the best known and loved reggae artist in the world, and you'll see his face on T-shirts and hear his music emanating from record stores, cafés, and car windows throughout the islands.

FOOD

Authentic Caribbean food is terrific, with a subtle blend of unusual flavors, often hot and pungent, always colorful and fresh. Delicious continental and nouvelle cuisine are available in resort areas and hotel restaurants. But don't worry, hamburgers and pizza are standard menu items on most islands. Of course *you'll* want to sample the local cuisine, but will your kids? A few delicious local dishes may tempt them.

Many traditional Caribbean recipes come down from the "make do" days when what grew locally—tropical fruits, root vegetables, pigeon peas, chicken, fish, goats, spices, and leaves—were staples. Some recipes are based on African fare, some came across on a boat from Europe, and some were invented on the islands.

Fresh fish is available everywhere, prepared in a variety of ways. A local favorite is the old wife, or triggerfish, which most children really like. The skin of this fish is so rough it was once used to scrub floors. Conch (pronounced conk), the animal that lives in the large shell with the shiny pink middle, is a mainstay of the local diet. You can find it prepared in chowder, salad, spicy garlic sauce, or dunked in batter and deep fried. Most children will try the fritters, usually accompanied by a key lime sauce.

Here are a few other Caribbean favorites:

Bullfoot soup is a thick stew of meat and vegetables flavored with local seasonings.
Callaloo is a big green leafy vegetable whose leaves taste like spinach, and it is often made into a popular soup made with the greens, ham, and crab.
Coconut water is the liquid found in large green coconuts. It's a refreshing treat.

Fungi, pronounced *foon-jee,* is a staple made from cornmeal and okra, often served with fish.

Johnny cakes are unleavened fried bread—plain but tasty.

Plantains are similar to bananas, though slightly less sweet, and are fried rather than eaten raw.

Pate turnovers, often sold at sidewalk stands, are pastries filled with spiced beef or salt fish.

Pepperpot soup is a rich savory stew containing beef, pork, vegetables, and spices.

Seamoss drink is locally considered an aphrodisiac, described with a wink as a "manly" drink.

Soursop, a green-skinned fruit with a sweet and sour citrus taste, is eaten raw or made into a drink that helps put babies to sleep.

Anguilla

Small, uncrowded, and tranquil, Anguilla—one of the northernmost of the Leeward Islands—has several of the Caribbean's most elegant superluxurious resorts, as well as casual and affordable beachfront retreats. Its thirty immaculate white-sand beaches with hidden coves and grottos circle the island and are surrounded by a coral reef that transforms the translucent turquoise waters into a giant aquarium. Snorkelers can go eyeball to eyeball with fish, eels, and octopus just offshore. Over the years, the government has sunk nine surplus hulls in order to create habitats for marine life, making it popular with scuba divers, too.

The long and skinny eel-shaped island is just 3 miles across at its widest point and 213 feet high at its greatest elevation. The rocky limestone soil is unsuitable for agriculture, so sugar was never cultivated there. Instead, the island's economy has been based on fishing and boat building (and more recently tourism), and many colorful and swift seacraft can be spotted in the harbors today. Not surprisingly, the national sport is boat racing. Races are a part of every public holiday and are usually accompanied by beachside barbecues, jump-ups, and betting. The sport reaches its high point during the first week of August when Anguilla celebrates three holidays and stages its riotous multicolored carnival.

Fast Facts:

Visitor Information: Website: www.anguilla-vacation.com, *US and Canada* Tourist Information and Reservations c/o Medhurst and Associates, Inc., 1208 Washington Drive, Centerport, NY 11721 (800-553-4939, 516-425-0900, fax 516-425-0903), *Anguilla* Anguilla Tourist Board, P.O. Box 1388, The Valley, Anguilla, BWI (800-553-4939, 264-497-2759, fax 264-497-3389).

Arriving and Departing: Passports are preferred for American and Canadian citizens, but an original birth certificate with a photo ID can be used instead.

Visitors must show an onward or return ticket. A departure tax of $10 per person is charged.

Currency: U.S. dollars are widely accepted, although the official currency is the Eastern Caribbean Dollar (EC$)

Language: A British possession for almost 350 years, Anguilla remains an English-speaking colony today.

Best Sweet Treat: Head to Randy and Joe's Ice Cream Parlor in the historical cotton gin building for creamy confections in tropical flavors.

WHERE TO STAY

Expensive: over $225
Moderate: $125–$225
Budget: under $125

Expensive

Cap Juluca

Address: P.O. Box 240, Maunday's Bay, Anguilla, BWI
Telephone: 888-858-5822 or 264-497-6666, fax 264-497-6617
Website: www.capjuluca.com

Looking a little like something out of Lawrence of Arabia, with its North African architecture and furnishings from Moroccan souks, deluxe Cap Juluca spreads along a gleaming one-mile strand of white sand at Maunday's Bay near the southwestern end of the island. Its white Moorish-style villas with domes, arches, and flowered courtyards are spacious and elegantly decorated. A romantic open-air restaurant sits right at the water's edge. The place is the ultimate in a luxurious, slowed-down vacation, yet enjoys its youngest guests, offering children's menus in the restaurants, children's rooms at half price, and a special program, Juluca's Fun House, in summer. There's also the full range of watersports and tennis courts with lights for night play. Adults and children who want to perfect their croquet game can take a thirty-minute "primer" for beginners and experienced players on the resort's immaculate regulation croquet court.

For Kids: Complimentary children's activities take place from June 1–October 31. Ten- to fourteen-year-olds enjoy one-hour clinics to improve their skills in a variety of sports such as water-skiing, windsurfing, snorkeling, sailing, and swimming. Three- to nine-year-olds meet in the children's clubhouse next to the junior Olympic-size pool from 10 A.M. to 8:30 P.M. and can drop in and out of activities as they wish. A daily schedule offers nature walks, arts and crafts, and beach activities in the morning; and pool swimming, tennis, story hour, and a movie in the afternoon. The program breaks for dinner and resumes at 7 P.M. when a movie is shown.

Accommodations: Eighteen villas house fifty-eight private rooms, seven suites, and six complete villas, several of which have three to five bedrooms and their own private pool. All have marble bathrooms, huge tubs, ceiling fans, air-conditioning, refrigerators, private terraces, louvered doors and windows, and elegant Moroccan-style furnishings.

Special Features: beach, pool, three tennis courts (two lit for night play), putting green, croquet, sunfish sailing, snorkeling, kayaking, windsurfing, waterskiing, fishing trips, children's program, baby-sitting, fitness center, nature trails, library, board games, shop, restaurant, bar.

$$$: Adjoining rooms for children are half price from June through October, and prices in general drop dramatically during the summer. Daily rates, double occupancy: rooms $300–$675, one- and two-bedroom suites, $575–$2,050, villas $2,010–$4,895.

Malliouhana Hotel

Address: P.O. Box 173, Meads Bay, Anguilla, BWI
Telephone: 800-835-0796, 264-497-6011, fax 264-497-6011
Website: www.malliouhana.com

Malliouhana is known for its sophistication, service, world-class French cuisine, and wine cellar, but will your kids care? They're more likely to notice the elaborate, supervised children's play area built along the beach at this elegant five-star resort. Its luxurious guest rooms cover twenty-five acres of tropical grounds on a bluff overlooking soft white-sand beaches and a secluded cove. A waterfall connects two freshwater pools, and the tennis courts, managed by Peter Burwash International, have lights and wind shields. Plus, there are two speed boats for waterskiing, and all kinds of other watersports. Dining is a large part of the Malliouhana experience, and the superb cuisine is French with a Caribbean twist. A TV video room has a selection of two hundred videos, including some just for kids.

For Kids: The adventure playground has equipment for both toddlers and older children, a wading pool and spray fountain and a covered games area with little tables and chairs, and a Ping-Pong table. It's supervised daily from 8:30 A.M. to 5 P.M. by a childcare counselor and assistant; structured activities are based on the number and ages of the children present. There is a one-on-one basketball court, Nintendo, Ping-Pong, tire swings, sandbox, tiny spinning carousel, and seesaw. The program is complimentary for two- to twelve-year-olds.

Accommodations: Fifty-five rooms and suites. There is a choice of double rooms, junior suites, and one- and two-bedroom suites, and all are spacious with exquisite furnishings, covered patios, and marble bathrooms. Many rooms have connecting doors. Seven villas are located on the beach, the bluff, or in the gardens that can be rented as individual rooms or as an entire villa.

Special Features: beach, two swimming pools, a Jacuzzi, fishing excursions, shops, hairdresser, library, board games, playground, windsurfers, sailboats, waterskiing, boat excursions, complimentary snorkeling gear, four tennis courts, fitness center, massage, restaurant, bar.

$$$: Daily rates, double occupancy: $340–$1,085. Rates include watersports. Credit cards are not accepted; personal checks by special arrangement only. Closed in September and October.

Moderate

Mariners Beach Resort

Address: Box 139, Sandy Ground, Anguilla, BWI
Telephone: 264-497-2671, fax 264-497-2901
Website: www.offshore.com.ai/mariners

Tucked between one of the island's prettiest white-sand beaches and a gentle green hillside is this cottage hotel with quaint gingerbread cottages and latticed verandas. Its watersports shop offers chartered fishing trips and sunset cruises in addition to more standard snorkeling, windsurfing, and sailing. There's also a swimming pool and tennis courts. The breezy beachside restaurant has barbecue buffets and a traditional West Indian buffet once a week, often with live music.

Accommodations: An alternative to the standard single- and double-room arrangement is one of the twenty cottages that are set up as "triplets": studios are in the middle and have small kitchenettes, with a bedroom and bath on either side. You can rent all or part of a cottage, depending on how much space you need.

Special Features: beach, swimming pool, restaurant, fishing, cruises, lit tennis court, scuba, sailing, snorkel gear, windsurfers.

$$$: Daily rates, double occupancy: $150–$675. All-inclusive packages are available.

Paradise Cove Resort

Address: P.O. Box 135, The Cove, Anguilla, BWI
Telephone: 264-497-6603, fax 264-497-6927
E-mail: para-cove@anguillanet.com

An Olympic-size swimming pool, kiddy pool, children's playground, croquet court, and a very homey atmosphere make these fourteen fully-furnished one- and two-bedroom suite/apartments attractive to families. As a bonus, the kitchens are especially spacious, and units have easy access to washers and dryers. The tropically landscaped property is about five hundred yards from the beach or you can drive to beautiful Cove Bay Beach; the resort staff will arrange car rentals and bike rentals before you arrive. Its main pool bar and small café serve breakfast and lunch.

Accommodations: Fourteen one- and two-bedroom suites: two-bedroom suites have twin beds in one bedroom and a queen bed in the other. All units have fully equipped kitchens with microwaves, air-conditioning, ceiling fans, cable TV, daily maid service. Private cooks can be arranged.

Special Features: beach, swimming pool, kiddy pool, Jacuzzi, children's playground with playhouse, seesaw, slides, laundry facilities, cribs, high chairs, and baby-sitting services available.

$$$: Daily rates, double occupancy: $155–$385.

Budget

Seashore Apartments
Address: Rendezvous Bay, Anguilla, BWI
Telephone: 264-497-6750, fax 264-497-6756

Seahorse's six one-bedroom cottages right on the beach at quiet Rendezvous Bay are one of Anguilla's best buys. Children under twelve are not accepted in season (December 15 to April 14), but families visit regularly during the rest of the year. The small beach has very safe, calm waters and excellent snorkeling is found just offshore. All guests are welcome to use the barbecue area and picnic tables near the water's edge. You'll want a car for mobility, and car rentals can be arranged in advance.

Accommodations: Spacious and spotless one-bedroom cottages have full kitchens, full baths, and maid service six days a week. Bedrooms have king-size beds, and one or two roll-away beds can be added for children (advance notice required). All cottages are cooled by ceiling fans and have large porches with table and chairs.

Special Features: baby-sitting.

$$$: high season: $95–$200.

Villa Rentals
Anguilla Connection specializes in villa rentals. They meet you at the airport, get you started with a bag of groceries, and are a phone call away if you have any problems (264-497-4403, 264-407-4402).

WHAT TO SEE AND DO
There are a couple of casual family-friendly eateries on Anguilla where you can make an afternoon of lunch:

Uncle Ernie's on Shoal Beach is an unpretentious bar and restaurant, with barbecued chicken, barbecued spare ribs, and local snapper specialties. The kids can play on the beach while you linger over some of the best chicken you've ever tasted. A local band entertains on Sunday. Open daily from 10 A.M. to 8 P.M.

Gorgeous Scilly Cay and its silly-sounding name is a favorite of many kids. Take the free boat ride to the private eastern island in Island Harbour Sound for lunch. One of the most popular dishes with locals and guests alike is the Caribbean lobster, or *longenese*. After you've finished your meal, lounge on the beach, take a swim, and snorkel the nearby coral reefs. Open 11 A.M. to 5 P.M. Closed Mondays. Live music on Wednesday, steel bands on Fridays, and reggae on Sundays.

Antigua

Three hundred and sixty-five sandy coves and beaches surround the island; that's one for each day of the year. Some are nearly deserted, while many others are hemmed in by resorts of all sizes. Coral reefs protect much of the shoreline, offering calm water and exceptional snorkeling no matter where you flip your fins. Antigua is a good place to perfect your tan, as it receives the least rainfall of all islands in the eastern Caribbean.

Columbus "discovered" the island on his second voyage to the West Indies in 1493, but several Amerindian groups had settled there first. History buffs will want to visit English Harbor where Captain Horatio Nelson took command of the British naval yard in 1784 in anticipation of invasions by the French and the other European powers who played king-of-the-hill over various Caribbean islands. Antigua remained a British territory until 1981, when it received its independence with neighboring sister island Barbuda.

Summer carnival takes place in August with ten days of parades, wild costumes, and calypso and steel band competitions. Race week in late April consists of seven days of ocean racing and parties. Kids will enjoy Dockyard Day when there is a tug of war competition between sailing crews, a greased pole race, and spinnaker flying contest.

Fast Facts:

Visitor Information: Website: www.antigua-barbuda.org. US: 610 Fifth Avenue, Suite 311, New York, NY 10020 (212-541-4117); Canada: 60 St. Clair Avenue East, Toronto, Ontario M4T1N5 (416-961-3083); Antigua: Department of Tourism, Thames Street and Long Street in St. Johns.

Arriving and Departing: You'll need a current U.S. passport or a birth certificate to enter Antigua. There is an airport departure fee of $10 per person.

Money: Antiguans use the Eastern Caribbean Dollar (EC$) but U.S. dollars are accepted throughout the island.

Best Sweet Treat: Ducana is a pudding made from grated sweet potato and coconut, mixed with sugar and spices, and boiled in a banana leaf.

WHERE TO STAY

Antigua has inclusive resorts and those that charge for the room only. When you're comparing prices, take this into consideration. Inclusive resorts will appear to be more expensive but usually offer more for the money.

Expensive: over $225
Moderate: $125–$225
Inexpensive: under $125

Expensive

Sunsail Beach Club
Address: Hodges Bay, Antigua, WI

Telephone: 800-734-7716, 410-280-2553, fax 410-280-2406
Website: www.sunsail.com

Sunsail Beach Club is Sunsail Sailing Vacation's first land-based resort in the Caribbean. Sunsail offers the novel option of combining a land vacation with a week sailing through nearby islands. Their claim to have enough equipment for every guest over the age of seven to be on the water at any one time means nonstop water fun for your kids. Sailing instructors are available for older children. There's a kids' program that includes a nursery for babies.

Accommodations: 123 guest rooms including suites and three-bedroom villas feature Caribbean-inspired colors, Italian tile, air-conditioning, mini-fridge, in-room safes, and satellite TV.

For Kids: The resort's complimentary children's club is available for kids ages two to sixteen at no extra charge. A miniclub for babies from four months to two years is available at an extra charge. Nannies are also available.

Special Features: two beaches, swimming pool, night-lit tennis court, beach volleyball, table tennis, windsurfing, dinghies, day cruising yachts, waterskiing, inner tube rides, scuba, snorkeling, sailing, restaurants, pizzeria, two bars.

$$$: For a seven night stay, adults $870–$1,250; children four months to sixteen years $499.

St. James Club

Address: P.O. Box 63, Mamora Bay, Antigua, WI
Telephone: 800-345-0356 or 268-460-5000, fax 268-460-3015
Website: www.saintjamesclub.com
E-mail: reservations @antigua-resorts.com

Long cream-colored sand beaches wrap around this resort's private peninsula, which separates Mamora Bay from the Caribbean. On the calm bay side, you'll find the watersports center, beach cabanas, sunbathing decks, and wonderful swimming opportunities in the tranquil saltwater. The other side of the resort faces the Caribbean Sea, and its water is rougher and more challenging for swimmers. The gated property is safe enough for older kids to roam wherever they wish—to the playground, the croquet court, the Ping-Pong table, or the game room. The club also has three pools, several restaurants, a European-style casino, and a good tennis program. Horseback riding along the beach and through the countryside starts from stables on the property. From December 20 to January 2, rates are all-inclusive only.

Accommodations: 105 rooms, 73 villas. Families usually stay in The Village, where separate two-story, two-bedroom villas have roomy kitchens with dishwashers, decks with barbecues, and two full bathrooms. Spacious dining areas and comfortable living rooms have cable TV and beautiful furnishings. Club Suite rooms, closer to the main resort, have two rooms, one a bedroom with a queen size bed, and the other a sitting room that can accommodate several roll-aways.

For Kids: Club Kidz is a supervised activity program for children ages two to twelve, divided into age groups of two to six (block building, ball games, reading, nature walks, cookie baking, movies) and seven to twelve (kayaking, fishing, beach picnics, kite flying, soccer, jewelry making). A separate playroom houses the children's program, open daily from 8 A.M. to 5 P.M. Teenz Club for ages thirteen to sixteen offers a host of watersports plus tennis tournaments, horseback riding, and soccer matches. Programs are complimentary.

Special Features: three pools, two beaches, horseback riding, scuba, fitness center, seven tennis courts (five lit for night play), volleyball, croquet, table tennis, children's playroom, playground, baby-sitting, car rentals, scuba, windsurfing, Sunfish sailing, pedal boats, snorkeling, kayaking, boating and fishing excursions, beauty salon, shops, deli.

$$$: Daily rates: villas $475–$640, rooms $235–$370. December 20–January 2 rates are all inclusive: villas (2 adults) $1,340, rooms $430. Additional child $65.

Moderate

Rex Halcyon Cove Beach
Address: Box 251, Dickenson Bay, St. Johns Antigua, WI
Telephone: 800-255-5859, 268-462-0256, fax 268-462-0271
Website: www.rexcaribbean.com

This full-fledged resort with many different watersports and nightly entertainment has its own ice cream parlor and a restaurant perched on stilts above the water that serves lunch and dinner. It's about ten minutes from St. John and twenty minutes from the airport on Dickenson Bay. Most of the action takes place around the pool and busy soft-sand beach. Watersports such as Sunfish Sailing, windsurfing, beach volleyball, snorkeling, and daytime tennis have a charge. Waterskiing, watersports tuition, nighttime tennis, and scuba cost extra.

Accommodations: 210 rooms: All rooms have air-conditioning; but vary in other amenities such as TV and refrigerators. A minimarket is nearby.

For Kids: Supervised activities operate weekdays from 9 A.M. to 4 P.M. for four- to twelve-year-olds, with a midday break for lunch. The program changes according to the ages of the kids present, but count on field trips, swimming, sports, games, and arts and crafts.

Special Features: beach, swimming pool, Sunfish sailing, windsurfing, beach volleyball, snorkeling, tennis, waterskiing, scuba, restaurants, bar, ice cream parlor.

$$$: On the inclusive plan, all children under two stay and eat free, one child age two to twelve stays free and second child pays $20 per day. Adults double occupancy: $400–$610 per day. Room only $185–$470.

Inexpensive

Falmouth Harbor Beach Apartments
Address: P.O. Box 713, St. Johns, Antigua WI
Telephone: 800-223-5695, 268-460-1027, fax 268-463-1534

Twelve fully equipped apartments are right on the beach at Falmouth Bay on the southern coast of the island; sixteen more perch on the hillside above the protected cove, just a short walk from the lively scene of English Harbor and its restaurants, shops, and historical sights. Its beach is on busy Falmouth Bay harbor, with lots of boating activity to observe. To relax on the sand, you're better off heading to quieter Pigeon Beach, a ten-minute walk away. Snorkel gear and sunfish are included in the very reasonable rate.

Accommodations: All units have three single beds, two of which can be made into a king. Roll-aways or cribs are available. Units are on the small side and haven't been renovated recently, but they are sparkling clean and have outdoor decks or patios with table, chairs, and lounge chairs. Some rooms have interior connecting doors. Daily housekeeping service, which includes dishwashing, is included in the rate.

Special Features: beach, snorkeling, sailing, boating, windsurfing, car rental.

$$$: Daily rate, double occupancy: $68–$134. Each child under sixteen sharing the apartment with their parents is $15 per night.

WHAT TO SEE AND DO

Visit **St. John's Market** on a Saturday to see the colorful and noisy scene crammed with fruit and vegetable stands, fish and spice vendors, and buyers haggling for a good deal.

Nelson's Dockyard: The British fleet in the West Indies called this dockyard headquarters and home from 1704 to 1889. Its most famous commander, Admiral Horatio Nelson, arrived in 1784 to protect it from the French, but little action was seen. After the British navy abandoned it in 1889, it slowly decayed, until a preservation group restored it to its former glory. The "new" Nelson's Dockyard opened in 1961 with colonial naval buildings standing as they did in the 1780s. The Admiral's house has been made into a museum with elaborate ships' models, maps, prints, and a model of English Harbor. Stop for a drink or lunch at Admiral's Inn, built of the ballast bricks of sailing ships, where the yachting crowd gather. The **Dow's Hill Interpretation Centre** traces the history of Antigua and Barbuda form prehistoric times to the present using a multimedia presentation. Time your visit to the dockyard so that cruise ship visitors are not present. Open 8 A.M.–6 P.M.

Just north of Nelson's Dockyard are the ruins of **Shirley Heights,** which include fortifications, barracks, and powder magazines that serve as great lookout points. Plan to be there on a Sunday afternoon for a tasty barbecue meal and reggae and steel band entertainment (make reservations at Shirley Heights Lookout). The steel band plays from 3 P.M. to 6 P.M., and the reggae band from 6 P.M. to 9 P.M. If you can't go on Sunday, you can still enjoy fresh fish or hamburgers any day of the week. From 9 A.M. to 10 P.M. (809-460-1785).

In St. John, the **Museum of Antigua and Barbuda** is a please-touch-style museum, with a life-size Arawak house, models of a sugar plantation, a wattle and daub house, and more. Early Indian items have been collected from 120 prehistoric sites on the island (Church and Market Streets, 809-463-1060).

Cricket is a popular spectator sport, and you can see formal regional and international matches called Test Matches played at the recreational grounds in St. John, or see a "knockabout" played casually on the beach, street corner, or playground.

Wind surfing is excellent for beginners along the west coast, while advanced wind surfers tend to prefer the much more challenging east coast surf. Lessons for all abilities are offered at Jolly Beach Hotel's Wind Surfing Sailing School (one of the best in the world) and Patrick Scales Water Sports at Lord Nelson Beach Hotel.

Tours of sister island **Barbuda,** twenty-six miles north of Antigua, can be undertaken in one day. The frigate bird sanctuary is accessible by small boat, through mangrove bushes that stretch for miles. In among the mangroves are nesting grounds for over five thousand frigate birds, known locally as man-o'-war. They make their nests in the mangroves just a few feet above the water.

Aruba

Aruba's beaches are legendary for their broad stretches of snow white sand flanked by startling turquoise water and showered with constant sunshine. In recent years, Aruba's most popular seven-mile strand of beach has sprouted a long line of resorts, casinos, restaurants, and boutiques. While you certainly won't be alone on the beach, families can often find a good package deal that includes airfare and accommodations and possibly meals and activities. Quite a few of the large island's resorts offer children's activity programs and special prices for families.

This flat, dry, deserty island buffeted by trade wind breezes is prime wind-surfing territory for beginners and experts alike. Beginners can start in quiet and shallow beach waters while crack windsurfers whip through the air on the high waves of Boca Grandi on the southeast coast. In June, tournament wind-surfers compete for the Annual Hi-Winds Pro Am World Cup.

Pack your strongest pair of jeans so you can sample the official sport of sand dune sliding; the fast and gritty slopes sandpaper thin shorts right off your backside. Zooming across the sand and fields in a sailcart is another unusual sport to try.

Aruba is the A of the ABC islands (Bonaire and Curaçao) off the coast of Venezuela. It was once part of the Netherland Antilles, but became an independent entity within the Netherlands in 1986. Its February carnival has a children's carnival in Oranjestad, usually held a week before the main carnival parade.

In recent years Aruba has become a popular place for timeshares to set up shop, and many tourists are courted with offers of free dinners or amenities if they spend a few hours listening to the pitch. Unless you're really serious about buying into a timeshare, be ready with a simple no-thank-you so you can spend your time where you belong—on the beach and in the pool.

Fast Facts:

Visitor Information: Website:www.aruba.com *U.S.:* Aruba Tourism Authority, 1000 Harbor Boulevard, Weekawken, NJ 07087 (201-330-0800 or 800-862-7822). *Canada:* 86 Bloor Street West, Suite 204, Toronto, Ontario MS 1M5 (800-268-3042, Ontario and Quebec 416-975-1950, fax 416-975-1947). *Aruba:* Aruba Tourism Authority, L.G. Smith Boulevard 172, Aruba (2978-21019, fax 2978-34702).

Arriving and Departing: A passport, a birth certificate, or a voter registration card with official photograph are required for entry. Departure tax is $20.

Money: The Aruba florin or A.FL is the official currency.

Language: Dutch is the official language, but Papiamento—which evolved from Spanish, Dutch, Portuguese, and a sprinkling of Indian, English, and French influences—is the native language of Aruba. English is often spoken by people in the tourist industries.

Best Sweet Treat: Caramel flan is an island speciality.

WHERE TO STAY
Expensive

Hyatt Regency Aruba Resort and Casino

Address: J. E. Irausquin Boulevard 85, Palm Beach, Aruba
Telephone: 800-233-1234, 297-8-61234, fax 297-8-61682
Website: www.hyatt.com

When children hear the name Hyatt, they think *awesome swimming pool,* and this resort doesn't disappoint; its sprawling three-level pool complex has cascading waterfalls, a two-story spiraling water slide, and a 5,000-square-foot lagoon stocked with tropical fish and wildlife. Other features include a full array of watersports, perfect white-powder sand beach, tennis, health spa, a 54-foot catamaran, and a beach volleyball court. Meanwhile, the elegant decor, four excellent restaurants, and superb service satisfy parents, too. This Hyatt continues to be one of the most popular full-service resorts on Palm Beach, arguably the prettiest beach on the island, but one that can be a bit crowded in season.

Accommodations: 360 rooms have air-conditioning, minibar, ceiling fan, oversized bathrooms, and digital safes. All rooms are the same size, and the view determines the difference in price. The top floor is reserved for Regency Club suites, which are more spacious and deluxe and loaded with amenities.

For Kids: Camp Hyatt offers three- to twelve-year-olds a newly renovated 5,000-square-foot facility. There's an extensive game room and a wealth of supervised activities such as nature walks. Papiamento language lessons, sandcastle building, arts and crafts, dancing lessons, movies, wildlife tours, and water slide fun. Camp Hyatt operates daily throughout the year with a variety of program times. Half-day programs are from 9 A.M. to 12 P.M. ($18 per child), and 1 P.M. to 5 P.M. ($24 per child). The whole-day program is from 9 A.M.

to 3 P.M. ($46 per child), and the evening from 6 P.M. to 10 P.M. ($34 per child). Lunch is served for an additional $10 and extends the morning session until 1 P.M.; dinner is offered in the evening session but not included.

Special Features: beach, pool complex, canoes, windsurfing, snorkeling, scuba diving, catamaran cruises, eighteen-hole golf, restaurants, bars, casino, fitness center, two night-lit tennis courts, shops, baby-sitting, jogging path.

$$$: Kids under eighteen are free in their parents' room. A second room, half price for children, is available year-round depending on availability. Roll-aways are free but advanced notice is required. Daily rates, double occupancy: $215–$495.

Costa Linda Beach Resort Aruba

Address: J. E. Irausquin Boulevard 59, P.O. Box 1345, Aruba
Telephone: 800-992-2015, 297-8-38000, fax 297-8-36040
Website: www.arubaonline.com/costalinda

Families can spread out in spacious comfort in two- or three-bedroom suites, all with a private balcony overlooking the sea and a kitchen for late-night snack and daytime meals. This all-suite resort is on Eagle Beach on the island's southern coast. A casual kids program, gorgeous beach, and free-form tropical swimming pools exhaust even the most energetic child. Plus, there's a playground, game room, tennis, fitness center, whirlpool, and nightly entertainment.

Accommodations: 139 two-bedroom suites: all face the ocean, with fully equipped kitchens, air-conditioning and fold-out couches in the living room. Washers and dryers are located on every floor. Baby cribs, playpens, and high chairs, are available.

For Kids: Five- to twelve-year-olds can attend the casual drop-in program weekdays from 10:30 A.M. to 3:30 P.M. and weekends until 4 P.M. to 5 P.M. Activities range from face painting, T-shirt painting, and carnival mask making to beach games and sports.

Special Features: beach, swimming pool, kiddy pool, children's playground, game room, shuffleboard, volleyball, car rental, shopping arcade, whirlpool, lit tennis courts, fitness center, restaurants, bars, nightly entertainment, laundry facilities.

$$$: Up to six people can stay in two-bedroom units: two-bedroom $298–$500. The resort offers many special promotions throughout the year; be sure to inquire.

Moderate

La Cabana All Suite Beach Resort and Casino

Address: J. E. Irausquin Boulevard 250, Oranjestad, Aruba
Telephone: 800-835-7193, 297-8-79000, fax 297-8-70834
Website: www.lacabana.com/resort
E-mail: lacabana@setarnet.aw

Every studio, one- , two- , or three-bedroom suite has a kitchenette in this enormous all-suite hotel on Eagle Beach. Three free-form swimming pools, a children's pool, a water slide, a playground, and the Club Cabana Nana Children's program are aimed specifically at youngsters, but there's plenty to do for every age. There's every conceivable watersport, squash and racquet ball courts, basketball, shuffleboard, aerobics classes, tennis clinics, and jogging trails. This small city-of-a-resort houses a 600-seat theater, the Caribbean's largest casino, a minimarket, pharmacy, boutiques, health spa, and beauty salon.

Accommodations: 811 suites come in studios, one- , two- , and three-bedroom styles in two sizes. All have master bedrooms, pull-out queen sofas and fully equipped kitchenettes with extras like microwaves and blenders, air-conditioning, ceiling fans, private balconies or patio, and laundry facilities on each floor.

For Kids: Club Cabana Nana for children five to twelve keeps youngsters on the go from 10:30 A.M. until 3:30 P.M. every day except Wednesday when the program shifts to the evening (5:30 P.M. to 8:30 P.M.) for movies and a pizza party, and Saturday, when there is no camp. Days are filled with minigolf, bowling, beach games, sports, and creative activities. The Club Cabana Nana package is priced at $80 per child weekly and includes daily lunch from the children's menu. Teenagers thirteen to seventeen are entertained with a beach disco party, bowling, tennis, windsurfing and snorkeling lessons, pizza night, table games, pool volleyball, and more. Separate fees are charged for some of their activities.

Special Features: beach, three swimming pools (one with slide and swim-up bar), kiddy pool, ice cream shop, shops, library, minigolf, bowling, shuffleboard, video game room, horseback riding, aerobics classes, volleyball, five lit tennis courts, racquetball, fitness center, casino, Laundromats, beauty salon, car rental, night club.

$$$: Up to two kids under twelve stay free when accompanied by two adults. Additional person over twelve in room, $15–$20 per night. Studio $150–$225 per night, one bedroom $160–$340, two bedroom $425–$655, three bedroom $450–$880.

Aruba Marriott Resort and Casino

Address: L. G. Smith Boulevard, Palm Beach, Aruba
Telephone: 800-223-6388, 297-8-69000, fax 297-8-60649
The Marriott's section of beachfront on spectacular Palm Beach tends to be a bit quieter than some of the other resorts on this popular stretch of sand, as it's situated at the very end of the line. You'll find families lounging in the sun, playing in the waves, or splashing in the resort's free-form pool with its cascading waterfalls and swim-up bar. Many parents take advantage of the enormous Stellaris Casino, offering 10,700 square feet of gaming space. Parents with older kids should take advantage of the resort's Vela Highwinds Center, which offers windsurfing instruction and rentals on this island famed for its perfect tradewinds.

Accommodations: 411 rooms including 20 suites. All rooms are air-conditioned and have their own 100-square-foot balcony.

For Kids: The Marriott has a kid's camp for five- to twelve-year-olds weekdays from 8:30 A.M. to 4 P.M. The $45 fee includes a camp T-shirt, lunch, prizes, and activities such as windsurfing, beach games, mini-Olympics, pool aerobics, and arts and crafts. Children can stay at camp at an hourly rate as well: $15 for two hours, $6 for each additional hour, and an added $10 for lunch and $25 for dinner. Two hours advance registration and personal sun protection is required.

Special Features: beach, swimming pool, kids program, casino, sailing, sportfishing, scuba, snorkeling, windsurfing, health club, baby-sitting, excursion, shops, restaurants, bars, swim-up bar.

$$$: Daily rates, double occupancy: $135–$750. There is a maximum of four people per room, and roll-aways are $20 per night. Kids under 12 eat for free.

Burshiri Beach Resort

Address: L. G. Smith Boulevard 35, Oranjestad, Aruba
Telephone: 297-8-25216, fax 297-8-26789

This beachfront property is part of the Aruba Hospitality Trades Training Center, and the cheerful and fresh-faced young staff who apprentice here are always eager to please, although the service can be rather uneven. Inclusive rates cover all meals, drinks, watersports, tips, taxes, and nightly entertainment. Adults keep busy with weekly tournaments, sightseeing tours, pool volleyball, snorkeling instruction, Papiamento lessons, dance classes, and theme parties. Kids have their own planned fun. A poolside barbecue offers hot dogs, hamburgers, and ribs throughout the day and evening, should you need a between-meal snack.

Accommodations: 155 rooms. Simple standard rooms have two double beds, deluxe rooms have two queen-size beds or one queen and one pull-out sofa. All are air-conditioned.

For Kids: Camp Bounty for four- to twelve-year-olds operates from 9 A.M. to 5 P.M. but can be adjusted to include children two to four and twelve to fifteen as well. Indoor and outdoor games and activities such as "beach Olympics," charades, shell and scavenger hunts, arts and crafts, theme parties, movies, and cooking lessons are regular features. Baby-sitting can be arranged after 6 P.M. with advance notice.

Special Features: beach, swimming pool, Jacuzzi, tennis, fitness center, watersports, scuba, entertainment, restaurants, bars.

$$$: Children under two stay free in their parents' room; cost for each child of ages two to eleven $50–$60 per day. Daily rates, per person: $100–$145. Extra beds and cribs for children are available at no extra charge.

Wyndham Aruba Beach Resort and Casino

Address: J. E. Irausquin Boulevard 77, Palm Beach, Aruba
Telephone: 800-996-3426 or 297-8-64466, fax 297-8-63403

Website: www.wyndham.com

Families who travel to this eighteen-story high-rise on popular Palm Beach get an exceptional deal if they visit from May 1 to September 30, when the kids on us program operates and children under age twelve eat and stay free when sharing a room with the adults in the existing bedding. There's a "Kids Klub" that operates during these months yet plenty for kids to do if they want to hang out with Mom and Dad. When the kids tire of swimming in the ocean waves, they'll be thrilled with the 8,000-square-foot swimming pool complete with fountains tucked into the lush tropical landscape. Kids under twelve eat free any time of year.

Accommodations: 421 rooms. Guest rooms and suites begin on the fifth floor, all with private balconies and an ocean view.

For Kids: The Kids Klub is for children ages five to twelve who can select from a full-day session, a half-day session, or an evening session.

Special Features: beach, pool, fitness center, tennis, sailing, snorkeling, windsurfing, parasailing, waterskiing, restaurants, bars, evening entertainment, two car rental, casino, baby-sitting.

$$$: Daily rate, double occupancy: $135–$300. Children under age eighteen free in their parents' room.

Aruba Sonesta Beach Hotel Suites, and Casinos

Address: L. G. Smith Boulevard 9, Oranjestad, Aruba
Telephone: 800-SONESTA, 297-8-36000, fax 297-8-34389
Website: www.sonesta.com

A short water-taxi ride takes guests to Sonesta's exclusive forty-acre tropical garden island with six beaches, watersports, tennis, a fitness center, and restaurants. Sonesta has two hotels that use the island, and both are in Oranjestad along the waterfront overlooking the city and water in the Seaport Village Complex which is filled with shops, restaurants, and a movie theater. The Aruba Sonesta Resort is a traditional hotel with standard rooms, and the other, Aruba Sonesta Suites, is best for families, with one-bedroom suites and two enormous free-form pools. Sonesta Island is the headquarters for the watersports program, where guests can scuba dive, snorkel, and windsurf. Deep-sea fishing, sailing cruises, parasailing, and waterskiing can be arranged. Eighteen-hole golf is fifteen minutes away from the hotel and suites.

Accommodations: The Aruba Sonesta Resort, a one-minute walk from the beach, is the hotel part of the property, with traditional hotel rooms. The shuttle to the island leaves from the resort. Aruba Sonesta Suites has one-bedroom suites with kitchenettes and is right on the beach.

For Kids: Kids who visit the "Just Us Kids" program for five- to twelve-year-olds take daily field trips to places like the caves, nature trails, and natural bridges of Aruba, and swim and play games the rest of the day. The program is offered to guests at no extra charge and operates from the Sonesta Suites Hotel. Children can participate in whatever they wish. The daily year-round program runs from 10 A.M. to 4:30 P.M. and 6 P.M. to 10 P.M. Evenings offer bingo, movie night, miniature golf, and arts and crafts.

Special Features: beach, swimming pools, health club, entertainment, restaurants, bars, scuba, kayak, snorkeling, aquacycle, room service, car rental.

$$$: Daily rates, double occupancy $145–$350. Children under twelve free in their parents' room.

Tamarijn Aruba Beach Resort
Address: J. E. Irausquin Boulevard 41, Oranjestad, Aruba
Telephone: 800-554-2008, 297-8-24150, Fax 297-8-34002
Website: www.tamarijnaruba.com

Guests can borrow bicycles to explore the surrounding neighborhood, and aqua cycles to cruise the aquamarine waters offshore. This all-inclusive resort offers some well-priced family packages from April through early December and plenty of activities to keep the fun rolling. There's every kind of theme night imaginable—from carnival to toga parties—plus goofy races, sunset cruises, beach volleyball, and unlimited food and drinks. Kids can spoil their dinner with self-service popcorn, pizza, or frozen yogurt day or night. More action can be found around the swimming pool and watersports center. Two room styles are available, the more deluxe of which allows guests complimentary use of the sister resort, Divi Aruba, next door.

Accommodations: 236 rooms in two-story low-rise buildings, all with air-conditioning, private balcony, and terrace. Rooms have one king or two double beds.

For Kids: A children's camp for ages three through twelve begins with an orientation and features group nature walks, shirt decorating, dancing, a carnival fiesta, sand sculpture, cooking, storytelling, and movies, as well as a weekly golf clinic for children eight and over.

Special Features: pool, bicycles, fitness area, volleyball, tennis, Sunfish sailing, water bikes, canoes, snorkeling, windsurfing, baby-sitting, shops, restaurants, bars, nightly entertainment.

$$$: Daily rate, per adult $150–$175. Two children free (under seventeen) staying in parents' room from April 15–December 20. Two children free (under eleven) from December 21 to April 14.

Divi Aruba Beach Resort
Address: J. E. Irausquin Boulevard 45, Orangestaad, Aruba
Telephone: 800-554-2008, 297-8-23300, Fax 297-8-34002
Website: www.diviaruba.com

For real value, head to Divi Aruba Beach Resort between mid-April and mid-September and your children can stay and eat from the kid's menu for free when they share your room. This all inclusive resort packs in all meals, unlimited beverages, use of nonmotorized watersports, bicycles, tennis, evening entertainment, and airport transfers. Guests at this resort enjoy reciprocal privileges at the adjacent Tamarijn Aruba Beach resort (see above). A tram runs between the two. Divi is slightly more deluxe.

Accommodations: 203 air-conditioned rooms in one- to three-story buildings, all with balconies or terraces and air-conditioning.

For Kids: The children's program takes place at the Tamarijn Resort next door. Children three to eleven get a variety of activities such as nature walks, a carnival fiesta, movies, cooking projects, and dancing. Kids eight and up have a weekly golf clinic. The program operates between 10 A.M. and 3 P.M. year-round.

Special Features: beach, two swimming pools, kayaks, paddle boats, snorkeling, Sunfish sailing, scuba, banana boats, windsurfing, tennis, volleyball, shops, beauty salon, casino.

$$$: Daily rates: adults $160–$205. Two children are free (under seventeen) in their parents' room April 15–December 20; under eleven December 21–April 14.

WHAT TO SEE AND DO

Enjoy the pleasures of scuba diving without getting wet, on an **Atlantis Submarine** tour. A catamaran cruise takes you to board the battery-powered environmentally friendly sub. Once you're inside and have positioned yourself in front of your porthole window, the submarine descends and cruises past elaborate coral formations, lacy sea fans, and multicolored tropical fish. A crew member identifies the various sea plants and animals and is available to answer any questions. Discounts are available for families of four and up and for children ages four to sixteen. Departs from the Seaport Village marina, information: 297-8-37077, fax 297-8-26944; reservations 297-8-36090, fax 297-8-37277.

Snorkeling and Scuba Diving—Water visibility of up to one hundred feet makes Aruba a popular dive spot. One favorite dive site is the *Antilla,* referred to locally as the ghost ship, a German freighter sunk in World War II that is the largest wreck in the Caribbean. It offers divers many pockets to explore along its 400-foot length. Most resorts are affiliated with certified dive operations.

Landsailing and Dune Sliding—Imagine a go-cart body with a windsurfer sail and you've got a breeze-powered sailcart that speeds across the fields. Aruba Sailcart supplies the carts, helmets, gloves, and instruction (297-8133 or 35133).

You can join the locals for some sand-sliding fun at Boca Prins on the north coast, the best location for the best dune sliding. Dress in jeans or heavy pants, and strong shoes.

The Caves—Native Arawak drawings remain visible on the ceilings of the Fontein cave, where the Indians once dwelled. Nearby at the Guadirikiri cave, sunlight filters through two inner chambers where a 100-foot-long tunnel houses hundreds of bats. The Tunnel of Love gets its name from its heart-shaped entrance, which leads to a 300-foot tunnel winding though eerie rock formations and barrow passages. Rent helmets and flashlights at the entrances of the Guadirikiri and Tunnel of Love caves.

Bahamas

These easy islands are just a short plane ride away for many Americans living in the southern part of the United States, and an easy commute for those in the Northeast and Midwest. With over seven hundred islands, cays, reefs, and beaches, the Bahamas have a little bit of everything to offer visitors. Action-oriented families will find full-service megaresorts with all kinds of activities, and smaller off-the-beaten track establishments with all kinds of watersports. Those wanting to simply stretch out and soak up the sun will find alluring stretches of soft white and pink sand just about anywhere they turn.

The islands stretch for more than 650 miles from the eastern coast of Florida to the southeastern tip of Cuba. They vary in size, with Andros being the largest. Only thirty of the islands are inhabited and the most-visited islands include Grand Providence Island, home to Nassau/Paradise Island and the Abacos chain. All of the islands are somewhat flat, with lovely soft-sand beaches, thick pine forests, palm trees, mangroves, lagoons, and lakes.

Cricket is a popular pastime. The cricket season runs March through November, and games are played on Saturday and Sunday. If you're interested in attending a game, contact the Bahamas Cricket Association at 242-322-1875.

While winter is usually balmy and warm, an occasional cold front can move in, so plan your visit in spring, summer, or fall to be sure of warm weather. It's best to avoid the Bahamas during college spring break when cheap charter flights lure masses of partying students.

Fast Facts:

Visitor Information: Website: www.interknowledge.com/bahamas: Bahamas U.S.: Tourist Office. 800-BAHAMAS or Atlanta 404-633-1793; Dallas, 214-742-1886; Miami 305-932-0051; Chicago 773-693-1500; Los Angeles 213-385-0033; New York City 212-758-2777. Canada: 121 Street East, Suite 1101, Toronto, Ontario 144W 3MS 800-677-3777, 416-968-2999. Bahamas: PO Box N3701, Nassau, 242-322-7500.

Arriving and Departing: U.S. and Canadian citizens need proof of citizenship in the form of a passport or certified birth certificate and photo identification. Voter registration cards are not accepted. A departure tax of $15 per person is charged.

Currency: Bahamian dollar (B$), but American money is readily accepted.

Language: English is spoken throughout the Bahamas.

Best Sweet Treat: Guava duff is a delicious rolled and sliced dessert filled with guava and topped with guava butter and brandy sauce.

NASSAU AREA

WHERE TO STAY
Expensive

Compass Point
Address: P.O. Box CB13842, West Bay Street, Gambler, Nassau, Bahamas
Telephone: 800-OUTPOST, 242-377-4500, fax 242-327-3299
Website: www.islandoutpost.com

This one-of-a-kind casual resort has brightly painted cottages on stilts overlooking the water. Part of the chic Island Outpost chain, its colorful accommodations come in a variety of sizes making them perfect for families. Just twenty minutes from Paradise Island and Nassau, it's a quirky yet upscale oceanfront retreat close to plenty of action if you want it but on a quiet slice of turf for those wanting a great getaway. The interiors of the cottages are soothingly decorated in natural wood and batik fabrics. Huge decks face the ocean, and louvered windows catch the breeze. Guests have an elaborate entertainment center in their cottage and can borrow videos and CD's (including excellent world music selections from sister company Island Records) for their enjoyment. An excellent restaurant serves breakfast, lunch, and dinner.

Accommodations: One- and two-bedroom cottages have king or queen beds, in room safes, and open air kitchens.

Special Features: beach, pool, dive shop, snorkeling, sailing, tennis, fishing, restaurant.

$$$ Daily rates: one-bedroom $230–$315, two-bedroom $330–$425, three-bedroom penthouse $625–$800.

Moderate

Atlantis Paradise Island Resort
Address: Paradise Island, New Providence, Bahamas
Telephone: 800-321-3000, 242-363-3000, fax 242-363-2593
Website: www.sunint.com

This immense playland at the beach has everything a vacationing family can ever need and then some. Fourteen acres of water gardens surround this elaborate family fun park on Paradise Island with nonstop activities for all ages. There's a spectacular open-air saltwater aquarium with a 100-foot-long clear tunnel visitors can walk beneath to view tropical fish—and even sharks—swimming overhead. Water fun, the preferred activity at the resort, never stops. Choose from the Mayan Temple with five heart stopping water slides, a winding quarter-mile Lazy River Ride that kids traverse on an inner tube, water tricycles to ride, an Adventure Water Walk with geysers and fountains, a snorkeling lagoon, and of course, a glorious white-sand beach. "The Dig" is a life-size replica of the Lost Continent of Atlantis. Its maze of underground rooms and corridors contains an invention room, map room, and crystal chamber. Guests wander the underground chambers at their leisure. There are plenty of options for dining, with numerous restaurants to choose from, including one that has an underwater viewing window. This place is an amusement park of tropical family fun.

Accommodations: 1,147 rooms are in three different towers. Rooms have private balconies, minibar, air-conditioning, and in-room safe.

For Kids: The Discovery Channel Camp for Kids ages five to twelve operates year-round with a program that blends nature, history, science, and technology. With a camper to counselor ratio of five to one, campers enjoy the vast resources of both the Discovery Channel and Atlantis Resort. They explore a replica of the *Atocha,* a Spanish treasure ship that went down off the coast of Nassau in the seventeenth century; learn to maneuver glass-bottom kayaks in the lagoon; and learn about the constellations and myths behind them in one of Atlantis' Starlab planetariums. Day sessions last 3½ hours; evening sessions are four hours. A fee is charged.

Special Features: beach, two free form-pools, water slides, river pools, marina, water rides, watersports, casino, 38 restaurants and lounge, live entertainment, man-made lagoons, tennis, spa, shops, sports center, basketball, mini-golf, golf, arcade.

$$$: Children under age eighteen free in their parents' room. Daily rates, double occupancy: $160–$350. Packages and meal plans are available.

Nassau Marriott Resort and the Crystal Palace Casino

Address: Box N-8306, Cable Beach, Bahamas
Telephone: 800-222-7466, 242-327-6200, fax 242-327-6801
Website: www.marriott.com/marriott/nasbs

Cable Beach is another stretch of fine white sand, and this large resort has a beautiful piece of it. The Marriott is known for its nightlife, with a huge 35,000-square-foot casino and flashy Las Vegas–style revue. All the balconies facing the ocean are brightly lit with colored lights, giving the hotel a rainbow appearance from the beach and over the water. Daily activities for all ages take place by the pool; and there's a Caribbean-style review in the "Rainforest Theatre," and a mini-golf course right on the beach.

Accommodations: 867 rooms all have air-conditioning, private balconies, and satellite TVs.

For Kids: The Marriotter Kids Club for children ages four and up has scavenger hunts, beach games, and theme days in a supervised program based in its own pavilion. Teens enjoy party nights with pizza pig-outs and video productions. The kids program is open from 9 A.M. to 5 P.M. Thursday through Saturday.

Special Features: beach, pool with fresh water swimming lagoon, twelve restaurants and lounges, watersports, boating, fishing, tennis, mini-golf, fitness center, tennis, shops.

$$$: Children under eighteen are free in their parents' room. Daily rates, double occupancy: $169–$279.

Budget

Orange Hill Inn

Address: P.O. Box 8583, Nassau, Bahamas
Telephone: 242-327-7157, fax 242-327-5186

This small family-run country-style inn is just across the street from the beach on the grounds of a former orange plantation with its own private swimming pool. Set on a hilltop overlooking the ocean, it offers apartments and rooms that can accommodate families comfortably. The rooms are spread out over the attractively landscaped property which has swing sets placed at the top of the hill offering lovely views of the ocean. Orange Hill Beach is quiet during the week, and a bit busier on the weekend. The lobby is a central gathering area for guests, and videos are available to view, with plenty of children's titles, on the lobby TV/VCR. Games, puzzles and books may also be checked out. The hotel will help you arrange tours of the area, with scuba a specialty. Baby-sitting can be arranged.

Accommodations: 32 rooms: superior rooms can accommodate up to four and have a minifridge and stove; apartments have a full kitchen and two queens or a queen and two twin beds, depending on the request.

Special Features: pool, kayaks, croquet, games, restaurant, bar.

$$$: Children eleven or younger stay free in parents' room. Superior rooms $92–$133, apartments $107–$165.

GRAND BAHAMA ISLAND

The Lucayan

Address: P.O. Box F-42500, Royal Palm Way, Lucaya, Grand Bahama Island, Bahamas
Telephone: 800-LUCAYAN, 242-373-1444, fax 242-373-4056
Website: www.thelucayan.com

A gorgeous Manor House is the centerpiece for this enormous resort, one of newest on Grand Bahama Island that is being built in three phases. It enjoys the largest white sand beach on Grand Bahama Island and all kinds of watersports. When phase three of the building plan is completed the resort will have two eighteen-hole golf courses, a casino, a huge Village Market filled with shops and a theater, and a children's program in addition to restaurants galore and all kinds of activities. At press time, phases one and two were completed. Watersports activities are geared to both children and adults. The Lucayan also offers educational programs for children and adults in partnership with UNEXSO (Underwater Explorers Society) on marine life, nature, and the ecosystem. Beginners have the chance to learn to scuba dive and snorkel and more seasoned divers have the chance to explore, too.

Accommodations: 1,350 brightly colored rooms and suites, all with air conditioning, in-room safes, and two queens or a king bed in each room.

For Kids: Camp Lucaya has its own building that is colorfully decorated with several rooms including an activities and TV room. A kiddy pool with fountains is nearby.

Special Features: beach, pool, snorkeling, scuba, parasailing, windsurfing, waterskiing, wave runners, Hobie cats, kayaking, spa, tennis, shops, restaurants, bars, eighteen-hole golf course, movie theater, ice cream store.

$$$: Daily rates, double occupancy $110-$230. Two children twelve and under free in parents' room.

Club Med Eleuthera

Address: French Leave, P.O. Box 25080, Governor's Harbour, Eleuthera, Bahamas
Telephone: 800-CLUBMED, 242-332-2270, fax 242-332-2855
Website: www.clubmed.com

Club Med Eleuthera offers a well-priced inclusive package that combines meals, recreational activities, a children's program, and evening entertainment. Situated in a quiet corner of Eleuthera, the village fronts a gorgeous stretch of pink sand and has a marina with a watersports center just a three-minute shuttle ride away. The Circus Workshop is a trademark of a number of Club Med Family Villages, and Eleuthera is one of them, offering the high and low tightrope, juggling, and trampolining, along with trapeze. While the kids swing by their knees or romp in any one of the organized clubs for children as young as two, ambitious parents can play in tennis round-robins, take aerobics classes, or even attempt the trapeze themselves. Guest rooms are simple—no phones or TVs—but are clean and comfortable. The food is surprisingly good for an all-inclusive buffet, and features several theme nights.

Accommodations: Rooms have either beach or garden views. Each has a king bed or two double beds and a private bath; all are air-conditioned and some rooms connect.

For Kids: A children's program begins at age two and keeps little ones busy throughout the day with all kinds of activities. There's a petite club and a mini club.

Special Features: beach, pool, fishing, waterskiing, sailing, scuba diving, archery, boccie ball, Ping-Pong, soccer, softball, tennis, volleyball, basketball, aerobics, evening entertainment, two restaurants, two bars, theater.

$$$: Inclusive rates per night based on double occupancy: adults $121–$150, children four–eleven $48–$60, children two–three $12–$14. Air packages are available; be sure to inquire.

WHAT TO SEE AND DO—GRAND PROVIDENCE ISLAND

Atlantis Submarines offer nondivers the chance to see the colorful sights of the coral reefs from the air-conditioned and pressurized comfort of a real submarine. Subs go down to a depth of eighty feet and tour the reefs and fish, as well as a Cessna aircraft that was wrecked for the filming of *Jaws 2*. Departure from the west end of the island near Lyford Cay.

Hartley's Undersea Walk is a throwback to the early days of skin diving, when divers wore watertight helmets attached to an air line. That's exactly what you and your kids can do, and the old-fashioned brass helmet looks just like it did in the old days. It's a good idea to reserve this when you book your hotel stay, as excursions fill up quickly (242-393-8234).

Blue Lagoon Island has a popular dolphin encounter program along with many other activities. If you can't get into the dolphin encounter, you can swim with the stingrays, lounge on the beach or in a hammock, or sample any number of watersports at this uninhabited island about a half hour away from Paradise Island. In this case uninhabited means there is no overnight lodging. But it's a popular day trip and the island regularly fills up with visitors. Make reservations for the Dolphin Encounter at least two months in advance by calling 242-363-1003. For general information on the programs call 242-327-5066.

Barbados

The courteous and good-natured residents of Barbados, known as Bajans, are among the best liked in the Caribbean. Ask any recent visitors, and along with their vivid descriptions of white sandy beaches and balmy turquoise waters, you'll hear praises for the Bajan's warmth and their gracious hospitality. Good manners are expected in return, and its' a pleasure to see how quickly visiting children incorporate "good morning," "good evening," "please," and "thank you" into their daily routine.

Off the beaten track and the most easterly of all the Caribbean islands, Barbados went unseen by Columbus on his four expeditions to the West Indies. The British were the first Europeans to settle the island in the 1600s. Unlike most other Caribbean islands, Barbados remained protected from invasion by other European colonizers, thanks to the trade winds that blow east to west, making it difficult to sail to Barbados from the other islands. Although Barbados achieved independence in 1966, many British customs, such as afternoon tea and a passion for cricket, have taken firm root here.

The rugged and windy east coast of Barbados softens the breeze of the trade winds making the protected west coast relatively calm and sunny. As you might expect, the bulk of the tourist development is along the western and southern edges of the island, where you can find everything from extremely elegant hotels and lavish villas to simple cottages and rather ordinary condos. The hills and valleys in the interior are thick with sugarcane. Bridgetown, the capital city, houses about half of Barbados's population and sits at its southwest corner.

Fast Facts:

Visitor Information: Barbados Tourism Authority: Website: www. barbados.org. *U.S.:* 800 Second Avenue, New York, NY 10017 (800-221-9831, 212-986-6516); or 3440 Wilshire Boulevard, Suite 1215, Los Angeles 90010 (213-380-2199). *Canada:* 20105 Adelaide Street West, Suite 1010, Toronto,

Ontario M5H 1P9 (416-214-9880, fax 416-214-9882). *Barbados:* Barbados Board of Tourism, Harbour Road, Bridgetown, Barbados, WI (246-427-2623).

Arriving and Departing: U.S. and Canadian citizens need a valid passport or original birth certificate and photo ID (a voter registration card is not sufficient), and a return ticket. A departure tax of $12.50 per person is charged.

Money: Barbados has its own currency, the Barbados dollar (BD$) but U.S. and Canadian dollars are widely accepted.

Best Sweet Treat: coconut ice cream

WHERE TO STAY
Expensive

Sandy Lane
Address: St. James, Barbados, WI
Telephone: 800-223-6800 or 407-432-1311, fax 407-432-2954
Website: www.sandylane.com

Sandy Lane keeps getting more luxurious. Its most recent renovation has increased the size of guest rooms and terraces, revamped the already lavish pools, and added a 20,000-square-foot health spa. The luxurious and refined resort is located on 380 acres of a former sugarcane plantation and overlooks a half-mile crescent of sandy beach. The resort's gourmet cuisine, world-class service, and sheer elegance have long drawn sophisticated guests. Now their sophisticated offspring can enjoy one of the Caribbean's most celebrated resorts. The golf course, designed by Tom Fazio, has 45 holes designed to please golfers of all abilities.

Accommodations: Choose from thirty elegant suites, most of which overlook the ocean, or from ninety double rooms. All have air-conditioning, room safes, minibars, and private patios or balconies. Two oceanfront restaurants serve fine cuisine, and a poolside snack bar offers more casual meals.

For Kids: Located in the hotel gardens, the Tree House Club has indoor and outdoor play areas and a schedule that includes arts and crafts, sports, games, stories, nature walks, beach time, and movies. Activities change daily. Parents can participate in the activities with their kids or drop the children off anytime between 10 A.M. and 8 P.M. The program is complimentary and includes dinner but not lunch, which costs $10.

$$$: Rates include breakfast and dinner daily, airport transfers, unlimited golf, and tennis. Daily rates, double occupancy: $485–$600 per person.

Almond Beach Village
Address: Vauxhall, St. James, Barbados, WI
Telephone: 800-4-ALMOND, 407-432-7840, fax 407-432-2115
Website: www.almondresorts.com

Almond Beach Village is becoming known in family travel circles for its attention to the tiniest travelers—those under the age of five. There are just a few resorts that cater to this age, and Almond Beach does a nice job of it.

Their special nursery for babies and toddlers is separated from the bigger, noisier kids. And the bigger, noisier kids will feel right at home, as families have their own separate "village" complete with comfortable accommodations, a family restaurant, a children's center, playgrounds, and a family pool, all at one end of the thirty-acre property. Couples and honeymooners (and families, too, if they want), stay in other secluded low-rise buildings in a villagelike atmosphere. The property stretches along a one-mile strand of beach, and one price includes absolutely everything, even hair braiding! Almond Beach Village is large enough and so action packed that you may never want to leave, but do plan a trip to explore some of the fascinating sights of this pleasant island.

Accommodations: 288 rooms, all with balcony or patio, air-conditioning, coffee machine, and safe. One-bedroom suites have a living area with a fold-out couch, and a spacious bedroom. Laundry facilities are available.

Children's Program: Children can drop in daily between 9 A.M. and 5 P.M. and are divided into three age groups: two to four, five to nine, and nine to thirteen. The large kids' room has video games, board games, toys, and computers with educational software. Kids are treated to nature walks, story time, pool and beach games, watersports, instruction in steel pan music and calypso and reggae dance, basketry, and boat rides.

Special Features: five tennis courts, nine-hole golf course, squash courts, one pool, Sunfish, catamaran, snorkeling, waterskiing, windsurfing, reef fishing, aquacycle, kayaking, banana boat rides, fitness center, shops, laundry facilities, evening entertainment.

$$$: An all-inclusive price includes meals, afternoon tea, drinks, watersports, room service for lunch and dinner, kids' program, field trips, nightly entertainment, island tours, airport transfers, and all gratuities, tips, and service charges. First child under twelve with parents free except for standard rooms. All other children under twelve, $50 per child per night. Per night, double occupancy, junior and one bedroom suites: $280–$630 depending on season, size, and view.

Budget

Silver Sands Resort
Address: Christ Church, Barbados, WI
Telephone: 800-GO-BAJAN, 246-428-6001, fax 246-428-3758

An excellent budget option, Silver Sands is right on a stretch of powdery soft white sand with a large freshwater swimming pool and a special children's pool. You can pick up groceries at the tiny minimart grocery store on the premises or take advantage of the resorts three-times-weekly bus service to Bridgetown. During the winter months, the shifting trade winds create perfect conditions for windsurfing, and the Club Mistral Windsurfing Centre operates from the property November to May.

Accommodations: 41 rooms and 89 studios and suites: are all air-conditioned with telephones, radios, and balconies or patios. Studios and suites have kitchen facilities.

Special Features: swimming pool, children's pool, beach bar, minimart, souvenir shop, varied weekly entertainment, washer and dryers, two tennis courts, volley ball, Ping-Pong, restaurant, bar, beauty salon, weekly rum punch party.

$$$: Children twelve and under sharing a studio or suite with their parents are complimentary. Daily rates, double occupancy: rooms $65–$140; studios $75–$170; suites $85–$200.

Villa and Condo Rentals

Villas and Apartments Abroad, 420 Madison Avenue, New York, NY 10017 (212-759-1025, 800-433-3020, fax 212-755-8316).
At Home Abroad (212-421-9145).
Barbados Board of Tourism lists rental properties (407-427-2623).
WIMCO also handles villa rentals (401-849-8012).

WHAT TO SEE AND DO

Snorkelers can follow marked underwater snorkeling trails around seven-mile-long Dottin's Reef at **Folkstone Underwater Park**, north of Holetown. The reef is teeming with colorful fish, sea anemones, human-sized fans, soft corals, and sea lilies. Glass-bottom boats are available for those who don't want to get their feet wet. Folkstone Park has a playground and picnicking area and a small restaurant. A small marine museum open Monday through Friday 10 A.M.–5 P.M., Saturday and Sunday 10 A.M.–6 P.M., shows the life of the sea.

Underground streams have carved out spectacular limestone caverns over the centuries at **Harrison's Cave**. A small electric tram carries you through subterranean passages and chambers that glow with actively growing crystalline stalagmites and stalactites. Near the lowest point of the cave, visitors traverse the side of a dramatic forty-foot waterfall that crashes into a deep blue-green pool. Tours are given every hour from 9 A.M. to 4 P.M. Night tours of the cavern are combined with a dinner served on top of the cave, cleverly staged so it appears you are dining deep inside the caverns (407-438-6640).

Tiny sea anemones that look like delicate flowers as they open and close their tentacles have given **Animal Flower Cave** at North Point its name. The cave has been eroded by wave action and drips with stalactites and stalagmites; it is open to visitors for a small fee. You can tour the cave and see the tiny creatures, also known as seaworms, and then pause when you're done for a cold glass of lemonade at the quirky refreshment stand/café run by Winston and Manuel Ward. Ask to see their pet sheep and her 7-Up-drinking talent-show trick (407-439-8797).

Footpaths through a lush glade of mahogany trees at the **Barbados Wildlife Reserve** (on Highway 1 near Spreightstown on the west coast) travel past groups of green monkey families playing, feeding their babies, and foraging for food. Other animals such as raccoons, box turtles, peacocks, deer, wallabies, and otters can be viewed. Squawking parrots converse in the aviary. Open daily 10 A.M.–5 P.M.(407-422-8826).

Sam Lord's Castle was built by the infamous and treacherous buccaneer who made his reputation (and much of his fortune) by lighting lanterns to trick ships' captains into thinking they had reached a safe harbor. After the ships foundered on the rocks and reefs, he would plunder them and carry off their treasures. Legend has it that some of his loot is still buried on the castle grounds. The castle is now a resort, but you can view the old building and see its magnificent mahogany columns, plaster ceiling, and the furniture he imported and used. Keep an eye out for the ghosts that are said to haunt the castle.

Atlantis Submarine descends as deep as 150 feet to explore shipwrecks and coral reefs and the creatures who inhabit them. The battery-run environmentally friendly sub gives a scuba diver's-eye view of the magnificent underwater world of Barbados. Hour-long tours are offered for ages four and up with special discounts for children (407-436-8929 or 407-436-8932).

Horseback Riding—Valley Hill Stables in Christ Church (407-423-6180) will pick you up at your hotel. Ye Old Congo Road Stables in St. Philip (407-423-8293) specializes in rides through sugar plantations and Brighton Stables (407-425-9381) on the west coast offers sunrise and sunset walks along beaches and through palm groves.

Bonaire

Bonaire is the "B" in the ABC islands (Aruba and Curaçao are the other two) that lie just off the coast of Venezuela. Bonaire is famous around the world for its unparalleled diving and snorkeling in one of the world's most unspoiled and protected coral reef systems. Since the island is out of the hurricane belt, its reefs have never been destroyed by storms, nor are they clouded by freshwater runoff, since only about twelve inches of rain falls annually. Water visibility of 100 to 150 feet is common.

Credit for the farsighted preservation of the island's pristine underwater paradise goes to the government and people of Bonaire who created the Bonaire Marine Park. The park includes the entire island's coastline down to a depth of two hundred feet, and strict rules govern its use.

The lush and spectacular underwater landscape, bursting with crowds of coral and throngs of fish, is in direct contrast to the flat and dry conditions above the water. The entire desertlike northern section of the island has been set aside as 13,500-acre Washington-Slagbaai National Park and is either home or way station to 190 different species of birds. Snorkeling and bird-watching are watching are superb here. Unique ground-bound Bonairian animal species include the blue lizard and the anole tree lizard with its distinctive yellow dewlap. At the southern end of the island, adjacent to salt ponds still in operation, is a sanctuary for the island's largest pink flamingo nesting ground.

The eastern side of Bonaire is subject to violent trade winds, serious surf, and dangerous undertows. Beware snorkeling or diving in this area.

Carnival is a lively affair held from late February to early March, but the island's biggest celebration is the International Sailing Regatta in October, when the island delights in boat racing, steel band music, dancing, and feasting.

Bonaire is not particularly known for its beaches, but the places listed in this book are on small beaches so that family members who enjoy a pail and shovel are satisfied.

Fast Facts:

Visitor Information: Website: www.infobonaire.com *U.S.*: Bonaire Government Tourist Office 444 Madison Avenue, Suite 2403, New York, NY 10022, (212-832-0779, 800-266-2473, fax 212-838-3407). *Canada*: 512 Duplex Avenue, Toronto, Ontario, M4R 2E3 (416-484-4864, 800-267-7600, fax 416-485-8256). *Bonaire*: Kaya Simon Bolivar 12, Kralendijk, Bonaire, N.A. (599-7-8322 or 8639).

Arriving and Departing: U.S. and Canadian citizens need a passport or notarized birth certificate or voter registration card and a return or ongoing ticket. A departure tax of $6 for visitors going to Curaçao and $10 for all other destinations is charged.

Language: The official language is Dutch but most people speak Papiamento, a mix of Spanish, Portuguese, Dutch, English, African, and French. English is spoken by most people who work in the tourist industry.

Money: The official currency is the Netherlands Antilles florin or guilder (NAfl or Afl) but U.S. dollars are accepted everywhere.

Best Sweet Treat: Try *cocada*, a coconut candy traditionally served on broken bits of coconut shell.

WHERE TO STAY

In this scuba-centered island, most hotels offer dive packages with unlimited use of tanks, unlimited shore diving, boat trips, meals, and more. Rates are:

Expensive: $225 and up
Moderate: $125 to $225
Budget: under $125

Expensive

Harbour Village Beach Resort

Address: P.O. Box 312, Kralendijk, Bonaire
Telephone: 800-424-0004, 5997-7500, fax 5997-7507
Website: www.harbourvillage.com

This 100-acre resort combines all the attributes of an elegant Caribbean beach resort with a hardworking dive operation. A full-service spa, the only of its type on Bonaire, offers all kinds of luxurious treatments and beauty services and its quarter mile of sandy beach is better than the others on the island. Guests enjoy a complimentary continental breakfast and live weekly entertainment. There is a library of children's books, videos, and board games in the guest service lounge. Next door lies the Yacht Harbour, the resort's sixty-slip marina. Many boaters stay aboard their yachts at night and use the services of Habour Village by day. Classes are offered in wreck diving, marine photography, and underwater navigation.

Accommodations: 73 rooms on one hundred acres. Rooms have two double beds or a king bed; beachfront one- and two-bedroom suites have a living area with a queen sofa bed, two or three full baths, and a king bed in each bedroom. All have air conditioning, ceiling fans, and safes. One- , two- , and three-bedroom villas are also available.

For Kids: A children's program operates during vacation time for ages five to eleven during carnival week in February, Easter, and Christmas. Kids enjoy arts and crafts, beach games in both morning and afternoon sessions.

Special Features: beach, swimming pool, four tennis courts, kayaks, Sunfish, small sailboats, waterskiing, fishing excursions, spa with whirlpool, steam, sauna and treatments, fitness center, two bars, two restaurants, dive center, dive lockers at beach, bicycles, baby-sitting, marina, shop, car rental, VCR, video rentals.

$$$: Children up to twelve sleep free in parents' room with two adults sharing existing bedding. Daily rates, double occupancy rooms: $305–$550, suites $510–$840, Villas $565–$1,100.

Captain Don's Habitat

Address: P.O. Box 88, Kralendijk, Bonaire
Telephone: 800-327-6709, 599-7-8290, fax 599-7-8240
Website: www.maduro.com

Captain Don Stewart has developed a local reputation as a raconteur, a diver extraordinaire, and the driving force behind efforts to preserve Bonaire's reefs and marine life. His resort is best known as a five-star dive-training facility, but he also has welcomed families for many years. People come to Captain Don's to dive, and they get what they come for, with unlimited round-the-clock shore dives, two boat dives a day with most packages, and unlimited boat dives with upgraded packages. Dive guides present slide shows on marine creatures Sunday and Monday nights throughout the year, and Captain Don himself shows up once or twice a week to entertain his guests with stories of life in the deep.

Accommodations: All units are air-conditioned with private baths. Two-bedroom cottages and villa deluxe suites sleep four and have kitchens, living rooms, and patios. Standard hotel rooms face the ocean. All units can accommodate an extra person.

Special Features: restaurant, bar, swimming pool, dive shop next door.

$$$: Children twelve and under are free with two paying adults. Family packages are available. Five days, four nights, per adult: $624–$824 depending on accommodations and number of dives. Includes daily buffet breakfast, airport transfer, service charges and taxes, unlimited shore diving.

Moderate

Sand Dollar Resort

Address: Kayagobernador N. Debrot 79, P.O. Box 262, Bonaire
Telephone: 800-288-4773, 599-7-8738, 8738, fax 599-7-8760.
Website: www.interknowledge.com/bonaire/sand-dollar

This resort's spacious time-share apartments and five-star dive center and photo shop attract serious divers and their families. There's not much beach, but an innovative kids program has children in the pool and the ocean learning how to snorkel and exploring the underwater world just offshore. Teens can work toward their junior scuba certification on the property. The Sand-Dollar Club for children offers supervised activities for a few hours each week during the year, and more during the month of August. The resort sits on a low bluff overlooking the Caribbean, and there's an Olympic-size swimming pool and a tiny beach right in front. Snorkelers can jump off the dive platform, swim a few strokes, and come to Bari Reef just offshore, where views of orange elephant-ear sponges and purple tube sponges provide a backdrop for schools of carnival-costumed fish.

Accommodations: 84 units. Comfortable studios, and one- , two- , and three-bedroom condominiums have air-conditioning, private patios or balconies, and complete kitchens. Living room couches turn into beds, and each unit's contemporary tropical decor varies a bit according to the individual owner's taste. Studios can take two adults and two children as can one-bedroom units. Two-bedroom units can sleep four adults and two kids, and three bedroom units house up to six adults and two kids.

For Kids: Two programs operate for children: Sand Penny Club for ages three to six, and Ocean Classroom for children six to fifteen (must be able to swim). Sand Penny Club operates Monday, Wednesday, and Friday mornings from 8:30 A.M. to noon. The free program includes arts and crafts, pool games, and movies. Ocean classroom is offered Monday through Friday from 8:30 A.M. to 12:15 P.M. with 24-hour advance notice, and a fee is charged. Kids enjoy hands-on learning about the oceans and its inhabitants, and learn to snorkel safely.

Special Features: small beach, swimming pool, PADI, five-star dive shop, dock, kayaks, slide shows, restaurant, bar, ice cream parlor, tennis, market, photo lab, car rental.

$$$: Children twelve and under free in parents' room (maximum two kids). Meal plans and scuba equipment rentals are available. Daily rates, double occupancy: studio $155–$180; one-bedroom condo $180–$250; two bedroom condo $200–$270; three bedroom condo $310–$380.

Budget

Divi Flamingo Beach Resort and Casino

Address: J. A. Abraham Boulevard, Kralendijk, Bonaire
Telephone: 800-367-3484, 599-5-8285, fax 599-7-8238

Website: www.diviresorts.com

With more beach to offer than other hotels, this resort gets its fair share of families. Parents who dive take advantage of the five-star dive shop, and the entire family can splash around in a special safe area roped off for swimming on the beach overlooking Calabas Reef. The property, originally called the Zeebad, opened in 1952 as Bonaire's first hotel, but it's been redone many times since. Informal, friendly, and lively, the active beachfront is the scene for beach games and contests for kids and adults.

Accommodations: Hotel rooms and studio apartments are available, all air-conditioned. Most rooms have two double beds, and a roll-away may be added for a small daily fee. The studios have kitchenettes, two double beds, plus a sofa bed.

Special Features: beach, freshwater swimming pools, a tennis court, two open-air dining rooms, dive shop.

$$$: Children under sixteen (two maximum) sharing a room with two parents' are free. A special inclusive family package is offered in August; call for prices. Rooms $100–$255; studios $190–$315.

WHAT TO SEE AND DO

Bonaire Marine Park—The World Wildlife Fund, in cooperation with the government, supplied seed money to ensure that Bonaire's magnificent coral reefs would remain undeveloped and in pristine condition for future generations. Virtually the entire coastline and the offshore island of Klein Bonaire are protected down to two hundred feet. Visitors may not take anything, dead or alive, from this area, and permanent moorings minimize anchor damage. Divers pay an admission charge of $10, which entitles them to unlimited diving for one calendar year. Fees are used to maintain the park and can be paid at all scuba facilities or at the Marine Park headquarters in the Old Fort at Kralendijk. Pick up a copy of the guidebook, *The Guide to Bonaire Marine Park*, which lists forty-four dive sites that have been marked by moorings, and their degrees of difficulty (599-7-8444).

Salt Flats—Head south out of Kralendijk along the southern scenic route, and you'll come to one of the world's most powerful radio transmitters, the 810,000-watt Trans World Radio. Continue south along the shore full of seabirds till you reach mountains of white sea salt where AKZO Antilles International Salt Company maintains its salt-gathering operation. The distillation process starts with seawater flowing into a rectangular pond. The sun and winds cause the water to evaporate and the remainder is pumped into a second pond where more water evaporates; this continues until the water is completely evaporated. Pink flamingos can be seen feeding in the briny, multicolored ponds.

Salt production was once Bonaire's most important source of revenue since it didn't have the fertile soil or water to support sugar, and slaves were imported to the island to work the salt pans. Workers had to live in horribly cramped **slave huts**, which have been reconstructed in Rode Pan. The men who worked the salt pans walked seven hours each Friday afternoon to visit their families on another part of the island. On Sunday they returned to their labor camp.

Pink flamingos also feed and nest at **Goto Meer**, a beautiful saltwater lagoon with an island in the middle in the northern part of Bonaire. Their main nesting season is between January and June. Bonaire is home to fifteen thousand of the spindly leg creatures.

Washington-Slagbaai National Park is a 13,500-acre tract of tropical desert terrain that can be explored with a four-wheel drive or on foot (bring lots of sunscreen and water). Pick up an excursion guide at the entrance to the park to learn about its geography, history, geology, and plant and animal life. Keep a sharp lookout for iguanas, donkeys, and goats. Salina Mathjis, a salt flat inside the national park, is another good spot for viewing flamingos. The park is open daily from 8 A.M.–5 P.M.

Windsurfing—Lac Bay on Bonaire's windward side is the ultimate windsurf location due to its steady on-shore winds and protected cove. Windsurfing Bonaire rents boards and offers lessons for beginning to advanced windsurfers. They pick up twice a day at all hotels on the island (800-748-8733, fax 599-7-5363).

Oscarina Yacht Charters takes families on a special Treasure Hunt Cruise. Kids are picked up at the waterfront of their hotels for a tradewind sail to Klein Bonaire—a 1,500-acre island due west of Kralendijk. Guided by a special treasure map, the search for treasure begins, followed by a swim or snorkel and a pizza party.

Toys Grand Café is a playful place where toy trains and puppets seem to pop out of the walls, and murals of all sorts—Mickey Mouse to Elvis—decorate the walls. The food is Indonesian influenced, which doesn't always work for the kids, but when in doubt, you can always order rice. J. A. Abraham Boulevard, Kralendijk (599-7-6666).

The British Virgin Islands

Dozens of hidden islands and secret coves once lured pirates to the British Virgin Islands (BVI) to stage raids on galleons carrying Mexican and Peruvian gold and silver. Legend has it that some of the nefarious sea dogs hid their stolen treasure in concealed caves and never returned to retrieve it. Tales of pirate treasure hidden on Norman Island, just south of Tortola, inspired Robert Louis Stevenson's classic tale, *Treasure Island*. Another uninhabited British Virgin Island, Deadman's Chest Island, inspired the song, "Fifteen Men on the Deadmen's Chest, (Yo, Ho, Ho, and a Bottle of Rum)," after the infamous Long John Silver punished fifteen of his crew by leaving them on this tiny island without food or water for a week. Other well-known pirates who made the British Virgin Islands their headquarters were Blackbeard Teach, Bluebeard, Captain Kidd, and Sir Francis Drake.

To this day, the islands' calm waters, steady breezes, and beautiful island anchorages make them a first-class sailing destination. You can charter a yacht for a day, a week, or a month and spend lazy hours on a different private island beach every day.

The British Virgin Islands are a major center for crewed charter boats and host the largest concentration of bare boats (boats rented without crew, to experienced sailors) in the world.

The clarity of the water and the protection from winds and currents the islands provide combine to offer exceptional snorkeling and diving. Most popular with pint-size snorkelers are the four caves at Norman Island where schools of tropical fish swim by close enough to touch, and legends of hidden treasure motivate the most reluctant swimmer to take a deeper look.

Hundreds of wrecks coated in coral lie offshore. The most famous of these, the RMS *Rhone,* sank in 1867 and sits in seventy-five feet of water, but her rudder juts up to within fifteen feet of the surface, allowing snorkelers to enjoy the view. The *Rhone* is the centerpiece of Rhone National Marine Park, which includes underwater coral caves, Blonde Rock (a submerged rock pinnacle), and Dead Chest Island, a nesting site for seabirds.

Resorts in the British Virgin Islands tend to be small and personal, since no building can be higher than the tallest palm tree. Virgin Gorda and Tortola, the two largest islands, handle the core of the tourist trade, but neither is very crowded.

Fast Facts:

Visitor Information: Website: www.bviwelcome.com *U.S.:* British Virgin Island Tourist Board, 370 Lexington Avenue, New York, NY 10017 (800-835-8530 or 212-696-0400), or 1804 Union Street, San Francisco, CA 94123 (800-835-8530 or 415-775-0344), *British Virgin Islands:* Social Security Building, Waterfront Street, Road Town, Tortola (284-494-3134).

Arriving and Departing: You'll need a passport, voter registration card, or birth certificate with a photo ID to enter the islands. Departure tax is $10 per person leaving by air and $5 leaving by sea.

Money: The U.S. dollar is the official currency.

Language: English is spoken throughout the British Virgin Islands.

Best Sweet Treat: Try *Ting,* a refreshing local soft drink, and potato pudding, a very sweet and common dessert.

TORTOLA

Steep green hills traverse the narrow length of this slow-paced, easygoing island. If you plan to rent a car, you'll need a four-wheel drive to maneuver the roads' hairpin turns and steep grades. At Tortola's southern edge, jagged mountain peaks soar 1,700 feet; and on its northern shore, you'll find sugar-fine white sand and tropical groves. The island is twelve miles long and three miles wide, so you're never far from a beautiful beach or breathtaking view.

WHERE TO STAY
Expensive: over $225
Moderate: $125–$225
Inexpensive: under $125

Moderate

Long Bay Beach Resort and Villas
Address: Box 433, Road Town, Tortola, BVI
Telephone: 800-729-9599, 284-495-4252, fax 284-495-4677
Website: www.longbay.com
E-mail: reservations@longbay.com

Families wanting to headquarter in spacious surroundings can have all the comforts of home (plus daily housekeeping service—the staff even washes the dishes) in Long Bay's two- and three-bedroom private villas set on a hill above a long sparkling white beach. These beautifully decorated units feature large outside terraces with barbecues and completely outfitted kitchens. Other smaller yet equally elegant accommodations are tucked into the hills or sit on stilts at the water's edge. A new pool complex charms families with its water slide, lap swimming area, and kiddy pool. A second pool and watersports desk are adjacent to the beach. In summer, snorkel right offshore in calm waters, and in winter, good bodysurfing keeps kids in the water for hours at a time. On-site car rental allows guests to rent for a day or two at a time.

Accommodations: 115 units. Simple hillside rooms overlook the ocean; studios farther up the hill are larger; and beachfront cabanas at the water's edge have their own hammocks. All have refrigerators, toaster ovens, coffee machines, air-conditioning, and safes. Completely outfitted two- and three-bedroom villas have ocean views; the largest have pools.

Special Features: two swimming pools, one with water slide and swim-up bar, children's pool, Jacuzzi, three tennis courts (two night lit), snorkeling equipment, surf boards, excursions desk, shops, snorkeling, restaurants, snack bar, bars, shops, car rental, baby-sitting.

$$$: Children under twelve are free if sharing a bedroom with their parents. Two children sharing a separate room are charged the single rate. Each additional adult is $30 in any accommodation. Ask about the Family Escape package that includes rooms, airport transfers, eight dinners, daily breakfast, rental car for three days, sailing trip, and other extras. Daily rates, double occupancy: rooms $145–$375, villas $280–$825.

Fort Recovery
Address: Box 239, Road Town, Tortola, BVI
Telephone: 800-367-8455, 284-495-4354, fax 284-495-4036
Website: www.fortrecovery.com

Ten charming little bungalows are steps away from their own white-sand beach on the calm Caribbean side of the island. Built around the remains of a seventeenth-century fort, the clean and fully equipped cottages create their own friendly small community. Boat trips, car rentals, and island tour arrangements can be made from the front desk. It's best to have a car to pick up groceries and explore some of the island's other magnificent beaches. Rates include a continental breakfast, and a restaurant serves other meals when you tire of cooking. A supermarket is a ten-minute walk away.

Accommodations: Villas accommodate two to eight people in units with one to four bedrooms. All have air-conditioning, full kitchens, and daily maid service.

Special features: swimming pool, children's library, baby-sitting, video rentals, massage, yoga classes, car rentals, boating excursion desk.

$$$: Daily rates: two bedroom villa for four people $215–$350. One bedroom unit $135–$240. Additional people in villas are $35 a night. Cribs are $10 per night.

Budget

Rhymer's Beach Hotel
Address: P.O. Box 570, Cane Garden Bay, Tortola, BVI
Telephone: 284-495-4639, 284-495-4820
Website: www.briguide.com/rhymers

Remember the places you stayed on the cheap as a college student, with small and tired rooms but great locations? If raising kids has reduced your vacation budget to that of your college days, Rhymer's is a real bargain. It's situated on the west coast of Tortola, right on white-sand Cane Bay Beach, backed by towering green hills. All units have tiny kitchenettes and air-conditioning, and its market on the ground floor has a wide selection of fresh produce, dairy products, and groceries at decent prices. Rhymer's is also known for its lively beachfront bar and restaurant. The police station sits directly behind the hotel across the street, so the college students who do stay here can't get too wild.

Accommodations: Very basic rooms all have private baths and a queen bed; a single bed can be easily added. Rooms can connect through the balcony, making it a good option if you have several older kids. Don't expect much in the way of service, but maids do clean and supply fresh linens daily. A Laundromat is on the premises.

$$$: The lowest priced we found anywhere in the Virgin Islands that was *on* the beach and safe. Daily rates, double occupancy: $45–$100, triples $55–$110.

Heritage Villas Vacation Apartments
Address: P.O. Box 2019, Carrot Bay, Tortola, BVI
Telephone: 284-494-5842, fax 284-495-4100
Website: www.GO-BVI.com/heritagevillas

Heritage's plain one- and two-bedroom apartments are perched on a cliff overlooking a scalloped line of some of Tortola's most beautiful white-sand beaches, along the island's north coast. You'll need a car to get to the beaches, but if you are looking for a low-priced clean place where you can cook and sleep, this is an excellent option. The resort has recently added a pool with a small deck and at the Jus' Limin Bar and Grille, which features fresh-caught fish and lobster.

Accommodations: Six one-bedroom and two-bedroom apartments are a little tired and very simply furnished but have the basics you need for vacation living, including breathtaking views. All have kitchens with microwaves, coffeemaker, toaster, stove, and fridge.

Special Features: swimming pool, restaurant, bar, car rentals.

$$$: $85–$200 per day, $595–$1,400 per week.

VIRGIN GORDA

WHERE TO STAY
Expensive

Bitter End Yacht Club

Address: P.O. Box 46, Virgin Gorda, BVI
Telephone: 800-872-2392, 284-494-2746, fax 284-494-4756
Website: www.beyc.com

I don't know a mistral from a mainsail, but staying at the Bitter End makes me want to haul out my bell bottoms and deck shoes. Accomplished sailors make it their hangout, but raw beginners like myself can take advantage of a full fleet of boats—and sailing classes so we know what to do with them. Spread along its own mile-long private cove backed by steep cliffs thick with tropical gardens, the resort is accessible only by boat and has a distinctive personality that is as far from a bland chain resort as you can get.

My seven-year-old son adored hanging out at the sailing docks, watching sailors come in and out to resupply their vessels in the store, tinker with their boats in the shop, or just venture ashore to enjoy a meal or a drink and some company on dry land. Guests can stay on one of the resort's Freedom 30 yachts, or in comfortable rooms along the beach or hillside. My favorite station was the hammock on our porch that overlooked the beach, the North Sound, and the Atlantic Ocean beyond.

The Bitter End's Junior Program for kids seven and older gave my two a real head start on their mother—they learned to windsurf and sail, and enjoyed storytelling, nature walks, and beach games. Local excursions (with an accomplished sailor at the helm) take guests to places like the awe-inspiring bouldery Baths, secret caves, hidden snorkeling coves, and deserted islands.

The watersports center is the hub of the place, but there's also action at the large pool (with a bar and grill) and at each of the three different beaches roped off for swimming, complete with rafts and diving boards. Fins are furnished, but bring your own mask and snorkel.

Accommodations: Two types of rooms are available. Beachfront rooms are rustic and cooled by ceiling fans and window-screen ventilation. All have small refrigerators, decks with hammocks and lounge chairs, ventwood closets and partitions, and no phone or TV. Beachfront units are duplex and one family can get both sides, connecting through the deck. Commodore rooms are much more elegant, with air-conditioning, phones, TVs, and VCRs by request. They have two queen beds or a king-size bed, refrigerator, coffeemaker, fans, and screened garden shower. As in the beachfront, there are connecting doors through the decks. Eight live-aboard charter yachts are provisioned and can accommodate up to six people.

There are no room keys. Safety deposit boxes are available in the office, and a security guard walks the property at night. No cribs, high chairs, or baby supplies.

For Kids: Kids Program for children ages five and older includes storytelling, beach games, sand painting, and an introduction to windsurfing, sailing, and snorkeling. The program operates most of the year. Children must be able to swim, and enjoy a morning session. The program can depend on the numbers of children at the resort.

Special Features: beaches, swimming pools, restaurants, bars, every kind of boat imaginable, boat excursions, sailing school, windsurfing, entertainment, shops.

$$$: Two different family vacation packages offer a good value at this pricey resort. Admiral's Family Vacation packages allows you two connecting rooms for the price of one and boating, snorkeling, etc. With the Family Thanksgiving Week package you get all the above plus Sail Caribbean sailing program $5,600. Daily rate, winter $700 double, summer $600 double. An extra child six to sixteen in a parents' room is always $100 per day.

Biras Creek Resort

Address: P.O. Box 54, Virgin Gorda, BVI
Telephone: 800-223-1108, 284-494-3555, fax 284-494-3557
Website: www.biras.com

Each guest is assigned a fat-tire bicycle at check-in for his or her own personal use on the paths at Biras Creek's 150 secluded acres. Since the country estate–like resort is accessible only by boat and is entirely self-contained, it's a safe place to let your children explore on their own while you relax in the sun. Accommodations are very private, with one-story villas housing two separate suites—perfect for a family of four or more. Supervised lessons are available for children who want to learn to windsurf, sail, snorkel, waterski, or play tennis. The resort has a lovely swimming pool, and nature trails for hiking and jogging crisscross the property. The full array of complimentary watersports are available, and your meals are included in one price and served in a castlelike hilltop dining room with panoramic views in all directions. Everything here is done well. Children must be six years old.

Accommodations: 32 suites and one private villa. Suites have sitting rooms, separate bedrooms, patios, and ceiling fans. Grand suites have air-conditioned bedrooms and oversized living room terraces. A two-bedroom private villa with its own kitchen is available for families wanting the ultimate in privacy. All overlook the ocean or gardens.

Special Features: swimming pool, snorkeling, windsurfing, sailboards, Hobie Cats, motorboating, night-lit tennis courts, boat excursions, jet skiing, waterskiing, scuba, restaurants, shops, pool, snooker table, nature trails, bicycles.

$$$: Summer Family Break package from June through October offers a second suite free, plus all meals and a variety of recreational options, $4,725 for two adults and up to three kids ages six to twelve for seven nights. Daily rates, double occupancy: rooms $350–$695, villas $600–$995.

Little Dix Bay
Address: P.O. Box 70, Virgin Gorda, BVI
Telephone: 284-495-5555, fax 284-495-5661
Website: www.rosewood-hotels.com

"Casual elegance" is the phrase often used to describe the beauty and service at Little Dix Bay in the northwest corner of Virgin Gorda. Set on a half-mile crescent-shaped bay and protected by a coral reef, this resort offers hilltop rooms with views of the sea beyond or seaside rooms where the beach is a few steps from the door. Families are welcomed in many ways. Children have a lovely new indoor/outdoor facility and teens have their own room with CDs, videos, a paperback book library, and board games. There are childrens menus in the restaurants, and a special pirates' party takes place weekly at the same time as the managers cocktail party so parents can enjoy adult company and conversation without interruption.

This secluded resort, accessible only by high-speed ferry, operates at an elegantly slow pace, with interesting boat excursions and a complimentary water taxi that ferries guests to other island beaches. There are thatched *palapas,* or umbrellas, to shade beach lovers from the intense tropical sun. (Note that the month of February is adults only and kids are not allowed.)

Accommodations: Rooms differ in location more than interior amenities, although the premium rooms have air-conditioning and the others are cooled by ceiling fans; all sleep a maximum of three people. Cottages are one large hexagonal room on or near the beach. One-bedroom beachfront suites are also available and are quite comfortable for families of four. Connecting rooms are available.

For Kids: The childrens program is in "Children's Grove," a 2,500-square-foot-interior space housing a miniature Caribbean Chattel House, a dress-up parlor, arts and craft center, dining area, and an outside play area. Activities include nature walks, shell collecting, treasure hunts, Caribbean folk art, stories, and music as well as free play. It's open Monday through Saturday from 9 A.M. to 4:30 P.M. and 6 P.M. to 9:30 P.M. Children must be over the age of three.

Special Features: beach, pools, Sunfish, sailboats, kayaks, waterskiing, snorkel gear, tennis, sailing excursions, horseback riding, scuba diving, fishing, and boat charters, bars, restaurants, baby-sitting, car rental, fitness center.

$$$: From June 1 to October 31, a second bedroom for children accompanying their parents is 50 percent off; kids up to sixteen are free in the parents' room but only three people may stay in a bedroom. Daily rates, double occupancy: rooms $250–$675; cottages $450–$750; suites $700–$1,300.

Budget

Guavaberry Spring Bay Vacation Homes
Address: Box 20, Virgin Gorda, BVI
Telephone: 284-495-5227, fax 284-495-5283
Website: www.guavaberryspringbay.com

Reasonable prices, fully equipped kitchens, and a great location within walking distance of a good swimming beach and Virgin Gorda's famous Baths make these vacation homes an excellent value for families who want a self-catering holiday. Sixteen modern, fully equipped one- and two-bedroom homes are elevated to provide views of Sir Francis Drake Channel, especially attractive at dusk when glorious sunset colors play over the water. A small, well-stocked "minimart" operates on the honor system, and the office is open daily to help guests with dinner reservations, car rentals, day sail charters, and snorkel trips. A restaurant and bar is just a five-minute walk from the property.

Accommodations: One- and two-bedroom houses are completely equipped with full-size refrigerators and stoves, linens and beach towels. Each house has a barbecue and daily maid service. Two-bedroom houses have two baths and can accommodate five people; one-bedroom units can accommodate only two people. The owners also manage privately owned deluxe homes in the vicinity, some with their own pools and tennis courts.

Special Features: minimart, car rental.

$$$: One-bedroom homes $95–$140. Extra person add $15 per day summer and $20 per day winter. Two bedroom $150–$210. Three-bedroom villas $265–$450. Fifth person add $15 per day summer and $20 per day winter.

WHAT TO SEE AND DO

Named for the huge granite boulders that form a natural sculpture display, **The Baths** offer superb snorkeling in calm weather. Walk the beach trail through the giant boulders and weave in and out of tide pools, across skinny wooden bridges, and through narrow crevices. The Baths can be crowded with day-trippers, but are still worth a visit. A complex with a restaurant, swimming pool, and gift shops at the top of the path offers refreshing snacks and souvenirs.

The Cayman Islands

Scuba enthusiasts from all over the globe rank the Cayman Islands as one of the world's top dive destinations, but if your children are too young to strap on a tank of compressed air, the diverse and abundant sea life and crystalline waters are just as rewarding to explore with mask and snorkel. Dozens of spectacular underwater sites offer views of colorful fish, elaborate coral formations, sea turtles, hidden caves, and shipwrecks. The government has created marine park systems on all three islands—Grand Cayman, Cayman Brac, and Little Cayman—to protect these undersea treasures.

Stingray City in North Sound off Grand Cayman is one of the Cayman's most famous underwater sites, and certainly one not to miss, where Atlantic stingrays frolic with snorkelers and swimmers in very shallow water. About thirty of the huge pancake-flat rays fly through the water at any one time, hoping for a handout and a gentle rub on the stomach. They're soft and slippery and will give you a hickey with their vacuum cleaner–like mouths, if you're not careful.

Gorgeous beaches entice sun worshipers just as the hidden caves and coves once lured pirates like Blackbeard and Sir Henry Morgan, who darted out to plunder Spanish galleons carrying gold from Mexico and South America. Sea turtles were once so abundant that Columbus named the islands Las Tortugas when he spotted them in 1503, but the name was later changed to Cayman. Sailors and fishermen brought the turtles to the edge of extinction but these creatures are now protected.

Tourism and banking drive the Caymanian economy, with Grand Cayman, the largest and most populated island, carrying most of the activity. Full-service resorts with children's programs and spacious beachfront condos line the edges of Grand Cayman's sparkling Seven Mile Beach, and many families headquarter here to enjoy the sun, sand, and convenient services. No building may be taller than the tallest palm trees, and enough trees and vegetation line the beach so that even in peak season the place doesn't seem too full. Those wanting total quiet and seclusion head to other parts of Grand Cayman or to Little Cayman and Cayman Brac.

Fast Facts:

Visitor Information Website: www.caymanislands.ky, *U.S.: Miami*: Cayman Islands Department of Tourism, 6100 Waterford Building, 6100 Blue Lagoon Drive, Suite 150, Miami, FL 33126-2085 (305-266-2300); *Houston*: 2 Memorial City Plaza, 820 Gessner, Suite 170, Houston, TX 77024 (714-461-1317); *New York*: 420 Lexington Avenue, Suite 2733, New York, NY 10170 (212-682-5582); *Illinois*: 9525 Bryn Mawr Avenue, Suite 160, Rosemont, IL 60018 (708-678-6446); *Los Angeles*: 3440 Wilshire Boulevard, Suite 1202, Los Angeles, CA 90010 (213-738-1969). *Canada*: Cayman Islands Department of Tourism, 234 Eglinton Avenue E, Suite, 306, Toronto M4P 1K5 (416-485-1550). *Grand Cayman*: Department of Tourism, N. Church Street, Georgetown (345-949-0623). Island-wide tourist hotline 345-949-8989.

Arriving and Departing: Americans and Canadians need proof of citizenship, either a passport, a birth certificate, or a voter registration card with photo ID, and a return ticket. A departure tax of $10 is charged.

Currency: The Caymanian dollar is worth about $1.25, but U.S. dollars are widely accepted.

Best Sweet Treat: Tortuga Rum Cake, the island's largest-selling export item, is a moist and flavorful cake.

GRAND CAYMAN

WHERE TO STAY
The long powdery ribbon of sand known as Seven Mile Beach (although it's really 5½ miles long) has most of the island's hotels and condominium complexes. Families trying to economize will do best renting a condominium so they can do their own cooking. It's a very safe and clean stretch of beach.

Expensive

Westin Causarina Resort
Address: West Bay Road, Grand Cayman Island, BWI
Telephone: 800-228-3000, 345-945-3800, fax 345-949-5825
Website: www.westin.com
One of the nicest resorts on Seven Mile Beach, this full-service operation is a comfortable place to headquarter to enjoy all that Grand Cayman has to offer. Its beach is one of the best on powder-soft Seven Mile Beach, and Casaurina pine trees, for which the resort is named, shade a swath of its shoreline. Guests relax in the cool shade of the trees, heading into the water for a swim or snorkel and back to the swim-up pool bar for a treat. Every watersport you can dream up is available from the watersports desk, and golf is just out the back door. All Westin Resorts have a year-round kids program, and this one operates from a fan-cooled tent down by the beach.

Accommodations: 340 rooms and one-, two-, and three-bedroom suites. All have a king bed or two double beds and a minibar, ceiling fans, and air-conditioning, coffeemaker, and in-room safes.

For Kids: The Westin Kids Club operates every day of the year from its home-base tent out on the beach. Daily activities include excursions to the Turtle Farm, snorkeling lessons (my kids perfected the art of snorkeling here), face painting, pool play, and arts and crafts. Kids four to twelve are cared for between 9 A.M. and 5 P.M.; a fee is charged, and mornings- or afternoons-only is available.

Special Features: beach, pool, swim-up bar, snorkeling, scuba diving and instruction, jet skis, catamaran excursions, windsurfers, sailboats, kayaks, waterskiing, parasailing, waverunners, fishing charters, health club, two lit tennis courts, restaurants, bars, hair salon, day spa, baby-sitting.

$$$: Children under eighteen are free in their parents' room. Daily rates, double occupancy: $214–$600.

Hyatt Regency Grand Cayman Resort and Villas

Address: P.O. Box 1588, Grand Cayman, BWI
Telephone: 800-228-900, 345-949-1234, fax 345-949-8528
Website: www.hyatt.com

Elegant sky-blue colonial-style low-rise buildings overlook a private waterway and eighteen-hole golf course designed by Jack Nicklaus at this premiere Caymanian resort. Three pools, including one with a swim-up bar, maintain the Hyatt trademark of water fun. Most of the resort is across the street from the beach, although a newer section of villas and a restaurant and pool are beachfront on the Hyatt property. There has been talk of adding an elevated crosswalk to make it easy to cross the busy street, but at press time, guests still had to wait for the light to change and then cross. There are tennis courts, every kind of imaginable watersport including sunset cruises and parasailing, three restaurants, and nightly entertainment. Bedrooms are elegant and spacious with marble baths and French doors. Bike rentals and scooters are available on the property. Night golf, with a glow in the dark ball, is a hit with kids.

Children's Program: Camp Hyatt for three- to twelve-year-olds operates on weekends, during holiday periods, and throughout the summer. The program includes swimming, windsurfing lessons, sand-castle building, movies, games, and arts and crafts. You must sign up in advance and pay a fee.

Accommodations: Rooms, suites, and villas are available; all are air-conditioned and have minibars, safes, and hair dryers. One- and two-bedroom villas are along the golf course and have fully furnished kitchens and washers and dryers. Special Regency Club rooms offer a higher level of personal service, continental breakfast, and upgraded amenities.

Special Features: beach, swimming pools, baby-sitting, bicycle rentals, fishing charters, golf, hair salon, beauty spa, parasailing, restaurants, ferry to Rum Point, shops, two night-lit tennis courts.

$$$: Children eighteen and under stay free in room with parents (limit two kids). A second room for the kids, when traveling with their parents is 50 percent off, subject to availability. Daily rates, double occupancy: $240–$600 rooms, villas $315–$735.

The Avalon Condominiums

Address: P.O. Box 32136SMB, Grand Cayman, BWI
Telephone: 345-945-4171, fax 345-945-4189

These attractive upscale condominiums are some of the most luxurious on Seven Mile Beach. Each unit can accommodate a large family, or even two smaller families, as there are three bedrooms and three baths in each spacious unit. The fully equipped kitchens have top-of-the-line appliances, and luxurious touches abound, from the decorator fabrics in lively tropical prints on the curtains and beds to French doors opening onto screened lanais showing off spectacular ocean views. The pool and Jacuzzi are just steps from the sand

and the resort's quiet beach is complete with beach chairs. If you take a first-floor unit, simply step outside to the beach.

Accommodations: Of the twenty-seven units, fifteen are in the rental pool. Three-bedroom, three-bath condos are air-conditioned with fully equipped kitchens, tile floors, screened lanais, and washer and dryer. Kitchen has service for twelve although six is the maximum allowed in each unit.

Special Features: beach, swimming pool, Jacuzzi, tennis courts, fitness room.

$$$: Daily rates: $415–$690.

The Beachcomber
Adress: Box 1799, Grand Cayman, BWI
Telephone: 345-945-4470, fax 345-945-5019
Website: www.arsl.com/beachcomber

A good buy on a great beach, the Beachcomber is another comfortable condominium resort on a quiet section of Seven Mile Beach. Quite a few shops and restaurants are located within a five-minute walk of the place, including a grocery deli, so you can stock up on goodies for your fully equipped kitchen.

Accommodations: Each apartment has an ocean view, screened patio, fully equipped kitchens, two full baths, air-conditioning, ceiling fans, cable TV, and telephone.

Special Features: beach, pool, barbecue grills, beach huts, beach towels, daily maid service, laundry facilities, baby-sitting services.

$$$: two-bedroom apartments: $230–$275, two-bedroom apartments with den: $270–$525.

Moderate

Indies Suites
Address: Box 2070, Grand Cayman, BWI
Telephone: 800-654-3130, 345-947-5025, fax 345-947-5024
E-mail: Indiessuites@att.net.

Although Indies Suites' one- and two-bedroom suites are not on the beach, they are just across the street where guests will find beach chairs and towels for their use. This resort is a favorite of divers, and the resort's custom-built dive boats take you to the best diving and snorkeling sights around the island. Guests receive a complimentary introduction to scuba in the pool, and the fully equipped dive shop has all sorts of equipment. Rooms in this attractive all-suite hotel are airy and amply sized. A swimming pool surrounded by lush tropical gardens stretches along the middle of the U-shaped hotel. Ground floor units have dive lockers, and upper floors have balconies for hanging wet dive equipment. This is an excellent value for families, and the kitchens help you further economize by allowing you to do your own cooking. An air-conditioned van takes you to the resort dock in comfort.

They have kids' sizes in snorkel masks and fins, and are PADI certified. On Tuesday nights the resort offers sunset cruises. You can get pizza and meat patties at the pool bar.

Accommodations: Forty units, thirty-eight one-bedroom, and two two-bedrooms units; most have a sofa bed in the living room and either a king or two double beds in the bedroom. Spacious kitchenettes have burners, a microwave, coffeemaker, and refrigerator. Roll-aways can be added for an extra child and cribs are available.

Special Features: continental breakfast daily in lobby, dive shop with instruction, washers and dryers on the premises, freshwater pool and Jacuzzi, pool bar, snack shop with sundries, equipment rental with scuba gear, snorkel vests and masks, wet suits, etc.

$$$: Children ages eleven and under stay free; additional person twelve and over $10 per person per night. Double rates: one-bedroom unit $170–$285 night; two-bedroom units $200–$340.

Tarquynn Manor

Address: P.O. Box 1362, G.T. Grand Cayman, BWI
Telephone: 345-945-4038, fax 345-945-5060
Website: www.armadainteractive.com/Tarquynn

Along a peaceful section of Seven Mile Beach, Tarquynn Manor's two- and three-bedroom condominiums offer families great comfort at moderate prices, especially off-season. A pool flanked by brightly striped umbrellas, thatched roof *palapas*, and lounge chairs is situated right at the edge of the beach. A broad grassy lawn, shaded in places by trees and edged by flowers, is a delightful place for children to romp when you're tired of cleaning sand out of their hair. Tame sea turtles swim offshore, and some guests have gotten close enough to touch them.

Accommodations: Eighteen units. Units come with either two bedrooms, or two bedrooms with a den, or in a three-bedroom penthouse configuration. All have central air, fully equipped kitchens, cable TV, telephones, and private screen-enclosed balconies.

Special Features: beach, pool, game room with Ping-Pong, barbecues, daily maid service

$$$: Daily rates, double occupancy:$158–$485.

Treasure Island Resort

Address: P.O. Box 1817, Seven Mile Beach, Grand Cayman, BWI
Telephone: 800-327-8777 or 345-949-7777, fax 345-949-8672
Website: www.treasureislandresort.net

A five-minute swim offshore takes you to Treasure Island's breathtaking coral reef, which stretches along the beach for about three hundred yards. It's marked with its own underwater snorkel trail with crystal clear visibility in fifteen to thirty feet of water.

The resort has two swimming pools: waterfalls spill into the undulating free-form pool with its own tropically landscaped island in the middle. Older kids can belly up to the swim-up bar of the second pool for a Shirley Temple or strawberry smoothie while the Barney set splashes in their own separate wading pool. There's a dive shop and watersports center on the premises, and two tennis courts. Be sure to ask about the summer and winter sale rate, which is available for a limited number of rooms year-round.

Accommodations: 280 rooms. Three different categories of rooms differ only in their location. All have king beds or two double beds, (connecting doors are available), air-conditioning, ceiling fans, balconies or patios, and minibars.

$$$: Children seventeen and under are free in their parents' room. Daily rates, double occupancy: $220–$275.

Condo Rentals
The Cayman Islands Department of Tourism (see above) has a list of condos and apartments available for rent.

WHAT TO SEE AND DO
Grand Cayman's capital city, **George Town,** has a small **National Museum** that showcases the natural and cultural history of the islands; old coins, ship-building tools, books, and rope-making techniques are among the items on display. Harbour Drive. Open Monday through Saturday 9:30 A.M. to 4:30 P.M. (345-949-8368).

Tiny turtle hatchlings, adolescents, and full-grown breeding adults are on display in enormous circulating water tanks at the **Cayman Turtle Farm.** Kids can hold yearling sea turtles above a special tank, and watch tiny babies paddle furiously after food. Each year, a number of hatchlings and yearlings are released to repopulate the region's waters; others not so lucky are sold for food, and the turtle meat dishes you taste on the islands most likely have come from here. Other animals are on display as well, such as iguanas, agoutis, parrots, and crocodile. A café has snacks (including turtle soup), and a gift shop sells all kinds of turtle-themed memorabilia, but remember that it is against the law to bring anything made of turtle back into the United States. West Bay Road. Open daily 9 A.M. to 5 P.M. (345-949-3893).

Cardinal D's Park is a fun and funky place to spend a few hours and is definitely worth a stop. You'll find over sixty species of exotic birds, some adorable miniature ponies, blue iguanas tame enough to pet, emus, turtles, agoutis, and more. We bought food for various creatures and enjoyed spoiling the birds with sunflower seeds and petting the tiny colt about the size of a beagle. Open Monday through Friday 10 A.M.–6 P.M., and Saturday and Sunday 12 P.M.–6 P.M. Off Courts Road (345-949-8855, fax 949-8885).

Atlantis Submarine takes passengers deep down in air-conditioned comfort along the Cayman wall to view the island's spectacular coral reefs, sponges, turtles, and brilliantly colored tropical fish. Guides identify sea life as it passes by the porthole windows. Kids need to be four and older to take the trip. Reduced rates are available for families. The sub is battery powered and nonpolluting. Night dives are available on Fridays. Georgetown (345-949-7700).

Snuba is a great way for kids 8 years and older to get a taste of scuba diving without the tanks, training, or worries. You can dive up to 20 feet attached to an air tank that floats on the surface on an inflatable raft. Trips are guided and safe. After a brief introduction, explore coral formations shipwrecks, tropical fish. Several dives are available each day. From Calico Jacks (345-949-4373).

Grab a **Rum Point Ferry** from the Hyatt Marina for a trip with several delightful stops—one to **Stingray City** to cavort with friendly stingrays, another stop for some spectacular snorkeling, and then grab a bite to eat from the Rum Point Restaurant. Evening rides are available too. Ferries depart six times a day and into the evening (345-949-9098).

Parents who take their kids to the tiny village of **Hell** can get a postcard and postmark or T-shirt to prove it to their friends back home. The fascinating stark volcanic rock formations around Hell inspired the town's name.

CAYMAN BRAC

Diving and fishing are the big attractions on Cayman Brac, named for the 140-foot bluff dotted with ancient pirate caves that dominates the island.

WHERE TO STAY
Moderate

Brac Caribbean Beach Village
Address: P.O. Box 4, Stake Bay, Cayman Brac, BWI
Telephone: 800-327-8777, 345-948-2265, fax 345-948-2206
Website: www.bracarib@candw.ky

Living rooms and master bedrooms overlook the sea in these comfortable two-bedroom condominiums on a reef-protected white-sand beach. The kitchen is stocked upon your arrival with snacks, sodas, and breakfast foods—everything you need until you get started, and you can get the pantry filled for the week if you request it.

Accommodations: All units are air-conditioned, and have shady verandas or balconies and French doors. Both the master bedroom and guest bedroom have private bathrooms.

$$$: Children eleven and under are free of charge. Daily rate, double occupancy: $165–$185.

Curaçao

Rows of pastel-colored gabled houses dominate the view in Willemstad, capital city of Curaçao, where homeowners were once forbidden by law to paint their homes white. Government officials deemed white too blinding in the tropical sun, and the city's penchant for pastels was born. Willemstad is one of the most photogenic cities in the Caribbean, and its architecture and historical heritage make it one of the island's big draws. A trolley takes passengers throughout the old part of the city. Other attractions are dependably sunny weather and superb snorkeling and scuba, especially in Curaçao Underwater Marine Park, which encompasses almost a third of the island's southern diving waters. Constant year-round winds and wave conditions have put Curaçao on the World Cup Windsurfing Tour in mid-June.

The island's austere countryside reflects its dry climate, and Dutch windmills that are still used for irrigation are seen all over. Historic plantation houses bordered by cactus and divi-divi trees sculpted by the wind have the same quaint Dutch style as buildings in the capital city. Several of these manors now house restaurants; one is a restored museum; and one offers a weekly folklore show.

Mikve Israel, the oldest synagogue in continuous use in the western hemisphere, was built in Curaçao in 1732. Jewish settlement of the island began in 1651 when twelve families from Amsterdam arrived and were followed by Jews escaping religious persecution from Portugal, Spain, and Brazil.

Curaçao is the biggest of the ABC islands (Aruba and Bonaire are the A and B) and the largest of the five-and-a-half islands constituting the Netherlands Antilles (Saba, St. Eustatius, and the Dutch half of St. Martin are the windward cousins of the ABC islands, separated from them by some five hundred miles of open Caribbean Sea). Just thirty-five miles north of Venezuela, its population is a lively mix of Latin, European, and African roots. Tourism is a relatively new industry, and visitors are warmly welcomed.

Fast Facts:

Tourist Information: Website: www.curacao-tourism.com, *U.S and Canada:* Curaçao Tourist Board, 475 Park Avenue South, Suite 2000, New York, NY 10016 (800-332-8266, 212-683-7660) or 330 Biscayne Boulevard, Miami, FL 33132 (800-445-8266, 305-374-5811, fax 305-374-6741). E-mail curacao@ix.net.com. *Curacao:* At Pietermaii No. 19 in Willemstad (599-9-61600)

Arrivals and Departures: U.S. and Canadian citizens need passports or birth certificates accompanied by a photo ID. All visitors must have a return or continuing ticket. Airport departure tax, per person, is $12.50 for international flights and $5.65 for interisland flights to another Netherland Antilles Island.

Money: The official currency is the guilder or florin, but the U.S. dollar is accepted everywhere.

Language: Dutch is the official language, but many inhabitants speak Papiamento, a mixture of Dutch, Portuguese, Spanish, and English. The language developed during the eighteenth century as the means of communication among slaves and landowners. Today children learn English (and Spanish) in school, and anyone connected with tourism speaks English.

Best Sweet Treat: Lover's Ice Cream—a company that's the Ben and Jerry's of Curaçao, has little shops around the island including one at Waterford Arches. For a tropical treat, try coconut, banana-pineapple, pistachio, or piña colada. Tamarind is used to make a *palu friu,* like a Popsicle. Another speciality is tamarind candy, where the tamarind fruit is boiled with brown sugar and turns into a pasty, gooey, delicious confection.

WHERE TO STAY
Expensive: over $225
Moderate: $125–$225
Inexpensive: under $125

Moderate

Sonesta Beach Hotel and Casino Curaçao
Address: P.O. Box 6003, Piscadera Bay, Curaçao
Telephone: 800-SONESTA, 599-9-736-8800, fax 599-9-462-7502
Website: www.sonesta.com
A stunning beach front location, five-star rating, and a large free-form swimming pool surrounded by lavishly landscaped grounds make this sun-drenched resort a favorite getaway for families. The architecture is faintly reminiscent of Curaçao's famous land-houses, although it's certainly modern in its amenities and services. Special "Family Fun" packages let kids twelve and under stay free and eat breakfast and lunch on the house from the kid's menu. Windsurfing, waterskiing, scuba diving, and snorkeling can be arranged from the watersports desk. Little ones can splash in their own shallow wading pool. Two tennis courts are lit for night play.

Accommodations: 248 rooms and suites all have a terrace or balcony, air-conditioning, in-room safe, TV, and minibar. Guest rooms, many with connecting doors, have two queen beds, two doubles, or a king. Suites have bedrooms and living areas with fold-out couches, and a deluxe presidential suite is available.

For Kids: Just Us Kids is a complimentary program that operates Wednesday through Sunday from 10 A.M. to 4:30 P.M for children between five and twelve years old. Kids leave the program to eat lunch with their parents and can return again to participate in treasure hunts, sand sculpture, arts and crafts, and movies. A special pizza and movie party Saturday night operates from 6:30 P.M. to 9 P.M. A Just Us Kids T-shirt is given to every child who enrolls.

Special Features: beach restaurants, casino, wading pool, swimming pool, swim-up bar, windsurfing, waterskiing, scuba diving, snorkeling, two night-lit tennis courts, playground, fitness center, children's program, shops.

$$$: Ask about the Family Fun package (three nights and four days) where kids age twelve and under stay and eat free. Daily rates, double occupancy: $180–$975.

Princess Beach Resort and Casino
Address: Martin Luther King Boulevard 8, Curaçao
Telephone: 800-992-2015, 599-9-736-7888, fax 599-9-614-131
Website: www.princessbeach.com

The beach at the Princess is one of the finest on the island and right in front of the protected Marine Water Park. There are two pools, a special children's pool, gorgeous tropical gardens, and the Seaquarium and Underwater Park are a short taxi ride away. It's a lively property that is spread out over a number of acres so you don't feel like you're constricted. This comfortable low-rise hotel has restaurants for every taste.

Accommodations: 310 rooms and suites. Large and comfortable rooms have a king or two queen beds and roll-aways can be added. Suites have fold-out couches in living areas.

For Kids: Ages two to twelve can participate in the complimentary daily program anytime between 9 A.M. and 5 P.M. in a special toy-stocked room. Youngsters play indoor and outdoor games, enjoy the children's playground, participate in arts and crafts, etc. A schedule of activities is published and changes daily, and the program operates year round.

Special Features: beach, pool, pool bar, restaurants, shops, dive shop, tennis, casino.

$$$: Children nineteen and under stay free in their parents' rooms. Daily rates, double occupancy: rooms $140–$205, one-bedroom suites start $205–$285.

Kadushi Cliffs

Address: P.O. Box 3673, Curaçao
Telephone: 800-KADUSHI, 599-9-8640200, fax 599-9-864-0282
E-mail: kadushi@cura.net

Twelve luxurious two-bedroom condos are on a hill above a beautiful crescent of beach sheltered by rocky cliffs on a secluded part of the island far from the more hectic pace of the beach strip. Fantastic snorkeling is just offshore. Private "villas," as they call them, are decorated in tropical motifs and can accommodate up to six people. Each villa has a patio with a gas grill, a Jacuzzi in the master bedroom, and dishwasher and microwave in the modern kitchen. A central reception area has a swimming pool and open-air restaurant that offers magnificent sunset views. All watersports can be arranged. You'll need a rental car, as the property is about forty-five minutes from Wilemstad.

Accommodation: 12 villas have two bedrooms, modern kitchens, living rooms with pull-out couch, safe, TVs, patios, and terraces. Baby cribs and baby-sitting are available.

Special Features: beach, pool, tennis court, watersports, restaurant, shop Laundromat, bicycles, and a walking/jogging trail.

$$$: Daily rates: villas for one to two people $195; for three to six people $295.

WHAT TO SEE AND DO

Curaçao Maritime Museum—Exhibits trace the story of Curaçao beginning with the arrival of the island's original inhabitants in 600 B.C. Forty permanent displays use video and multimedia technology to discuss the development of Curaçao's harbor, the role of the island as one of the largest slave depots in the Caribbean, and a virtual reality look at French and English pirates. Other exhibits contain artifacts such as seventeenth-century ship miniatures and maps (some dating as far back as 1500). The museum is located in a newly renovated mansion originally built in 1729 and has a small gift shop and café. Open Tuesday through Sunday 10 A.M. to 4 P.M. 9-560-5792.

Curaçao Seaquarium—Learn to identify the sea creatures that live around the island before you go out snorkeling. Indoor tanks exhibit four hundred varieties of fish and vegetation, and outdoor tanks contain sea turtles, sharks, and sea lions. A "semi-submarine" (really a stationary underwater observatory) takes forty-six people at a time below water level to view an underwater garden where fish, lobsters, stingrays, sharks, and turtles cavort in the crystalline water. Divers and snorkelers can swim outside of the sub, explore a shipwreck, and visit the Shark Encounter where humans are protected behind a sheet of Plexiglas set into a fenced area under water. Special feeding holes allow swimmers to feed the sharks who gather waiting for a handout; be sure to bring your underwater camera. The Seaquariums's beach is worth a stop to sun and swim. Open daily 10 A.M. to 10 P.M. Tel 599-9-616666.

You could find **Coney Island,** a fair with a merry-go-round, swimming pirate boat, and Ferris wheel, just about anywhere in North America. But, if you happen to be on the island on one of the two weekends per month that it's open, the kids will get a kick out of a fair with a West Indian flair. Next to the water plant—check with the tourist office for open days and times.

Hato Caves are actually old coral reefs that emerged out of the water when the island's landmass lifted and the sea level dropped, forming Curaçao. Hourly tours are given of the chambers studded with hundreds of stalactites and stalagmites and gleaming quartz crystals. Look closely to see the fossil coral formations and different species that made up the former reef. Outside, children can see iguanas, and a wooded path leads to Indian carvings etched into the rocks. Open Tuesday through Sunday. Tel. 599-9-680379.

Curaçao Underwater Marine Park, a 12½-mile unspoiled coral reef, is protected by national park status. Snorkel the marked 875-foot underwater trail of coral beds, sheer undersea walls, and shallow well-preserved shipwrecks. Normal visibility is sixty to eighty feet and even better on especially good days.

The deep bay of **Vaersenbaai** has little sand and a rocky entry, but teens will enjoy jumping of the pier and swimming out to a floating platform while little ones splash in the wading pool and enjoy the small playgrounds. Parents can sip drinks on the shaded terrace overlooking the water.

Grenada

Ice cream is the unofficial national food of Grenada. You can sample varieties of the creamy frozen confection flavored by whatever exotic tropical fruit is in season—papaya, coconut, banana, lime, mango, and even avocado. Rich and aromatic nutmeg ice cream is available year-round, and no wonder, since the fragrant spice is Grenada's number one export. Even tourism comes in second to nutmeg in Grenada's economy.

Three inhabited islands—Grenada, Carriacou, and Petite Martinique—and a few tiny uninhabited islands make up the island nation of Grenada. The largest, Grenada, is often remembered as the place U.S. troops invaded following an internal coup d'état in 1983, ostensibly to evacuate American students at St. George's Medical School. Small and quiet Carriacou and Petite Martinique have beautiful beaches and very little tourism. Prices are much lower here than in tonier parts of the Caribbean.

Grenada's tidy farming towns and quaint fishing villages are testimonials to the island's unspoiled character. The island's hillsides are thick with banana, nutmeg, and cocoa crops. Shimmering green rain forests shrouded in mist hide dramatic waterfalls and breathtaking hiking trails. Tourism is concentrated on the southwest corner along Grand Anse Beach, a sparkling two-mile crescent of white sand bordered by palm trees and the brilliant turquoise Caribbean Sea, where vendors amble by sunbathers, offering coconut milk straight from the coconut. In the early morning small boys play cricket by the water's edge. The word "grog" originated on the island, standing for grand rum of Grenada.

Fast Facts:

Visitor Information: Website.www.grenada.org/, *US:* Grenada Board of Tourism, Suite 900D, 820 Second Avenue, New York, NY 10017 (800-927-9554 or 212-687-9554). *Canada:* Grenada Board of Tourism, Suite 820, 439 University Avenue, Toronto, Ontario M5G 1Y8 (416-595-1339). *Grenada:* Grenada Board of Tourism, The Carenage, St. George's (809-440-2279).

Arriving and Departing: U.S. and Canadian citizens need a passport or birth certificate with a photo ID and an onward or return ticket. The departure tax is $10 per person; children under five are exempt.

Currency: The Eastern Caribbean Dollar (EC$) is the local currency. You can use U.S. dollars in many shops, hotels, and restaurants, but you'll get a better rate of exchange using EC dollars.

Language: English is spoken throughout Grenada.

Best Sweet Treat: Tropical flavored ice cream

WHERE TO STAY
Moderate

Blue Horizons Cottage Hotel

Address: P.O. Box 41, St. George's, Grenada, WI
Telephone: 800-223-9815, 473-444-4316, fax 473-444-2815
Website: www.cpscaribnet.com/ads/blue/blue

A warm and homey atmosphere brings many of Blue Horizon's international guests back year after year. Its excellent value makes it popular with families who want an informal housekeeping cottage near a good beach. Grand Anse Beach is just a five-minute walk down the hill, where hotel guests can use the beach chairs and complimentary watersports at the resort's sister property, the

Spice Island Inn. The hotel's highly regarded La Belle Creole Restaurant, one of the best on the island, specializes in imaginatively prepared local cuisine. This charming getaway has a swimming pool and small playground set in 6½ acres of tropical gardens.

Accommodations: Thirty-two rooms have fully equipped kitchenettes, ceiling fans, hair dryers, air-conditioning, TV, radios, and private patios. One-bedroom and two-bedroom units are also available.

Special Features: swimming pool, pool bar with snacks, restaurant, whirlpool, car rental, lounge with games. At sister resort, Spice Island Inn, guests can use beach, tennis court, paddle boats, small sailboats, snorkel equipment, and windsurfers; they can waterski and scuba dive and use the fitness center, shops, and car rental services.

$$$: In winter season, children under twelve stay free; in summer children under eighteen stay free. Per night, double occupancy: one bedroom $120–$180; two bedrooms $230–$340.

Coyaba Beach Resort
Address: P.O. Box 336, St. George's, Grenada, WI
Telephone: 800-223-9815, 473-444-4129, fax 473-444-4808
Website: www.coyaba.com

Situated directly on Grande Anse Beach about midway down the two-mile expanse of ecru sand, all of Coyaba's guest rooms feature private verandas and patios with views of the Caribbean Sea or St. George's Harbor. Seven rather undistinguished buildings, each with ten guest rooms, surround the resort's outdoor pool, which features Grenada's only swim-up bar. A small playground and the pool keep the kids happy when they tire of the beach. The restaurant on the premises serves local and international cuisine, and a more casual open-air dining room serves breakfast. A complimentary tea is served each afternoon. Their watersports center, Grand Anse Aquatics Ltd., has PADI-certified instructors and conducts scuba and snorkeling trips around Grenada, Carriacou, and Petite Martinique. Windsurfing rental and instruction are available.

Accommodations: Seventy rooms have two double beds or one king, all with air-conditioning, balconies or patios, and hair dryers. Cribs and roll-aways are available.

Special Features: beach, tennis, snorkel gear, canoes, Sunfish sailboats, pool, swim-up bar, volleyball, restaurants.

$$$: For children two to twelve sharing parents' room, add $15 per child in summer, $25 per child in winter. Daily rates, double occupancy: $120–$200.

Rex Grenadian
Address: Point Salines, P.O. Box 893, St. George's, Grenada, WI
Telephone: 800-255-5859, 809-444-3333, fax 473-444-1111

One of the biggest hotels on the island, this resort is the only one with a small children's program. Its three-acre lake, one beach for swimming and sunbathing and another for watersports, a free-form swimming pool with a waterfall, plus a busy schedule of activities attract families who like plenty to do. Many rooms have views across the soft white sands and turquoise waters of Tamarind Bay to St. George's in the distance. Windsurfing, sunfish sailing, and snorkeling equipment are complimentary, while a fee is charged for scuba diving, parasailing, waterskiing, high performance windsurfing boards, and sports lessons. A children's menu is available for lunch and dinner.

Accommodations: 212 rooms and suites, in six different styles and sizes. Least expensive rooms have fans, the rest have air-conditioning.

For Kids: Supervised activities for four- to twelve-year-olds take place Monday through Friday from either 9 A.M. to 12 P.M., or 2 P.M. to 4 P.M. Planned activities include mask making, beach play, painting, treasure hunts, parties, kite making, movies, and music games.

Special Features: beach, pool, windsurfing, Sunfish sailing, snorkeling, scuba diving, parasailing, waterskiing, restaurants, baby-sitting.

$$$: Children under two eat and stay free, children under twelve stay free and eat at half price. Rooms daily rates, double occupancy: $185–$210. Inclusive rates also available.

True Blue Bay Resort
Address: P.O. Box 1414, Grand Anse, St. George's, Grenada, WI
Telephone: 473-443-TRUE, fax 473-444-1247
Website: www.truebluebay.com

Spacious lawns slope down to beautiful True Blue Bay where a small dock reaches out into the azure Caribbean Sea. Guests can use the resort's dinghy to explore nearby coves and offshore reefs. The quiet setting, away from St. George's on a private peninsula, doesn't have much of a beach, but you can swim in the ocean from a platform at the end of the dock or in the freshwater swimming pool. Grande Anse and Morne Rouge beaches are just a few minutes away. It's a very small family-run property, with just seven units, all with full kitchens. A dive outfit operates from the dock. Indigo's Restaurant and Bar is available for breakfast, lunch, and dinner when you are tired of cooking, and a waterfront bar serves snacks and drinks. You'll want a car for mobility.

Accommodations: Children under twelve are only allowed in the two-bedroom cottages nestled in tropical gardens. All have ceiling fans, air-conditioning, pull-out sofa beds, cable TV, and daily maid service.

Special Features: beach, swimming pool, dock, restaurant, bar, dive shop.

$$$: Daily rates: two-bedroom cottages $125–$195 for up to four people, additional person $25–$40.

WHAT TO SEE AND DO
The **People to People** program brings together visitors to the island with Grenadine residents who share similar interests for visits and outings. Write to New Trends Tours before you go, requesting an introduction. Be sure to specify your interests and your children's interests and ages. There is no charge, but it's always most gracious to treat your host to any outing. P.O. Box 797, St. George's. 473-444-1236 and fax 473-444-4836.

Plan to visit **St. George's,** Grenada's capital city and major port, on Tuesday afternoons to see the loading of the boats with crates and bags of fruits and vegetables bound for Trinidad. **Market day** in St. George's takes place every Saturday morning. Arrive early to see its exotic fruits and vegetables and aromatic spices. Ask permission before shooting any photos. You can buy little baskets of cinnamon, nutmeg, mace, bay leaves, vanilla, and ginger at shops in the market or around town.

Nearby, the **Grenada National Museum** houses archaeological finds, mounted specimens of native fauna, historical memorabilia, and the Empress Josephine Bonaparte's marble bathtub. Open weekdays 9 A.M. to 1:30 P.M., Saturday 10 A.M. to 1:30 P.M. The most comprehensive exhibit traces the Indian cultures of Grenada.

Fort George, built by the French in 1705, still has ancient cannons standing on its ramparts. You can visit the adjacent botanical garden and small zoo with tropical trees and flowers and rare Caribbean birds and animals. Open daily.

Find out how nutmeg goes from the tree to the dusting on cookies, eggnog, and rum punch at the **Nutmeg Processing Station** in the west coast town of Gouyave, the center of Grenada's nutmeg industry. You'll see old wooden shelling and cracking machinery still at work, sacks of fragrant spices, and nutmeg and mace (the dried fibrous covering of the nutmeg seed, which is removed and used as a spice in its own right) being prepared for export in much the same way the Grenadians have been preparing them for centuries. Handfuls of nutmeg are passed out as souvenirs at the end of your visit. Open Monday through Friday 8 A.M. to 4 P.M. and Saturday 8 A.M. to noon.

Just inland, stop in at **Dougaldston Estate,** where cloves, cinnamon, mace, nutmeg, and cocoa are prepared and sorted. Employees will explain how the spices grow, discuss their uses, and show you the large trays where the spices are set to sun dry before being painstakingly separated by hand. Open Monday through Friday 9 A.M. to 3:30 P.M. and Saturday 9 A.M. to noon (809-444-8213).

Pack a picnic lunch and take the coast road eight miles north from St. George's to breathtaking **Concord Falls**. A two-mile hike will take you to the more dramatic part of the falls, where water cascades down a fifty-foot fall into a deep blue pool. After swimming beneath the waterfall, hike along the river through the tropical forest for about an hour to a more remote fall. There's a small changing room at the main falls where you can slip into your swimsuit.

The centerpiece of **Grand Étang National Park** is a large volcanic crater that has become a lake. A number of magnificent waterfalls offer perfect sites for a refreshing swim and picnic. Annandale Falls is just off Grand Etang Road.

La Sagresse Nature Center offers hiking trials, wild birds, a banana plantation with guided nature walks, an extensive beach, and a café for lunch and refreshments.

Saturday is **market day in Grenville,** known as Grenada's bread basket. This large, colorful market offers fish, spices, fruits, vegetables, pastries, and Grenadian delicacies prepared on the spot.

With visibility often close to two hundred feet, **scuba and snorkeling** opportunities are manifold. Grenada's waters are home to the largest shipwreck in the Caribbean, The *Bianca C*, a cruise ship that caught fire and went down in 1961, eventually settling into waters more than one hundred feet deep. Turtles, eagle rays, and all kinds of brilliantly colored tropical fish now make it their home.

The superb **sailing** between Grenada and the island chain of the Grenadines is best for experienced sailors, although inexperienced sailors can easily rent a crewed boat. **The Moorings,** one of the best charter yacht operators in the Caribbean, have facilities at Secret Harbour Hotel.

Guadeloupe

Like a large butterfly floating on a sea of blue, Guadeloupe is really two islands. One wing of the butterfly, Grande-Terre, has tantalizing beaches and a haute scene, and as you might guess, it's the center of resort life. The other wing, the rugged and mountainous Basse-Terre, contains a national park and concerns itself with more natural splendors. A seawater channel called the Rivière Salée separates the two wings, and a drawbridge allows passage between them.

When travelers Deidre Hamilton and John Swift took their two boys, ages eleven and fourteen, they stayed a few days on each side of the island and had distinctly different experiences: "We loved exploring the little towns, beautiful beaches, and lively resort scene of Grande-Terre," said Deidre, "but Basse-Terre was tremendous fun, too, with more gorgeous beaches and some spectacular waterfalls to hike to. The boys swam in the pools and we picnicked with the local people who were enjoying the beautiful natural setting."

Sophisticated gourmands rank Guadeloupe's cuisine as one of the best in the Caribbean. The top restaurants and hotels offer elegant meals prepared in the classical French manner, but there are also more than one hundred small bistros, beachside cafés, and funky diners where you'll find spicy, out-of-this world Creole cooking.

The island's French influence can be seen in more than the cuisine. Shops close for the ritual of a long lunch with wine, as they do all over France; bakeries offer light and flaky French pastries; and itsy bitsy French bikinis become even smaller when the tops are removed to ensure the perfect tan. The hotels have been set up to cater to French vacationers who often vacation for two weeks or more, and many properties have studio- and apartment-style units with small kitchens and greater elbow room.

Windsurfing or *planche-a-voile* is excellent on the island, and several major international competitions are held here. Cycling is a popular pastime, and bicycles can be rented at a variety of bike shops throughout the island. The Tour de Guadeloupe, a ten-day international race is held each August. Note that scuba divers use the French CMAS system rather than PADI or NAUI.

Fast Facts:

Visitor Information: Website: www.guadeloupe.com, *U.S.:* Guadeloupe

Tourist Office: 161 Washington Valley Road, Suite 205, Warren, NJ 07059 (732-302-1223, fax 732-302-0809); French Government Tourist Office, 444 Madison Avenue, New York, NY 10022; or 9454 Wilshire Boulevard, Suite 715, CA 90212 (310-271-6665); 676 N. Michigan Ave., Suite 3360, Chicago, IL 60611 (312-751-7800). *Canada:* French Government Tourist Office, #490 1981 McGill College, Montreal, Quebec, H3A 2W9 (514-845-4868) and #700, 30 Patrick St., Toronto, Ontario M5G 1Z3 (416-593-6427, fax 416-979-7587). *Guadeloupe:* Office Départemental du Tourisme de Guadeloupe, 5 Square de la Banque, Pointe-a-Pître, Guadeloupe, WI (590-82-09-30). The staff speaks English.

Arriving and Departing: A passport, notarized birth certificate with raised seal, or voter registration card with official ID are required for U.S. and Canadian citizens. You must show an ongoing or return ticket. There is no departure tax unless you are part of a charter group.

Money: The French franc is the official currency, but dollars are widely accepted.

Language: French is spoken everywhere and street signs, shops signs, and menus are in French. If you don't *parlez Français* you'll be better off staying in one of the larger hotels where some staff speak English.

Best Sweet Treat: Street vendors sell banana and coconut ice cream that is out of this world.

WHERE TO STAY

Just as in the hotels in France, the bedrooms and bathrooms in Guadeloupe's hotels are rather small by American standards.

Moderate

Le Méridien St. François

Address: St-François 97118, Guadeloupe, FWI
Telephone: 800-543-4300, 590-88-51-00, fax 590-88-40-71
Website: www.lemeridien-hotels.com.

This 150-acre resort is jam-packed with sports and leisure activities, right on St. François beach adjacent to the Robert Trent Jones golf course. For dining, select one of the two restaurants right on the beach. All sorts of sports are offered free of charge: windsurfing, sailing, snorkeling, aerobics, and volleyball. Full- and half-day excursions to other islands can be arranged for a fee. There's also evening entertainment such as steel band, jazz music, and dance performances. One child under twelve stays free in parents' room, and all guests enjoy a complimentary breakfast. Both French and English are spoken.

Accommodations: 265 rooms. Rooms have one double bed or two twin beds and one child can stay in parents' room. Connecting doors are available. All rooms are air-conditioned, and some have a minibar and small sitting area.

Special Features: beach, swimming pool, windsurfing, kayaks, pedal boats, aqua gymnastics, snorkeling, small catamarans, canoes, waterpolo, boccie ball, volleyball, Ping-Pong, aerobics, gym, archery, tennis courts, daytime tours, two restaurants, bar.

$$$: One child under twelve is complimentary in parents' rooms. Double occupancy, per night, high season: $150–$476.

Le Méridien Cocoteraie

Address: Avenue des Europe, St-François, Guadeloupe, FWI
Telephone: 800-543-4300, 590-8879-81, fax 590-8879-33
Website: www.lemeridien-hotels.com

Families looking for two-room suites with the services of a hotel can find comfort and style in this resort at which guests get the complete use of facilities at its sister resort, Le Méridien (see above). It enjoys the same Robert Trent Jones golf course and boating marina, but is a quieter, smaller, more upscale option. Each suite is decorated in Creole style with terraces overlooking the pool and sea. The beach is a bit small, but guests who stay in the beach suites are barely six yards from the beach.

Accommodations: Fifty suites. A convertible sofa in the sitting room will accommodate one adult or two children; the bedroom contains one kingbed or two twin beds. All units are fully air-conditioned with phones, satellite TV, VCR, minibar, in-room safe, and hair dryer. Connecting rooms are available

Special Features: beach, eighteen-hole golf course, massage and fitness equipment, catamaran at property marina, swimming pool, tennis courts, windsurfing, sailing, waterskiing, scuba, deep sea fishing, jet skiing, jogging trail, room service.

$$$: Daily rates, double occupancy: $175–$500. Children under twelve can stay free in their parents' room.

Hotel Marissol

Address: Bas-du-Fort 97190, Gosier, Guadeloupe, FWI
Telephone: 800-221-4542, 590-90-84-44, fax 590-90-83-32

Set in a huge ten-acre park at the edge of the sea, this resort has all the watersports, a holiday children's program, and standard hotel rooms or bungalows with two to four rooms each. Folklore shows are offered at least once a week, and there are several restaurants, a disco, and all kinds of "light" sports such as Ping-Pong, pétanque, volleyball, archery, and board games. Rates include a lovely buffet breakfast.

Accommodations: 195 guest rooms, including standard rooms, and 48 bungalow-style accommodations. All rooms are air-conditioned and have terrace or balcony, minibars, radio, and TV. Connecting rooms are available. Bungalows have two to four rooms, and a few sit at the edge of the beach.

For Kids: Dolphi Club children's program operates daily during French school holidays from 9 A.M. to 7 P.M. Children six to twelve are invited to participate in watersports, games, and arts and crafts for a daily fee of 100 French francs (about $20). Watersports are monitored by certified staff, and kids are given a weekly schedule and welcome gifts when they first register. Each week, children present a show to the hotel's guests.

Special Features: beach, health club, massage, windsurfing, waterskiing, scuba diving, sea excursions, restaurants, bars, tennis, swimming pool, babysitting, entertainment, volleyball, archery.

$$$: One child under the age of sixteen may stay free in parents' room. Daily rates, double occupancy: $120–$240, triple occupancy $152–$290, bungalows $134–$340.

Budget

Residence Canella Beach

Address: Pointe de la Verdure, P.O. Box 73, Gosier, 97190, Guadeloupe, FWI
Telephone: 800-223-9815, 590-90-44-00, fax 590-90-44-44

Adults rave about the highly regarded French cuisine at this resort's La Verandah Restaurant, while their offspring report on the beach activities, pool, and children's playground. Built to resemble a Creole village, Canella Beach has studios and duplexes with terrace kitchenettes in three-story buildings. Snorkeling equipment, paddle boats, canoes, and daytime tennis are complimentary; other watersports such as scuba, windsurfing, catamaran trips, jet skiing and waterskiing have an additional fee. The resort's restaurants and snack bars have children's menus and low cal options. This resort is in the Gosier area, which is full of resort hotels lining the beach. At peak season, the beach can get a bit crowded, but this location offers all kinds of restaurants, shops, and nightclubs within walking distance of the hotel. If you've happened to bring your French poodle with you, she may stay, as long as she weighs no more than seven pounds.

Accommodations: 146 units, studios, junior suites that can accommodate up to four, and duplexes that can accommodate five to six people. All have small kitchenettes, air-conditioning, full baths, in-room safe, twin or queen beds, living area with sofa bed, TV, radio, and phone.

Special Features: swimming pool, children's wading pool, pedal boats, canoes, snorkeling, scuba diving, windsurfing, sailboats, waterskiing, massage, restaurants, bars.

$$$: Children under twelve are free in their parents' room: Daily rates, double occupancy: studios $98–$160, junior suite $134–$190, duplex apartment $175–$260. Extra person 12 and over $30 per day except in apartment.

WHAT TO SEE AND DO

Guadeloupe Aquarium is one of the best aquariums in the entire Caribbean. Plan to visit early in your vacation so you can learn to identify the tropical fish, coral species, and sponges before you go snorkeling or diving. Place Créole, off Route N4. 590-90-92-38.

Parc National de la Guadeloupe —Forty-two thousand acres of rain forest, a volcano, and dramatic waterfalls make up the national park that takes up a third of Basse-Terre. Well-marked nature trails that lead through the rain forest begin behind the visitors center on the Route de la Traversée. Favorites include the **Cascade aux Ecrévisses,** a sparkling waterfall and pond perfect for a refreshing dip and the **Parc Bras David** with walking tours of varying lengths. The **Zoological Park and Botanical Gardens** displays animals such as iguanas, turtles, and cockatoos. La Traversée. 590-98-83-52. Open daily 9 A.M.–5 P.M. The park's best-known attraction is **La Soufrière**, a volcano whose last eruption in 1976 prompted the evacuation of seventy thousand people. You can hike to the top without a guide on several trails to see its 5-acre center of bubbling lava and weird rock formations. **Carbet Falls,** on a hillside of La Soufrière, is a dramatic three-level waterfall that you can easily hike to in about thirty minutes. Park headquarters can be reached at 590-80-24-25, fax 590-80-05-46.

Cousteau Underwater Park—Jacques Cousteau spent time in the waters off Guadeloupe and described the area around Pigeon Island as one of the worlds ten best snorkeling and scuba spots. His underwater reserve stretches along Basse-Terre's scenic western coast. The glass-bottom *Nautilus* takes passengers out to view the reef and stops for snorkeling and swimming off Pigeon Island. Boat reservations 590-98-89-08.

Jamaica

Jamaica is home to the Caribbean's greatest concentration of all-inclusive resorts, and some of these have been built just to cater to families. Keeping in mind that Mom and Dad's idea of fun may not be quite what the kids had in mind and vice versa, these resorts make it possible for adults to doze in the sun while the kids exhaust themselves with every watersport imaginable. They have children's programs, nannies, washers and dryers, and virtually everything necessary for a *no problem* family vacation.

Jamaica is the third largest and one of the most beautiful of the Caribbean islands. About the size of Connecticut, it was originally called Xaymaca, Arawak for "land of wood and water," from which the current word Jamaica comes. The 120 rivers that run through the island have thrilling rapids for riding, waterfalls for climbing, and gentle waters for swimming and canoeing. Verdant mountain ranges rich in limestone, marble, porphyry, alabaster, shale, and sandstone cover almost half of the island. The dramatic coastline has some of the world's most beautiful beaches, caves, coves, and reefs.

Jamaican cuisine is slightly different than food on some of the other islands. Pimento or allspice is indigenous to Jamaica and constitutes the backbone of Jamaican cooking. Jerk sauces use pimento as well as hot pepper and spices, and jerk chicken and pork are Jamaican specialties in which the meats are marinated for hours in the delicious aromatic sauce. *Bammie* is a toasted flat cassava wafer eaten with fried fish. *Ackee,* Jamaica's unofficial National vegetable, was originally brought from Africa. "Pickapeppa" sauce is found on every café table.

Jamaica has gained a reputation in recent years as a rough place where crime and street vendor hassling is the worst in all the Caribbean, and many travelers, once bitten, never return. Crime exists in Jamaica just as it does in any city in the United States or Canada. The difference between the haves (who are often visitors) and the have-nots (who are often local residents) is often extreme and fuels the incidence of crime. Take the same precautions you would at home: be aware of your surroundings, keep your rental car locked, and don't carry valuables with you. Eager entrepreneurs will approach you on the beach and streets to ask you to buy just about anything, including drugs. A pleasant but firm, "No thank you" will usually discourage them.

Fast Facts:

Visitor Information: Website: Jamaicatravel.com, *U.S: Los Angeles:* 3440 Wilshire Blvd., #805, Los Angeles CA 90010 (213-384-1123, fax 213-384-1780). *Chicago area:* 500 North Michigan Avenue, Suite 1030 Chicago IL 60603 (312-527-1296, fax 312-527-1472). *New York:* 801 Second Avenue, 20th floor, New York, NY 10017 (212-856-9727, fax 212-856-9730). *Florida:* 1320 S. Dixies Highway #1101, Coral Gables FL 33146 (305-665-0557, fax 305-666-7239). *Canada:* Jamaican Tourist Board (1 Eglington Avenue E. Suite 616, Toronto, Ontario M4P3A1 (416-482-7850, fax 416-482-1730). *Jamaica:* 2 St. Lucia Avenue, New Kingston 5 (876-929-9200, fax 876-929-9375). Cornwall Beach P.O. Box 67, Montego Bay (952-4425, fax 952-3587).

Arriving and Departing: Because airlines offer direct flights from the United States and Canada into both of Jamaica's international airports (Kingstown and Montego Bay), you don't have to change planes in Miami or Puerto Rico like you do for many of the other islands. U.S. and Canadian citizens need a passport, birth certificate, or voter registration card with a photo ID. A departure tax of $21 is charged.

Currency: Jamaican dollars are the legal tender, although U.S. and Canadian dollars are accepted in many tourist-oriented businesses.

Language: English is the official language but the Jamaican patois you will hear has a vocabulary all its own. There are lots of words that mean great, cool or A-OK, such as *irie* and *cool runnin's;* the meanings of others, like *soon come,* are easier to decipher.

Meet the People: If you make arrangements before you go, you can hook up with some Jamaican families who have similar interests and spend some of what may turn out to be your most interesting time on the island. Contact the Jamaican tourist board (see above) before you go and tell them when you're arriving and the ages of the family members in your group. They'll try to match you up with a similar volunteer family. If you're about to leave, contact the tourist office in the area in which you're staying.

Best Sweet Treat: Jamaica has some delicious drinks to sample: homemade limeade is out of this world, cola champagne is similar to a light cream soda with a trace of orange and root beer, and Jamaican fruit punch is different wherever you go; it's blended from whatever fresh fruit is on hand or in season and a little coconut milk.

WHERE TO STAY

Keep in mind that comparing the prices for an inclusive resort to a hotel room is misleading. The inclusives cost more per day, putting them into a more expensive category in this book, but you get more for your daily dollar.

Expensive: $250 and up
Moderate: $150–$250
Inexpensive: under $150

MONTEGO BAY

Known affectionately as Mo'Bay, the tourism capital of the country was dubbed "The Gulf of Good Weather" by Christopher Columbus. It's the second largest city in Jamaica and it offers the largest number of guest rooms of any resort area on the island. An international airport makes it easy to come and go, and its stretch of glittering sandy coastline makes it hard to leave.

Expensive

Half Moon Golf, Tennis, and Beach Club and Half Moon Village Villas

Address: P.O. Box 80, Rose Hall, Montego Bay, Jamaica, WI
Telephone: 800-626-0692, 876-953-2211, fax 876-953-2731
Website: www.halfmoon.com.jm

Glamorous Half Moon Club has one of the most comprehensive sports facilities in Jamaica with horseback riding, golf, tennis, and a full selection of watersports. Add to that spacious and luxurious accommodations including villas, a full-service spa, and a lively children's program, and you've got an action-packed vacation done up in a deluxe package. The resort's equestrian center is one of the best in the Caribbean and its international show jumping events have attracted riding luminaries such as Captain Mark Phillips (former husband to Princess Anne). Anyone, even beginners, can saddle up one of their horses and ride along the beach and through the Jamaican countryside or take a lesson in how to play polo. Pony rides for little ones are complimentary.

The main body of the resort houses the hotel, beach, watersports center, eighteen-hole golf course, and riding stables. Another part of the resort, Villa Village, is located across a natural wetlands filled with bird life. It has its own beach, a croquet court, a putting green, shops, and restaurants. Guests are given the use of a car or golf cart so they can easily travel between the two properties.

After playing all day in the kids program or with their parents, children can relax in the Kiddies Lounge on large comfortable throw cushions in the care of nannies (additional cost) who are available to families during their stay. Teens enjoy the Bob Marley movie theater and disco. In case you develop a serious case of sunburn or something more serious, a new medical facility has opened up on the premises to serve residents of the Montego Bay area as well as guests.

Children's Program: The lavishly landscaped grounds that surround the Children's Activity Center have a duck pond, kiddy pool, sandboxes, swings, horseshoes, and a tennis court. Tightly planned daily activities from 8 A.M.– 12 P.M. and 2 P.M.–6 P.M. are arranged for three age groups: three to seven, seven to twelve, and twelve to fourteen, and include nature walks, swimming, games, reggae dance lessons, arts and crafts, and ice cream parties. Private nanny service is available for an extra fee.

Accommodations: 418 accommodations include villas, rooms, and suites. The five- to seven-bedroom villas are situated along the beach and each has a private pool, chef, maid, and butler. Other guest rooms and suites are in cottages along the beachfront, or around a courtyard enclosing a swimming pool. Guests can opt for a number of inclusive plans, all with children's rates.

Special Features: beach, pools, equestrian center, eighteen-hole golf course, shops, beauty salon, restaurants, bars, croquet, squash courts, tennis courts, spa, fitness center, scuba, snorkeling, glass-bottom boat tours, windsurfing, volleyball.

$$$: Daily rates, double occupancy (except villas): rooms $220–$330, suites $280–$600, villas $440–$2,400. Children stay free between April 15 and December 15, otherwise they pay extra.

Round Hill Hotel and Villas

Address: P.O. Box 64, Montego Bay, Jamaica, WI
Telephone: 876-956-7050, fax 876-956-7505
Website: www.roundhilljamaica.com

The secluded enclave of Round Hill rambles across a 98-acre former pineapple plantation fronted by a slender curve of white-sand beach that has an enormous enclosed swimming area with several rafts floating in it. While international jet-setters and film stars make this elegant resort that exudes "old money Jamaica vacation" their retreat, especially in winter, its summer season family discounts are so good that it allows us plebeians to enjoy all that it has to offer. Discounts occur from May through October when a Just for Families program allows children under sixteen to stay free in adjoining hotel rooms. Complimentary nanny service is available for up to five hours each day, and children under twelve are offered 50 percent discount on any meals plan.

If you want a preview of Round Hill's old-style luxury, rent a copy of *How Stella Got Her Groove Back,* which was filmed at the resort. All the stars, including Angela Bassett and Whoopie Goldberg stayed at Round Hill while on location. Other stars throughout the ages who have made Round Hill their vacation stopover include Paul and Linda McCartney, Grace Kelly, Steven Spielberg and family, and Goldie Hawn.

Accommodations: Thirty-six rooms and twenty-seven villas with seventy-four suites. All rooms have refrigerators. The private villas have two to four suites, each with a veranda and living area. Each villa unit has a kitchen where housekeepers cook breakfast and serve it in guests' rooms. Parents can have two rooms for the price of one during the off season.

For Kids: Complimentary nanny service is available for up to five hours each day. Activities include a free tennis clinic daily for kids, donkey rides at the Monday night beach party, and games on the beach. Children's videos are available.

Special Features: swimming pools, private beach, scuba diving, deep sea fishing, five tennis courts (two lit for night play), fitness center, jogging path, shops, shopping shuttle, restaurants, bar, complimentary afternoon tea, evening entertainment.

$$$: Daily rates, double occupancy: suites $340–780, villas $240–$470.

Moderate

Wyndam Rose Hall Beach Resort
Address: P.O. Box 999, Rose Hall, Montego Bay, Jamaica, WI
Telephone: 800-996-3426, 953-2650, fax 953-953-2617
Website: www.wyndham.com

A lavish new water park is helping this well-priced resort reclaim a position as a major player in the Jamaican family resort scene. Handsomely situated at the water's edge on an old 400-acre sugar plantation, it has its own golf course and eighteenth-century great house, Rose Hall, whose murderous mistress is just one of the historical building's claims to fame. The water park is indeed, spectacular, with a lazy river complete with currents for rafting or tubing, two swim-up bars, a water tunnel and rapids area, a 280-foot-long thrill slide, enormous swimming pools, and a 15,000-square-foot pool deck so you shouldn't have too much difficulty finding a deck chair. The stairs to the slide are cleverly concealed in a windmill ruin, and from the top they can venture down the slide or walk to the top of the three terraced pools that cascade down and connect together with short slides. The resort itself is enormous, largely consisting of two concrete blocks of rooms that overlook the pool complex.

Accommodations: 489 standard hotel rooms have two queen beds or one king bed and air-conditioning, patios, or balconies. One- and two-bedroom suites are available.

Children's Program: A supervised program for ages five to twelve is broken into two age groups: five- to eight-year-olds, who enjoy activities such as sing-alongs and scavenger hunts; and nine- to twelve-year-olds who get to tie-dye their own T-shirts and participate in swimming races. The schedule of activities changes each day and includes other fun, such as building sand castles, competing in a mini-Olympics, and volleyball.

Special Features: beach, pools, Jacuzzi, windsurfing, snorkeling, sailboats, tennis, volleyball, golf, shops, fitness center, restaurants, bars.

$$$: From May through September, kids twelve and under eat free and stay free in their parents' room. Discounts of up to 50 percent are given on adjoining rooms. Daily rate, double occupancy: $145–$220.

Sunset Beach Resort and Spa

Address: P.O. Box 1168, Freeport, Montego Bay, Jamaica, WI
Telephone: 876-979-8800, fax 876-953-6744
Website: www.sunsetbeach.com.jm

Newly opened Sunset Beach Resort and Spa is the latest entry in the wide selection of inclusives for which Jamaica is known. Its all-inclusive rates cover just about everything, except for spa services which are paid for à la carte. Two children's programs are offered: one for ages three to ten, another for teens, and they operate throughout the day and into the evening. Formerly the Sea-wind Resort, the recently renovated Sunset is located on a peninsula just outside of Montego Bay on twenty acres landscaped with tropical foliage and swaying palm trees. Many different sports are offered with complimentary instruction. Two of the resort's three swimming pools have swim-up bars, and there are four restaurants so that guests don't get tired of just one menu.

Accommodations: 420 rooms, in three different buildings, all featuring one king bed or two double beds, voice mail, cable TV, in-room safes, and private balconies.

For Kids: For Kid's Sake, the supervised children's program for three- to ten-year-olds offers a variety of activities that focus on ecology, island culture, and arts and crafts. There's building and seashell collecting, magic shows and pajama parties, and even visits from local schoolchildren complete with a pen pal club. For teens, the S-H-A-R-K (which stands for smart, hyped, and radically cool) Club is an activity program of snorkeling trips, tennis tournaments, pool and Olympic games, video game competitions, kayak races, and dancing contests.

Special Features: three swimming pools, four tennis courts, snorkeling, Sunfish sailing, kayaking, windsurfing, paddle boats, hobie cats, shuffleboard, giant chess and checkers, beach volleyball, nightly entertainment, fitness center, disco, electronic slot machine, casino, baby-sitting, beauty salon, shops, car rentals, restaurants, bars, shops.

$$$: Inclusive rates: two adults $268–$595 per night. Children two to twelve $35. Children under two are free.

Holiday Inn Sunspree Resort

Address: P.O. Box 480, Rose Hall, Montego Bay, Jamaica, WI
Telephone: 800-HOLIDAY, 876-953-2485, fax 876-953-9480
Website: www.holiday-in.com

Just five miles from Montego Bay's airport, this Holiday Inn Sunspree propertyoffers all-inclusive options or à la carte hotel rooms with deeply discounted prices for families from April through mid-December, and prices that are quite reasonable during high season. The free-form lagoon-style pools are the central action on the pleasant grounds with a half mile of beach front.

Hotel rooms are plain but clean and attractive, and this resort offers an excellent buy for an inclusive vacation. Children under twelve stay and eat free when sharing a room with their parents. There are programs for all ages of kids, from six months through the teen years that start at 9 in the morning and run until 9 at night. Teens have their own clubhouse on the beach, and disco dance parties and lots of sports. It's a big resort with 523 rooms, which can mean that in peak season you may need to claim a lounge chair around the various freshwater swimming pools early in the day.

Accommodations: 523 rooms and suites are situated around the twelve-acre property in eight different buildings. All have air-conditioning, cable TV, and private balconies or patios.

For Kids: Kids four and up meet at the fully supervised Kids Spree Activity Center where they enjoy organized activity such as pool and beach games, reggae dance parties, puppet shows, crab races, story time, and more. If there are no scheduled activities, children are free to play on the outdoor play equipment and in the wading pool. Older children can take advantage of basketball, volleyball, tennis courts, outdoor billiards, or Ping-Pong. Babies six months and toddlers through age three go to Granny's Nursery, where Jamaican nannies care for them; there are cribs, a soft area for storytelling, toys, videos and books, and special activities depending on the number of kids and their ages. Teens have a clubhouse on the beach, and separate activities such as regular movies, dance parties, and all the sports facilities of the resort.

Special Features: swimming pool, beach, four night-lit tennis courts, basketball, volleyball, fitness center, electronic gaming, disco, nine-hole mini golf, Jacuzzi, kiddie pool, video game room, bars and restaurants, kids disco, and movie room.

$$$: Kids nineteen and under sharing a room with their parents stay free, and twelve and under eat free. Daily rates double occupancy: $135–$180.

NEGRIL

WHERE TO STAY
Moderate

Negril Cabins

Address: Norman Manley Boulevard, P.O. Box 118 Negril, Jamaica, WI
Telephone: 876-957-5350, fax 876-957-5381
Website: www.Negril-cabins.com

Situated at Negril's northern edge, this eco-friendly resort has open-air pavilions housing its restaurants, and charming cabins up on stilts amid swaying palms and tropical plants. Each cabin has two spacious bedrooms with private baths and the real kid pleaser—a tree level balcony. If your family enjoys nature and wants to feel like it's camping without the inconveniences, this is a fun place to unpack your suitcase. The resort grounds are beautiful with a lush junglelike feel, but you'll have to cross a two-lane road to get to the beach. Once you cross the street, there are chairs and chaise lounges on the resort's own section of sand. Guests rooms have standard hotel amenities like hair dryers, in-room safes, and room service, but the Swiss Family Robinson–style setup amid the flora and fauna moves this resort far above the ambience of any chain hotel. Several options for meals are available; the airy Coconut Palm Restaurant serves buffet breakfasts and à la carte dining featuring Caribbean and international cuisine. A relaxed open-air restaurant, Alfresco, features buffet dinners during the week. A poolside bar and grill and beach snack bar feed you while your on the move. Directly behind the property is the Royal Palms reserve.

Accommodations: Ninety rooms, all with telephone, ceiling fans, in-room safes, and balconies. Upgraded rooms have satellite TVs, air-conditioning, and private baths; one-bedroom suites have living and dining areas, pull-out sofas, minibar, patios, air-conditioning, and satellite TVs; some have odd decor like rust-colored shag carpets and leather furniture that doesn't really match the tropical eco-resort feel of the outdoor spaces.

For Kids: There is no official children's program but there are special activities set up throughout the day or week for children—arts and crafts, story time, computer games. A fun scooter excursion for families to hidden areas of Negril is available.

Special Features: tennis, pool volleyball, daily activities, board games, baby-sitting, playground on the beach, restaurants, bars.

$$$: Children under twelve stay free with an adult. Daily rates, double occupancy: rooms (up to three people) $145–$195, suites (up to four people) $250–$300.

FALMOUTH

WHERE TO STAY
Expensive

Franklyn D Resort
Address: Franklyn D Resort, Main Street, Runaway Bay, St. Ann, Jamaica, WI
Telephone: 800-654-1FDR, 516-223-1786, fax 516-223-4815; In Jamaica 876-973-3067, fax 876-973-3071
Website: www.fdrholidays.com

A Girl Friday trained in child care and cooking is assigned to every family at FDR for the duration of their stay. Their job is to make you happy; they'll take the children to the swimming pool, feed or change a baby, prepare the meal of your choice, or disappear when you require privacy. If you want to dine in privacy after the nanny's complimentary 9 A.M. to 4:30 P.M. shift is over, you pay just $3 per hour for after-hours baby-sitting.

The resort's planners have thought of every detail, from the baby gate at the top of the stairways to a children's stool in the bathroom. There's even a permission slip parents must sign in order for their children to play video games. Meals, drinks, excursions, the nanny, and the children's programs are included in the price. There are two small beaches—one protected and shallow and safe for young ones, and the other for teens and adults, with deeper water and interesting coral and fish life. Live entertainment every evening can be attended by just Mom and Dad or by the entire clan.

The Children's Program: FDR cleverly slips education into its program. Children learn about Jamaica's culture and heritage and learn to speak patois. They collect leaves and shells, learn their names, and then use them in crafts projects. The Kiddies Center has eight computers, educational games, and all kinds of toys, and all kinds of toys, and is open from 9 A.M. to 10 P.M. for children ages two to eleven.

Teens have their own supervised daily activities such as bike tours, arts and crafts lessons, trips to nearby Ochos Rios, hikes, treasure hunts, and rap sessions. They can play pinball, pool, and basketball anytime they want.

Accommodations: Each family has its own spacious one- or two-bedroom suite with a kitchen, dining area, and large living room with balcony.

$$$: Prices include all meals, wine, bar drinks, transfers to and from the airport, and use of all sports and entertainment facilities. Children under sixteen are free. Daily rates, double occupancy: $265–$345.

FDR Pebbles

Address: Trelawny Post Office, Jamaica, WI
Telephone: 800-654-1FDR
Website: www.fdrholidays.com

FDR's latest all-incusive property, Pebbles, offers what they call a "soft adventure holiday" that emphasizes learning and outdoor fun. Their signature vacation nanny service is also a part of this new resort. Teens have their own supervised tropical "campsite" where they camp beneath the stars. They also are taken on supervised trips, to beach parties, for hiking, cycling, and on field trips. Dining options include an all-day buffet, and a barbecue area with Jamaican jerk specialties, hamburgers, and hot dogs. Accommodations are in attractive two-story wooden structures on the seafront.

Accommodations: Ninety-six suites have air-conditioning, terrace, two twin beds or one king, and a day-bed.

For Kids: The Small World Kids Club features the latest computer games and an array of supervised activities such as donkey rides, goat races, picnics, shell collecting, and arts and crafts.

Special Features: beach, swimming pool, windsurfing, sailing, scuba, kayaks, snorkeling, glass bottom boat rides, tennis, beach volleyball, basketball, tours, restaurants, bars, disco, fitness center, bicycles.

$$$: Children under 16 stay and eat free. Daily rates per person $175–200.

OCHOS RIOS AREA

WHERE TO STAY
Expensive

Boscobel Beach Resort
Address: Box 63, Ochos Rios, Jamaica, WI
Telephone: 800-859-SUPER, 876-974-3291, fax 876-975-3270
Website: www.superclubs.com

Toddlers through teens who like to stay busy with others their own age will find plenty of action at Boscobel, Jamaica's first all-inclusive resort designed and built specifically for families. Parents will find opportunities for rest and recuperation while the kids are in programs that run from 9 A.M. to 9 P.M., and they may even get a bit of family time if they can lure the kids away from the organized fun. Managed by SuperClubs, who have inclusive resorts throughout the Caribbean, Boscobel is for families who like the beach, big buffets, group activities, and a reasonable price tag. Inclusive here means accommodations, all meals, snacks, cocktails, the children's center, unlimited use of all sports facilities including equipment rental and instruction, entertainment, taxes, and airport transfers with no tipping allowed.

A new "super adventure" adds extreme sports such as rock wall climbing, skateboarding, rollerblading, and flying trapeze to the lineup of activities included in the rates. Optional "extreme" sports such as jet skiing, parasailing, swimming with horses, and mountain biking can be added for an extra fee, all available to older kids as well as adults. The kids program is vast. A special nursery cares for babies and toddlers, the Kids Club offers activities for four- to twelve-year-olds, and teens have a "Jump Up" club all their own. Besides a gorgeous white-sand beach (albeit a bit small) and clear Caribbean waters, there is a minizoo, adventure playground, snorkeling, scuba, kayaking, windsurfing, waterskiing, and tennis. Stay in shape with the fitness center, bicycle rides, and golf.

Accommodations: 207 deluxe rooms and suites have double or king-size beds with single, pull-out sofa beds, twin or bunk beds. All are air-conditioned with minirefrigerators, cable TV, safety deposit boxes, coffeemakers, and CD players. One-bedroom suites and larger junior suites have king-size beds in the bedroom and queen-size sofa beds in the living room. Lanai rooms are suitable for older children or families with one baby.

Children's Program: The Kids Centers are open from 9 A.M. until 10 P.M. daily, with separate daily activities tailored to two- to three-year-olds, four- to seven-year-olds, and eight- to twelve-year-olds. Activities might include tie-dying T-shirts, working in the computer lab, learning tennis, and taking bike excursions. A supervised Teens Jump Up Club has computers, Ping-Pong, pool tables, a movie theater, jukebox and dance floor, and is open from 9 A.M. to 10:30 P.M. Private nannies are available for a small fee, twenty-four hours a day, to watch children of any age.

Special Features: swimming pool, four lit tennis courts, golf (at sister resort, Breezes) volleyball, pool volleyball, fitness room, exercise classes, windsurfing, waterskiing, scuba (with resort certification), snorkeling, kayaking, sailing, banana boat rides, Hobie cat rides, shops, hair salon, laundry, bicycle tours, minifarm, playground.

$$$: Up to two children under fourteen (one per parent), sharing a room with parents, stays, plays, and eats free. Everything is included in the price: meals, snacks, bar drinks, wine, trips and excursions, sports, and tips. Per adult, per night: $179–$479.

Renaissance Grande

Telephone: 800-HOTELS-1, 876-974-2201, fax 876-974-2289
Address: P.O. Box 100, Ochos Rios, St. Ann, Jamaica, WI
Website: www.renaissancehotels.com

This mega-resort—once three separate resorts—has been unified with a central reception area. Now, with 720 rooms, it can get a bit crowded at the beach and pool when the place is full. It doesn't cater exclusively to families, encouraging honeymooners and couples as well, but it does enthusiastically throw the welcome mat out to families. Its kids program, Club Mongoose, has a novel twist: visiting children get to spend time each week at a local elementary school to meet some of the local youngsters, a visit your children are likely to remember for years. The pool is a family favorite, with caves, waterscapes, and a swinging bridge; lucky for the honeymooners that there's a quiet pool just for them.

Accommodations: 720 rooms, all simple, comfortable, and a tiny bit worn. Cabana rooms are larger and have patios that open directly onto the lawn and the beach beyond.

For Kids: Club Mongoose is for two- to twelve-year-olds and has both indoor and outdoor play areas. Meals and snacks are provided on site, and activities might include plant and garden walks, pony rides, reggae dance lessons, slumber parties, and kiddie disco jams.

Special Features: beach, pools, tennis courts, watersports, slot machines, restaurants, bars, disco.

$$$: All-inclusive daily rates, double occupancy: $320–$400; two children under the age of twelve are free.

Moderate

Shaw Park Beach Hotel

Address: P.O. Box 17, Cutlass Bay, Ochos Rios, St. Ann, Jamaica, WI
Telephone: 876-974-2552-4
Website: www.shawparkbchhtl@vwjamaica.com

All rooms have an ocean view at this three-story complex on its own 1,600 foot beach. You can opt for a plan that includes all meals, if you wish, and children nine and under stay free and enjoy a complimentary breakfast, while kids ages ten to twelve stay free.

Accommodations: 118 rooms and two-bedrooms suites.

For Kids: The Minnow Club operates daily from 9 A.M. to 5 P.M., taking a break for lunch. Children between the ages of two and twelve are invited to participate in scavenger hunts, board games, origami, movies, and arts and crafts.

Special Features: pool, beach, sailing, snorkeling scuba, fitness center.

$$$: Daily rates, double occupancy: rooms $123–$226, suites $207–$358

Villa and Apartment Rentals

JAVA (Jamaican Association of Villas and Apartments) has been in business for over thirty years and represents more than three hundred villas, cottages, and condos. 800-VILLAS or 312-883-3485.

WHAT TO SEE AND DO

MoBay Undersea Tours—Nondivers can see the treasures of the undersea realm in a fifty-passenger air-conditioned submarine. The trip past coral reefs and colorful tropical fish and through Montego Bay's marine sanctuary is narrated by experts. 876-979-2281.

Wilderness Resorts, outside of Ochos Rios, offers excursions off the beaten track—jeep excursions, hiking, fishing where if you catch your own, they'll cook it for lunch, tubing, boat rides on a pond, and a mini–petting zoo. 876-974-5189.

Anancy Family Fun and Nature Park in Negril was named for "Anancy" the mischievous spider character in Jamaican folktales and children's storybooks. The park was developed to provide entertainment for the entire family while developing more of an appreciation for the history, culture, and natural beauty of Jamaica. Here's where you can ride a go-cart and then observe cultural exhibits of Jamaican folk arts and crafts, or take a spin on a carousel followed by a walk along a marked nature trail. You will also find an eighteen-hole mini–golf course, minijeeps, a boating lake and a fishing pond where the motto is "you catch it we cook it." Bait and fishing poles are available for a nominal fee. Across from the Poinciana Beach Resort. 876-957-4100 or 800-468-6728.

Valley Hikes out of Port Antonio offers guided walks through the Rio Grande Valley and the John Crow mountains. All day, half day and two-hour hikes of varying degrees of difficulty are led by fascinating and experienced guides who stop along the way to point out plants, herbs, and vegetables and explain how they are used. You'll explore caves with stalagmites and stalactites, and gorgeous waterfalls where you can swim in the pools. These hikes are in remote areas and offer visitors a true Jamaican "backcountry" experience where you won't see many other tourists. 876-993-3881.

Rafting on the gentle Martha Brae River outside of Montego Bay is a popular trip for families, who sit on bamboo rafts steered by experienced pole-wielding raftsmen. You'll cover 3½ miles in about 1½ hours past fern groves, bamboo, bananas, and sugarcane. The river was named for an Arawak Indian who refused to reveal the location of a gold mine to the greedy Spanish. Instead, she took them to the site of the mine and used magic to change the course of the river, drowning herself and the Spaniards. You can book raft trips through most hotels. 876-954-5168.

Rafting on the Rio Grande in Port Antonio carries tourists past people washing clothes, swimming, and bathing in the river. Occasionally musicians serenade from passing rafts in hopes of a tip. Other floating vendors offer cold drinks and souvenirs. Keep a look out to see where the local kids are swimming to identify the best swimming holes, and ask your raftsman to stop for a refreshing dip. The trip takes about three hours, longer if you stop to cool off frequently. 876-993-5778.

Rafting on the Great River in Montego Bay allows you to float along the river surrounded by flora and fauna, led by guides who point sights along the way. You can stop at a riverside stand and grab something to eat and drink. On Thursday nights, a candlelit raft ride takes place with entertainment and food at the end of the journey. 876-952-3732, 876-971-2436, or 876-912-0020.

Walk up **Dunn's River Falls**, a cascading series of broad stone "steps" carved by the swath of cool mountain water that spills to the sea outside of Ochos Rios. Wear your swimsuit, grab the hand of the person above you, and climb the slippery steps. It's best to visit at times or on days when cruise ship passengers are not present, to avoid crowds. $3 adults, $1 children.

Off-shore **scuba diving** is most prominent along the west and north coasts of the island. Montego Bay is famous for its wall dives, and Kingston has Port Royal, the sunken city with sunken ships and beautiful reefs.

Martinique

Le soleil shines brightly on the white-, gray-, and black-sand beaches of Martinique's coastlines. The island's leeward side is classically Caribbean, with soft and gentle waves lapping smooth, calm shores. On its opposite windward Atlantic Ocean shore, the terrain is more rugged, with rough waters crashing on pretty coved beaches and rough-hewn cliffs. The island holds a surprising variety of attractions, with more than just gorgeous beaches to draw visitors.

Centuries ago the Carib Indians called it "Madinina," meaning "Isle of Flowers," and hibiscus, frangipani, bougainvillea, poinsettia, orchids, and anthuriums still cover the land. Fields that once grew sugarcane are now rich in guava, mango, papaya, bananas, pineapple, cinnamon, and coffee. In the tropical rain forests, hikers come across giant breadfruit trees and ferns as big as a house.

A mass of intensely hot gas from Mt. Pelée, accompanied by ash and cinders, smothered the Martinican city of Saint-Pierre in 1902, killing all but one inhabitant. Ruins and a small museum in the rebuilt city, now just a fragment of its former glory, offer the chance to see its touching artifacts.

Martinique is West Indian with a French twist. Haute cuisine mixes with island delicacies from the sea and garden creating a memorable culinary experience almost anywhere you dine. Your sons and daughters may be wide-eyed at the topless sunbathing on most of the beaches, but they are sure to enjoy the mouthwatering baguettes and chocolate brioches they'll find in the local patisseries. English is spoken in most hotels, but the official language is French and it is useful to bring along a French phrase book.

The capital city, Fort-de-France is backed by lush mountains, and criss-crossed by narrow balconied streets. On the other side of the bay opposite Fort-de-France, there are beautiful beaches and the island's greatest concentration of resort hotels.

Fast Facts

Visitor Information: Website: www.martinique.com, or www.martinique. org. *U.S.:* Martinique Promotion Bureau, 444 Madison Avenue, New York, NY 10022 (800-391-4909, 212-838-7855, fax 212-247-6468). *Canada:* French Government Tourist Office, 1981 McGill Avenue, Suite 490, Montreal H3A 2W9 (514-288-4264), or 1 Dundas Street, W, Suite 2405, Toronto Ontario M5G 1Z3 (416-593-4723 or 800-361-9099). *Martinique:* Along the waterfront in Fort-de-France on Boulevard Alfassa (63-79-60). Also at Lamentin Airport.

Arriving and Departing: U.S. and Canadian citizens need passports (even if they've expired within the last five years), original birth certificates, or voter registration cards accompanied by an official photo ID. You must show an ongoing or return ticket. There is no arrival or departure tax unless you are on a charter flight.

Currency: The French franc is the official currency, but U.S. and Canadian dollars are accepted almost everywhere.

Language: French is the official language, and Creole, a blend of French and Spanish, is spoken in rapid-fire speed by many locals. English is spoken in major tourist areas.

Best Sweet Treat: Mouthwatering french pastries are found throughout the island.

WHERE TO STAY

Quite a few family accommodations in Martinique have outdoor kitchenettes on a terrace. Prices show daily rates:

Expensive: over $225
Moderate: $125–$225
Budget: under $125

Moderate

Hotel Sofitel Backoua
Address: Box 589, Fort de France, Martinique, FWI
Telephone: 800-322-2223, 800-763-4835, 800-221-4542, 596-66-02-02 fax 596-66-00-41.
Website: www.frenchcaribbean.com

One of the most stylish resort hotels on the island, the Backoua in the Trois Ilets area south of Fort-de-France is on a beautiful, albeit small, white-sand beach. Guest rooms are in four buildings on the hillside or along the beach. Families are most comfortable in the garden-view building whose rooms connect through communicating doors. A large swimming pool, which seems to spill over one edge into the sea, and the complete watersports center are the center of resort activity during the day. Three restaurants, two bars, and nightly live entertainment draw guests from other hotels. There are two tennis courts, croquet, a golf driving range, and scuba and waterskiing at an extra charge.

Accommodations: All 132 rooms have air-conditioning, balconies or terraces, king-size beds, safe, minibar, terrace. One child under twelve is allowed in garden-view rooms on a roll-away bed. Larger families must reserve rooms with connecting doors.

Special features: beach, swimming pool, two tennis courts, croquet, golf driving range, scuba, waterskiing, restaurants, evening entertainment, bars.

$$$: One extra child under twelve is free in their parents' room. Rates include buffet breakfast and taxes. Daily rates, double occupancy: $157-$716

Moderate

Anse Caritan Beach
Address: P.O. Box 24, Anse Caritan, 97227 Ste-Anne, Martinique, WI
Telephone: 596-76-74-12, fax 596-76-72-59

A hotel popular with French families is Anse Caritan Beach in St. Anne on the southern tip of the island. Its two-bedroom units and studios all have kitchenettes and are scattered around a central entertainment complex containing a restaurant, bar, and complete watersports center. Rates include a full American breakfast.

Accommodations: 140 rooms with kitchenettes on terrace, air-conditioning, and personal safes. Studios hold two people, and two-bedroom units accommodate four.

Special Features: beach, swimming pool, windsurfing, sailing, waterskiing, scuba, canoeing, paddle boat, snorkeling, boat rides, volleyball, boccie ball, billiards, Ping-Pong, car rental, restaurants, and evening entertainment such as dance bands and fashion shows.

$$$: Daily rates, double occupancy: $170-$250.

Diamant Mercure
Address: Point de la Chery near Diamant, Martinique, FWI
Telephone: 800-221-4542 or 596-76-46-00, fax 596-76-2599
Website: www.hotelweb.fr

Many French families stay at this self-contained apartment complex with accommodations in units that seem to spill down a hillside to the sea. All rooms feature views of the azure sea and Diamond Rock. The main hotel building is at the top of the 100-foot hillside, and the climb down to the beach is easy and exciting as little ones anticipate their fun in the sea and sand. But the climb back up at the end of a busy day can seem longer than it really is, so bring a few bribes to motivate tired youngsters. A long water slide whisks kids into a lagoon-shaped freshwater swimming pool and all watersports can be arranged from the resorts watersports center. A shuttle takes guests to Le Diamant and Fort-de-France. Full American-style buffet breakfasts are included in the rates.

Accommodations: Each of the 150 small apartments is basically a sleeping room with a kitchenette on the terrace. The main room has a sofa sleeper and king-size bed, and the kitchen is outfitted with a refrigerator, a two-burner stove, and cookware and utensils.

Special Features: beach, pool, volleyball, Ping-Pong, a game room, and two tennis courts.

$$$: One child under twelve is free in the parents' room. Daily rates, double occupancy: start at $123.

Budget

Hotel Novotel Diamant
Address: Pointe de la Chery, 97223 Le Diamant, Martinique, FWI
Telephone: 800-322-2223, 596-76-42-42, fax 596-76-22-87
Website: www.hotelweb.fr

Tiny kids get their own paddling pool while adults and older children swim and splash in the "grown-up" pool at this popular three-star resort. It spreads over five acres on a peninsula overlooking Diamond Rock and has lovely gardens filled with palm trees, bougainvillea, and other colorful tropical plants. Several restaurants and bars offer everything from fine Creole cuisine to casual poolside lunch-time snacks, and evening entertainment often includes steel band music. A fee is charged for dive trips and waterskiing, Hobie cats, and deep sea fishing trips. Horseback riding trips begin from the ranch next door. The staff speaks English.

For Kids: Available for children ages six to twelve, the Dolphi Club program features a range of recreational and artistic activities such as land- and watersports, games, arts and crafts, canoe outings, and archery. The program operates during July, August, and the winter holiday season from 9 A.M. to 7 P.M.

Accommodations: 181 rooms, including 6 suites all overlook the sea, pool, or gardens and have air-conditioning, a bed and sofa bed, and safe. Connecting rooms are available.

Special Features: swimming pool, windsurfing, canoes, pedal boats, snorkeling, sailboats, introduction to scuba in the pool, two tennis courts, volleyball, excursions, three restaurants, evening entertainment, bars, baby-sitting.

$$$: Two children under the age of sixteen can stay free in their parents' room. Rates include full American breakfast. Daily rates, double occupancy start at $134.

Villas and Gites

The Villa Rental Service run by the Martinique Tourist Office can arrange vacation home rentals. Most of the rentals are in the southern part of the island near good beaches and rented by the week or month 596-63-79-60.

WHAT TO SEE AND DO

St-Pierre on the upper west coast was known as the Paris of the West Indies until 1902, when the Mount Pelée volcano erupted in an avalanche of fire, gas, and molten rock. Three minutes later, all inhabitants of the town were dead except for one person—a prisoner who was jailed in a thick-walled underground dungeon and survived to become a Barnum and Bailey Circus sideshow attraction. The ruins of his cell and other vulcanized buildings still stand. The **Musée Vulcanologique** portrays the tragedy through old photographs and relics excavated from the site, including a melted tuba, blackened spaghetti, and clocks stopped at 8:00 A.M., the time when the disaster struck. Tel. 596-78-15-16. Open 9 A.M.–12 P.M. and 3 P.M.–5 P.M.

Cyparis Express is a little train that tours the historic town. A rather new submarine tour of the Bay of St-Pierre take visitors to see wrecks of ships lost in the volcanic eruption. Reassure your children that the mountain is now very dormant. Contact your hotel for details.

South of St-Pierre, **Le Carbet,** the site where Columbus is believed to have stopped in 1502, is home to the **Zoo de Carbet,** also called the Amazona Zoo. You can get up close and personal with animals from the Caribbean, Amazonas, and Africa, including rare birds, caimans, snakes, and wildcats. Open daily 9 A.M.–6 P.M.. 596-78-00-64.

The dolls in **Musée de Poupées Végétales** are so delicately crafted that from a distance they resemble small porcelain figurines. Upon closer inspection you can see the leaf overskirts, bark dresses, and flower hats that turn them into famous French historical figures. Open daily 7 A.M.–5 P.M. 596-78-53-92. The **Leyritz Plantation,** which houses the Musée, has a hotel, sugarcane factory, and lovely gardens.

The **Martinique Aquarium** displays marine animals from the surrounding water and is a smart stop before heading out on a snorkeling expedition. Don't worry about the piranhas on display; the only ones you'll see on Martinique are in this aquarium. 3 Boulevard de la Marne. 596-73-02-09. Open daily 9–7.

The **Museum of Seashell Art** in Anse a l'Ane has an extensive shell collection as well as shell artwork depicting scenes of daily life on Martinique. Displays include tiny shell farms worked by shell farmers, complete with cows and chickens, a sugarcane harvest, and a seashell depiction of Napoléon's coronation. Open Wednesday to Monday, 9 A.M.–12 P.M. and 3 P.M.–5 P.M. 596-68-34-97.

Puerto Rico

Easy-to-get-to Puerto Rico is just a four-hour flight from New York and a little over two from Miami. Since it's a commonwealth of the United States, American travelers need not hassle passports, foreign money, or long immigration lines. The island was first named Borinquien and was inhabited by several Indian tribes before its "discovery" by Christopher Columbus on his second voyage in 1493. It was renamed San Juan and finally Puerto Rico, which means "rich port." Ponce de León, who was best known as the seeker of the fountain of youth, established a settlement on the island in 1508. His plans for eternal life were thwarted when he died an early death from a poison-tipped arrow in the jungles of Florida. Spain ceded the island to the United States in 1898 following the Spanish-American War, and Puerto Ricans became U.S. citizens in 1917.

Old San Juan, founded by de León in 1521 on the Atlantic (north) coast of the island, is the oldest capital city under the U.S. flag. It's now a National Historic zone with some of the most authentic examples of sixteenth- and seventeenth-century Spanish colonial architecture in the western hemisphere. Visitors can tour the narrow cobblestone streets and see fanciful wrought-iron balconies, plazas, and sidewalk cafés. The two massive forts that once guarded the city still stand strong and invite exploration. Bustling New San Juan is the island's center of business and commerce.

Less than an hour away from San Juan is a lush tropical rain forest and nature reserve known as El Yunque, the only tropical rain forest in the U.S. forest system. Numerous hiking trails wind past 240 species of trees, as well as flowers, waterfalls, and birds.

Hundreds of beaches surround the island. The Atlantic side is popular with surfers, as its powerful waves make for thrilling rides. The calmer Caribbean side of the island has gentle waves and better swimming for little ones.

Puerto Rico's cuisine has been influenced by Spanish, Creole, and native Indian cultures. Local vegetables are used frequently. Delicious plantains are cooked in many different ways, and a variety of beans—especially white beans and garbanzos (chick peas)—are common. *Sofrito,* a garlic, onion, sweet pepper, oregano, tomato puree, and coriander mix, is used as a base for many dishes. Fritters are fast-food snacks found at roadside stands. These include *empanadillas,* stuffed fried turnovers; *surrullitos,* cheese-stuffed corn sticks; *alcapurias,* stuffed green banana croquettes; and *bacalaitos,* codfish fritters. A Cubano sandwich is made with roast pork, ham, Swiss cheese, pickles, and mustard.

Fast Facts:

Visitor Information Website: www.prtourism.com or www. meet-puertorico.com, *U.S.:* Puerto Rico Tourism Company. In New York: 575 Fifth Avenue, 23rd Floor, New York, NY 10017 (212-599-6262 and 800-223-6530). Miami: 901 Ponce de Leon Boulevard., Suite 604, Coral Gables, FL 33134 (305-445-9112 or 800-815-7391). Los Angeles: 3575 W. Cahuenga

Boulevard, Suite 405, Los Angeles, CA 90068 (213-874-5991 or 800-874-1230). *Canada:* Puerto Rico Tourism Company, 41-43 Colbourne Street, Suite 301, Toronto, Ontario M5E 1E3 (416-368-2680, 800-667-0394—within Canada only). *Puerto Rico:* The Puerto Rico Tourism Company's main office is in a restored former nineteenth-century prison on Paseo la Princesa, Old San Juan, Puerto Rico 00902 (787-721-2400).

Arriving and Departing: Puerto Rico is a commonwealth of the United States, and U.S. citizens can travel freely to and from the island. Canadian citizens need proof of citizenship, and a passport is preferred. There is no departure tax.

Currency: American dollars are the official currency.

Language: Spanish is the official language of Puerto Rico, but English is widely spoken.

Caution: Crime is a problem in Puerto Rico, just as it is in many places at home. Avoid deserted beaches, and don't walk alone on a beach at night, even in highly populated areas. Avoid renting an open-air jeep for touring, and plot your route carefully so you don get lost in unfamiliar territory.

On a Budget: Families can save with the Le Lo Lai VIP (Value in Puerto Rico) program. For $10 per person, visitors gain access to a week's worth of activities that highlight the island's musical, folkloric, cultural, and natural attractions. The card can also be used for discounted sightseeing tours of Old San Juan, El Yunque, the Rio Camuy Cave Park, and more. For more information call 787-723-3135 or 787-722-1513.

Puerto Rican music, dance groups, and orchestras perform, and local painters and sculptors display their wares every Saturday at the Puerto Rico Tourism Company's "La Casita" Tourism Information Center located at Plaza Darsenas, adjacent to Pier 1 in Old San Juan. For more information call 787-722-1709.

Best Sweet Treat: The national dessert of Puerto Rico is flan, a delicious condensed milk and vanilla custard with variations made by adding cream cheese, coconut milk, mashed pumpkin, or breadfruit. Stop and try the fresh guarapo juice (sugarcane) at roadside trucks.

SAN JUAN AREA

WHERE TO STAY
Expensive

El San Juan Hotel and Casino
Address: Avenue Isla Verde, Box 2872, San Juan, Puerto Rico 00902
Telephone: 800-468-2818 787-791-1000, fax 787-791-6985
Website: www.wyndham.com

The hand-carved mahogany ceilings and rose marble floors of El San Juan's luxurious lobby exude old world elegance and distinction. Well located, the hotel is ten minutes from the airport, and a short complimentary shuttle bus ride from Old San Juan and El Morro Castle. If you want to explore Old San Juan and your children are too young to appreciate history (or shopping), the resort has a children's program to keep them occupied. The resort is on a busy strand of beach that is lined with high-rise hotels, but its secluded tropical gardens surrounding a large swimming pool complex and patio area make you feel worlds away.

Accommodations: 392 rooms have one king bed or two double beds, air-conditioning, and many amenities. Junior suites have a small separate sitting area and a king-size bed; kitchenettes can be added. One- and two-bedroom suites have a full-size Murphy bed in the living room.

For Kids: Afternoon story time is in the shade of the garden at this full-day program that runs from 10 A.M. to 4 P.M. Children five to twelve are divided into separate age groups to enjoy water basketball, tennis clinics, treasure hunts on the beach, arts and crafts, Spanish lessons, storytelling, and botanical garden tours. The fee includes lunch and all kinds of souvenirs. Teenagers learn merengue and salsa at their own Paradise Club.

Special Features: beach, swimming pools, three tennis courts, shopping arcade, health club, Jacuzzi, shoppers shuttle, watersports, disco, casino, restaurants, bars, baby-sitting, 24-hour room service.

$$$: Children under twelve are free in their parents' room. Daily rate, double occupancy: rooms $355–$595, suites $595–$815.

Caribe Hilton International

Address: Box 1272, San Juan, Puerto Rico 00902
Telephone: 800-468-8585 or 787-721-0303, fax 787-722-2910
Website: www.hilton.com

A boardwalk for strolling is situated along the length of private beach on this deluxe property. Its atrium lobby is beautifully decorated with rose marble, waterfalls, and colorful tropical plants, and its lush grounds even have an antique fort. A children's program operates during the summer and over holiday periods, and Old San Juan is a short taxi ride away.

Accommodations: 668 rooms have two double beds or one king bed and balconies, and roll-aways or cribs can be added. A variety of suites and a full apartment are available.

For Kids: Each week, Holiday Camp Coco has a different theme such as "Ecology Awareness," "Peace on Earth," and "Health and Fitness," with games, arts and crafts, parties, water games, and more revolving around the theme. The camp is offered during Presidents' week, Easter, Summer, Christmas, and Thanksgiving. A special youth center for teens lets them meet other kids, play games, watch movies, dance, and hang out under supervision during Christmas, Easter, and Thanksgiving holidays.

Special Features: beach, two swimming pools, six tennis courts lit for night play, air-conditioned squash and racquetball courts, all kinds of watersports, restaurants, bars, room service, baby-sitting, fitness center.

$$$: Children sixteen and under are free in parents' room. Daily rates double occupancy: $210–$550.

Moderate

The Ritz-Carlton, San Juan
Address: 6961 State Road, #187, Isla Verde, Carolina, Puerto Rico 00979
Telephone: 800-241-3333, 787-253-1700, fax 787-253-0700
Website: www.ritzcarlton.com
   Much to the benefit of its guests, the Ritz-Carlton greedily takes up eight acres of prime oceanfront real estate and lives up to the Ritz-Carlton's reputation by being the ultimate in luxury. The hotel swimming pool edges up to the sapphire blue waters of the ocean, restrained only by lush vegetation. Seven different dining and lounge areas offer guests a complete range of foods from Caribbean to Mediterranean. Daily afternoon tea and drinks are available as well. The Ritz offers a variety of activities, both day and night, from their casino to roaming the cobblestone streets of old San Juan and visiting Spanish mansions and military monuments. The hotel restaurants offer children's menus, so kids can eat all the peanut butter and jelly sandwiches and ice cream sundaes they want.
   Accommodation: 414 rooms and suites with fully stocked refrigerators and honor bars, marble bathrooms with hair dryers, color TV with sports channels and movies, heating and air-conditioning, personal safes. The Ritz-Carlton Club offers seventy-two private luxury rooms, with five complimentary food and beverage presentations throughout the day, and a club concierge.
   For Kids: The Ritz Kids activities program, for ages four to fourteen, invites children to participate in supervised activities such as watersports, arts and crafts, cooking and tennis classes, and spa treatments including manicures, pedicures, facials, and clothed massages.
   Special Features: casino, the spa and fitness center featuring everything from yoga to bodywraps, two lit tennis courts, poolside massages, restaurants, bars, 24-hour room service, an outdoor Jacuzzi, and retail shops. Golf, fishing, horseback riding, and race tracks, waterskiing, sailing, and reefs for diving and snorkeling are all nearby.
   $$$: Daily rates, up to four people: $195–$395

WHAT TO SEE AND DO
Old San Juan—Free open-air trolleys take you through the narrow streets of Old San Juan, past shops filled with folk art from all over the Caribbean, slow-paced sidewalk cafés, department stores, balconied homes, small gardens, and formal squares. Two forts are at either flank, El Morro and San Cristóbal.
   El Morro was constructed by the Spanish from 1540 to 1586 to protect the harbor from invasions, especially from the notorious Sir Francis Drake. Its windswept battlements rise 140 feet above the sea and offer panoramic views of the harbor. Climb through dungeons, towers, and barracks and visit the small museum that explains the history of the fortress. Calle Norzagaray. Open 9 A.M.–4 P.M. daily, 787-729-6960.
   Casa Blanca was built for Ponce de León, who died in the jungles of Florida before he could inhabit it. It now houses the Juan Ponce de León Museum and

the Taino Indian Ethno-Historic Museum, which recreates the life and culture of the Puerto Rico's first inhabitants. Exhibits include a model Indian village and displays of crop cultivation, hunting, and canoe building. Be sure to see the sixteenth-century European maps of the world, reproductions of paintings of Columbus, and charts of his voyage. Tuesday through Sunday 9 A.M.–12 P.M. and 1 P.M.–4:30 P.M., 1 Calle San Sebastián. 787-724-4102.

San Cristóbal was an eighteenth-century fortress designed to guard the city from a land attack. Even bigger than El Morro, it was known once as the Gibraltar of the West Indies. Open 9:15 A.M.–5:45 P.M., 787-724-1974.

Paseo de la Princesa, near the port, is a broad boulevard with flowers, trees, and a playground where the **Children's Theater** has puppet shows, storytelling, and performances every Sunday afternoon.

On Saturdays, prominent Puerto Rican musicians, dance troupes, and orchestras perform; puppet shows are staged; and local painters and sculptors show their work at **La Cast Tourism Center**, Plaza Darkness across from Pier 1 in San Juan.

Puerto Rico's **winter baseball league** features games nearly every night from November through January at San Juan's Hiram Bithorn Stadium. Tickets are about $6 for the finest seats.

Museo del Niño (Children's Museum) is a ten-minute walk from El Morro. Here, small children enter the museum through the legs of a large wooden figure. Hands-on exhibits include a village of playhouses and a puppet theater. Open Tuesday through Sunday, 9 A.M.–3:30 P.M. and weekends 11 A.M.–4 P.M., 787-725-7214. 150 Cristo Street, Old San Juan.

WHERE TO STAY BEYOND SAN JUAN
Expensive

Hyatt Regency Cerromar Beach
Address: Highway 693, Dorado, Puerto Rico 00646
Telephone: 800-233-1234, 787-796-1234, fax 787-796-4647
Website: www.hyatt.com

One of the world's best pools. It's as simple as that. You *might* find a more elaborate water playland somewhere, but you won't find one hidden in more lavish tropical gardens. The Hyatt's 1,776-foot-long river pool cuts a path under waving palm trees, scarlet hibiscus, and blazing purple bougainvillea, through pools connected by curving water slides, past the swim-up bar and a dramatic rocky grotto hiding a large Jacuzzi, under crashing waterfalls, and eventually spills out into a behemoth of a swimming pool flanked by a twisty tube slide. When parents aren't bobbing merrily along with their kids, you'll find them sprawled out on lounge chairs with good books, offering cheery waves as the kids float past. If you can ever get out of the pool, there's a decent beach, ten all-weather tennis courts, a full-service spa and fitness center, and every watersport you can dream up.

The golf courses match the pools in both abundance and quality. There are four of them for a total of seventy-two holes—two eighteen-hole golf courses at Hyatt Cerromar Beach and another two at its sister resort Hyatt Dorado next door—and they offer some of the best play in the Caribbean. When parents are ready to tee off, they can arrange for their kids to sample Camp Hyatt, which offers carefully planned daily fun for kids.

Accommodations: 504 rooms in a modern seven-story building all have a king bed or two queen beds, air-conditioning, spacious bathrooms, and attractive furnishings, in-room safe. Luxurious suites are available on the top floor.

Children's Program: Camp Hyatt for three- to twelve-year-olds is headed by CPR-certified counselors who lead outdoor games, swimming, tennis, and arts and crafts during the day. In the evening, the program features clown and mime shows, movies, talent shows and video games. Parents of children enrolled in Camp Hyatt can obtain a second hotel room, if available, at a 50 percent discount. The camp, which charges a fee, operates from 9–4 and 6–10 and requires registration in advance.

Special Features: four golf courses, tennis, swimming pool, beach, snorkeling, full-service spa, health club, beauty center, bicycling, waterskiing, skate rentals, deep sea fishing, windsurfing, excursions, movies, games, shops, beauty salon, golf and tennis pro shops, car rental, playground, restaurants, casino.

Accommodations: Rooms have two double beds or one king bed, air-conditioning, and suites and connecting rooms are available. A concierge floor makes up the top level with extra services.

$$$: Children eighteen and under free in their parents' room. Daily rates, double occupancy: $215–$465.

Hyatt Dorado Beach Resort and Casino
Address: Highway 693, Dorado, PR 00646
Telephone: 800-233-1234, 787-796-1234, fax 787-796-6065
Website: www.hyatt.com

You won't find the spectacular pool complex at this sister property next door to Hyatt Cerromar beach, but you'll find Hyatt Dorado more intimate and perhaps more elegant. Guests at each resort have charging privileges and the use of all facilities of both establishments, including the pools (Hyatt Dorado has two) and children's programs; shuttles run every thirty minutes between the two. Windsurfing instruction is based here as are other watersports such as deep-sea fishing, jet skiing, parasailing, waterskiing, kayaking, and canoeing.

Accommodations: 298 rooms are in two-story buildings scattered throughout the palm-studded, lavishly landscaped one thousand acres. Ground-floor units have patios. All have a king bed or two double beds, minibars, cable TV, in-room safes, and views of the pool, golf course, or beach. One-bedroom suites are available.

Special Features: two pools, including a lap pool with five lanes, Lisa Penfield Windsurfing School, jet skis, catamaran rides, deep sea fishing, excursions, baby-sitting, car rental, beauty salon, shops, health spa, golf pro shops, restaurants, bars, seven tennis courts, golf courses, movies, bicycles.

$$$: During high season, breakfast and dinner is required; double occupancy adults: $589–$669. Children's meal plan $32 per child three through fifteen; under three free. Room rates rest of year: $175–$350.

El Conquistador Resort and Country Club
Address: Fajardo, PR 00738
Telephone: 800-468-8365, 787-863-1000 fax 787-863-6500
Website: www.wyndham.com

Perched on top of a cliff where the Atlantic and Caribbean Oceans merge, El Conquistador is like a city unto itself with four resort environments including a grand hotel and three distinctive villages, an eighteen-hole golf course, five swimming pools, and its own private island. Water taxis regularly hop the short distance to Palomino Island, a 100-acre private paradise where the children's day camp and watersports center are headquartered. Complimentary snorkeling equipment helps guests explore the coral reefs a few feet from the shore. White-sand beaches fringe the island, and nature trails lead to secluded beaches on all sides of the island.

The main pool complex features three different freshwater swimming pools totaling two acres of pool. A 55-slip marina is the point of departure for deep-sea-fishing charters, sailboat and catamaran trips. El Yunque rain forest is very close by.

Accommodations: Las Casitas Village, designed in the style of Old San Juan, has one-, two-, and three-bedroom villas with full kitchens. La Marna Village has deluxe accommodations overlooking the harbor with its own park and swimming pool. Las Olas Village is tucked into the cliffside, with a glass funicular traversing the cliff, and the grand hotel features everything from standard to superdeluxe hotel-type rooms.

For Kids: Named after Puerto Rico's indigenous singing tree frog, Camp Coqui offers supervised activities seven days a week from 9 A.M.–3 P.M. Daily sessions incorporate cultural and educational activities along with the fun: marine biology talks are followed by snorkeling excursions; children learn to play Taino ball games, native to the Puerto Rican Indians who inhabited the island before European came; and there are scavenger hunts, arts and crafts, and dance and cooking lessons. Ages three to nine and nine to thirteen have separate activities, and older teens have pool parties, Ping-Pong tournaments, sports Olympics, and bonfires. All counselors are Red Cross and Lifeguard certified.

Special Features: beach, five swimming pools, eighteen-hole golf course, seven tennis courts, shopping arcade, fitness center, marina, Sunfish sailing, windsurfers (miniwindsurfers are available for kids), kayaks, boat excursions, restaurants, bars, nightclub.

$$$: Ask about their packages, especially the Family Holiday package during the summer. One-, two-, and three-bedroom casitas $375–$2,170. Grand Hotel rooms $205–$595.

Westin Rio Mar Beach Resort and Casino

Address: 6000 Río Mar Boulevard, Río Grande, PR 00745-6100
Telephone: 800-WESTIN-1, 787-888-6000, fax 787-888-6600
Website: www.westin.com

Golf and tennis fanatics get a lot of mileage at this relatively new resort on Puerto Rico's northeast coast, about nineteen miles east of the international airport. A Peter Burwash Tennis center features thirteen Har-Tru courts with their own shop and center, and two golf courses, designed by international golf star Greg Norman, feature a river flowing through one course and an ocean setting for the other. A 35,000-square-foot clubhouse has a restaurant, golf shops, and full spa facilities. Water lovers find plenty to do, too, as the resort's two oceanfront swimming pools, kiddy pool, and watersports center offers more than most—you'll find jet skis, banana boat rides, and waterskiing, along with more traditional fare. The Camp Iguana program for kids operates during most of the day, and well into the evening, taking a short break for dinner. The seven-story resort buildings stretch along a mile-long broad swath of ecru beach, with lounge chairs and umbrellas studding the sand. All guest rooms, each with a balcony or terrace, look onto the ocean or the Caribbean National Forest, El Yunque. The resort is situated on 481 tropical acres.

Accommodations: 600 guest rooms all feature a king bed or two double beds with private balconies or patios, in-rooms safes, cable TV, coffeemakers, and minibar.

For Kids: Camp Iguana is comprised of three rooms: an arts and crafts room, a general playroom, and a TV room that is convertible to a sleeping room for late-night campers, since the program runs from 9 A.M. to 3 P.M. and again from 5 P.M. to midnight. A range of both indoor and outdoor activities is offered, such as sailing clinics, tennis and golf lessons, arts and crafts, and video games, Morning and afternoon or full days can be booked at a set fee. The evening program chargers an hourly rate of $5 for its young guests. Sleeping mats are provided.

Special Features: beach, pools, two golf courses, thirteen tennis courts, jet skis, wave runners, windsurfers, kayaks, Hobie cats, Sunfish, banana boat rides, parasailing, waterskiing, volleyball, horseback riding, scuba, deep sea fishing, spa, fitness center, children's program, baby-sitting, business center, shops, beauty salon, laundry facilities, 24-hour room service, concierge level, eleven restaurants and bars, full-service casino, day trips to the Bahamas, car rental.

$$$: Daily rates, double occupancy: $475–$575. Children under seventeen free in their parents' room.

Moderate

Ponce Hilton and Casino

Address: Box 7149, Ponce, Puerto Rico 00732
Telephone: 800-HILTONS or 787-259-7777, fax 787-259-7674
Website: www.hilton.com

This attractive upscale resort on eighty acres of lavishly landscaped grounds has a man-made lagoon and beach and offers a summer children's program with daily activities. It is about ten minutes outside of the beautifully restored historical town of Ponce. There's a pool with a waterfall, children's playground, golf practice range, four tennis courts lit for night play, bikes for rent, and all the watersports.

Accommodations: Standard rooms have air-conditioning, ceiling fans, balconies, tile floors, minibar, coffeemaker, and a king bed or two double beds. Suites have bedrooms with king beds and a parlor with fold-out couch, and a Jacuzzi bath.

For Kids: The complimentary youth program is offered during July and August for six- to twelve-year-olds. Kids enjoy crafts, swimming, games, and sports.

Special Features: beach, pool, playground, four tennis courts, bike rentals, three restaurants, casino, shopping arcade, beauty salon, room service.

$$$: Children sixteen and under free in their parents' room. Daily rates, double occupancy: $205–$230. Children have discounts on meals in family programs.

Budget

Parador Villa Antonio

Address: P.O. Box 68, Rincon, Puerto Rico 00677
Telephone: 787-823-2645, fax 787-823-3380

This intimate and pleasant property is in Rincon on the island's west coast near Puerto Rico's championship surfing beaches. Board riders in search of the perfect wave stay here, and so do people who like to sail, snorkel, and go deep-sea fishing. Nearby attractions include surfing beaches such as Los Almendros, Black Eagle, Crash Boat, Aguadilla beach, and Wilderness Aguadilla public beach. There is a swimming pool, tennis courts, and a children's playground on the property.

Accommodations: All fifty-five one-bedroom housekeeping apartments have kitchens. Some units sleep three in a double bed and twin beds, while others can sleep up to six in a double bed, two twin beds, and additional cots.

Special Features: beach, swimming pool, tennis courts, a children's playground.

$$$: Up to two children under twelve stay free in their parents' room in existing bedding. Daily rates, double occupancy $80–$130.

WHAT TO SEE AND DO ON OTHER PARTS OF THE ISLAND

More than 100 billion gallons of water fall annually on **El Yunque,** a vast 28,000-acre rain forest thirty-five miles east of San Juan. It is dripping with waterfalls, crawling with vines, and home to more than twenty kinds of wild orchids, fifty varieties of ferns including giant ferns, and 240 species of trees. Tiny tree frogs calling out lend atmosphere, and many birds, including the rare Puerto Rican parrot, call it home. It's the only tropical rain forest in the U.S. national park system, and it is smart to see it with a tour so as to visit the best waterfalls, viewpoints, and swimming holes. Adjacent Luquillo Beach is shaded by majestic coconut palms and should be visited although it is crowded on weekends. If you forget your picnic basket, local *kioskos* can supply you with something to eat, plus there are lockers and changing rooms. Many hotels provide tours of El Yunque, or you can arrange tours in the park's Sierra Palm Interpretive Center on Route 191 at km 11.6, which is open daily from 9:30 A.M.–5 P.M. General park information: 787-887-2875 or 787-766-5335.

Two hours from San Juan on the north coast is **Arecibo Observatory,** the world's largest radar-radio telescope—as big as thirteen football fields. Scientists study planets and distant galaxies by gathering radio waves from space and operating SETI, the Search for Extraterrestrial Intelligence. Tours are self-guided and you can view the telescope from an observation platform. No admission charge. Tuesday through Friday 2 P.M.–3 P.M., Sunday 1 P.M.–4 P.M. Route 625, Arecibo. 787-787-2612.

Rio Camuy Cave Park, west of San Juan near Arecibo, is an enormous cave system carved out by the world's third largest underground river. Trams take visitors to the mouth, where a foot path winds through the cave to deeper views. Another tram trip leads to a 650-foot-wide sinkhole with platforms suspended over the Camuy River 400 feet below. Call to make reservations before you go. On Route 129 at km 18.9. Open Wednesday through Sunday and holidays 8 A.M.–4 P.M. 787-765-5555 or 787-893-3100.

Las Cabezas Nature Reserve is about an hour-and-a-half from San Juan with a restored nineteenth-century Spanish colonial lighthouse that has breathtaking views of islands as far off as St. Thomas. Boardwalk trails wind through mangrove islands and a bioluminescent lagoon. Ospreys, sea turtles, and an occasional manatee can be seen from the windswept promontories and rocky beach. Route 987. Admission by reservation only on weekdays. Tours to the general public on Friday, Saturday, and Sunday begin at 9:30 A.M., 10:30 A.M. and 1:30 P.M. 787-722-5882.

Centuries-old **Ponce** has a restored area with trolleys, horse drawn carriage rides, and many recently restored historic buildings that might remind you of New Orleans or Barcelona. Its distinctive architecture dates from the mid-1800s to the 1930s when it was the intellectual epicenter of the island. The legacy thrives today in lively art galleries, museums, theaters, and a remarkable number of professional schools and universities for a town this size. Its beautiful downtown plaza has fountains, park benches, gardens, and sidewalk cafés. There are many beautiful buildings within walking distance of the main plaza, but your children will especially enjoy red-and-black-striped **Parque de Bombas Firehouse Museum,** on one side of the plaza, with its antique firetrucks, equipment, and memorabilia. Open Wednesday–Monday 9:30 A.M.–6 P.M. 787-284-4141, ext. 342.

Just outside of town is the oldest-known Indian burial site in the area, **Tibes Indian Ceremonial Park,** where you can explore seven ceremonial ball courts, two dance grounds, and a re-created Taino Indian village. A museum on the premises displays Indian ceremonial objects, jewelry, and pottery. Open Tuesday–Sunday 8 A.M.–4 P.M.. Route 503 at km. 2.7. 787-840-2255.

Mayagüez, Puerto Rico's third largest city, has the **Mayagüez Zoo,** showing off forty-five acres of tigers, reptiles, birds, and mammals plus a lake and children's playground. Route 108 at Barrio Miradero. 787-834-8110. Open Tuesday–Sunday 9 A.M.–4:30 P.M..

Phosphorescent Bay at La Parguera—The sea comes alive with dazzling sparks of life on moonless nights in La Parguera. Boats leave for the bay about every half hour from just past dusk to 10:30 P.M. The millions of microscopic dinoflagellates light up when they are disturbed by movement. Boat crews dump buckets of seawater on the deck so you can see the "fireflies of the sea" up close. $4 per person.

The **baseball** season runs from October through April, and stadiums are in San Juan, Ponce, Santurce, Caguas, Arecibo, and Mayagüez. The tourist office can give you a schedule of games, or contact Professional Baseball of Puerto Rico at 787-765-6285.

St. Barthélemy

St. Barts is fashionably French, with its haute cuisine, French bakeries, sidewalk cafés, and monokinis. Yet it maintains a strong element of "Caribbean casual" throughout its 8 square miles of low green mountains, its sparkling coral sand beaches, and quaint red-tile-roofed capital port city. Its understated glamour is reflected in its stylish continental visitors and its *trés chic* prices.

Columbus "discovered" this island in 1493 and named it for his brother Bartolomeo, but the Carib Indians living on the island called it Ouanalao, meaning "Land of the Hummingbirds." Now nicknamed St. Barts, its first successful European settlers were colonists from Brittany and Normandy. Later, the island became a popular port of call for pirates, privateers, and buccaneers who provided defense and protection for the inhabitants in exchange for provisions. The islanders were more than happy to have the pirates spend their quickly gained fortunes in the island's shops and taverns. St. Bart's most famous pirate was Captain Montbars (also known as Montbars the Exterminator), a Frenchman who is thought to have buried his treasure on the island.

The buccaneers dubbed the capital Carenage, as it was here that the careening (scraping of barnacles from the hulls) of their ships took place. Later its name was changed to Gustavia.

Renting a villa is the most popular way to vacation on the island, and there is a large selection of styles, sizes, and prices. It's an easy island to explore by car, and you should plan to rent one whether you stay in a villa or hotel. Be sure to book it when you make your reservations, as cars can get scarce during high season. St. Barts is known for its fine cuisine.

Fast Facts:

Visitor Information Website: www.st.barths.com. *U.S.:* France on Call 202-659-7779, French Government Tourist Office, 444 Madison Avenue, New York, NY 10022, or 9454 Wilshire Boulevard, Suite 715, Beverly Hills, CA 90212 (310-271-6665), or 676 N. Michigan Avenue, Suite 3360, Chicago, IL 60611 (312-751-7800). *Canada:* French Government Tourist Office, 1981 McGill College Avenue, Suite 490, Montreal, Québec H3A 2W9 (514-288-4264). *St. Barts:* Office du Tourisme on the Quai Général de Gaulle across from the Capitainerie in Gustavia (590-27-87-27, fax 590-27-74-47). Mailing Address: St. Barts Tourist Office B.P. 113, Gustavia, 97098 Cedex, St. Barthélemy, FWI.

Arriving and Departing: U.S. and Canadian citizens need proof of citizenship in the form of a valid or recently expired passport or a voter registration card or notarized birth certificate, both accompanied by official photo IDs. A departure tax of 30 francs (about $6) is charged.

Language: The official language of St. Barts is French, although many hotel and restaurant staff speak a little English.

Money: The official monetary unit is the French franc, but many stores and restaurants accept American dollars.

Best Sweet Treat: Stop at any of the French *patisseries* for delicious pastries and cakes.

WHERE TO STAY

Expensive: over $225
Moderate: $125–$225
Budget: under $125

Expensive

Guanahani

Address: Box 609, Grand Cul de Sac, St. Barthelmy 97098 FWI
Telephone: 800-223-6800 or 590-27-66-60, fax 590-27-70-70
Website: www.st-barths.com/guanahani

This posh resort, the island's largest, is situated between two rather different beaches, one protected and calm, and the other with rolling ocean waves. Its seven acres of gardens and West Indian–style cottages trimmed with gingerbread spill down a hill crest of Grande Cul de Sac Beach. A magnificent freshwater swimming pool and Jacuzzi overlook the exclusive beach, and many rooms have their own private pools. Coral reefs just offshore feature excellent snorkeling. There are two restaurants, one casual, serving breakfast and lunch by the pool, and one serving French cuisine. Cookies and ice are delivered to your room each afternoon. Two night-lit tennis courts, a full watersports facility, boutiques, and room service are all available.

Accommodations: The resort's seventy-five rooms are housed in bunga-lows, all have air-conditioning, ceiling fans, minibar, satellite TV and VCRs. One- and two-bedroom suites and deluxe rooms can be combined in a variety of ways for families. Suites consist of a living room and bedroom and have private pools or Jacuzzis.

Special Features: two swimming pools, fishing, snorkeling, peddle boats, canoes, windsurfers, waterskiing, deep-sea fishing, aerobics classes, boat ex-cursions, beauty salon, massage, shop, library, car rental, 24-hour room ser-vice, Jacuzzi, fitness center, two night-lit tennis courts, tennis pro, nonmotorized watersports.

$$$: Children under six are free in their parents' room. Rates include con-tinental breakfast served in your room or American breakfast buffet, all service charges, and taxes. Daily rates, double occupancy: deluxe rooms $250–$800, suites $530–$1,400.

Filao Beach
Address: Box 667, St. Barthelmy 97899 FWI
Telephone: 590-27-64-84, fax 590-27-62-24

Breakfast is served on your private terrace or by the pool at this Relais et Chateau hotel on bustling St. Tropez–style St. Jean beach, one of St. Barts's most popular sandy strands. The breakfast is included in your rates, and is American style during the winter and continental during the off-season. A pool, complete watersports center, boat charter, good service, and casual French scene keep many guests coming back year after year.

Accommodations: Thirty rooms in fifteen bungalows vary in price accord-ing to proximity to the beach. All have air-conditioning, a refrigerator, double and single beds, and small sitting area. Roll-aways are available; rooms are big enough to accept one extra child or a small child and a baby.

Special Features: beach, pool, watersports, restaurant, bar.

$$$: Children are free to age three in room with parents; third person $50–$60 per night. Daily rate, double occupancy: $240–$640.

Moderate

Emeraude Plage
Address: Baie de Saint-Jean, St. Barthelmy, 97133 FWI
Telephone: 590-27-64-78, fax 590-27-83-08

Right next door to Filao Beach Hotel on the lively beach at St. Jean with its chic bistros and sidewalk cafés, this bungalow-style hotel has spacious family-style units with outdoor kitchenettes on the terrace. It's situated around a green lawn and tropical gardens bordered by beautiful white sands—just step out of your bungalow and you're on the beach. Supermarkets, shops, and cafés are in easy walking distance of this hotel. Kids under thirteen are free in their parents' room, which is a rarity in the French Caribbean.

Accommodations: Thirty bungalows with one or two bedrooms have air-conditioning and ceiling fans. Bungalows have an equipped kitchenette outside on the terrace.

Special Features: beach, sailing, scuba, snorkeling, windsurfing, wave runners, volleyball, library.

$$$: Daily rates, double occupancy: $135–$380.

Villa rentals

Many people prefer renting their own private villa when they visit St. Barts, and the hillsides are dotted with everything from simple accommodations to the most luxurious. The following companies handle a large number of villas. Most of them have staff who greet guests at the airport, escort them to their villa, and are their on-island contacts should there be any problems.

St. Barth Properties, Inc. handle simple to ultradeluxe private villas scattered throughout the hills of St. Barts. 2 Master Drive, Franklin, MA 02038 (800-421-3396 or 508-528-7727, fax 508-528-7789).

SIBARTH (tel. 590-27.62.38) is managed in the U.S. and Canada by WIMCO 800-932-3222, Newport, Rhode Island; they are the rental agency for two hundred villas and apartments throughout the island.

WHAT TO SEE AND DO

St. Bart's capital city **Gustavia** has the charm of a small port city. A steady stream of dinghies and small boats enters and leaves the harbor. Pleasant walkways and plenty of sidewalk cafés invite visitors to stop, snack, and watch the action. The **Musée de St. Barthélemy** showcases the island's history through photographs, documents, costumes, etc. Open Monday–Friday 8:30 A.M.–12:30 P.M.and 2:30 P.M.–5:30 P.M. (no phone), Saturday 8:30–noon. Kids under twelve are free.

All of St. Barts's beaches are lovely, but a few are worthy of special mention. Secluded **Anse du Gouverneur Beach** is reputed to have buried treasure somewhere under its sands. From it, in clear weather, you can see the islands of Saba, St. Eustatius, and St. Kitts. **Anse du Grand Galet** near Gustavia is known as shell beach, and you can spend happy hours sifting for natural treasures from the sea.

In the town of **Corossol,** visit the **Ingénu Magras Inter-Oceans Museum,** a remarkable collection of 100,000 seashells that is the second-largest private seashell museum in the world. Open daily 9 A.M.–5 P.M. (Tel. 590-27-62-97). Residents of the town are known for the exquisite woven hats, bags, and mobiles they offer for sale. Some of the older women still wear the white sunbonnets called quichenottes (kiss-me-not-hats).

Scuba Diving is known as "Plongée" in the French-speaking part of the Caribbean. The most popular dive spots are around the islet of Pain du Sucre because of its sheer drop-off, cave, coral, and sponges. Les Petits Saintes—several small islets off the western edge of Gustavia harbor—are home to sea turtles. If your hotel doesn't have a dive center, Club Labulle Oceanmust (590-27-62-25) caters to beginners and children.

St. Kitts and Nevis

St. Kitts and Nevis have more monkeys than people. The French brought the African green or vervet monkeys centuries ago as food tasters, and now these hardy creatures make themselves comfortable in the islands' rain forests. Another imported animal that still thrives, the mongoose, was brought from India to rid sugarcane fields of rats. Unfortunately, the rats slept during the day and mongoose slept at night, so the rats remained and the mongoose flourished at the expense of nonpest native species. Sugarcane is still grown on St. Kitts, the larger of the two islands, while tourism has replaced cane as the leading source of revenue on Nevis.

Columbus sighted St. Kitts in 1493 and named it Saint Christopher after the patron saint of travelers. Its nickname, St. Kitts, stuck, and its British colonizers in 1623 changed its name permanently. Don't miss the chance to explore Brimstone Hill Fortress, a gigantic fort the British strategically placed at the crest of a hill overlooking the island and sea. It took over one hundred years to construct.

Nevis was named by Columbus during his second voyage to the New World upon seeing its mountain peak topped with snowy white clouds. *Nieves* is the Spanish word for snow. Greener and less developed than St. Kitts, it is known for its gracious plantation inns and as the birthplace of Alexander Hamilton, born in Charlestown in 1755. Hamilton left the island at age seventeen to continue his education, and ultimately died in a duel with Aaron Burr. His former home now contains the museum of Nevis history. Two special Nevisian resorts have much to offer families: the posh Four Seasons and the nature-rich Golden Rock Inn.

Fast Facts:

Visitor Information: Website: www.stkitts-nevis.com or www.stkitts nevis.com, *U.S.:* St. Kitts and Nevis Tourist Board: 414 East 75th Street, New York, NY 10021 (212-535-1234, 800-582-6208, fax 212-734-6511). *Canada:* St. Kitts and Nevis Tourist Office, 365 Bay Street, Suite 806, Toronto, Ontario, M58 2V1 (416-368-6707). *St. Kitts:* Tourist Board, P.O. Box 132, Pelican Mall, Basseterre (869-465-4040). *Nevis:* Tourism Office, Main Street, Charlestown (869-469-1042, fax 869-465-1066).

Arriving and Departing: U.S. and Canadian citizens need to show passports or original birth certificates with an official photo ID. All visitor's must show a return or ongoing ticket. A 45-minute ferry service between Basseterre on St. Kitts, and Charlestown on Nevis, runs regularly. Departure tax of $11.50.

Currency: Eastern Caribbean dollar (EC$) is the official currency, but American dollars are widely accepted.

Best Sweet Treat: The island has rich and creamy coconut fudge.

ST. KITTS

WHERE TO STAY
Moderate

Ocean Terrace Inn
Address: P.O. Box 65, Basseterre, St. Kitts, WI
Telephone: 800-524-0512, 800-742-4276, fax 800-524-1057 or 869-465-2754
E-mail: tdcoti@caribsurf.com

Manicured tropical garden terraces spill down a lush green hillside over-looking the Basseterre harbor. The landscaped gardens have antique cannons, caged parrots, a rock grotto, bench swings, and several swimming pools, including one with a grotto-themed waterfall and swim-up bar. Comfortable suites with kitchens are most suitable for families.

The OTI, as the locals call it, is a ten-minute walk from downtown Basseterre. The resort's three swimming pools (and most rooms) have views of the Basseterre harbor and the sea beyond. A daily shuttle goes to Turtle Beach, one of St. Kitts's most beautiful beaches on the northeast peninsula where the hotel has a watersports center (complimentary snorkeling equipment) and a restaurant/grill; guests have signing privileges at both.

Accommodations: Seventy-three rooms, all with air-conditioning. One-bedroom suites have full kitchens, spacious dining areas, two queen beds in the bedroom and a living area with a fold-out couch. A second bedroom can be added. Other rooms in the hotel have connecting doors.

Special Features: three swimming pools, restaurants, beach shuttle, beach bar, snorkeling.

$$$: Children under twelve are free in their parents' room. Daily rates, double occupancy: hotel rooms $130–$170.

Sun 'n Sand Beach Village
Address: Frigate Bay, P.O. Box 341, Basseterre, St. Kitts, WI
Telephone: 800-223-6510, 869-465-8037, fax 869-465-6745

An Ice Cream Parlor, well-stocked minimarket, bank, and gift shop are a few steps away from the resort's simple studio and two-bedroom cottages that allow families to save by doing their own cooking. At the back of the resort is the Atlantic beach, great for building sand castles but a bit rough for swimming on most days. The Caribbean beach is a 10-minute walk away. A freshwater pool with a slide is in the middle of the rather plain grounds and a separate pool is designated just for adults. It's a popular enclave for British guests, who economize by renting a car to explore the island for a few days and headquarter for the rest of their stay at the Sun 'n Sand.

Accommodations: Two-bedroom cottages and studio apartments aren't fancy but are very serviceable. A well-stocked minimarket has anything you need. Other condo and apartment renters in the area come here to stock up, too.

Special features: pool, beach, restaurant, bar, market, bank, shop.

$$$: Daily rates, double occupancy: studios $95–$190, cottages $170–$280. Extra person in room $20 per day. Baby cribs are $5 per day.

WHAT TO SEE AND DO

Brimstone Hill Fortress sprawls across a strategic hillside eight hundred feet above the Caribbean. Its massive walls were built of igneous rock by thousands of slaves who worked over the course of a century. One of the best-preserved fortresses of its type in the Caribbean, it was once so intimidating that ship captains changed course rather than come within range of its powerful cannons. A tour of this fort fuels a child's imagination; stand in the damp dark rooms of the officers quarters; marvel at the immensity of each volcanic brick and the tremendous effort and skill required to cut and place them; straddle any of the many cannons and imagine crowds of militia getting blasted by volleyball-size iron balls. Green grassy areas and stone stairways separate areas of the fort, allowing for plenty of exercise. On the main road northwest of Basseterre. Open daily 9:30 A.M.–5:30 P.M. No phone. A small admissions fee is charged.

Signs off Main Road near Old Road Town direct you to Romney Manor, which houses **Caribelle Batik**, where artisans handprint fabric by the ancient Indonesian method. Visitors can watch the artisans work; questions are welcomed. The manor is set in a large tropical garden. Open Monday through Friday from 8:30 A.M. to 4:00 P.M. 869-465-6253.

Young stamp collectors should stop in at the **St. Kitts Philatelic Bureau** (open weekdays from 8 A.M. to 4 P.M.) on the second floor of the Social Security building on Bay Street in capital city Basseterre (869-465-2521).

A colorful **produce market**, weekends only, takes place on Bay Street.

The Sugar Factory tour shows kids how sugar is made during the cutting season, from February through July. Call the Department of Tourism for details. The factory is between the airport and Basseterre.

NEVIS

WHERE TO STAY
Expensive

Four Seasons

Address: Box 565 Charlestown, Nevis, WI
Telephone: 800-332-3442, in Canada 800-268-6288, 869-469-1111, fax 869-469-1112.
Website: www.fourseasons.com or www.fshr.com

It's hard to find a superluxury resort with world-class cuisine and exquisite service that is truly welcoming to families, but this Four Seasons manages to put out the welcome mat with warmth and style. Situated along a strand of sparkling white sand, there is every watersport imaginable, a spectacular golf course (voted one of 1997's top five golf resorts in the world by *Condé Nast* readers), swimming pools, tennis, and one of the most creative children's programs in the Caribbean.

Pricey and posh, this resort pampers with a vengeance; guests need not even wipe their own brows as staffers patrol the beach and pool offering sunbathers cooling spritzes of chilled Evian and iced facecloths. The kids program (best for ages three to nine) operates on a drop-in basis and integrates the culture of the islands—food, folktales, crafts, animals, and music—into its lively and varied daily program. Well-trained baby-sitters are easily arranged any time of day or evening for children under three. Children can order from the children's menu or order half portions from the adult menu, half price.

Guests can swing rackets on ten tennis courts, play golf, get a message, play croquet on a perfectly manicured croquet court, or work out in the Four Seasons well-equipped exercise room. Children's beach toys are available at the watersports center, as are all kinds of boats and adult water toys.

Guests stay in two-story "cottages" that are oddly reminiscent of elongated Swiss chalets. Each cottage contains twelve spacious and lavishly appointed rooms or suites, many with connecting doors, and either a second-story screened porch or a first-floor patio just steps from the beach. Villas can be rented along the golf course overlooking the sea.

Accommodations: 196 rooms. Spacious standard rooms have two queen beds or one king (a roll-away can be easily added). Suites are larger and have varied configurations. Many rooms have connecting doors for families, and all have air-conditioning and ceiling fans and window screens, coffeemakers, personal safes. A complimentary washer and dryer is located in all buildings, each of which houses twelve of the rooms, called "cottages." Upstairs rooms have large screened porches with lounge chairs while bottom-floor rooms have patios. Luxury villas have multiple bedrooms.

Children's Program: This well-planned program for children ages three to nine operates from 8 A.M. to 6 P.M. in a cheerful room filled with all kinds of enticing toys. Different local foods, folktales, music, plants, and wildlife are highlighted each morning with stories, outdoor exploration, and art and cooking projects. Croquet, tennis, and outdoor games take place during the early morning and late afternoon to avoid the intense midday tropical sun. Breakfast and lunch are provided through room service. Parents can bring kids under three to play with the many toys, but they must remain with their children. Baby-sitters are available anytime for the younger children. Three days a week a junior snorkeling program is offered for children ages eight to twelve, and tiny tots tennis lessons (ages three to six) and Mousersize workouts (ages three to six) are also offered.

Special Features: ten tennis courts (four clay, six all weather), three night lit, snorkeling, scuba diving, windsurfing, sailing, waterskiing, two swimming pools, Jacuzzi, fitness center, hair salon, daily exercise classes, lawn croquet, horseshoes, volleyball, two restaurants, three bars, car rental, 24-hour room service, weekly West Indian nights, children's menus.

$$$: Daily rates, double occupancy: rooms $275–$685, suites $810–$1,860. Be sure to inquire about summer family packages, which can reduce the posted low-season rate.

Moderate

Oualie Beach Hotel
Address: Nevis, WI
Telephone: 800-682-5431, 869-469-9735, fax 869-4469-9176
Website: www.oualie.com

Situated on a beautiful white-sand beach in a sheltered bay with calm shallow water, Oualie Beach Club has one of the island's most complete watersports center with Sunfish sailing, snorkeling, fishing excursions, and yacht charters. Its dive shop, the only one on the island, has a NAUI certified instructor and two thirty-foot custom dive boats. Forty different dive sites are currently visited. Twenty-two rooms in pastel gingerbread cottages all have ocean views. Saturday night is Caribbean night with a string band and a carnival masquerade troupe dancing to traditional drumming rhythms and a west Indian buffet. The children's menu is simple, healthy, and sensible. The resort also handles villa rentals above the bay. Windsurfing right off the beach is popular and the on-site windsurfing school, Windsurfin Nevis, supplies Mistral equipment, and the trade winds provide the power. Mountain bike tours also operate from the hotel, and rides take you around the island and through historic trails with rides to suit all levels of ability. On Sundays Oualie Beach features a round-the-island bike ride with members of the Team Nevis race club that is open to anyone who wishes to join—it's a great way to tour Nevis.

Accommodations: Twenty-two rooms, all with screened verandas and ceiling fans, in-room safes, refrigerators, cable TV, minibar, air-conditioning, and one queen bed or two double beds. Studios have full kitchens and can connect to adjoining bedrooms.

Special Features: beach, scuba diving, windsurfing, deep-sea fishing, snorkeling, boat charters, Sunfish sailing, mountain bikes, island tours, restaurant, bar, nightly entertainment.

$$$: Children twelve and under stay free in parents' room. Daily rates, double occupancy: rooms $140–$225, studios $203–$255. Scuba and windsurfing packages are available.

Golden Rock Plantation Inn
Address: Box 493, Gingerland, Nevis, WI
Telephone: 869-469-3346, fax 869-469-2113

Wild African green monkeys frequently play in this unusual plantation inn's gardens where families can stay in a restored two-story sugar mill made of hand-carved lava stones. Take the Golden Rock Nature Trail into the rain forest behind the hotel to see more of the local monkeys or peek from behind the monkey blind for a view of the frolicking primates—the resort sits on a ninety-six-acre natural preserve. Golden Rock is located in Gingerland, the lushest part of Nevis, where gardens flourish and ginger was once grown for export. Naturalist programs such as guided hikes, slide shows, and cultural programs are a trademark of Golden Rock and are tailored to guests' interests and ages. If you're staying elsewhere on Nevis, arrange to come for lunch so your children can hike the nature trail and explore the monkey-filled grounds.

The hotel has a pavilion on Pinneys Beach with lounge chairs, its own a restaurant bar, and a watersports center with towels, and a free shuttle leaves the resort at 10:30 A.M. and returns at 3 P.M. Activities for guests include West Indian storytelling, slide shows on native flora and fauna, and other cultural programs throughout the week. The hotel's large spring-fed swimming pool is a good place to cool off after a hike.

Accommodations: Sixteen rooms. Twelve cottages overlook the Caribbean Sea; most are separated into two bedrooms that connect through the deck, one with a king-size bed, one with two single beds; each have bathrooms. The largest cottage has three bedrooms. The sugar mill has a king and a double and two single beds on two levels, with full bathrooms on both floors. Cribs are available. An excellent restaurant serves breakfast, lunch, and dinner.

Special Features: beach accessible via shuttle, spring-fed swimming pool, game room with bumper pool, board games, books, and chess, restaurant, nature walks, tennis court.

$$$: Daily rates, double occupancy: $130–$235. Breakfast or dinner can be included in the rates. Food charge for kids thirteen and under is 50 percent off with modified American plan.

WHAT TO SEE AND DO

Caribbean Cove—Located about one mile outside of capital city of Charlestown, this two-acre facility, nicknamed "the Cove," features an eighteen-hole miniature golf course that follows the history of Nevis, bumper boats, an arcade, entertainment, and a restaurant/bar. Open noon to midnight during the tourist season. 869-469-1286.

Glass Bottom Catamaran rides—Daily cruises that tour along the coastline of St. Kitts include lunch and snorkel stops. A sunset cruise is available in the late afternoon. Trips start at Cades Bay Beach from the Mariners pub.

ST. LUCIA

A drive-through volcano? You *can* view the bubbling, belching, stinky, steaming seven-acre crater through the car window if you want, but you'll feel the heat and smell the sharp sulfur fumes if you explore the rocky moonscape of dormant Mt. Soufrière on foot. More evidence of St. Lucia's volcanic past can be seen in the twin peaks, known as the Pitons, that dominate the landscape and rise abruptly from the sea for almost a half mile.

But don't think for a minute that St. Lucia is harsh and covered in lava. It's one of the most lush and beautiful islands in the Caribbean, combining acres of emerald green hillsides and banana plantations with near-perfect beaches. A protected national rain forest covers nineteen thousand acres of mountains and valleys with giant ferns, wild orchids, and exotic wildlife. This mango-shaped island grows enormous quantities of mangoes, (over one hundred varieties), breadfruit, coffee, limes, vanilla, nutmegs, and other fruits, vegetables, and spices, and is one of the leading banana exporters in the Caribbean

St. Lucia didn't escape the island battles that took place throughout the Caribbean, and in the eighteenth century alone, it changed hands fourteen times between the French and British. The British finally won out, but St. Lucia still has a strong French influence, particularly in the dialect spoken by the people.

The island has become a center for yacht charters, especially at the beautiful anchorage town of Marigot Bay where the Moorings' fleet is headquartered. St. Lucia's location in the southern Caribbean between Martinique and St. Vincent means that many islands are within easy sailing distance.

Fast Facts:

Visitor Information: Website: www.stlucia.org. *U.S.:* 800 Second Avenue, Suite 400-J New York, NY 10017 (212-867-2950 or 888-4-STLUCIA, fax 212-867-2795) *Canada:* 4975 Dundas Street West, Suite 457, Etobicoke "D" Islington, Ontario M9A 4X4 (800-456-3984 or 416-236-0939, fax 416-236-0937). *St. Lucia:* St. Lucia Tourist Board at Pointe Seraphine complex on Castries Harbor (758-452-4094, fax 758-453-1121).

Arriving and Departing: U.S. and Canadian citizens must present a valid passport and an ongoing or return ticket. Departure tax is $20 per person.

Language: English is the official language of St. Lucia, but a French-based patois can be heard due to the islands early French influence.

Currency: The official currency is the Eastern Caribbean dollar (EC$), but U.S. dollars are readily accepted.

Best Sweet Treat: nutmeg ice cream is an island speciality.

WHERE TO STAY

St. Lucia has a number of all-inclusive resorts that fall into the expensive category of accommodations. Note that you get many extras, including food and activities, for the price listed when you comparison shop. Daily rates:

Expensive: over $225
Moderate: $125–$225
Budget: under $125

Expensive

Windjammer Landing
Address: Box 1504, Labrelotte Bay, Castries, St. Lucia, WI
Telephone: 800-743-9609, 758-452-0913, fax 758-452-0907
Website: www.wlv-resort.com

Patterned after a white-washed, red-tile-roofed Mediterranean village, Windjammer Landing offers private villas (many with their own plunge pools), the concierge services of a hotel, and a full-scale daily children's program. The spacious villas are tucked away with seclusion in mind within Windjammer's fifty-five acres of scented gardens, waterfalls, footpaths, and foliage. Five different restaurants offer everything from local Caribbean dishes and wood-oven fired pizza to fancy international cuisine.

All guests enjoy complimentary watersports. In addition there's tennis, a children's playground, two large pools, a children's pool, and a beautiful crescent of white-sand beach.

Accommodations: One- to four-bedroom three-story villas have ceiling fans, air-conditioning, living and dining rooms, full kitchens, and plunge pools. Some villas have sofa beds (you must request them), but most accommodate two people in each bedroom. If a family does not want an entire villa, the villas can be divided into superior and deluxe rooms, both of which have private baths, minifridge, coffeemakers, and small sitting areas.

For Kids: The complimentary program for four-to-twelve-year-olds is open year-round from 10 A.M. until 4 P.M. Kids can drop in and out as they wish, and participate in beach Olympics, treasure hunts, nature walks, art classes, peddle-boat rides, calypso and limbo lessons, and more.

Special Features: beach, swimming pools, wading pool, waterskiing, windsurfing, snorkeling, banana boat rides, scuba fishing charters, restaurant, bar, shop, baby-sitting.

$$$: Children under twelve stay free in villas (up to two kids), children four and under stay free in deluxe and superior rooms. Daily rates, double occupancy, superior or deluxe rooms $240–$390. Villas $360–$1,070.

Wyndham Morgan Bay Resort

Address: Box 2216 Gros Islet, St. Lucia, WI
Telephone: 800-WYNDHAM, 758-450-2511, fax 758-450-1050
Website: www.wyndham.com

Waterskiing clinics, tennis lessons with oversize rackets, and a grill next to the beach that serves hamburgers, hot dogs, and ice cream all day long are a few of the activities this 240-room all-inclusive beachfront resort has in place to attract families. All watersports, meals, and drinks are included in one price, and a children's program operates year-round with all kinds of activities. If you're traveling with babies, baby-sitting can be arranged through the concierge. The property is a bit stark for this lush island, with dormitory-like buildings atop grassy fields not far from the beach. In peak season the medium-sized beach can feel crowded—get out there early to claim your lounge chair.

Accommodations: 238 rooms in three-story buildings contain rooms having views of the garden area or beach. All rooms have either one king bed or two twin beds, marble bathrooms, air-conditioning, windows that open, coffeemakers, and balconies. A total of three people are allowed in each room, but connecting rooms are available.

For Kids: In the summer, the resort has a complimentary drop-in program for ages four to seven and ages eight to twelve. The schedule (from 10 A.M.–4 P.M.) includes arts and crafts, sand-castle building, scavenger and shell hunts, nature walks, volleyball, pool games, swim races, and dance lessons. Kids Klub Program for ages five to twelve, seven days a week from 10 A.M. to 5:30 P.M. complimentary. Activities include playground, treasure hunt, pool games, boat rides, tie dying, arts and crafts, tennis, cricket, and soccer.

Special Features: beach, swimming pool, limbo dancing, waterskiing, snorkeling, windsurfing, volleyball, three-hole golf course, archery, chess, Ping-Pong, pool, pedal boats, tennis, Hobie cats, two restaurants, two bars, baby-sitting, day and night tennis, windsurfing, Sunfish and catamaran sailing, snorkeling, pedal boats, badminton, croquet, fitness room, steam room, whirlpool, nightly entertainment, car rental, gift shop, laundry.

$$$: Rates include all meals, drinks, taxes, gratuities, watersports, and activities except for scuba diving and deep-sea fishing. Daily rates per person double occupancy: $275–$630, depending on room size and time of year. Kids on Us program from May to September allows children under age eighteen and stay free in their parents' room, and children under age twelve to eat and stay free. Rest of year, children ages three to twelve $55, thirteen to eighteen $75 per day.

Odyssey St. Lucia

Address: Box 915, Smugglers Village, Castries, St. Lucia, WI
Telephone: 800-777-1250 or 758-450-0551, fax 758-450-0281
Website: www.odysseyresorts.com

This excellent value all-inclusive resort with nonstop fun keeps adults and children busy day and night. It's divided into five smaller villages, each with its own character and check-in center. The villages are clustered around a main town center and there's continuous shuttle service around the property. There's an extensive children's program, free evening baby-sitting, and all kinds of activities. There's an excellent tennis center on the property, all kinds of watersports, a spa (and a children's spa), a rollerblade track, and evening activities including a nightclub theater with live entertainment and a disco. The swimming pool features slides, water cascades, and a swim-up bar. The resort is all inclusive and children under twelve stay free (one per paying adult).

Accommodations: 372 rooms. One-bedroom family suites have living rooms with sofa bed and patios. Most standard rooms have one king-size bed and can accommodate an extra twin. All rooms have air-conditioning, coffee-makers, and TVs.

For Kids: Four daily kids clubs are offered: the Baby Parrots Nest for infants to three years old; and separate clubs for four to nine years olds, nine to twelve years old, and teens.

Special Features: beach swimming pool, roller blade track, spa, kids park, sailing, waterskiing, windsurfing, paddleboats, canoes, snorkeling, scuba instruction, tennis, squash, Ping-Pong, board games, tennis, disco, evening entertainment, shops.

$$$: Rates include all meals, drinks, taxes, gratuities, and watersports. Daily rates, adults $99–$189, children under twelve stay free (one per paying adult) with a maximum of two children staying in a family room. Specials are in effect at different times of the year offering even more savings for guests.

Jalousie Hilton Resort and Spa

Address: Box 251, Soufrière, St. Lucia, WI
Telephone: 800-445-8667, 758-459-7666, fax 758-458-7667
Website: www.hilton.com

Lounge by the pool with the dramatic green pitons soaring on either side of you and a velvety gray volcanic sand beach just a few steps away. The 325-acre resort on the secluded southwest coast is lowered by a tropical rain forest and the blue waters of Jalousie Bay. A world-class spa lets you pamper yourself with a massage and seaweed wrap, facial, or any number of other luxurious treatments. All accommodations include a private plunge pool and veranda set in a tropical garden. Non-motorized watersports are complimentary and there's a PADI dive center on the property, plus an expansive fitness center.

Accommodations: 114 rooms in villas, villa suites, and sugarmill buildings. All have air-conditioning, ceiling fans, minibars, coffeemakers, and electronic safes. The resort's banana and soursop trees are used to produce organic juices for guests, and the hydroponic garden grows other fruits, vegetables, herbs, and spices used in meals.

For Kids: The complimentary children's program operates daily year-round from 10 A.M.–5 P.M. Kids ages four to twelve are entertained with nature walks, crafts, aerobics, water sports, and island tours. A small fee is charged for the island tours.

Special Features: beach, pools, four tennis courts, squash, racquet ball courts, putting and chipping green, windsurfing, snorkeling, waterskiing, scuba diving, restaurants, bars, shops, 24-hour room service, car rental, island tours, baby-sitting.

$$$: Virtually everything is included, even taxes and services charges. Children under age five stay free in parents' room. Children ages five to fifteen add $125 per night; sixteen and over are classified as adults and cost $175 per night. Daily rates, double occupancy: $250–$600.

Club Med St. Lucia

Address: P.O. Box 246, Vieux Fort, St. Lucia, WI
Telephone: 800-CLUBMED or 758-454-6546, fax 758-454-9641
Website: www.clubmed.com

Newly renovated, this Club Med village has upgraded its guest rooms and added telephones to each one. The Mini Club program for kids two to eleven is one of its star attractions. There's an intensive English riding program for the horse-loving set, and a full circus workshop for all ages making this Club Med an action-packed vacation choice for just about any family. Preschoolers to grandparents can participate in the circus workshop—learning trapeze skills, juggling, acrobatics, vaulting, clowning, and walking the tightrope. A windsurfing beach for experienced windsurfers is four minutes away and a shuttle runs every twenty minutes. A supervised children's program for two- to eleven-year-olds offers parents the time to perfect their windsurfing skills or relax uninterrupted on the beach. (The beach, on the Atlantic side, is a bit rough.) In addition to the laundry list of activities, adults can take 2½ hours of riding instruction daily, including dressage, jumping, and trail rides.

Accommodations: 254 rooms on three floors. (No elevators.) Each room is air-conditioned with a personal safe, terrace, private bath, and two double beds. Some rooms have connecting doors. Families of five or more must take two rooms.

For Kids: Operating from an activities center within the vacation village, kids can drop by anytime from 9 A.M.–9 P.M. for activities such as waterskiing, sailing, golf, archery, arts and crafts, boat rides, pony rides, go-carting, excursions, and puppet shows. The Mini Club for kids two to eleven is divided into age groups and housed in three separate buildings built around the special pool for kids. Early supervised lunches and dinners are offered for youngsters.

Special Features: beach, swimming pool with lanes for lap swimming, eight flood-it tennis courts, aerobics classes, archery, fitness center, eight-hole pitch-and-putt golf course, horseback riding, go-carts, in-line skating, Ping-Pong, scuba diving, volleyball, basketball, windsurfing, two restaurants, bar, nightclub.

$$$: All-inclusive rates cover everything but drinks. Kids ages two to five stay free (one per full-paying parent) for certain weeks of the year, usually from mid-November to mid-December and during certain weeks of January through March. The full horseback riding program, golf, scuba trips, and special excursions cost extra. Nightly rates, double occupancy, per adults (ages 12 and over) $105–$125; children three to eleven $42–$52; children two to three $11–$13; under two free. Special air packages are available.

Budget

Harmony Marina Suites

Address: P.O. Box 155, Castries, St. Lucia, WI
Telephone: 800-223-6510 or 758-452-8756, fax 758-452-8677
Website: www.hotelbook.com

Renuit Beach is a short walk away from this two-story family-owned apartment hotel whose affordable rates, good location, and one-bedroom apartments have always attracted vacationing families. The ground-level poolside apartments are quietest and most convenient, allowing little ones and their escorts to step out the door, cross the lawn, and head straight to the pool. Complimentary watersports include windsurfing and canoeing, and other watersports are easily arranged. There's a restaurant, bar, small market/deli, and car rental on the property. Rodney Bay Marina and other restaurants are nearby.

Accommodations: Four one-bedroom suites have kitchenettes and sofa sleepers. Eighteen one-bedroom suites have refrigerators, coffeemakers, and wet bars but no other kitchen appliances. All have twin or king beds, air-conditioning, and balcony or terraces.

Special Features: pool, windsurfing, canoes, restaurant, bar, shop, car rental.

$$$: Daily rates: one-bedroom luxury suites with kitchenettes: $90–$200.

Villa Rentals

Tropical Villas can help you arrange to rent a villa on St. Lucia. From the U.S.: 800-387-2715, 800-367-2720, or 800-387-2726. In Canada: 800-265-6070 or 800-387-1201 (Ontario, Quebec). P.O. Box 189, Castries, St. Lucia, WI. 758-450-8340, fax 758-450-8089.

WHAT TO SEE AND DO

The town of **Soufrière,** south of Castries, was named after the nearby volcano, **La Soufrière,** which has been dubbed the world's only drive-in volcano. Most of the island's mangoes, breadfruit, tomatoes, limes, and oranges, are grown in this lush and fertile region. **Soufrière Estate** has a small zoo and botanical gardens with an operational waterwheel. Next to the estate are the **Diamond Falls Botanical Gardens and Mineral Baths** which were built during the time of Louis XVI and restored in the 1960s. For a small fee, you can tour the grounds and gardens and enjoy a steaming bath fed by an underground stream of water from nearby sulfur springs. Morne Coubaril estates in Soufrière re-creates an eighteenth-century family cocoa plantation. There's a sugar mill, a cocoa house (where a demonstration of cocoa processing takes place), a re-created slave village, and farm animals such as goats and pigs. Open daily 9 A.M.–5 P.M. (459-7340).

Union Nature Trail in the northern part of island near Rodney Bay, has an easy-to-walk nature trail good for children and visitors who want to acquaint themselves with the animals and woodland landscape of the island. The trail takes forty-five minutes to complete and meanders past Caribbean pine, cashew, cinnamon, calabash, and mahogany trees. A nature center has a medicinal garden and a miniature zoo with agouti, iguanas, and boa constrictors.

Pigeon Point Island, on the northwest coast, was once frequented by pirates. Later a causeway was built to connect it to the mainland. The notorious French buccaneer Jambe de Bois (the name means "wooden leg") used to hide out on this forty-acre island, which is now a national park featuring the ruins of a British fort, picnic spots, long stretches of sandy beaches, and tranquil waters for swimming. The Pigeon Point Interpretive Center houses a small display on the history of St. Lucia. Open 9 A.M. to 5 P.M. daily. A pub beneath the center serves snacks, and a restaurant nearby serves lunch only.

St. Vincent and The Grenadines

Thirty idyllic islands and cays make up St. Vincent and the Grenadines, a fully independent country within the British Commonwealth. Fertile St. Vincent, larger than all the Grenadines put together, handles the bulk of the tourist trade. Its green volcanic mountain slopes are covered with banana, breadfruit, lime, and nutmeg trees, and its valleys are lined with blooming flowers, coconut palms, and arrowroot leading to beautiful black- or white-sand beaches.

Bequia (pronounced BECK-way), just nine miles south of St. Vincent, is the second largest of the islands. Best known of the smaller islands is Mustique, for its chic homes-away-from-home of Princess Margaret, David Bowie and Iman, and Mick Jagger. All of the Grenadines have kind and welcoming people and splendid beaches.

This island chain is the place to be if you want a quiet vacation with few planned activities other than the ones you and your family create and enjoy for yourselves. The sailing crowd has long enjoyed the area's quiet bays, easy island anchorages, secluded sandy coves, and magnificent snorkeling and diving opportunities. Prices are lower here than at more glamorous island destinations. Tourism is gaining a prominent place in the economy, but bananas, or "green gold," as they're often called, supply St. Vincent with half of its foreign exchange earnings.

Fast Facts:

Visitor Information: Website: www.vincy.com/svg. *U.S.* 801 Second Avenue, Twenty-first Floor, New York, NY 10017 (800-729-1726 or 212-687-4981, fax 212-949-5946). Or, 6505 Cove Creek Place, Dallas, TX 75240 (800-235-3029 or 214-239-6451, fax 214-239-1002). *Canada:* 32 Park Road, Toronto, Ontario M4W 2N4 (416-924-5796, fax 416-924-5844). *St. Vincent:* on Bay Street, P.O. Box 834, Kingstown, St. Vincent, WI (809-457-1502, fax 809-456-2610).

Arrivals and Departures: U.S. and Canadian citizens need a passport, a birth certificate, or a voter registration card and a photo ID to visit, plus a return or onward ticket. Departure tax is $12. Most visitors from the United States and Canada fly into Barbados and then fly LIAT (Leeward Islands Air Transport) or Mustique Airways into St. Vincent and the Grenadines. Daily ferry service is available to Bequia; and three days a week, mail boats and freight-carrying schooners can take you to Canouan, Mayreau, and Union islands. Mustique, Canouan, and Union islands all have airstrips that allow small planes to land.

Money: The larger resorts accept U.S. currency, but the Eastern Caribbean dollars (EC$) is used in most other places.

Language: English is the official language of St. Vincent and the Grenadines.

Best Sweet Treat: Golden apple pie is an island treat. The fruit is not related to North American apples, but has a sweet tangy taste, golden flesh and skin, and a large seed in the center.

ST. VINCENT

WHERE TO STAY
Expensive

Young Island
Address: P.O. Box 211, Young Island, St. Vincent, WI
Telephone: 800-223-1108 or 809-458-4826, fax 809-457-4567
Website: www.youngisland.com

At this small, private island resort just two hundred yards off the southern shore of St. Vincent, guests have thirty-five acres of fruit frees, flowers, ferns, turtle ponds, and beaches to explore. Hammocks hang under thatched roofs, and the island's swim-up bar is in the ocean instead of the pool; a coconut bar is attached to a small dock and serves drinks in coconut shells, giving lingerers the nourishment they need for the short swim or walk back to shore. On Friday night guests can attend a cocktail party on a small rocky island behind Young Island. Ferries to the mainland are complimentary and run twenty-four hours on demand.

Accommodations: All guests are housed in cottages with a refrigerator, king-size or twin beds, a ceiling fan, and a private patio. Four of the cottages have an alcove that can hold extra beds to accommodate families of three or four.

Special Features: beach, dock, swimming pool, windsurfing, snorkeling, glass-bottom boat rides, restaurant, bars.

$$$: Room rates include breakfast and dinner. Daily rates, double occupancy: $275–$590. Children under age twelve sharing their parents' room is $40 per child (for meals). Discounts and other bonuses such as airport pickup and boat trips are offered for seven- and ten-night stays.

Moderate

Grand View Beach Hotel
Address: P.O. Box 173, Villa Point, St. Vincent, WI
Telephone: 800-223-6510 (in the United States), 800-424-5500 (in Canada), 784-458-4811, fax 784-457-4174.

This old cotton plantation great house on eight acres of tropical gardens in southern St. Vincent has been turned into a gracious hotel run by the Sardine family. Its secluded beach has spectacular snorkeling, and the terrace next to the free-form swimming pool offers staggeringly beautiful views of Young Island and the Grenadines beyond. Rates include a complimentary breakfast.

Accommodations: All rooms have both air-conditioning and ceiling fans and can accommodate up to four people.

Special Features: beach, pool, snorkeling, tennis and squash, aerobics classes, a small gym, and a watersports center.

$$$: Daily rate, double occupancy: start at $130–$270. Each child between ages two and twelve sharing a room with parents pays $30 per day. Children under age two stay free.

Budget

Casa de Columbus

Telephone: P.O. Box 993, Kingstown, St. Vincent, WI
Address: 784-458-4001, fax 784-457-4777

Located on Indian Bay Beach, this very reasonably priced unit has one- and two-bedroom units, and daily housekeeping service. Its beachfront restaurant serves Caribbean and international cuisine, and fresh seafood is a specialty. The hotel's own beach can keep you busy for hours and watersports such as snorkeling, scuba, and sailing are available nearby. This is a great headquarters for enjoying the beach, but you'll want to rent a car if you plan to participate in any watersports or explore the island. A full breakfast is included in the rates.

Accommodations: 10 rooms with two twin or double beds can accommodate families up to four people. All are air-conditioned.

Special Features: beach, restaurant.

$$$: Daily rates, double occupancy: $75, additional people $10 per night, includes breakfast. Roll-aways are available for $10.

WHAT TO SEE AND DO

Your hotel or the tourist office can help you arrange a boat trip to the **Falls of Baleine** near the northern tip of the island; and getting there is half the fun as you skim along the blue Caribbean Sea, glimpsing the lush green island scenery. Be prepared to hop off the boat into shallow water and wade to shore. The falls are a ten- to fifteen-minute hike from the shoreline. Bring water shoes or sneakers, since you'll be walking through the stream to get to the falls. Swim and splash in the pool at the foot of the falls.

In addition to being the oldest such gardens in the Western Hemisphere, St. Vincent's **Botanical Gardens'** claim to fame is a breadfruit tree grown from the original plant brought by Captain Bligh of the H.M.S. *Bounty* in 1793. St. Vincent's endangered endemic parrot, Amazona guildingii, is represented at a small aviary here. In Kingstown, 809-457-1003. Open weekdays 7 A.M.–4 P.M.; Saturdays 7 A.M.–11 P.M., and Sundays 7 A.M.–6 P.M.

BEQUIA

WHERE TO STAY
Moderate

Plantation House Hotel

Address: P.O. Box 16, Admiralty Bay, Bequia, St. Vincent, WI
Telephone: 800-223-9832, 809-458-3425

Cottages and guest rooms overlook the beach or are tucked into palm-shaded gardens on eleven-acre Plantation House. Two beachfront cabanas have three bedrooms each, and cottages nestled into the gardens have one or two bedrooms. Five air-conditioned double rooms are in the main house; other rooms are cooled by trade-wind breezes.

Accommodations: Cottages and cabanas have ceiling fans and refrigerators. Deluxe accommodations in the main house have air-conditioning.

Special Features: beach, swimming pool, scuba diving, tennis, waterskiing, Italian restaurant, veranda bar, beach bar.

$$$: Daily rates double occupancy: $190–$290. The price includes a full English breakfast.

Budget

Fairmont Apartments

Address: Belmont, Bequia, St. Vincent, WI
Telephone: 809-457-1121, 809-458-4037 (after working hours), fax 809-456-2333

Comfortable apartments overlook Admiralty Bay on the island's west coast and are just a few minutes walk from restaurants, shopping, and the ferry service to St. Vincent. Each apartment features a large porch, a kitchen, living and dining rooms, and housekeeping service.

Accommodations: Studio apartments, one- and two-bedroom apartments, and a two-bedroom house with its own swimming pool are available.

$$$: Weekly rates: one-bedroom apartment $300–$450, two-bedroom apartment $350–$500, house $575–$700. Daily rate for one-bedroom units is $100 all year.

The Frangipani

Address: P.O. Box 1, Admiralty Bay, Bequia, St. Vincent, WI
Telephone: 809-458-3255, fax 809-458-3824

Once a family home, the Frangipani was converted into an inn two decades ago and is now owned by the prime minister of St. Vincent. Yachting enthusiasts gather here to stretch their sea legs while enjoying a meal and perhaps some evening entertainment. Thursday night steel band jump-ups at the beachfront bar are not to be missed, and folksingers and string bands perform throughout the week. The St. Vincent ferry stop is a several-minute walk away.

Accommodations: The inn has five simple rooms with shared bathrooms and cold water only, but the garden units and two-bedroom dwellings are larger, have hot and cold running water, a small refrigerator, and are better suited for families.

$$$: Daily rates, double occupancy: inn rooms $45, and garden units $95.

MUSTIQUE

WHERE TO STAY

More than forty luxury villas, one hotel, and a small guest house are the sum total of posh Mustique's tourist accommodations. You'll need to reserve villas up to a year in advance through House Rentals Department, Mustique Co., Ltd., P.O. Box 349, Mustique, St. Vincent, WI (809-458-4621, fax 809-456-4565), or WIMCO, P.O. Box 1461, Newport, RI 02840 (800-932-3222 or 401-849-8012, fax 401-847-6290). Most rentals cost about $3,000 to $15,000 per week, depending on the season and the amenities, size, and service you require. Mick's and David's houses are not for rent, but you can reserve Princess Margaret's pad for a week in the summer for about $3,600.

The Cotton House is the island's only hotel; if you want even greater spaciousness and seclusion you can rent one of the fifty sumptuous fully staffed villas scattered throughout the island.

Expensive

The Cotton House

Address: Mustique, St. Vincent and the Grenadines, WI
Telephone: 800-826-2809, 809-456-3414

Poised right at the edge of the calm aquamarine Caribbean Sea, the Cotton House has just twenty luxurious rooms, suites, and cottages. Well-suited for the family of any age but ideal for those with babies and toddlers, it offers special private nanny services to its clientele. Families with infants can add a crib to any of the guest rooms, but larger families will be most comfortable in the two-room deluxe suites. The hotel knows personal pampering means a lot to its glamorous guests: staff members unpack and press your clothing upon your arrival, at no charge, and there's a "pillow menu" of nine choices, including a special maternity pillow for the comfort of expectant mothers.

If you tire of tanning poolside or on the powdery white-sand beach, a watersports and dive shop can arrange more active fun and a sailing yacht is available for private excursions. Other island activities include sunset horseback rides, tennis, and hanging out at Basil's Bar, the hip place to see and be seen.

Accommodations: rooms and suites all have air-conditioning, ceiling fans, and elegant furnishings.

Special Features: beach, swimming pool, restaurant, bar, English tea.

$$$: Daily rates, double occupancy: April through August rooms $490–$740. A meal plan is available during the rest of year. Modified American plan (breakfast and dinner,) only rest of year: adults $590–$1,150. Children four to twelve pay $100 modified American plan when sharing a room with their parents. No charge for children under three.

Trinidad and Tobago

Musical Trinidad spawned the steel drum band and calypso, both of which now flourish throughout the Caribbean and beyond. Just seven miles off the Venezuelan coast, Trinidad is a geographical extension of South America, as is Tobago, twenty miles farther out. Residents of both melting pot islands trace their roots to every corner of the globe—Africa, India, China, and Great Britain.

The two sister islands, one bustling and commercial and the other quiet and shy by comparison, became independent from Britain in 1962 and have a fully democratic government. Originally sugar producers, the two-island nation now makes its living from oil and gas, petrochemical industries, manufacturing, and tourism. The national capital is Port of Spain in Trinidad.

Tobago has the world's oldest preserved rain forest, protected by law since 1776, and is home to 433 species of birds, and hundreds of types of butterflies. Enormous leatherback turtles nest on beaches in April and May on the northwestern coast from Great Courland Bay to Turtle Beach; several hotels offer wake-up call service to enable your family to see the lumbering giants lay their eggs and the tiny babies scramble to the sea. Tobago may have served as the fictional island in Daniel Defoe's *Robinson Crusoe*. Many people visit Trinidad for the action during carnival time or for one of the many other celebrations, and visit Tobago to enjoy the tranquillity and spectacular beaches.

Trinidad's carnival is the biggest, liveliest street party in the Caribbean. A children's carnival takes place on Saturday morning, when toddlers to teenagers come out in costumes as elaborate and beautiful as their adult counterparts. Carnival preparations begin early in the new year with Calypso "tents" (now concert spaces) scattered throughout the city hosting rehearsals and performances. Judges visit the tents, and select the best Calypso artists to compete in the semifinals. Steel pan musicians rehearse their numbers in Port of Spain's pan yards; you can visit them and listen as long as you like. *Mas* camps (*mas* means masquerade) throughout the city allow visitors to come in and order costumes, if they like what they see. Pick up your costume before carnival, and dance through the streets with other revelers who look just like you. Costumes are artistic and technical wonders, made of balsa wood, gauze, carved foam, shimmering fabrics, sequins, wheels, and everything else you can think of. Tourist publications list names and address of calypso, steel band, and *mas* tents.

Fast Facts:

Visitor Information: Website: www.visittnt.com. *U.S.:* 7000 Blvd. East, Guttenberg, NJ 07093 *Canada:* The RMR Group, Taurus House, 512 Duplex Avenue, Toronto, M4R 2E3 (416-485-8724 or 416-485-8256, 888-595-4TNT). *Trinidad:* Trinidad and Tobago Tourism Development Authority, 10–14 Phillips Street, Port of Spain, Trinidad, WI (868-623-1932, fax 868-623-3848). *Tobago:* Unit 12, TIDCO Mall, Sangster's Hill, Scarborough, Tobago (868-639-4333, fax 868-639-4514).

Arriving and Departing: U.S. and Canadian citizens need a valid passport for visits of less than two months. Longer visits require a visa. There is a ferry service between Trinidad and Tobago six days a week. An airport departure tax of $20 is charged that must be paid in local currency.

Money: The Trinidadian dollar (TT$) is the official currency.

Language: The official language of Trinidad and Tobago is English.

Best Sweet Treat: Try Sorrel drink, a bright red sweet-tasting libation that is made into a soft drink by Ting. Or sample a Rollie Pollie, a small soft cake with a spiral of pink in the middle.

TRINIDAD

WHERE TO STAY
Moderate

Trinidad Hilton
Address: P.O. Box 442, Lady Young Road, Port of Spain, Trinidad, WI
Telephone: 800-445-8667, 868-624-3211, fax 868-624-4485
Website: www.hilton.com

An Olympic-size pool cools down hot kids after they've explored Port of Spain, wandered through the zoo, or danced in the streets at Carnival. The hotel is above the city near Savannah Park and is especially well-suited to business travelers, but families wanting to stay in town find it convenient, too. Rooms are spacious and although more than three people may not stay in one room, connecting doors are available. Shopping districts are nearby. Note that the hotel can be a bit noisy because of its downtown location.

Accommodations: 394 rooms, all with balconies, a small sitting area, air-conditioning, TVs, and radios. Rooms have king, queen, or twin beds. Roll-aways and cribs are available.

Special Features: swimming pool, lawn tennis, Ping-Pong, buffets with entertainment by the pool, shops, hair salon, café.

$$$: Daily rate, double occupancy: $205-$450.

Budget

Hotel Normandie
Address: 10 Nook Avenue, St. Ann's Village, Port of Spain, Trinidad, WI
Telephone/fax: 868-624-1181

Located a short walk from the Savannah and Hilton Hotel, this establishment has comfortable rooms with sleeping lofts suitable for families, as well as more traditional hotel accommodations. A small swimming pool is bordered by patios and tropical gardens; most rooms face the pool. La Fantasie Restaurant is highly regarded in the city for its "nouvelle Creole" cuisine but their homemade ice cream is what your kids will savor. Room service is available until 11 P.M. The hotel is near a lively shopping area of crafts and clothing shops.

Accommodations: Standard rooms have one double bed or two twin beds; superior rooms have two double- or queen-size beds. Loft bedrooms have a queen-size bed and a double futon. All rooms are air-conditioned and have cable TV.

$$$: Kids under twelve are free in their parents' room. Daily rates, double occupancy: (except during Carnival when rates increase) standard room $90, superior $105, loft bedrooms $120.

WHAT TO SEE AND DO

Queen's Park Savannah in Port of Spain is a sprawling public park with lily ponds, playing fields, enormous trees, and manicured lawns. On its western edge sits a group of mansions called The Magnificent Seven. Built in 1904 by wealthy plantation owners, each tried to outdo the other with their showy architecture and opulence. Just north of the Savannah are the **Emperor Valley Zoo** and the **Botanical Gardens**. The zoo features animals and birds of the Caribbean region, in addition to animals from all over the world. They have a tame ocelot that you can pet. If you don't get a chance to see the scarlet ibis in the Caroni Bird Sanctuary (see below), you can see it here or get a close-up look at an enormous anaconda or python. Open daily 9 A.M.–6 P.M. Small admission fee. 868-622-3530.

Caroni Bird Sanctuary, about a thirty-minute drive from Port of Spain, is part large swamp and part lagoon with mangrove islands in the middle and waterways winding through it. Boats explore the swamp in the early morning and late afternoon, taking guests to see the thousands of brilliant scarlet ibis who leave at sunrise and arrive again at sunset to roost in the small islets in the middle of the sanctuary. Boats leave the roadside dock at 4:30 A.M. and 4 P.M., and reservations are essential (most hotels will make the arrangements for you). Keep a sharp eye out for other animals, too, such as the ant-eaters who can be spotted encircling a branch where they've coiled up to sleep. A good dose of insect repellent will help keep voracious mosquitoes at bay and a sweater will ward off any late evening chills. Tours of Caroni can be arranged through Winston Nanant (868-645-1305) or David Ramsahai (868-663-4767).

TOBAGO

WHERE TO STAY
Expensive

Plantation Beach Villas
Address: P.O. Box 435, Scarborough, Tobago, WI

Telephone: 868-639-9377, fax 868-639-0455
Website: www.wow.net.villas

Very comfortable and spacious two-story colonial-style plantation house villas are tucked into the hillside amid a grove of trees above a long palm-fringed beach. Views are quite spectacular. The beach is a favorite of nesting leatherback turtles (they're the biggest of all sea turtles and can grow up to 1,200 pounds). Guests who are interested can request a wake-up call to see the lumbering creatures climb up above the high-water mark, dig their nests, lay about one hundred eggs, and then cover and disguise their nest and head back to the ocean. The resort borders on the Alefounder Bird Sanctuary, and a wide variety of fascinating bird species can be seen from your villa's veranda.

Just fifteen minutes from the international airport, the resort's beach is quite calm, safe, and private, and the resort is quiet and tranquil, yet perfectly comfortable for families. An eighteen-hole golf course is about a mile from the hotel, and the supermarket is about three miles away. All kinds of watersports can be arranged. The housekeeper, who services your villa daily, can also be hired to cook.

Accommodations: Each of the six villas is a two-story, three-bedroom home (one bedroom has twin beds, two have queen beds) with huge verandas, private baths in each bedroom, complete kitchens, and washer and dryers. The villas are situated to catch the trade-wind breezes but rooms have both air-conditioning and ceiling fans. Cribs, roll-aways, and high chairs are available.

Special Features: swimming pool, guided rain forest hikes, snack bar, bar, car rental, games and puzzles for children, baby-sitting, barbecue pit.

$$$: Villas, up to four people $220–$500; up to six people, $280–$560. No charge for roll-away for child under twelve, or for crib and high chair.

Moderate

Footprints Eco Resort
Address: Culloden Bay Road via Golden Lane, Tobago, WI
Telephone: 800-814-1396
Website: www.footprintseco-resort.com

This delightful new eco-resort, on sixty-one acres of a former banana plantation, has been constructed carefully of local materials by island residents. Thatched-roof buildings are of teak and local hardwoods, and each unit features artwork of local artists. Wooden boardwalks run along the beach and a tree-planting program for guests helps ensure the property, designated a nature preserve, remains lush and full. Several nature trails lace the property with excellent bird-watching opportunities, and guests can have a guide accompany them or can explore on their own. Reference books on the island's flora and fauna are available in the small library. The resort grows its own fresh organic herbs and vegetables. The beach is a bit rocky and the water is rough in the winter months, but the rest of the year there is excellent snorkeling around Culloden Reef, just offshore. Kids love the bar—the bar itself is a beautiful fish tank. Two-bedroom, two-bathroom villas are very private and feature fun touches such as hammocks and their own solar-heated Jacuzzis. This is the kind of place that older kids can explore safely on their own.

Accommodations: Villas contain a master bedroom with a king bed and a loft bedroom with twin beds, ceiling fans, full kitchenettes, two bathrooms, a deck with a Jacuzzi and a gas barbecue, and a covered porch with a hammock. Suites are oceanfront with a bedroom with one king bed or two twins, two bathrooms, a sitting room with full-size pullout futon sofa, and a minifridge and electric kettle. All units have air-conditioning.

Special Features: saltwater swimming pools, restaurant, hobby and crafts weeks, snorkeling, convenience store, boutique, library.

$$$: Daily rates, double occupancy: villas $210–$275, suites $185–$225. Additional person $25 per night. Accommodations include round-trip airport transfers.

Rex Turtle Beach

Address: P.O. Box 201, Cortland Bay, Scarborough, Tobago, WI
Telephone: 800-255-5859, 868-639-2851, fax 868-639-1495
Website: www.rexcaribbean.com

Lumbering leatherback sea turtles lay their eggs from March to August, and tiny hatchlings scramble to the sea just a few steps from the guest rooms in this two- and three-story full-service resort hotel. Children under two receive free accommodations and meals, while two- to twelve-year-olds stay free in their parents' room and receive a 50 percent discount on meals. Two restaurants, one casual and the other more elegant, offer international, local, and vegetarian cuisine. The full compliment of watersports and activities are on the premises. Evening entertainment keeps the fun rolling into the wee hours with steel band performances, live bands, and dancing to folk drums. The resort is slightly in need of a renovation, but its location on a drop-dead gorgeous beach still makes it a good choice for families.

Accommodations: 125 superior rooms have various bed configurations and can house a maximum of two adults and two children. All rooms have balconies or terraces with a view of ocean, and air-conditioning.

For Kids: The Children's Club operates weekdays from 9 A.M.–4 P.M. with a short break at lunchtime. Kids ages four to twelve are invited to participate in supervised games and activities within the hotel grounds. Baby-sitting services can be arranged.

Special Features: beach, pool, windsurfing, Sunfish sailing, snorkeling, waterskiing, beach volleyball, shuffleboard, and table tennis.

$$$: Daily rates, double occupancy: $155–$210. Meal plans are available. Two children under twelve free in their parents' room.

WHAT TO SEE AND DO

Ornithologist and nature guide David Rooks takes visitors on **tours of the rain forest** to explore its plant, animal, and bird life. He will also design customized tours to accommodate your family's interests and ages, such as a walk to a waterfall and swimming hole with bird-watching along the way. Whatever the hike, he engages children easily, getting them involved looking at bugs, explaining about medicinal plants, or pointing out edible plants. One tour goes out by boat to Little Tobago Island where you can climb on the island to see birds. Children pay reduced prices (868-639-4276, fax 868-639-5440).

Turks and Caicos

Just ninety minutes from Miami between the tip of Florida and Puerto Rico, the Turks and Caicos island group is known for long silvery strands of soft sand, a safe atmosphere, and relatively uncrowded and unspoiled islands—forty of them in all—most of which are uninhabited. They are surrounded by one of the longest coral reefs in the world, and scuba diving and snorkeling are very popular pastimes. Turks and Caicos is also known as a popular offshore banking center for American corporations. The island of Providenciales, referred to as Provo, is the most populated island and is the center of the tourist industry, but despite that reputation, it is a quiet and low-key getaway compared to many other Caribbean islands. Seven other islands regularly receive visitors, too.

In addition to hosting some popular family-style inclusive resorts and small locally owned inns and hotels, Provo Island is know as the home of JoJo the dolphin. Now named a National Treasure, this Atlantic bottlenose dolphin has lived in the shallow waters around the island since 1980. JoJo is one of the few dolphins in the world who voluntarily interacts with humans in his own habitat—the ocean. The occasional lucky visitors swimming, snorkeling, or scuba diving offshore may have the chance to frolic in the water with JoJo.

Fast Facts:

Visitor Information: Website: interknowledge.com/turks-caicos. *U.S.*: Turks and Caicos Tourist Board, 11645 Biscayne Boulevard, Suite 302, North Miami Fl 33181. 800-241-0824, 305-891-4117, fax 305-891-7096. *Turks and Caicos:* P.O. Box 128, Ponds Street, Grand Turk, Turks and Caicos Islands.

Arriving and Departing: Proof of citizenship is required, such as an official birth certificate, a voter registration card with photo identification, or a passport. A departure tax of $15 is charged all visitors over age twelve.

Currency: The U.S. dollar is the official currency.

Language: English is the official language of Turks and Caicos.

WHERE TO STAY
Expensive

Beaches Turks and Caicos Resort and Spa
Address: Lower Bight Road, Providenciales, Turks and Caicos, BWI
Telephone: 800-BEACHES, 649-946-8000, fax 649-946-8001
Website: www.beaches.com

As if the long ribbon of white sand and numerous water sports weren't enough to keep the kids occupied for hours, Beaches has added a lavish children's activity center featuring an enormous wooden boat surrounded by a freshwater pool. The pool even has its own swim-up bar serving nonalcoholic drinks only, and since this resort is all-inclusive, your kids can sample as many as they like. There's a full-scale kids program for infants through teens, a Sega game center, a teen nightclub plus all kinds of other fun. Five restaurants allow for great dining variety and evening entertainment keeps the fun roaring into the wee hours. Beaches is a very upscale inclusive resort chain that is the family counterpart to its successful sister resorts, Sandals.

Accommodations: Rooms have a king or two double beds with air-conditioning, ceiling fans, private balconies, safes, and coffeemakers.

For Kids: Three separate programs are features for infants, kids, and teens. Infants have a special room just for them; kids four to seven and eight to twelve enjoy all kinds of fun activities and teens have a program just for them that includes a disco and dining area that is teens-only in the evening.

Special Features: beach, two pools, wading pool, scuba, snorkeling, kayaks, Sunfish sailboats, sea cycles, parasailing, mini golf, full service spa, tennis, beach volleyball, croquet, lawn chess, shuffleboard, fitness center, five restaurants, bars, nightly entertainment, car rental, shops, beauty salon.

$$$: Seven night stay, double occupancy adults $2,205-$7,175 each, children ages two to fifteen $490, under two free.

Ocean Club

Address: Box 240, Providenciales, Turks and Caicos, BWI
Telephone: 800-457-8787, 649-946-5880, fax 649-946-5845
Website: www.ocean-club.com

Right on twelve-mile Grace Bay Beach, this upscale all suite-resort offers families many of the services of a hotel with the convenience of extra space and fully outfitted kitchens and kitchenettes. The spectacular white sand beach will always be the resort's the main attraction, but action-oriented families will find an experienced dive operation on-site, plenty of watersports, deep sea fishing, and two swimming pools to keep them busy. The resort has an excellent restaurant of its own, but also offers guests a dining shuttle that operates nightly for drop-offs at island restaurants and a shopping shuttle so guests can get to the island supermarket. A golf course is nearby.

Accommodations: 86 studios, one- , two- , and three-bedroom suites have air-conditioning, private balconies, kitchenettes or full kitchens; all but studios have their own washer and dryer.

Special Features: beach, two swimming pools, scuba diving, kayaks, fishing, sailing, windsurfing, parasailing, restaurants, tennis, fitness center, bars, shops.

$$$ Two children under age twelve stay free in their parents' accommodation. Daily rates, double occupancy: suites $185–$420; one bedroom $225–$575; two-bedroom $375–$750; three-bedroom $500–$995.

The U.S. Virgin Islands

The three siblings that make up the U.S. Virgin Islands have distinctly different personalities. St. Thomas is a bustling vacation hub with world-renowned duty-free shopping and a wide selection of resorts, hotels, restaurants, and activities. Quieter St. Croix, once a large producer of sugarcane, now has abandoned sugar mills and rum distilleries scattered across rolling hills and valleys. Beautiful back-to-nature St. John, protected by its status as a national park, has pristine beaches of legendary beauty and a cover of lush jungle in its interior.

Columbus came across these islands on his second trip to the New World in 1493; and the English, French, Spanish, Knights of Malta, and Danes ruled over them at different times. In 1917 the United States purchased the islands for $25 million in gold from Denmark so as to protect U.S. interests in the Panama Canal. Despite the American flag, driving is on the left side of the road.

Fast Facts:

Visitor Information: Website: www.usvi-on-line.com. *U.S.:* 800-372-USVI or contact the office of tourism nearest you: *Atlanta:* 225 Peachtree Street N.E., Suite 760, Atlanta, GA 30303 (404-688-0906, fax 404-525-1102). *Chicago:* 500 North Michigan Avenue, Suite 2030, Chicago, IL 60611 (312-670-8784, fax 312-670-8788). *Los Angeles:* 3460 Wilshire Boulevard, Suite 412, Los Angeles, CA 90010 (213-739-0138, fax 213-739-2005). *Miami:* 2655 Le Jeune Road, Suite 907, Coral Gables, FL 33134 (305-442-7200, fax 305-445-9044). *New York City:* 1270 Avenue of the Americas, Suite 2108, New York, NY 10020 (212-332-2222, fax 212-332-2223). *Washington D.C.:* 444 North Capital Street, NW, Ste 298, Washington, DC 20001 (202-624-3590, fax 202-785-2542). *Canada:* 3300 Bloor Street, Ste. 3120, Centre Tower, Toronto M8X 2X3 (416-233-1414 or fax 416-233-9367). *St. Thomas:* P.O. Box 6400 Charlotte Amalie, USVI 00804 (340-774-8784, fax 340-774-4390). *St. Croix:* P.O. Box 4538, Christiansted, USVI 00822 (340-773-0495, fax 340-773-5074) and Fredericksted Custom House Building, Strand Street, USVI 00840 (340-772-0357). *St. John:* P.O. Box 200, Cruz Bay, USVI 00830 (340-776-6450).

Arriving and Departing: St. Thomas has the biggest airport; St. Croix has a smaller one, and St. John has none at all. A ferry runs regularly from either Charlotte Amalie and Red Hook on St. Thomas to Cruz Bay on St. John. A ferry service between St. Croix and St. Thomas makes daily round-trips between Christiansted on St. Croix and Charlotte Amalie on St. Thomas.

Language: English is the official language of the U.S. Virgin Islands.

Best Sweet Treat: Sidewalk vendors sell *fracos* made of shave ice, topped with flavored syrup and condensed milk

ST. THOMAS

St. Thomas is the number one cruise port in the West Indies and has been nicknamed the Manhattan of the Caribbean for its hustle, bustle, and traffic jams. The island was known more as a trading port than a plantation island in the seventeenth century; its main city, Charlotte Amalie, pronounced Amal-YAH (founded in 1672), was originally called Tappus by the Danes after the tap houses frequented by pirates and buccaneers.

Most of the hotels and condos are on the flatter east end where beautiful white-sand beaches stretch for miles. Steep green mountains provide breathtaking view throughout the island; it's thirteen miles long and less than four miles wide.

WHERE TO STAY
Expensive

Sapphire Beach Resort and Marina

Address: P.O. Box 8088, St. Thomas, USVI 00801
Telephone: 800-524-2090 or 340-775-6100, fax 340-777-3555
Website: www.usvi.net/hotel/sapphire

Sapphire Beach is the comfort food of the Caribbean resort world. It's wholesome, unpretentious, comfortable, and somehow reassuringly familiar—but with a tropical twist. It does manage to slip in plenty of classy nouveau family vacation features, like spacious and airy two-story condos (called villas) with full kitchens, a charming complimentary children's program, and a concierge service that can arrange anything you might want to do, but it's the unaffected and effortless ease permeating the place that sets the guests to relaxing right away.

While my family enjoys the quarter-acre freshwater swimming pool, the beach holds us captive for most of our days. Located on one of the island's best stretches of sand at the east end of St. Thomas, the resort is just a few minutes from the village of Red Hook, where you can catch ferries that leave for St. John and the British Virgin Islands. Toddlers and their families cavort in the bathtub-warm calm waters while teens can parasail offshore or play a rousing game of beach volleyball, overseen by the staffer whose job it is to get the games going. Since my kids are at the in-between age when just about anything goes, they snorkel, kayak, hunt shells, and visit with new pals they met earlier in the kid's program.

Accommodations: Luxurious beachfront suites accommodate up to four people, and two-story villas with private balconies accommodate families of up to six people. All have full kitchens, spacious living rooms, air-conditioning, ceiling fans, and daily maid service, and can adjoin other units through the deck. An inexpensive shopping shuttle takes guests to a nearby supermarket to stock up on necessities.

For Kids: Indoor and outdoor activities are well balanced at this quality, half and full day daily drop-in program for four- to twelve-year-olds. Kids can pop in for an hour or two to swim and work on arts and crafts or arrive at 8 A.M. and not leave until the program is over at 5:30 P.M. Lunch and snacks are part of the complimentary program. An evening program is available during certain vacation periods

Special Features: beach, pool, restaurants, bars, snorkeling, windsurfing, jet skis, scuba, volleyball, Sunfish sailing, room service, car rental.

$$$: Children under thirteen stay, play, and eat free when accompanied by parents. December 24 through April 15; suites (up to four people) $295–$350 and villas (up to six people) $355–$405. April 18 to December 22: suites $190–$245 and villas $235–$285.

The Ritz Carlton

Address: 6900 Great Bay, St. Thomas, USVI
Telephone: 800-241-3333, 340-775-3333, fax 340-775-4444
Website: www.ritzcarlton.com

The luxury and service that are trademarks of the Ritz Carlton hotel line are overlayed here with a comfortably elegant tropical ambience. Fifteen acres of exquisite gardens complement this beachfront estate designed to remind you of a Venetian palace. Six lemon yellow buildings, all named after the various flowers that decorate the landscape, face the Great Bay at the eastern end of St. Thomas. The Red Hook ferry to St. John and the British Virgin Islands is just a mile away. The buildings surround a pool and look out upon a half-mile stretch of bone-white sand and the islands beyond. The hotel's fifty-three-foot catamaran, the *Lady Lynsey*, takes guests on sunset cruises and snorkeling trips. All the resort's restaurants feature children's menus. This is luxury living with a warm welcome for the children.

Accommodations: 152 oceanview rooms and one-bedroom suites are in five separate buildings. All have private terraces, safe-deposit box, minibar, marble baths, and air-conditioning. Most rooms have king beds and some have two double beds. Some connecting rooms are available. Roll-aways can be added.

For Kids: Operating year-round, the Ritz Kids program offers a wide variety of games and educational activities for children ages four to twelve. You'll find sand-castle creations, tennis lessons, pirate treasure hunts, arts and crafts, volcano building, and even a noontime iguana feeding. The program operates daily during morning, afternoon, and evening hours, for a fee. The morning and full-day session include continental breakfast and lunch. The evening program operates from 6:30 A.M.–9:30 P.M.

Special Features: swimming pool, windsurfing, parasailing, scuba diving, Sunfish sailing, deep-sea fishing, sunset cruises, three night-lit tennis courts, fitness center, nanny service, beauty salon, shops, three restaurants, bars, in-room movies, aerobics classes, catamaran trips, floating mats, kayaks, power boat rentals, sailing class, snorkel gear, snorkel boat excursion, sport fishing, Suncat sailboats, wave runners, scuba certification, and diving, 24-hour room service.

$$$: Children under eighteen stay free in their parents' room. Daily rates, double occupancy (maximum of four in one room): $325–$1,700

Wyndham Sugar Bay Beach Club and Resort

Address: 6500 Estate Smith Bay, St. Thomas, USVI 00802
Telephone: 800-WYNDHAM, 340-777-7100, fax 340-772-7200
Website: www.wyndham.com

An all-inclusive program includes just about everything at this enormous white edifice that dominates thirty-one acres on the island's east end. Most of the family action takes place off to one side of the building where the swimming pool, bird lagoon, and beach sit. The sprawling pool complex is a Mecca for kids, who never seem to tire of its waterfalls, volleyball net, and hidden corners. The watersports center can arrange windsurfing and kayak rentals, and there are tennis courts and a fitness center. The all-inclusive package gets you all meals and drinks, all nonmotorized watersports, daily activity program, nightly entertainment, and unlimited ice cream from the ice cream bar. Movies, including children's, are shown in an indoor resort amphitheater—a welcome break from the sun and heat. The children's program operates every day for children three to twelve.

Accommodations: Rooms are standard but attractive hotel fare and have one king bed or two queen beds. All rooms have a small refrigerator, coffeemaker, and storage cupboards above, handy for late night snacks.

Children's Program: Operating year-round from 9:15 A.M. to 5 P.M., children three to twelve stay busy with kite flying, iguana hunts, shell crafts, crab races, and more.

Special features: beach, pool, restaurants, bars, evening entertainment, watersports, workout facility, movie theater.

$$$: Daily rates all inclusive double occupancy: $360–$580. Children twelve and under from May 1–September 30 stay and eat free off the children's menu. Rest of year $60 per day. Under three free.

Moderate

Marriott's Frenchman's Reef and Morning Star Resorts

Address: P.O. Box 7100, St. Thomas, USVI 00801-0100
Telephone: 800-524-2000, 340-776-8500, fax 340-715-6190
Website: www.marriott.vi

Popular with conventioneers, these two properties sit next to one another on the southern tip of St. Thomas overlooking the harbor of Charlotte Amalie and Morning Star Beach. The Morning Star part of the complex is situated right on the beach while Frenchman's Reef is a multistory pink building next door that wraps around the top of a point above the shore. Frenchman's pool area is bigger and has a swim-up bar and crashing waterfalls; if you want a sandy beach you'll have a slight hike. A rather new seaside pool with a wraparound terrace has been added for all guests in the Morning Star area. Morning Star is the pricier of the two, but it may be worth it if you have young children and want a golden beach just steps from your door. A fun water taxi transports guests to and from the town of Charlotte Amalie.

Accommodations: 496 rooms and suites at Frenchman's Reef and 96 units at Morning Star. All rooms have air-conditioning, refrigerator, coffeemaker, in-room safe, and in-room ice maker.

For Kids: Morning Star offers an evening story hour with tales of pirates adventures and exciting tales from the sea every Thursday evening from 8 P.M. to 9 P.M. Children must be accompanied by their parents.

Special Features: beach, three swimming pools, lit tennis courts, health club and spa, beach volleyball, kayaking, water aerobics, aerobics, jet skies, scuba diving, snorkeling, sailing, sunset cruises, fishing, parasailing, wind-surfing, shops, car rental, baby-sitting, beauty salon, tennis, restaurants, bars, nightclub, room service.

$$$: Children eighteen and under stay free in their parents' rooms. Daily rates, double occupancy: rooms $200–$425, suites $235–$1,200.

Renaissance Grand Beach Resort

Address: Smith Bay Road, Box 8267, St. Thomas, USVI 00801
Telephone: 800-HOTELS-1, 340-775-1510, fax 340-775-2185
Website: www.renaissancehotels.com

Tucked unobtrusively onto thirty-four acres of tropical flowers, ferns, and trees, the Renaissance has been carefully landscaped so that you don't see a lot of hotel. It's a full-service resort with several restaurants, a poolside grill and bar, a watersports center on the beach, and a car rental. An enormous free-form pool with a wading area is almost as popular as the thousand-foot white-sand beach. Children's menus are available in all restaurants.

A complete watersports center and dive shop rents sailboats, windsurfers, and kayaks, and arranges sailing trips, scuba, fishing expeditions, and para-sailing right off the dock. Six tennis courts and rackets are available for day or night play.

Accommodations: 297 rooms. Standard rooms have two queen beds, and superior and deluxe rooms offer more space. Two-story town houses and one-bedroom suites are popular with families.

For Kids: The Kids Club is a daily year-round program for kids ages four to twelve. Activities begin in the Kids Club Room, and move in and out to the beach, pool, and grounds throughout the session.

Special Features: beach, pool, sailing, windsurfing, scuba, tennis, snor-keling, kayaks, island tours, wave runners, parasailing, car rental, 24-hour room service, evening entertainment.

$$$: Daily rates, double occupancy: rooms $115–$299; suites $210–$400; townhouses $270–$460.

WHAT TO SEE AND DO

Charlotte Amalie has a dizzying number of shops, most catering to the cruise-ship trade. Its duty-free shops sell jewelry, watches, designer clothes, and many things younger kids couldn't care less about, but teens may enjoy.

Those too young to strap on a dive tank can descend through the translu-cent Caribbean waters to a depth of 150 feet on an **Atlantis Submarine** ride.

The battery-powered nonpolluting sub cruises past sponge gardens, flashy tropical fish, and sunken ships on its hour-long underwater journey. A boat picks up passengers at a dock and takes them out to an area rich with coral gardens, where the sub is anchored. After boarding the sub, it begins its descent. Cards identifying different marine plants and animals are placed by every window. Adults $65 per person, kids from minimum age of four to twelve pay $25. Teens thirteen to eighteen pay $35. Building IV, Havensight Mall. Tel. 800-253-0493, 340-776-5650.

Get a bird's-eye view of the town and harbor of Charlotte Amalie and its harbor on **Paradise Point Tramway**. Similar to a gondola at a ski lift, the three-and-a-half-minute tram ride takes you to the top of 697-foot Paradise peak where you can stop at the restaurant for a bite to eat and a breathtaking view. Leaves from the Havensight Mall area.

Blackbeard's Castle sits at the top of the city's **ninety-nine steps,** a staircase street built in the 1700s. Climb the steps, and stop for lunch. The kids can swim in the pool after they eat while Mom and Dad sip a cool drink and enjoy the panoramic vista of the town and harbor. The castle tower was built in 1679 and was thought to have been used by the notorious pirate Edward Teach. Today it is a lovely guest house and restaurant.

Drake's Seat, above Charlotte Amalie, is the mountain lookout from which Sir Francis Drake kept an eye on his fleet and watched for enemy ships. Come here in late afternoon or dusk to avoid the crowds.

Go nose to nose with fish, sea horses, giant rays, and sea turtles at **Coral World,** a marine complex that features an underwater observatory twenty feet below sea level. Windows look out at the fish rays, turtles, and other sea creatures going about their daily business. Saltwater tanks throughout the rest of the property contain excellent examples of the variety of sea life you'll view snorkeling around the islands. It's a good place to learn to identify the native coral and fish before heading out in fins and masks to see it on your own. In addition to the marine exhibits, there is a funny bird show, touch pond, tropical nature trail, sea turtle pool, and exotic bird habitat. Open daily 9 A.M. to 6 P.M. 6450 Coki Point. Tel. 340-775-1555, fax 340-775-9510.

After visiting Coral World, use one of their lockers to store your belongings and head next door to beautiful **Coki Beach,** known for its superior snorkeling and transparent waters. Showers are available.

Kayak and Snorkel Tours of the Marine Sanctuary are offered by Virgin Islands Ecotours. Trips last abut 2 ½ hours on stable kayaks that are easy for children and adults to master. Cruise past herons, ducks, and egrets, and peer into the waters to see rays, tarpon, and tiny reef fish. Reservations are required. 340-779-2155.

Magen's Bay on the northeast coast is one of the most beautiful long strands of beach in the Caribbean. A popular snorkeling spot, it has lifeguards, equipment rental, changing rooms, restaurants, and bars.

ST. CROIX

Once one of the most productive sugar producers of the West Indies, St. Croix at one time had more than 150 sugar plantations in operation. The crumbling stone remnants of the ruined sugar mills can still be seen throughout the island. Sea turtles nest on many of the island's beaches and areas have been protected to safeguard their eggs.

Its two quaint towns located at opposite ends of the island have a distinctly Danish flavor. Historic Christiansted has been the commercial center of the island for hundreds of years. Its eighteenth-century fort built to protect the harbor has been repeatedly damaged by hurricanes. In 1989, Hurricane Hugo's 200-mile-an-hour winds actually lifted boats out of the water and threw them against the fort's rock walls. At the other end of the island, Frederiksted's Fort Frederik was the site where the slaves from the Danish West Indies were freed in 1848. Buck Island, offshore, is a national monument with an underwater trail clearly marked for snorkelers and scuba.

WHERE TO STAY
Expensive

The Buccaneer
Address: Box 218, Christiansted, St. Croix, USVI 00821-0218
Telephone: 800-255-3881 or 340-773-2100, fax 340-773-0010
Website: www.thebuccaneer.com

First built in 1653, the pale pink plantation house that is the centerpiece of this classic Caribbean resort sits at the crest of a gentle hill overlooking a golf course on one side and the turquoise sea (at the eastern end of St. Croix, about a five-minute drive from Christiansted) on the other. Original walls, six- to eight-feet thick, made from bricks of crushed seashell and molasses, can still be seen in some places. Some of the resort's guest rooms are attached to this main building; the rest spill down the hill in small clusters to the shore. The picturesque ruins of a sugar mill still stand out front, and are the site of many gatherings and an occasional wedding. It's been recently renovated with a new floor and landscaping. The Buccaneer has been run by the Armstrong family for the past fifty years, and today it is managed by Elizabeth Armstrong, the granddaughter of the founders, who opened it as an eleven-room inn in 1948.

Two pools and three separate beaches offer unlimited sunning and swimming, but most of the action is on the palm-shaded beach by the watersports shack where kids can test complimentary snorkel gear, paddleboats, floats, and sand-castle building toys. The resort's private dock offers parasailing and a number of different excursions, but be sure to sail to Buck Island Reef National Monument for a chance to snorkel and explore the sandy island. Eight tennis courts host championships throughout the year.

Sea turtles nest on the Buccaneer's beaches, and families can help patrol the beaches each morning when the turtles are laying. The Buccaneer has been recognized for its contributions to sea turtle research. A lavish menu-ordered breakfast is included in the room rate, and excellent children's menus are available at the resort's restaurants.

Accommodations: Eight different types of accommodations are available, all with air-conditioning, small refrigerators, safes, private balconies and terraces; most have ceiling fans. Small families can fit into a standard, superior, or ocean view room, with two queen size beds (or one king and a roll-away) and views of golf course or ocean. Family cottages, hotel suites, and beachside doubloons feature a master bedroom with a king bed, and a sitting room with two daybeds or couch beds. Several suites that have connecting possibilities are available.

For Kids: A complimentary Pirate's Playhouse children's program operates during holidays and summer months from 10 A.M. to 2 P.M. for children ages four to twelve. Activities include local crafts such as calabash maracas made from local calabash trees, hair braiding and beading, plus games, swimming, and arts and crafts. A game room has a large Ping-Pong table, and kids can check out games and baseball bats and balls at the front desk any time of year.

Special Features: three beaches, eighteen-hole golf course, two pools, snorkeling, water bikes, floats, kayaks, Sunfish sailboats, windsurfers, cruises, scuba diving, glass-bottom boat rides, Hobie Cat, eight tennis courts (two lit for night play), spa, fitness center, jogging and nature trail, baby-sitting, entertainment, restaurants, bars.

$$$: Daily rates, double occupancy: rooms $170–$375, suites, family cottages, and doubloons $225–$525.

Moderate

Chenay Bay Beach Resort

Address: P.O. Box 24600 Christiansted, St. Croix, USVI 00820
Telephone: 800-548-4457 or 340-773-2918, fax 340-773-2918
Website: www.chenaybay.com

If your family can't make it through the night without a midnight snack, Chenay Bay's kitchenettes can help protect you from short-term famine (or at least the bothersome bellyaching of hungry kids). But if cooking on vacation makes you pale, breakfast, lunch, and dinner are served in the oceanfront restaurant. The resort's one-room cottages all come with enough gear to slap together a sandwich or cook a full meal, and a convenient shopper's shuttle will take you to the market to get the fixings.

You can load a picnic lunch in your beach bag, take a few steps, and there you are, standing on the broad white-sand beach that fades into a shallow and calm aquamarine sea, a perfect paddle pond for tiny guests. The same trade winds that ruffle the palm trees propel older kids on windsurfers to and fro across the translucent surface.

My children were delighted to check out their new playmates at Chenay Bay's children's program that operates during the summer months. When we finally convinced them to lounge with us adults for a day, we all took advantage of the complimentary watersports equipment and kayaked over to Green Cay, a small island preserve not far from Chenay Bay's beach, where we all flipped our fins over the undersea landscape.

Accommodations: Fifty one-bedroom cottages are outfitted as efficiency apartments with ocean or garden views; all have kitchenettes, air-conditioning, cable TV, and private decks.

For Kids: Cruzan Kids for children three to twelve operates over the summer months each weekday from 9 A.M. to 1 P.M. Active fun is their specialty—such as snorkel trips, tennis lessons, beach hikes, and shell hunts.

Special Features: beach, swimming pool, restaurant, shoppers shuttle, two tennis courts, complimentary snorkeling equipment, ocean kayaks, mats.

$$$: Kids under eighteen are free in a room with parents, third person over eighteen $25 per night. Daily rates, double occupancy: $135–$220.

Hibiscus Beach Hotel

Address: 4131 La Grande Princess, St. Croix, USVI 00820
Telephone: 800-442-0121, 340-773-4042, fax 340-773-7668
Website: hibiscus@worldnet.att.net

Situated right on the beach, these fresh plantation-style buildings with just thirty-eight rooms offer an unparalleled beachfront location at a moderate price. The resort doesn't have all the bells and whistles, such as watersports or fitness equipment, but it is a great buy in a pricey neighborhood, just ten minutes from Christiansted. Complimentary snorkel gear is available for guests, and an excellent Caribbean dance performance takes place each Friday night. Be sure to reserve tickets for it as people come to see it from all over the island. Endangered green and hawksbill turtles have been known to make Hibiscus Beach their nesting spot, and every once in awhile you can see them lumber up the beach to nest.

Accommodations: Thirty-eight rooms have either a king bed or two double beds; all have air-conditioning, cable TV, ceiling fans, minibars, and an in-room safe.

Special Features: beach, pool, snorkeling, bar, and restaurant.

$$$: Daily rates, double occupancy (children under twelve are free in existing bedding maximum two per room): $130–$200.

Budget

The Waves

Address: P.O. Box 1749 Kingshill, St. Croix, USVI 00851-1749
Telephone: 800-545-0603, 340-778-1804
Website: www.thewavesatcanebay.com

This reasonably priced property is a real find for families. Located on secluded Cane Bay, its eleven studios all have their own kitchens and private screened balconies overlooking the water. Guest rooms are literally built into the rock, and there is a seawater grotto pool that is flanked by lounge chairs. The water in the pool stays fresh, as waves spill over the edge bringing in an occasional fish; it's a great place to teach children to snorkel. Snorkeling and scuba diving are superb right from the resort's tiny beach, and a full-service dive center operates from the resort. Much larger Cane Bay Beach is a few hundred yards down the road. The restaurant on the property is open for dinner only. The Waves is run by Suzanne and Kevin Ryan, who along with their young daughter, give it a very personal flair.

Accommodations: Studios have a king bed or two twins; one roll-away can be added. All have kitchenettes, air-conditioning, ceiling fans, and TV. Adjoining rooms are available, as are cribs.

Special Features: restaurant, snorkel, scuba, saltwater pool.

$$$: Daily rates, double occupancy: $85–$195.

WHAT TO SEE AND DO

Building codes were used in **Christiansted** as early as 1747 to spare the town from fire. Consequently, the town looks much like it did in its heyday as a port in eighteenth and nineteenth centuries. Many of the original buildings built of thick coral brick or ballast bricks from sailing ships still stand. **Old Scalehouse** was built in 1856 to house the huge scale used to weigh merchandise coming into the harbor. Bright yellow **Fort Christiansvaern** (its color is typical of those used by the Danes) dates back to 1749. You can tour its dungeons and scramble about on its ramparts and old cannons. Open daily 8 A.M.–5 P.M. 340-773-1460.

Christian "Shan" Hendricks Market, built in 1735 as a slave market, is now used for market goods and produce. Company Street, open Wednesdays and Saturdays from 8 A.M. to 5 P.M.

Buck Island Reef National Monument is an 850-acre island and reef system with waters perfect for exploring marine life. In a depth of twelve feet with visibility of over one hundred feet, visitors can snorkel the spectacular marked underwater trail and experience a virtual rainbow of fish, sponges, and coral in a marine garden. The underwater snorkeling trail takes less than an hour, and there are many other areas to explore as well. If you don't want to get wet, you can inspect the reef from a glass-bottom boat. On Buck Island, two miles off St. Croix's north shore, visitors will find talcum-powder sand beaches, hiking trails, and an observation tower. We saw the remains of turtle eggs left behind by the tiny hatchlings who scrambled to the safety of the sea the night before. Ninety species of fish and several species of coral inhabit these waters. Mile Mark Charters has several trips a day and a good supply of snorkeling equipment in all sizes. 340-773-2628.

Estate Whim Plantation Museum is a restored sugar plantation with a windmill, cook house, and a look at life on a sugar plantation in the 1800s. Look closely at its building materials of native rock and coral with mortar made of seashells and sugar molasses. Open Tuesday–Saturday 10–4. Fredericksted. Tel. 340-772-0598.

Chris Columbus and his crew came ashore looking for fresh water at **Salt River** and tangled with the local Carib Indian population. His landing spot has been commemorated with a marker, and the area has been designated a national park. Its significance goes beyond Columbus, however, as Indian burial grounds and artifacts from three different native cultures have been discovered. You'll also find here the island's largest mangrove forests, twenty-seven species of threatened or endangered plants and animals, and a huge submarine canyon with superb scuba diving.

Sandy Point National Refuge, at the southwestern end of the island, offers protection to the endangered leatherback turtle. These massive sea reptiles nest here from March through June, while environmentalists work year-round to track the female turtles, save nests, and conduct research to help regenerate the population of leatherbacks. Hawksbill turtles and green turtles are also found here. To reserve a space to volunteer on night patrols during the turtles' nesting season with Earthwatch, call the **St. Croix Environmental Association** at 340-773-1989.

Hundreds of species pass through the tanks of **St. Croix Aquarium** each year. Owner Lonnie Kaczmarsky recycles the sea life that it has on display, setting specimens free and catching fresh examples. Come here before scuba diving or snorkeling to learn about the sea life of the area, or catch a lecture on the effect snorkelers and divers can have on the environment. Open Wednesday–Sunday 11 A.M.–4 P.M. Located on the Frederiksted waterfront, 3A Strand Street. 340-772-1345.

Take a **horseback ride** through rain forests, hidden Danish ruins, along the beach, and across hilltops with panoramic vistas of the Caribbean Sea at Paul and Jill's Equestrian Stables. Make reservations a day in advance. Reigning, trotting, cantering lessons are included for beginners. No children under eight accepted. Sprat Hall, Route 58. 340-772-2880 or 340-772-2627.

ST. JOHN

St. John is guaranteed to remain Caribbean postcard-perfect. Its spectacular white-sand beaches bordered by brilliant turquoise waters and emerald green hillsides thick with flowers are protected from any kind of development by its status as a national park. Laurence Rockefeller donated most of the island to the national park service in 1956. You'll find two world-class full-service resorts, villas tucked into tropical hillsides, and two unusual campgrounds. The rest of the island is full of unspoiled beaches, hiking trails through the woods, and a couple of small towns. Just a twenty-minute ferry ride from St. Thomas, St. John is a world away in slow-paced casual living. Many families rent a villa (and a car) to explore this unspoiled beauty of an island. Cruz Bay is the biggest city, although compared to Charlotte Amalie it's a small town.

WHERE TO STAY
Expensive

Westin St. John
Address: P.O. Box 8310, Great Cruz Bay, St. John, USVI 00831
Telephone: 800-WESTIN-1, 340-693-8000, fax 340-693-8888

Website: www.westin.com

A quarter-acre pool complex with islands, a waterfall, and a volleyball court is the centerpiece of this glamorous resort. If you can ever get the kids out of the pool, a fine white-sand beach is just steps away. The property was devastated by a direct hit from hurricane Marilyn several years back, and Westin resorts purchased it and began a series of renovations that repaired and upgraded the property. Its lush tropical landscape features forty-seven acres of bougainvillea, palm trees, and other tropical flowering plants and trees. The relaxed elegance for parents and guaranteed fun for kids makes this Westin an unbeatable destination for all family members. There are all kinds of watersports, a daily children's program, and six lit tennis courts. Golfers can head via ferry to the nearby Mahogany-run course on St. Thomas.

Accommodations: 285 guest rooms and suites and 96 fully equipped villas. Rooms all feature air-conditioning, in-room safes, coffeemaker, balcony or patio, minibar and in-room movies. Villas include studio, one-, two-, and three-bedroom units; many have their own private pools.

For Kids: The Westin Kids Club operates year-round for children ages five–twelve.

Special Features: beach, swimming pool, Jacuzzi, fitness center, six lit tennis courts, snorkeling, scuba diving, kayaking, windsurfing, sailing, fishing, parasailing, three restaurants, a deli, bar, excursions, shops, baby-sitting, car rental.

$$$: Children age eighteen and under stay free in their parents' room. Daily rates, double occupancy: rooms $245–$575, villas $600 and up. Family packages are available throughout the year.

Caneel Bay Resort

Address: P.O. Box 720, Cruz Bay, St. John USVI 00831-0720
Telephone: 800-928-8889 or 340-776-6111, fax 340-693-8280
Website: www.rosewood-hotels.com

Follow the sun from beach to beach—seven in all—as it warms posh Caneel Bay's 170-acre private peninsula that is completely surrounded by national park. Laurence Rockefeller purchased the land in 1952 when it was a sugar plantation, and began turning the junglelike environs into a discreet and elegant tropical vacation wonderland where guest cottages are concealed amongst jacarandas, tropical orchids, palm trees, bougainvillea, and the occasional wild donkey! Its service and delicious restaurants are legendary.

Turtle Town, a special area just for kids, houses the resort's children's program, which focuses on environmental appreciation of the resort and island. Children's games and videos can be checked out, and lessons in sailing, scuba, and tennis can be arranged. Nature trails head out into the primitive natural beauty of the Virgin Islands National Park. Rooms are spread throughout the grounds, and many guests ride about the property in an open-air bus that makes a complete loop of the property every twenty minutes. A ferry run by Caneel Bay picks guests up at the airport and carries them to the resort.

Accommodations: 168 guest rooms have air-conditioning, ceiling fans, hand-crafted furniture, patios, minibars, and in-room safes, and all have views of one or more of the seven beaches and gardens. There is a maximum of three people in a room, and price is determined by size and location. There are no telephones or TVs.

For Kids: Turtle Town's activities begin at 9 A.M. and end at 4 P.M. Parents may join their children if they desire. Activities include nature walks, searching for turtle nests, pirate treasure hunts, and magic shows. Reservations are required, a fee is charged, and half-day and full-day slots are available.

Special Features: beaches, swimming pool, snorkeling, Sunfish sailing, sea kayaks, windsurfing, scuba, private excursions with a marine naturalist, boat rentals, deep-sea fishing, nightly movie presentations, eleven tennis courts, baby-sitting, restaurants, jogging trails, nature tours, fitness center, aerobics classes, shop.

$$$: One child under seventeen is free in parents' room. Daily rates, double occupancy: $200–$700.

Budget

Cinnamon Bay Campground
Address: P.O. Box 720, Cruz Bay, St. John, USVI 00831-0720
Telephone: 340-776-6330, fax 340-776-6458
Website: www.virgin.islands.national-park.com

Situated on the island's north coast, on its longest stretch of white sand beach, Cinnamon Bay has cottages, completely outfitted tents, and bare campsites for those who like to pack and carry their own gear. The campground has many of the extras that you'll find at a full-service resort, such as a complete watersports center, a snack bar, a restaurant (with good food and reasonable prices), and superb snorkeling. A roped-off, safe swimming area extends to a tiny island a few hundred yards offshore so that snorkelers can avoid any interference from boats. Huge hermit crabs scale the palm trees and scuttle across paths, providing endless entertainment for children.

The watersports center has windsurfers, sea kayaks, sailboats and snorkeling equipment for rent. An attractively priced boat tour allows you to tailor a day trip to your interests. Park rangers lead daily tours of the Virgin Islands National Park, and guests have access to public phones, safe-deposit boxes, lockers, a general store, and a gift shop. The island's only snuba center operates from here for adults and children eight and up.

Accommodations: 26 tent sites, 44 tent platforms, 40 cottages. The fifteen-by-fifteen foot screened cottages have four twin beds, electric lights, and an outdoor terrace. Two extra cots can be added for a family of six, and linens are changed twice weekly. All units have a ceiling fan, picnic table, charcoal grill, propane gas stove, ice chest, water container, and cooking and eating utensils. The ten by-fourteen-foot canvas tents are on a solid floor and have cots, picnic tables, charcoal grills, propane gas stove, ice chest, water container, gas lantern, and cooking and eating utensils. Bare sites have a picnic table and charcoal grill. All are near central bathhouses. Taxi buses run frequently from Cinnamon Bay to other parts of the island.

Special Features: beach, shop, restaurant, snuba, boat rentals

$$$: Rates are nightly based on double occupancy: cottages $63–$105; tents $48–$75, bare sites $17. Children under three free of charge; extra person $5–$15.

Maho Bay Campground

Address: St. John, PO Box 310, USVI 00831
Telephone: 800-392-9004, 340-776-6204, fax 340-776-6226
Website: www.maho.org

Simple screened tent cabins are tucked into a hillside high above the beach and connected with Swiss Family Robinson–style wooden walkways. There are 105 tent cottage sites on fourteen acres; some offer spectacular Caribbean views, while others are hidden in the trees. A restaurant serves breakfast and dinner and has views of the sparkling aquamarine bay below. You won't need a car if your kids are good hikers, as nearby beaches offer wonderful snorkeling areas. A shuttle stops here several times a day and goes into town. The campground is not recommended for children under four, and some children under age seven find it a difficult place to stay because of the amount of walking up and down to the beach.

The activities desk will help you plan sailing, scuba diving, snorkeling, windsurfing, island boat tours, Sunfish sailing, rafting, and sea kayaking at a reasonable cost. Snorkeling equipment, beach chairs, and rubber rafts can be rented. Weekly slide shows describe the local flora and fauna.

Accommodations: Each tent cottage in Maho has an ice chest and pantry shelves and can comfortably sleep four or five people. Their translucent fabric screen and wood construction breathes with the trade winds. All housekeeping equipment is supplied (sheets, towels, pots, pans, dishes, and so on), and every unit has a propane stove, an ice cooler, and an electric fan. The store sells blocks of ice, basic groceries, and sundries. Communal bathhouses offer hot and cold water and flush toilets. No laundry facilities are available.

$$$: Daily rates, for double occupancy: $75–$125. Children under sixteen stay free from May 1 through November 15 in tent with parents. Rest of year $15 per night per person.

Maho Bay's Green Accommodations

Telephone: 800-392-9004, 340-776-6204, fax 340-776-6226
Website: www.maho.org

Ecology-minded travelers can stay in the more upscale "green" properties that offer the comforts of a traditional resort but are powered by the ubiquitous St. John sunshine. The dwellings were constructed of recycled materials: lumber made from discarded plastics, recycled clay tile floors, recycled steel nails, etc. *Harmony* is located above the tent cabins of Maho Bay, and *Estate Concordia* is twenty-five minutes away on Salt Pond Bay where the island's best snorkeling, shelling, and hiking are found. *Concordia Eco-tents* are just over the hill from Estate Concordia.

Accommodations: *Harmony* has two sizes of studios that sleep three to four people, all two-story with kitchens, full baths, and decks with spectacular views.

Ten *Estate Concordia* units sleep three to five people, and offer full kitchens, and more luxurious furnishings. They have their own swimming pool and more personal attention. You'll need a rental car because of their remote location.

Concordia Eco-tents are high-tech tent cottages with private baths, running water, solar and wind energy, and kitchen facilities with refrigerators. Each can sleep five or six people on twin beds and a queen-size sofa bed.

$$$: Daily rates, double occupancy: Harmony: $100–$215. Add $25 per night for an extra person, regardless of age. Concordia: $100–$215 minimum one week stay. Concordia Eco-tents: $70–$110; extra person $10–$25 per night.

Villas and Condos

Renting your own home by the week or month is one of the most popular ways to vacation on St. John. You can rent first-class luxury homes with private pools and cooks or simple cottages with only the basics, but all are just minutes from a magnificent white-sand beach. The following businesses offer all types of villas:

Catered To: 800-462-6641, 340-776-6641, fax 340-693-8191

Private Homes for Private Vacations: phone or fax 340-776-6876

St. John Villa and Condo Rentals: 800-338-0987

Vacation Homes: 340-776-6094

WHAT TO SEE AND DO

Virgin Islands National Park has well-mapped nature trails crisscrossing through it and some of the most beautiful unspoiled beaches in the world. The **Visitor Center** in Cruz Bay (340-776-6201) offers all kinds of nature talks and guided tours such as snorkel trips, bird walks, guided hikes to see petroglyphs and an old sugar mill, and seashore walks. Rangers set up evening programs at Maho Bay Camps, Cinnamon Bay, and Caneel Bay Resort.

The perfect first snorkel experience for kids is the self-guided 225-yard underwater trial at **Trunk Bay**. Large underwater signs clearly identify species of coral and other items of interest. There are changing rooms, equipment rentals, snack bar, showers, and a lifeguard. The more serious diving is done about two miles out. Check the cruise ship listings and pick the day when the fewest ships are docking, as many passengers come here to snorkel. **Annaberg Plantation,** a ruined plantation great house, has cultural demonstrations such as basket weaving and bread making.

5.

MEXICO

Our family loves Mexico. We can't get enough of the beaches—the long stretches of talcum-soft sand edged by impossibly blue, soothingly warm water. We snorkel, swim, splash, kayak, and bodysurf until we're so waterlogged we collapse on our beach towels or head back to our room to read a book or play a game. The unhurried, leisurely pace of life south of the border suits us just fine on vacation.

But just as much as we come for the recreation and relaxation, we also relish the warm and embracing Mexican culture, which extends a special welcome to little ones. We find that our children open many doors for us throughout the country. And our visits to Mexico have opened up a new world for our children—they've discovered that the world is a big and varied place, and that their neighborhood and youth culture is not the center of it all. Even more important, they've discovered the power of speaking a second language. Because children are present in all facets of life throughout Mexico, my two find ample opportunities to strike up a conversation or a game with local youngsters. At first they communicated using sign language and smiles, but they were soon motivated to learn Spanish words and phrases so they could play and chat with local children.

Plan your trip to allow plenty of time to experience the real Mexico by visiting some of the smaller towns and villages, rather than only the areas created just for tourists. You can headquarter on the beach and enjoy the sun, sea, and sand, and rent a car or, better yet, take a local bus to a nearby village to explore the marketplace, or stop for lunch or dinner at a restaurant around the *zócalo*, or town square, while you watch the life of the town.

Both the Caribbean and Pacific coasts have wonderful beach towns with a great variety of accommodations. Generally speaking, the Pacific coast has rougher waters than the Caribbean Sea, which has better visibility and is a better choice if you plan to concentrate on scuba diving or snorkeling. Families who want to tuck a little history into their sun, surf, and sand can head to the Yucatan peninsula and stay on a glorious beach, taking short excursions to some of the world's premier archaeological sites. Glamorous resort towns such as Puerto Vallarta not only have gorgeous beaches, but an active yachting scene

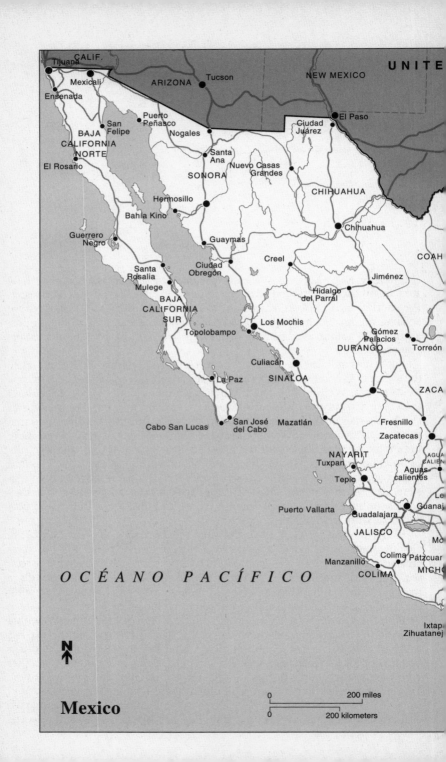

Mexico

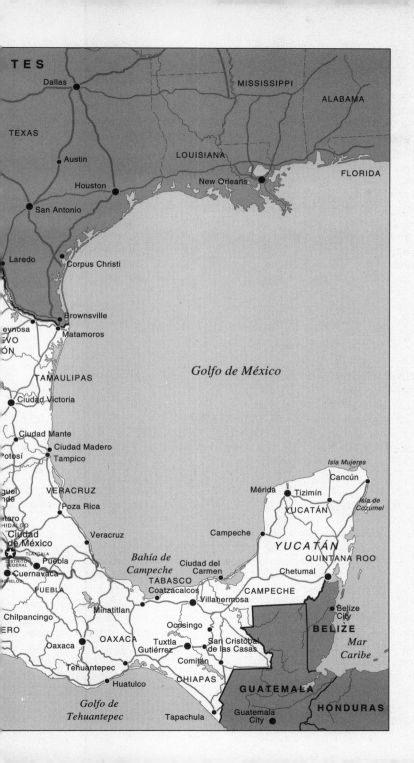

and some of the best restaurants outside of Mexico City. Quieter Manzanillo has spectacular beaches, excellent bodysurfing, and plenty of lodgings with kitchens, where you can spread out as if you were home. Aficionados of sport fishing should book a stay in Los Cabos or Mazatlan, which have some of the best ocean angling in the world. Baja California is a land of stark contrasts, where dramatic desert landscape is edged by a brilliant blue Pacific Ocean; surfers still make pilgrimages to its legendary beaches.

Some resort towns in Mexico, such as Puerto Vallarta and Mazatlan, have been transformed into their present state slowly over the past fifty years. But another group of resort areas were nothing more than sleepy fishing villages and empty white-sand beaches until about thirty years ago when the Mexico government decided to identify areas of the country that were well-suited to tourism. They added up the factors that they were looking for—perfect stretches of white sand bordered by crystalline aquamarine waters—and created made-for-tourist towns such as Cancún and Ixtapa where hotels now sit side by side along the sea.

Mexico has a vacation for every taste, and better yet, every pocketbook. Families can find truly affordable beachfront lodging throughout most of the country.

PLANNING YOUR TRIP
Visitor Information
Website: mexico-travel.com
Mexican Government Tourist Offices (MGTO)
United States: Chicago, IL (312-606-9252); Houston, TX (713-629-1611); Los Angeles, CA (310-203-8191); Miami, FL (305-443-9160); New York, NY (212-421-6655); Mexican Embassy Tourism Delegate, 1911 Pennsylvania Avenue, Washington, DC 20005 (202-728-1750). *Canada:* 1 Place Ville-Marie, Suite 1526, Montreal, QUEB H3B 2B5 (514-871-1052); 2 Bloor Street West, Suite 1801, Toronto, ON, M4W 3E2 (416-925-2753); 999 West Hastings, Suite 1610, Vancouver, BC, V6C 2W2 (604-669-2845)
Entry Requirements and Customs
A passport is always the best form of identification when you're traveling abroad. It's what most customs officials are used to and it will help you avoid delays at the border as well as making it easier to change money.

If you don't have a passport, you may enter Mexico with a photo ID, such as a driver's license plus proof of citizenship, an original birth certificate, or a notarized copy of a birth certificate. Remember to make photocopies of your passport's data page and leave it with someone at home, carrying a second copy with you separate from your passport. If you lose your passport, contact the nearest embassy and the local police. *American Citizens:* Each member of the family (even infants) will need their own passport. Obtain them through the Department of State Office of Passport Services at 1425 "K" Street, Washington, DC, 20522. Their information line is 202-647-0518. *Canadian Citizens:*

Children under sixteen may be included on a parent's passport, but they must have their own passport if they plan to travel alone. The passport office can give you information on where to obtain forms at 514-283-2152.

Note that the heaviest demand for passports starts in January and continues until August as people get ready for their summer vacation. It can take as much as eight weeks to process a passport application. Personal applications at regional offices can expedite the matter.

**Important Note: A parent traveling to Mexico with his or her children MUST get a bonded note from the other parent stating that he or she has permission to take the kids to Mexico. The letter should include your destination, the duration of your visit, and the name, phone number, and address of the parent not accompanying the child.

You are allowed to bring $400 worth of goods back into the United States duty free as long as the items are for your personal use and not for resale. Many articles are illegal, such as pre-Hispanic Indian art, Cuban cigars, lottery tickets, and fireworks. Avoid buying jewelry with tortoise shell or black coral, or anything made of endangered animals. The World Wildlife Fund's *Buyer Beware* (800-634-4444) brochure contains information about items illegal to bring into the United States. Always carry prescription drugs in their original containers accompanied by their prescriptions, if you have them, to avoid delays at the border.

When to Go

Mexico has two main travel seasons: high and low. High season begins about December 20 and runs through Easter. Prices are at their highest during this time, and resorts are more crowded, particularly during Christmas and Easter. Low season begins after Easter and runs through mid-December, when prices for accommodations and air/land packages run 20 to 50 percent lower. Many families travel in the summer months, and while many resort areas are cooled by tropical breezes, the farther south you go the hotter it gets. Rainy season begins in May and continues until mid-October, while dry season starts in mid-October and ends in late April. The rain storms tend to be in short bursts; they cool the air and shouldn't affect your travel plans. Avoid traveling to Mexico over spring break when American college students flock south and spend their days and nights partying with great abandon and ear-splitting volume.

Health and Safety

No special inoculations are required for entering Mexico, but your children should be up-to-date on their vaccinations and a tetanus shot is recommended for each member of the family. Other health concerns include:

Turista: Mexico's greatest health risk is traveler's diarrhea, also known as turista or Montezuma's revenge. To prevent it, be vigilant about what you and your family eat and drink. Drink only bottled water or water that has been boiled for twenty minutes. Most large tourist hotels have water purification systems and post signs in the bathroom stating that the water is safe to drink. Stick to fruits and vegetables that can be peeled. Avoid drinks with ice at nontourist establishments, and stay away from uncooked food and unpasturized milk and milk products. Make sure the food you eat has been freshly cooked and is still warm. Be wary of Mexican hamburger and pork dishes and avoid uncooked meat and seafood dishes such as ceviche or sushi. Be sure to bring along a good anti-diarrhea agent or bring Immodium or Pepto Bismol, which you can purchase at any drugstore. Some people have reported great success chewing Pepto Bismol tablets as a preventative measure before and during the trip.

If you do get sick, dehydration is the main danger, especially for children, so be sure to drink plenty of purified water. Eat bland foods (the BRAT diet—bananas, rice, applesauce and toast—is a good one for diarrhea) and rest until your symptoms lessen or disappear. Families with very young children may want to bring a small supply of Pedialyte, a rehydration solution that is also available in some Mexican pharmacies.

Mosquitoes: Other health risks for people traveling to certain rural areas of Mexico are dengue fever and malaria, both carried by mosquitoes. While most urban regions and resort areas have no problems, if you're worried, wear insect repellent that contains DEET, which is safe for your children only if used in a concentration of 35 percent or less (and 6 to 10 percent for toddlers and babies) and used according to the label instructions. Do not apply it to the hands of very young children as it may end up in their mouths, and take care when applying it near the eyes. Wash it off as soon as the risk of exposure has ended. Other precautions include wearing long clothing, using mosquito nets at dawn and dusk, and avoiding wearing highly scented perfumes. Insect repellent is available in many (but not all) tourist areas, so it's best to bring your own.

Sunburn: The Mexican sun is *caliente*, especially for gringos not used to hotter climates. Be sure to wear sunscreen (at least SPF 30) and apply it liberally and often. Try to stay out of the sun during peak hours, between 11 and 2 or 3, and cover up with a hat and loose, cool clothing. The most effective cure for a sunburn is to stay out of the sun for a few days.

Crime: Although Mexico's crime rate is much lower than that of the United States, tourists are always targets for pickpockets and thieves, as they are presumed to be wealthy (by Mexican standards) and carrying valuables. Take the same precautions you would anywhere: avoid beaches and empty streets at night, and never take valuables onto the beach. Instead, lock them in your hotel safe. Always lock your car, keeping valuables out of sight in your trunk. It's wise to wear a hidden money belt or keep your wallet on an inside pocket, carrying a small amount of cash in your pocket or purse when you explore a town or go shopping. Obtain travelers checks before you go, and keep a separate record of them in your luggage. Leave your expensive jewelry at home.

Important Phone Numbers:
- U.S. State Department Citizens Emergency Center Hotline: 202-647-5225
- National Center for Disease Control International Travelers Hotline: CDC, National Center for Infectious Diseases, Division of Quarantine, Traveler's Health Section, 1600 Clifton Road, M/S E-3, Atlanta, GA 30333 (404-332-4565) www.cdc.gov.

Traveling with Babies

It's perfectly safe to travel with babies in Mexico as long as you take certain precautions, especially with their food. While baby food, dry cereal, and formula are easily found in resort areas, it's often wise to bring your own to avoid a change in diet that might upset your little one's system. Be extra vigilant about bottled water with babies, making sure the bottles are sealed and state *agua purificada*. While larger hotels often purify the water used throughout their establishments, it's still best to buy sealed bottled water for babies just to be extra safe.

Disposable diapers are available throughout Mexico, but most local brands are of a poorer quality. Top name brands sold in the United States can be found south of the border, but usually at prices much higher than you're used to paying at home. Bring a healthy supply with you. Cribs are a rarity in many hotels, except the very biggest and most deluxe. Always ask before you go, in case you should bring a portacrib with you. Some families bring a portacrib because the safety standards of cribs in Mexico are slightly different than in the United States and Canada. If you plan to rent a car, double-check that car seats for infants are available or bring your own.

Make sure your accommodations have window screens to protect your baby from mosquito bites, and if your child is too young to wear insect repellent, dress your baby in long, loose-fitting clothing, and bring mosquito netting.

Money Matters

The Mexican monetary unit is called the *nuevo peso* or new peso. You can get a far better rate of exchange if you change your money once you're in Mexico, although it's helpful to have a small amount of pesos before you go to avoid the long lines at the airport change windows. It's most convenient to exchange money at *Casas de Cambio,* which are readily found throughout the cities and towns that cater to tourists. Exchanging money at Mexican banks can be extremely slow and often involves standing in a number of different long lines; avoid them if you can. Larger cities will have ATMs, which often have the best exchange rates, and large hotels usually will change travelers checks for you. Dollars are often accepted in the Cancún and Baja California areas. Carry with you only the money you think you'll need for the day, leaving the rest in your hotel safe.

Most tourist towns have set fees for taxi rides, but to be safe, settle on a fee before you step into a cab. Bargaining at the marketplace and sidewalk stands is permissible and expected, but many shops have set prices and will not bargain.

On a Budget

Prices in Mexico are usually favorable to American and Canadian tourists, and offer excellent value for the dollar. Unless you're staying in a first-class resort, which will most likely have similar prices to those of home, you'll find that everything costs a bit less than its counterpart in the United States and Canada.

To save money on accommodations, look for a small hotel or a condo with a kitchen so you can cook your own food. Visiting the market and bargaining for groceries is one of the great joys of a Mexican vacation and one your kids will remember long after you've returned home. Tomatoes, peppers, tiny bananas, and fruits and vegetables you've never laid eyes on before are piled high in row after colorful row. If bargaining for produce and other foodstuff intimidates you, there are small grocery stores in all towns, where you can shop as you do at home.

If you don't have a kitchen and plan to do most of your eating in restaurants, look for the *comida corrida,* the fixed-price meal, which usually offers an ample lunch or dinner at a reasonable price. Traditional Mexican dishes are priced lower than American or foreign fare, so sample the local cuisine. Buy Mexican-brand bottled water, and buy it at the market, not the hotel shop.

The plaza (called the *zócalo*) is the main square of a town and often consists of a small park with benches and a bandstand. Sidewalk cafés along the *zócalo* are a wonderful place to headquarter for people-watching, or to enjoy free entertainment on Sundays when band concerts often take place. For the price of a soft drink you can listen to mariachis and other musicians play music around the town square.

Take public transportation and ride Mexican buses; they are generally safe, reliable, colorful, and quite inexpensive. Avoid the Mexican train system, which needs a complete upgrade and is a risky business to ride.

Culture, Food, Music and Crafts

Mexico has some of the world's most talented artisans and craftsmen, and most tourist areas sell handicrafts, or *artesanias,* produced by people from all over the country. You'll find exquisite and quite affordable silverwork from Taxco, hand-painted folk art figurines from Oaxaca, pottery from Puebla, handwoven hammocks from the Yucatan, masks from Guerrero, and more. All cities have a marketplace that sells these handcrafted treasures, and most have shops that sell them as well. Resort areas also have tourist boutiques, shopping malls, and hotel shops that sell these items, usually at a higher price. You're expected to bargain in the market, so shop around to get a sense of prices and to know what is reasonable to pay. Quality may be inconsistent; take your time and inspect items you plan to buy carefully.

Be sure to keep all of your receipts; you will be asked to show customs officials what you've bought and you must fill out a form stating the value of each piece and the total value of all items purchased in the country.

Food

Mexican food isn't nearly as hot as its reputation has it. The heat is added at the table with chilies and sauces after it's been served and according to the diner's tastes. You'll rarely see a table in a Mexican restaurant without a bowl of chilies and a bottle of hot sauce or two. Mexican food tends to be simple and delicious, with tortillas, beans, tomatoes, chilies, and squash cooked in many different ways. Traditional tortillas are the best-known staple of Mexico and are eaten at breakfast, lunch, and dinner. They are often used in place of a fork and spoon to scoop up food off the plate. Lunch is the main meal, and dinner is served late, usually after 8 P.M.

Fresh fruits and vegetables should be sampled and enjoyed; be sure to wash those without a peel in water treated with a commercial disinfectant. Papaya, mango, guayaba, banana, jicama, and avocado are just of a few of the delicious fresh treats in store for your family. Fresh-squeezed fruit juices and fruit shakes, called *licuados* or *jugos des fruitas* are found throughout Mexico and are safe to sample in a restaurant with hygienic practices.

Music

Mexican music has an emotional and expressive power no matter what style you hear. Mariachi music, the staple of the tourist industry, is popular with the locals countrywide and is often played in plazas on Sunday afternoon. It's known for its big sound and violin and trumpet instrumentation. Other popular, more traditional sounds, are *norteño* music, with its accordion accompaniment and serious lyrics, and *ranchera* music loaded with melodramatic passions and characterized by cries of "aye yi yi yi." *Banda* music is a fusion of *norteña* style with brass instruments. The *bandas* dominate TV music programs and fill stadiums and music halls throughout the countryside. It's their names you'll see painted on the sides of buildings and along the roads.

WHERE TO STAY

The variety of accommodations in Mexico is as broad as in any tourist destination. In addition to glamorous high-rise luxury hotels and all-inclusive playgrounds where English rather than Spanish is the language of the staff, you'll find charming little palm-roofed bungalows on the beach and simple condominiums with kitchens. Shop the packages to find low-priced airfare and accommodations deals, but be sure to read the fine print before you sign on the dotted line. Generally speaking, lodging prices in Mexico, with the exception of Cancún and possibly Los Cabos, are lower than similar lodging in the Caribbean and Hawaii. Price categories in this chapter are rack rates, the highest price you'll pay for a room without any discounts, and they're for the purpose of comparison. Always inquire about discounts and package deals to get the lowest price possible.

Expensive: over $190 per night
Moderate: $90–$190 per night
Budget: $90 or under per night

Mayan Riviera

What's fondly referred to as the Mayan Riviera is really the Caribbean side of the Yucatan peninsula, where some of Mexico's most popular beachfront playgrounds stretch along the sand. The resort scene along this coast is anchored by Cancún, which sizzles with nonstop action from dawn until well past dusk. Hotels of all shapes and sizes sit shoulder to shoulder along the white sand, and restaurants, shopping, watersports, and excursions keep action-loving families happy for days on end.

Families wanting a quieter or less expensive beach vacation should pick Isla Mujeres, Cozumel, or Playa del Carmen for their stay. All feature smaller communities, beautiful beaches, spectacular snorkeling and diving, and still place you in close proximity to the fascinating Mayan archaeological sites in the region.

If you have limited time and can only spend one day touring the ancient Mayan treasures of the region, Chichen Itza is the archaeological site that will most impress your children and offer them the most to see. If you can, spend the night near the ruins so you can see the 9 P.M. English sound-and-light show and can get an early start viewing the ruins in the cool of the morning before the tour buses arrive at around 11.

Other amusements in the area are worth exploring, from the somewhat commercialized but delightfully fun snorkeling parks Xel-ha and Xcaret to secluded beaches and a spectacular biology reserve.

CANCÚN

When the weather turns cold in the Northeast and Midwest, families looking for package deals, sandy beaches, warm saltwater, and nonstop action head south to Cancún. Thirty years ago the area was an uninhabited fourteen-mile-long sun-soaked strip of spectacular beach bordered on one side by the Caribbean Sea and on the other by a placid lagoon. The government agency in charge of developing tourism throughout the country picked it as their first experiment in resort development. Today Cancún has more than 125 hotels and over 22,000 rooms. You name it, they've got it—time-shares, monolithic high-rise hotels, discos, shops, restaurants—a regular Miami Beach of options.

More than two million people—Americans, Canadians, Mexicans, and South Americans—visited Cancún last year. English is spoken everywhere and menus printed in several different languages offer both Mexican food and the food Americans are most familiar with. Cancún is not particularly authentic Mexico in feeling, but the beaches are some of the most beautiful in the world, and the snorkeling and scuba diving are among the best anywhere thanks to offshore coral reefs abundant with marine life. Surprisingly, the spectacular white sand never gets hot, not even in the middle of the day, since it's made of porous limestone, rather than coral, which does not hold the heat. Cancún has the best year round weather of all Mexican resorts and is very low on rainfall in the summer.

Cancún's proximity to prehistoric Mayan ruins lets you combine a recreational beach vacation with some fascinating education and history. Tours leave from Cancún and take guests in air-conditioned comfort to all three of the largest sites in the area—Chichén Itzá, Cobá, and Tulum. If your family is particularly interested in Mayan archaeology, rent your own car or make different transportation arrangements so you can spend the night and visit during the uncrowded and cooler morning hours.

There's no real budget lodging in Cancún's hotel zone (*Zona Hoteleria*) although there are plenty of other choices in the moderate and expensive range.

Best Sweet Treat: look for licuados—fruit drinks—made of cantaloupe, pineapple, watermelon, and other fruits

WHERE TO STAY
Expensive

Caesar Park Beach and Golf Resort
Address: Km 17 Paseo Kukulkán, Retorno Lacandones, 77500 Cancún, Quintana Roo, Mexico
Telephone: 800-228-3000, (52) 98-81-8000, fax (52) 98-81-8080
Website: www.westin.com

Caesar Park sits like a triangular palace surrounded by a carpet of rich grassy lawns and seven hundred yards of white-sand beach flanked by Caribbean waters so clear you can see reefs forty feet below. If you're not paddling in the sea, you can swim in seven interconnected pools that offer enough water acreage to stay uncrowded, even in the peak of the season when the resort's 426 rooms are filled. Caesar Park's own eighteen-hole par-72 golf course built around Mayan ruins is just across the street, and guests receive a discount on green fees. The three-tiered pyramid-like structure of the resort allows each room an unobstructed ocean view. A children's program operates during most of the year.

Accommodations: 426 deluxe rooms, 16 junior suites, 6 master suites, 80 Royal Beach Club rooms. Rooms have tiled floors with area rugs, rattan furniture, and local artwork. Each room has a minibar, in-room safe, and some have private terraces. Royal Beach Club rooms and suites are in separate two- to three-story buildings and have complimentary cocktails, air-conditioning, ceiling fan, coffeemakers, marble bathrooms, and Jacuzzi tubs.

For Kids: The Kids Club offers supervised activities as part of the gym program; baby-sitting is available, too.

Special Features: Seven connected pools, two Jacuzzis, health club with sauna and massage, gym, sailing, windsurfing, waterskiing, diving, fishing, two lit tennis courts, four restaurants, a lobby lounge, swim-up bar, eighteen-hole golf course, driving range, pro-shop, 24-hour room service, laundry.

$$$: Daily rates, double occupancy: $260–$1,600.

Camino Real

Address: Av. Kukulkán, 77500 Punta Cancún (Apdo. Postal 14), Cancún, Quintana Roo, Mexico
Telephone: 800-7-CAMINO, (52) 98-83-0100, fax (52) 98-83-1730
Website: www.caminoreal.com

One of the first luxury hotels on the peninsula, the Camino Real is surrounded by sea and lagoon and claims one of the best locations in Cancún. The original hotel is a low-rise masterpiece of "Mexican Minimalism," paying more attention to complementing nature's own beauty than to building a monstrous tribute to concrete. The newest addition to the hotel, an eighteen-story luxury tower, spoils some of the original ambience. The typical American high-rise is designed to accommodate as many guests as possible while taking up the least space, but in the meantime it obstructs the skyline. But nevertheless, the hotel is one of Cancún's nicest and all rooms are plush and comfortable with ocean or lagoon views and, in some cases, even hammocks on their balconies. A private saltwater lagoon, in which guests are allowed to practice their snorkeling, teems with tropical fish and sea turtles. A freshwater pool and stretch of beach covered with shady *palapas* are popular places for relaxing, and there is a dive shop, a windsurfing operation, and all kinds of watersports on the premises. Many of the hotel's restaurants overlook the beach. The Camino Real chain is known for its interest in keeping family travelers happy, and its children's club is offered during holiday periods throughout the year.

Accommodations: 296 rooms in the main building have balconies, a king bed or two doubles, marble floors, air-conditioning, minibar, cable TV, personal safe, and telephones. Suites have private terraces and Jacuzzis and are decorated with original Mexican folk art. Camino Real Club guests receive complimentary breakfasts, cocktails, and snacks. 85 rooms in the tower are concierge level.

For Kids: Children's program operates during holiday periods and the month of July. It's available for age five to twelve. Baby-sitting is easily arranged through the front desk.

Special Features: beach, fresh- and saltwater pools, tennis, volleyball, fishing, scuba diving, water- and jet skiing, sailing, snorkeling, and windsurfing, three restaurants, a bar featuring live Mexican music nightly, an ocean-view disco, excursions, 24-hour room service, car rentals, beauty salon, shops, fitness center.

$$$: Children twelve and under free in their parents' room. Daily rates, double occupancy rooms: $185–$415; Camino Real Club rates $200–$305, suites $1,320–$1,600.

Westin Regina Resort

Address: Km 20 Paseo Kukulkán, 77500 Cancún, Quintana Roo, Mexico
Telephone: 800-228-3000, (52) 98-85-0086, fax (52) 98-85-0779
Website: www.westin.com

The Westin lazily stretches along a strip of pure white sand that separates the tranquil Nipchutké lagoon from the open sea. Guest rooms are in a series of low-rise buildings that claim more of the beach than many of the tall high-rise hotels in other sections of Cancún. The sands are never too crowded and guests can sun or swim on either shore or in any one of five freshwater pools overlooking the ocean. It's one of the only hotels in Cancun that offers a children's program year-round, regardless of how many children are in the hotel. Though the Westin is a fair distance from the shops and restaurants of the hotel strip—about a twenty-minute cab ride—it's nice to be removed from the commercialism, and the Westin has plenty of its own bars, shops, and restaurants to keep guests busy. Rooms have white walls and pale marble floors and are decorated with brightly colored Mexican folk art.

Accommodations: 385 rooms and suites are spacious, with air-conditioning, ceiling fans, in-room safes, and minibars.

For Kids: The Westin Kids Club offers a day-care center for children ages five to twelve open daily throughout the year. Children enjoy a variety of indoor and outdoor activities. Baby-sitting can be arranged through the concierge.

Special Features: a quarter of a mile of beach, five pools, fitness and recreation center with aerobics classes, sauna, massages, and a huge indoor Jacuzzi, two lit tennis courts, scuba diving, snorkeling, boating, sunset cruises, waterskiing, fishing, 24-hour medical service, 24-hour room service, shops.

$$$: Children under age eighteen free in their parents' room. Daily rates, double occupancy: $180–$300.

Royal Caribbean

Address: Blvd. Kukulkán km. 16.5, Cancún, Quintana Roo, Mexico 77500
Telephone: 800-221-8090, (52) 98-81-0100, fax (52) 98-85-0032
Website: www.royalresorts.com

This condominium-style resort is the sister property to two other Royal Resort condominium/timeshare properties that sit side by side on a gorgeous stretch of white sand. The condos, called villas, are quite spacious and have one or two bedrooms and full kitchens, and can be rented by the week by families wanting extra space and the ability to cook. The three properties are all are linked by a long walkway with the Royal Caribbean in the middle, and all have large swimming pools, kiddy pools, restaurants, and a variety of watersports. The Royal is particularly well-suited for families since it contains an activities center where the children's program meets, free swim lessons for kids, and a boating marina.

Accommodations: 207 two-bedroom villas have a living/dining room and fully-equipped kitchen; one of the bedrooms has a king bed and the other has two twins; a sofa bed in the living room allows for two more people. The one-bedroom suite is the same living/dining kitchen set up but comes with the master bedroom only. Rooms only can be rented and come with the two twin beds. All rooms are air-conditioned.

For Kids: Organized children's activities are arranged for three age groups: Turtles (age two to five), Dolphins (age six to nine) and Seagulls (age ten to fourteen). Activities might include sports, games, swimming lessons, puppet shows, arts and crafts, pool volleyball, and treasure hunts. The program takes place daily from 10 A.M. to 3 P.M.

Special Features: beach, pools, bicycles, tennis, sailboats, snorkeling, swim lessons, marina, Ping Pong, volleyball, baby-sitting, restaurants, bars, grocery store, laundry facilities, shops, beauty salon.

$$$ Weekly rates: two-bedroom villa, $1,300–$3,000, one-bedroom $970–$2,500, rooms $672–$803.

Fiesta Americana Condesa

Address: Paseo Kukulkán, Km 16.5 (Box 5478), 77500 Cancún, Quintana Roo, Mexico
Telephone: 800-343-7821, (52) 98-85-1000, fax (52) fax 98-85-1650
Website: www.fiestaweb.com.mex

The Condesa has engaging Mediterranean-style architecture, with arches and balconies at every turn, and overlooks an intricate pattern of landscaping, *palapas,* streams, and swimming pools. The resort's three seven-story towers surround a landscaped courtyard, beyond which is a sandy beach. The centerpiece of the courtyard is a lagoonlike free-form swimming pool that winds its way past an ice cream parlor, restaurants, and a swim-up bar. There's a full watersports concession and daily activities program plus an attractive stretch of beach shaded with *palapas.* The hotel is just steps from the convention center and the Plaza Caracol Shopping Center.

Accommodations: 502 rooms have pink stucco walls, pale wood furnishings, and Mexican tile floors; standard rooms share a balcony with two other rooms, deluxe rooms have their own. Oceanfront suites have private terraces with Jacuzzis. Rooms have minibars, safety deposit box, and air-conditioning.

For Kids: The Fiesta Kids Club is offered during holiday periods and summer months, and baby-sitting can be arranged through the front desk.

Special Features: beach, swimming pools, spa, gymnasium, massage, golf, tennis, watersports, daily social activities, shopping arcade, beauty salon, car rental, post office, 24-hour room service, four restaurants, two bars, and an ice cream parlor.

$$$: Daily rates, double occupancy: $250–$275.

Moderate

Ritz Carlton Cancún

Address: Retorno del Rey #36, Zona Hotelera, Cancún, Q. Roo, 77500, Mexico
Telephone: 800-241-3333, (52) 98-81-0808, fax (52) 98-85-1015
Website: www.ritzcarlton com

Families wanting extra service and style will find it at this elegant resort designed to reflect the Spanish heritage of Mexico—with tiled roofs, wrought-iron railing, fountains, and private courtyards. Its unassuming exterior is rather nondescript but its elegant interior featuring a stunning stained-glass, domed atrium, nineteenth-century European paintings, and crystal chandeliers definitely has a Spanish aristocratic feel. Guest rooms have a similar sumptuous

European flair. This Ritz Carlton (along with a number of other Ritz Carltons throughout North America) has earned the American Automobile Association's (AAA) five-diamond award for its world-class service and facilities. Families are warmly welcomed with a pleasant children's program (available for full- or half-day care), a playground, baby-sitting, and children's menus in several of the restaurants. The beach is 1,200 feet long and filled with comfortable beach chairs and shady *palapas*. A watersports desk on the premises can arrange all kinds of activities for guests, no matter if the sport is found on the premises or off. There's access to an eighteen-hole golf course designed by Robert Trent Jones, and a variety of excellent restaurants and bars where guests can sample up to 120 different types of tequila. Private candlelight dinners for two, served anywhere in the resort, can be arranged when you're ready to hire a baby-sitter and steal an evening for yourselves.

Accommodations: 365 rooms all have ocean views and private balconies or terraces plus marble bathrooms, minibar, three phones, terry bathrobes, private safes, and air-conditioning.

For Kids: A fun-filled activities program for four-to-twelve-year-olds is offered year-round. Half- and full-day programs are available. Kids enjoy making piñatas, baking cookies, playing games on the beach, and arts and crafts. Baby-sitting can be arranged.

Special Features: beach, two pools, three lit tennis courts, watersports, fitness center, aerobics classes, spa services, business center, beauty salon, gift shops, restaurants, bars, 24-hour room service.

$$$: Daily rates, double occupancy: $155–$390. Children twelve and under free in their parents' room.

Presidente Inter-Continental

Address: Km 7.5 Pasea Kulkukán, 77500 Cancún, Quintana Roo, Mexico
Telephone: 800-327-0200, (52) 98-83-0200, fax (52) 98-83-2515

The Inter-Continental's ultramodern marble design could mislead visitors into thinking they are in a sophisticated urban hotel rather than a laid-back resort. But once they step through the sleek lobby onto the grounds and beach and spot the oversize pool, waterfall, and beach beyond, they will undoubtedly see the Presidente for what it really is—a truly relaxing vacation getaway. The beach is less crowded than at other hotels along the Cancún strip, because neighboring the Presidente are private homes and a golf course rather than high-rise hotels. Families vacationing during the months of July and August can take advantage of a complimentary children's program. On Caribbean Night, one of the hotel's several theme parties thrown during the week, guests can groove to the distinctive island sounds of steel drums and reggae music.

Accommodations: 298 rooms are furnished with pine and wicker furniture, and either two double beds or a king-size bed. All rooms have private balconies, air-conditioning, and in-room safes, and some on the first floor have patios with their own whirlpools.

For Kids: Chiqui Club provides activities for children up to age twelve during the months of July and August. Activities include Spanish language lessons, treasure hunts, cooking and craft classes, beach and pool games, aerobics, movies, magic lessons, and animation workshops. Kids can learn traditional Mexican songs and dances and listen to stories about local history. Enrollment in the club is complimentary.

Special Features: beach, three restaurants, two swimming pools, whirlpools, fitness center, lit tennis courts, watersports equipment rental, marina, room service, travel agency, car rental.

$$$: Children twelve and under stay free in parents' room. Daily rates, double occupancy: $155–$485.

Marriott Casamagna

Address: Km 20 Paseo Kukulkán, 77500 Cancún, Quintana Roo, Mexico
Telephone: 800-223-6388, (52) 988-52000, fax (52) 988-51731
Website: www.marriott.com

Six-story Casamagna, located along the main strip in Cancún, features a year-round children's program, Club Amigos, that is free during the summer months. It's an elegant resort shaped like a "U" surrounding a spacious pool and situated so that most rooms have ocean views or partial ocean views. Special activities for adults are offered each week, such as poolside Spanish classes, Mexican coooking lessons, and pottery painting. Guests can choose from four different restaurants; the casual open-air restaurant La Capilla is especially lovely as it offers views of the pool and sea. One of the resort's bars has mariachi music every night, and all kinds of excursions and watersports can be arranged.

Accommodations: 452 guest rooms and 38 suites. All units have balconies, air-conditioning, ceiling fans, minibar, and in-room safes. Standard rooms have either two double beds or a king-size bed; deluxe rooms have both a king bed and a sofa bed, and an ocean view.

For Kids: The Club Amigos Children's Camp provides daily activities from 10 A.M.–3 P.M. for kids ages five to twelve. The camp operates year-round. The supervised activities include snorkeling, Spanish lessons, beach games, arts and crafts, and indoor activities for the rare rainy days. During the summer, membership is free for participants in the Family Vacation package (two kids stay free in parents' room); a fee is charged the rest of the year. Baby-sitting for kids ages four and under can be arranged through the front desk.

Special Features: beach, pool, kiddy pool, volleyball, tennis lessons and tournaments, water aerobics, water polo, scuba diving lessons, snorkeling, sailing, jet skiing, and parasailing, boutiques, beauty salon, three bars, health club and a juice bar.

$$$: Children under eighteen free in their parents' room. Daily rates, double occupancy: rooms $135–$275, suites $300–$695.

WHAT TO SEE AND DO

Folkloric Ballets are held nightly in two different locations: the Cancún Convention Center has a nightly dinner show. Paseo Kukulkán, Km 9. 98-83-01-

99. The Hotel Continental Villas Plaza has an elaborate show with regional Mexican dances. Paseo Kukulkán, Km 11. 98-83-10-95.

Wet 'n Wild Water Park has all kinds of water fun such as a wave pool, twister slides, a lazy river ride, little kid's park and more. Paseo Kukulkán, KM 25, near the airport. 98-81-30-00

Sub-Sea-Explorer is a minisub that explores area reefs with four daily departures. 98-83-30-07.

Atlantis Submarines excursions take guests down in air-conditioned and pressurized comfort to view the spectacular sights of Cancún's coral reefs. Perfect for those who want to see sea life up close but who don't want to scuba dive. 98-83-30-21

BEYOND CANCÚN
ISLA MUJERES

A pleasant ferry ride about eight miles east of Cancún is Isla Mujeres, a small and unpretentious island with a quieter atmosphere, more moderate prices, and the feeling of a real Mexican town. Day-trippers head over from Cancún to play on the beaches or snorkel in one of the several reef areas, but despite the daytime crowds, the island remains a more peaceful and serene vacation retreat. There are plenty of restaurants and shops, plus an old pirate fortress, a turtle sanctuary, and Garrafon National Park, a popular beginning snorkel spot and aquarium.

Isla Mujeres, meaning "Island of Women," has several different stories about how it got its name. One version claims that Spaniard Hernandez de Cordoba first came upon the island in 1517 and discovered wooden idols of a Mayan goddess. Another story asserts that the Spaniards arrived on the fish-shaped island and found only women, since all the men were off on a fishing trip.

Most hotels, the ferry dock, and the center of town are within walking distance of each other. The older lodging properties are found in town, while the newer, more expensive, lodgings are usually beachfront around Playa Norte, the island's finest beach, and on the peninsula near the lagoon. No car rentals are available, so unless you bring your own vehicle across on the ferry, you'll need to rent bicycles, mopeds, or a golf cart, or hire a taxi to explore the island.

Visitor Information

At Plaza Isla Mujeres at the north end of the main shopping street. 987-7-03-16. Open weekdays 9–2 and 7–9.

Best Sweet Treat: Head into any Mexican bakery to sample the variety of sweet breads dusted with coarse sugar.

WHERE TO STAY
Moderate

Na Balam
Address: Calle Zacil-Ha 118, Isla Mujeres, Quintana Roo, Mexico

Telephone: (52) 987-7-02-79, fax (52) 987-7-04-46
Website: www.nabalam.com

This small beachfront inn on the best beach on the island offers spacious rooms at excellent prices. Town is a short cab ride away. Palm trees shade the simple grounds and a restaurant serves breakfast, lunch, and dinner (breakfast is especially good), although rooms come with refrigerators, allowing you to provide your own snacks and breakfast or lunch, if you wish. A large *palapa* contains hammocks, allowing you to swing in the shade with a drink or a good book. Reserve early as it's one of the best beachfront values in the area.

Accommodations: suites have two double beds and a terrace with an ocean view, a sofa, a dining table, and a refrigerator plus either a ceiling fan or air-conditioning.

Special Features: beach, pool, snorkeling, fishing, restaurant, juice bar, yoga classes, massage.

$$$: Daily rates: $110.

Cabañas Maria del Mar

Address: Av Carlos Lazo 1, Isla Mujeres, Quintana Roo, Mexico
Telephone: (52) 987-7-01-79, fax (52) 987-7-02-13

Well-located on Playa Norte, this simple hotel has several different types of rooms, some of which have hammocks as well as beds. The cabanas section has fifteen rooms with *palapas* and front porches in a garden. Tower rooms have private terraces that face the beach. Castle rooms are the nicest and newest of the units. A continental breakfast is included in the rate. The hotel is an excellent buy on a gorgeous stretch of beach, so reserve early.

Accommodations: rooms have air-conditioning, ceiling fans, refrigerators, and a combination of double or single beds.

Special Features: beach, pool, restaurant, bar, moped rental, travel services.

$$$: Daily rates, double occupancy: $95–$150

Budget

Posada del Mar Hotel

Address: Av Rueda Medina 15A, Isla Mujeres, Quintana Roo, Mexico
Telephone: (52) 987-7-02-12, fax (52) 987-7-02-66

This getaway is a long-time favorite with Isla Mujeres regulars and has one of the best swimming pools on the island. It's situated about four blocks from the main pier and three blocks from Playa Norte. There are pleasant gardens plus a dining room that serves breakfast, lunch, and dinner and a bar that has live music on weekend nights during the high season. Try to get one of the rooms in the main building.

Accommodations: fifty rooms, all with air-conditioning (which occasionally doesn't work) and louvered windows that let in the sea breezes.

Special Features: pool, shops, restaurant, bar.

$$$: Daily rates, double occupancy: $76–$86.

WHAT TO SEE AND DO ON ISLA MUJERES

Swim with the Dolphins at Dolphin Discovery, an organization that offers four swims each day at 9 A.M., 11 A.M., 1 P.M., and 3 P.M. Sessions last one hour and feature thirty minutes of video instruction and thirty minutes in the water with these gentle playful creatures. 987-7-07-42.

El Garrafon National Park and Marine Life Refuge has superb snorkeling that is perfect for beginners, and there's easy access to the expansive coral reef via a sandy-bottom entry path. Unfortunately sections of the coral reef are dead, due to overuse and Hurricane Gilbert. Arrive early to avoid the day-trippers from Cancún. Avenida Rueda Medina, no phone, daily 9 A.M.–5 P.M.

Tortuga Marina Turtle Farm—Dedicated to the study and preservation of sea turtles, visitors can tour during daylight hours and see tanks containing hundreds of hatchling sea turtles and youngsters of various species. Be sure to see the fenced-in beachfront area where turtles can be seen swimming in the ocean, nibbling on food. It's run by Eco-Carib, an organization that lovingly cares for and releases infant sea turtles to help preserve their numbers. 987-05-95. Daily 9 A.M.–5 P.M.

COZUMEL

Another quieter cousin to its flashy neighbor to the north, Cozumel is Mexico's largest island and is a forty-minute ferry ride from Playa del Carmen on the mainland. White sandy beaches and calm waters line the western side of the island, while eastern beaches have rough surf and rocky entrances. A legendary offshore reef encircles the entire island. Most of the interior of Cozumel is palm groves, tangled jungles, lagoons, and swamps. Only a few roads are paved, so you'll need to rent a jeep if you want to explore the island. The small town of San Miguel is charming to explore, although it should be avoided when the cruise ships have docked as it gets overwhelmed with visitors. However, thanks to the cruise ship trade it's developed an excellent crafts market well worth a visit.

Cozumel's lodgings are concentrated in three main areas on the western side of the island: in town (where you'll find most of the budget lodging); south of town where divers and snorklers like to go because of the proximity to the reefs; and north of town where you'll find the best beaches. In-town lodging is inexpensive because it's not next to the shore, but for a taxi ride (about $5) you can easily get to an idyllic stretch of sand and still save money in the long run, enjoying a delightful small town to explore as a bonus.

WHERE TO STAY
Expensive

Meliá Mayan Paradisus
Address: Carretera Norte, Km 5.8 (north end of road) 20411, Cozumel, Quintana Roo, Mexico

Telephone: 800-336-3542, (52) 98-72-0411, fax (52) 98-72-1599

The Meliá is a secluded all-inclusive resort located on the northernmost tip of Cozumel. Lying on the beach, you can almost imagine you are shipwrecked on a tropical isle, as the stretch of sand eventually fades away into a lush jungle undergrowth. Ocean conditions at this end of the island are almost always calm and are ideal for snorkeling. There is a swim-up bar covered by a huge thatched-roof *palapa* in the swimming pool, and small *palapas* and palm trees shade the private beach. True to its name, the Meliá Mayan Paradisus seems to occupy a piece of tropical paradise, a little secret the Mayans knew about long ago.

Accommodations: 200 rooms all with marble floors, cane furnishings, terraces, air-conditioning, and minibars. Not all have ocean views, so be sure to ask if this is important to you. Deluxe rooms have large private balconies with furniture.

Special Features: beach, two pools, two tennis courts, scuba excursions, snorkeling, sailing, windsurfing, restaurants, bars, evening entertainment.

$$$: All-inclusive daily rates: $264–$400 per night. Rates include three meals, all drinks, most recreation, tax, and service.

Moderate

Presidente Inter-Continental Cozumel
Address: Km 6 Costera Sur, 776000 Cozumel, Quintana Roo, Mexico
Telephone: 800-327-0200, (52) 98-72-0322, fax (52) 98-72-1360
Website: www.interconti.com

Set within a jungle-enclosed cove, the Presidente is one of the nicest hotels on Cozumel. Snorkelers are rewarded right offshore with numerous sightings of tropical fish such as sergeant majors and angelfish, while nearby reefs are home to an even greater diversity of exotic marine life. A stone stairway allows you to step right into the water in front of the resort and flip your fins. A full-service dive shop leads scuba trips and offers instruction if you want to get serious about underwater exploration. Farther along the beach is a softer sandy zone that will delight young guests who want to dig in the fluffy white sand. The beach is large enough to comfortably accommodate all guests even when the hotel is completely full. Private beach areas under the shade of *palapas* can be found to the north of the cove. One of the two hotel restaurants, Arrecife, has been called one of the best on the island. The other, El Caribeño, is a charming beachfront café under a large *palapa*.

Accommodations: 253 rooms and suites, all with air-conditioning, a king bed or two double beds, and rattan furnishings.

Special Features: beach, two lit tennis courts, swimming pool, windsurfing, waterskiing, sailing, snorkeling, deep-sea fishing, restaurants.

$$$: Kids under eighteen free in parents' room. Daily rates, double occupancy: rooms $155–$330, suites $595–$645.

Budget

Playa Azul Hotel

Address: Carretera Norte, Km 4 (between San Miguel and Punta Molas) 20199, 20043, Cozumel, Quintana Roo, Mexico

Telephone: (52) 98-72-0033, fax (52) 98-72-0110

Families feel right at home in this recently renovated resort—it's not particularly fancy or luxurious but its comfortable and casual attitude and excellent beach bring families back year after year. The shallow water is protected with a sea wall, and a pier provides access to the ocean (which is usually calm) for swimming and snorkeling. There are *palapas* on the beach for shade and a private dock for boat pick-ups. The staff will arrange for fishing, windsurfing, jet skiing, snorkeling, and scuba diving trips. Rooms are situated in several two- or three-story buildings, and a spacious restaurant serves three meals a day.

Accommodations: 60 rooms have tiled floors, balconies, air-conditioning, and showers but no tubs. Garden-view rooms are a little shabby; the ocean-view rooms are spacious, containing king-size beds and a sitting area. Suites are even larger with a sofa bed, bathrooms with two vanities, minirefrigerator, two double beds, and a large balcony.

Special Features: beach, swimming pool, restaurant, gift shop, lobby with a pool table, video room, library, beachfront snack bar, scooter and car rentals, room service, and massage.

$$$: Daily rate, double occupancy: rooms $65–$115, suites $100–$140. Two children under twelve are allowed to stay free with two adults.

Sol Cabañas Del Caribe

Address: Km 4.5 Carretera Santa Pilar (Apdo. Postal 9), 77600 Cozumel, Quintana Roo, Mexico

Telephone: 888-341-5993, (52) 98-72-0017, (52) 98-72-0072, fax (52) 98-72-1599

E-mail: paradisu@cozumel.czm.com.mz

This truly kid-friendly resort offers lodging in the form of small cottages situated around a peaceful cove. The Sol Cabañas were one of Cozumel's first accommodations (built in the 1960s) and are beginning to show their age. Kids will never notice the wear and tear, and parents will not need to worry about breakables or fancy furnishings, as the cottages are sturdy yet comfortable. Two newer buildings contain more modern rooms. The resort has a small wading pool for young children, and the protected cove is shallow and tranquil. The beachfront restaurant has a picturesque view of Caribbean sunsets.

Accommodations: The nine cabañas have kitchenettes, beachfront patios, brick floors, fold-out sofas, and queen-size beds. The forty-eight smallish rooms each have a double bed and a twin bed, and a private terrace. All accommodations have air-conditioning, ocean views, and showers, but no bathtubs, TVs, or telephones.

Special Features: beach, restaurant, pool-side snack shop, swimming pool, sailboats, jet skis, diving, snorkeling, windsurfing, a pharmacy, gift shop, and travel agency.

$$$: Daily rates, double occupancy: $69–$168.

Villa Rentals

At Home in Cozumel rents private one-to-eleven-bedroom villas, condos and townhouses in Cozumel, Playa del Carmen, and Akumal. Most are on the beach and have maid service. Website: www.akumal.net, 800-833-5971, 561-488-8938.

WHAT TO SEE AND DO IN COZUMEL

Glass-bottom boat rides—If you don't scuba dive, you can view the spectacular underwater coral and marine life through a glass-bottom boat. The Palapa Marina has two trips each day, one at 9 A.M. and one at 1 P.M., departing form the Sol Caribe pier near the car-ferry dock. Calle 1 Sur No. 177, tel 2-05-39.

PLAYA DEL CARMEN

About thirty miles from Cancún, people used to stop in Playa del Carmen just long enough to catch the ferry to Cozumel Island. But today, the open-air cafés, quaint shops, and ocean front *malecon* (boardwalk) attract visitors for a lengthier stay. You'll find a variety of accommodations and a convenient central location to enjoy day trips to interesting archaeological sites and diving spots around the Yucatan. Tulum and Cobá are less than an hour's drive south.

The town center is the waterfront plaza at the ferry dock, where you'll find a church, a playground, and sidewalk cafés. South of the town is the Playacar development which consists of a golf course, private homes, condos, and several hotels.

WHERE TO STAY
Expensive

Continental Plaza Playacar

Address: Km 62.5 Fracc. Playacar, 77710 Playa del Carmen, Quintana Roo, Mexico

Telephone: 800-88-CONTI, (52) 98-73-0100, fax (52) 98-73-0105

Part of the 880-acre Playacar development, the Continental is one of the nicer hotels found in Playa del Carmen. Its 308 acres are along a very long beach past the ferry pier. During construction of the hotel, two hundred Mayan ruins were found, most of which can now be seen around the resort. Room views vary considerably and are priced accordingly. The least expensive look out onto a parking lot or brick wall. About a third of the rooms have kitchenettes and the hotel is popular with the package tour group.

Accommodations: 188 rooms and 16 suites. All rooms have large marble bathrooms, wood furniture, satellite TV, in-rooms safes, purified tap water, tile floors, wet bars, and refrigerators.

Special Features: beach, two restaurants, a swim-up bar and lobby bar, swimming pool, watersports equipment, one lit tennis court, eighteen-hole golf course, baby-sitting, laundry and room service, shops, travel agency, tours to archaeological sites and lagoons.

$$$: $285–$485 per night for a double; package deals available.

Allegro Resort Playacar

Address: Hotelero No 7, Desarollo Playacar, Playa del Carmen, Quintana Roo, Mexico
Telephone: 800-858-2258, 98-73-0339, fax 305-444-4848 or 98-73-0346
Website: www.allegroresorts.com

Allegro resorts are becoming real players in the family inclusive market, and this Allegro has a beautiful piece of real estate to catapult it to the top of the charts. It's about twenty minutes away from Playa del Carmen, and part of the Playacar development. Guest rooms, housed in thatched-roof villas, are spread out along gentle hills along the ocean and are secluded enough to avoid the noise from the karaoke bar and the outdoor stage. The two freshwater swimming pools are separated, one side being used for games and lively splashing while the other is reserved for quieter pursuits like slipping in for a dip after lazing in your lounge chair in the warmth of the sun. The main dining room, bar, entertainment area, and lobby are all sheltered under one giant *palapa*.

Accommodations: 296 rooms have one king or two double beds. All have air-conditioning, ceiling fans, coffeemaker, safe.

For Kids: Kids program available for ages four through twelve that features a full program of games, lessons, and activities.

Special Features: beach, two pools, four tennis courts, windsurfing, snorkeling, paddle boating, volleyball, aerobics, shuffleboard, dive shop, three restaurants, bar, disco, evening entertainment, gift shops, car rental, and babysitting.

$$$: Rates are all-inclusive, with plentiful buffet and à la carte style meals. Double occupancy each adult $135–$170; children under thirteen $60 per night but can drop much lower during the off season.

Budget

Villa Catarina Rooms and Cabañas

Address: Calle Privada Nte. between 12 and 14, 77710 Playa del Carmen, Quintana Roo, Mexico
Telephone: (52) 98-73-0970, fax (52) 98-73-0968

Hidden in a grove of palm trees, the accommodations at Villa Catarina are pleasantly rustic. Rooms contain tasteful Mexican folk art and high quality furniture and are airy and free of mosquitoes and other pests, thanks to consistently screened windows. It is just one block from the beach, and the charming rooms are shaded and comfortable. It's an excellent value.

Accommodations: fifteen rooms with *palapa* roofs and terraces or reading lofts. Rooms have one or two double beds on wooden bases; tile floors are common to all rooms; and the larger rooms have sitting areas.

Special Features: Complimentary coffee available in the mornings.

$$$: Daily rates, double occupancy: $35–$75.

AKUMAL

Akumal means "Place of the Turtle," as the beach was once a nesting ground for thousands of sea turtles. It's now famous for its excellent diving and deep-sea fishing. Beaches are long and lovely, and the pace is much slower than the high-octane scene to the north.

WHERE TO STAY
Moderate

Club Akumal Caribe and Villas Maya

Address: Hwy 307, km 104, Akumal, Quintana Roo, Mexico

Telephone: 800-351-1622, (52) 95-800-351-1122

Website: www.hotelakumalcarib.com

Right at the edge of a pretty cove, the varied accommodations at the property include beachfront hotel rooms, simple bungalows in the garden, secluded one-, two-, and three-bedroom condominiums overlooking the pool and beach, and four villas a bit farther away from the beach. It's an excellent value. Two dive shops offer resort courses and PADI certification, and take guests to unusual spots such as cenotes and caves to dive. There are three restaurants, and a variety of watersports. The beach is shallow and calm, especially in winter, making it an excellent choice for families with young children. Older children enjoy a variety of activities. A screened-in dining area next to the beach allows you to eat without bugs and watch older children play in the sand.

Accommodations: twenty-one rooms, forty bungalows, four villas, five condos. Rooms and more spacious bungalows have balconies, a king or two double beds, air-conditioning, ceiling fan, minifridge. Villas have two or three bedrooms, air-conditioning and daily maid service. Condos are two bedroom with a complete kitchen.

For Kids: The Kids Club has an enclosed playground and a playroom with arts and crafts materials, games, videos, and even a crib for tiny tots. The program runs during the morning and evening hours, for an hourly rate.

Special Features: beach, pool, dive shops, three restaurants, bar, grocery, ice cream parlor, gift shop.

$$$: Daily rates: rooms $89–$130; bungalows $79–$99; condos $70–$170; villas $106–$317.

WHAT TO SEE AND DO AROUND THE REGION

Xcaret (pronounced ish-karet)—About an hour from Cancun, this tropical eco-archaeological amusement park offers many other activities in addition to its main feature—snorkeling and swimming along an underground river ride filled with coves, inlets, grottos, and cenotes—but nothing comes close to the thrill of the river ride. It's touristy, but your kids will never forget donning a life jacket and heading through two miles of winding underground river that is lit through holes in the ceiling. After you've had your fill of the river ride you can swim with the dolphins if you're one of the first guests to arrive in the morning (first come, first served each day), ride horseback, and wander through an aquarium, and butterfly and bird aviaries, or explore a botanical garden. The area was once an important trading center for the Mayans, and it's filled with beautiful ruins. Archaeologists believe that the sixty buildings uncovered to date are just the beginning of the excavations. You can tour a Mayan village replica and replicas of Mayan ruins, plus there's a mini-Mexican rodeo, restaurant, petting zoo, and lockers. Privately owned Xcaret has its own fleet of buses that picks up passengers in Cancún. Plan a full day to get the most out of all the activities, and avoid the river ride in the middle of the day when it's most crowded. 98-83-31-43. Open April to October 8:30 A.M. to 10 P.M. and November to March 8:30 A.M. to 8:30 P.M. Shorter hours on Sundays.

Xel-ha (pronounced Shell-Ha)—Xel-ha is known as a touristy snorkeling destination, and its natural aquarium-like setting covers ten acres of lagoons, coves, and inlets naturally carved into the area's soft limestone terrain that are home to countless species of tropical fish. Visitors get the opportunity to explore underwater caves, cenotes (sinkholes), and a partially submerged Mayan ruin. It's terrific fun and definitely worth a stop. You can rent snorkel gear on the premises to see the underwater sights, or head deep into the jungle to the far side of the lagoon to tour by glass-bottom boat. Xel-ha gets crowded in the middle of the day when the tour buses arrive after visiting Tulum. Plan to visit first thing in the morning to avoid the crowds. Located several miles south of Akumal, 98-84-94-12.

Tulum—The most visited of all of the Mayan sites, this ancient city has the most dramatic setting, against rocky cliffs and the crashing sea, of any of the Mayan ruins. Because it is rather close to the tourist centers of Cancún and Isla Mujeres, it is a very popular tour bus destination and can get extremely crowded. Come early in the morning or late in the day to avoid the crowds. The adults will truly appreciate the breathtaking setting of this ruin, as will some children, but because it is more a look-and-don't-touch kind of place, children tend to race through it rather quickly. Another more refreshing option is to head to the beach for a swim and enjoy viewing the ruins floating on your back in the water. If you have a limited amount of time, visit Chichén Itzá rather than Tulum for a dose of Mayan history.

Cobá—Thick tropical jungles still cover much of the archaeological site of Cobá, once the largest of the Mayan cities and one of the oldest known settlements on the peninsula. Archaeologists believe that at its peak, it covered fifty square kilometers and held forty thousand people. It was first built in 400 B.C. but developed into a full-scale city about A.D. 500 and was mysteriously abandoned in A.D. 1100. The ruins were discovered in 1891 by an Austrian archaeologist but serious excavation was only begun several decades ago and has barely scratched the surface. Because the jungle still looms so thick and mysterious around these ruins, you get the feeling that you're exploring uncharted territory. Distances between the excavated sites are far, so wear comfortable hiking shoes and apply plenty of insect repellent. Drink stands are situated at the entrance only, so bring a good supply of water with you. If you wish to spend the night, Villa Arqueologica Cobá offers comfortable rooms, and most important, a swimming pool.

You may see a number of Mayan men standing around the entrance offering themselves as tour guides. Most of them know a great deal about the site, and some have worked on the excavations. Their knowledge and ability to find their way around this vast site can greatly add to your family's enjoyment and they are well worth hiring. Use good judgment, make sure they can speak some English, and expect to pay between $15 and $30 for their services.

Sian Ka'an Biosphere Reserve—The Mexican government set aside over one million acres of tropical jungle, marsh, mangrove, a coral barrier reef, archaeological ruins, Caribbean beaches, and islands as a large biosphere reserve. In 1987, the United Nations designated it a World Heritage Site and incorporated it into UNESCO's World Network of Bioshphere Reserves. Filled with tropical butterflies, howler monkeys, ocelots, foxes, raccoons, eagles, and all kinds of other fauna, as well as small unrestored Mayan ruins, it is a fascinating place to explore if your family likes adventures in the outdoors. You can arrange a guided tour of it from Cancún or Playa del Carmen that covers different areas and topics depending on the season. Tours generally last about six hours and are guided by biologists. You'll get an in-depth explanation of the reserve and then head out in a motor launch to explore the winding channels and mangroves, stopping along the way to float with the current. Tours are operated by the nonprofit Amigos de Sian Ka'an, 98-84-95-83 at the Plaza America, Avenida Cobá, 3rd floor, suites 48–50, Cancún.

Chichén Itzá—This enormous Mayan site, more than 2-by-1½ miles is one of the most visited and best restored of all the Yucatan Peninsula's Mayan sites. Its massive structures have been extensively excavated and offer visitors a fascinating glimpse of Mayan civilization. From A.D. 450 to 1200 it was one of the most impressive centers of wealth and learning in the Mayan world. Many visitors make a day trip to Chichén Itzá, arriving around 11 A.M. just as the sun really begins to heat up the place. You're better off spending the night nearby and exploring the ruins in the late afternoon one day and in the early morning hours the following day, when temperatures have cooled and crowds have thinned. Hacienda Chichén (800-223-4084) is a convenient and moderately priced overnight option with a pool and restaurant. If you don't spend the night, arrive early and spend part of the middle of the day lingering over lunch in a nearby hotel restaurant that has a pool; many hotels will allow lunch guests to swim, so bring your swimsuits. Don't forget the insect repellent and plenty of drinking water, and wear very comfortable hiking shoes, hats, and cool clothing. There are public restrooms placed around the ruins.

Take the time to learn about the site before you go and select what you explore carefully as many children fade after a few hours. Children are usually most impressed with: 1) El Castillo, as they enjoy climbing its steep steps to be rewarded with a spectacular view of the entire site (note that it's very steep, especially on the way down); 2) the Principal Ball Court where the astonishing acoustics allow you to hear a conversation taking place at one end of the court 135 meters away at the other end. Clap your hands to hear the echo bouncing back and forth along the ball court walls. The stadium has two stone circles embedded high in the walls into which players once attempted to shoot a large ball using only their hips, elbows, and knees. During the Toltec period, the losing captain and perhaps his teammates were sacrificed; 3) the Sacred Cenote, a natural well about sixty meters in diameter and thirty-five meters deep and flanked by steep walls tangled in vegetation. Excavation conducted in the early part of the century brought up the remains of men, women, and children who were sacrificed here as well as priceless artifacts and gold and jade jewelry. As you explore the rest of the site, be sure to point out the exquisite stone carvings that have stood up to the elements over many centuries.

A sound and light show takes place at 9 P.M. in English and provides an entertaining overview of the city's history and the fall of the Mayan empire. Open 8 A.M.–5 P.M.

Pacific Coast

ACAPULCO

The oldest of Mexico's beach resorts and the closest to Mexico City, Acapulco first became a popular tourist destination in the 1930s and 1940s thanks to its beautiful broad blue bay backed by emerald green mountains and a long sandy beach. It was called the "Riviera of the West" in the 1940s and 1950s, when American jet-setters and movie stars such as Rita Hayworth, Eddie Fisher, and Cary Grant made this one of their favorite playgrounds. Nearly 80 percent of today's visitors come from within Mexico, and the rest fly in from North or South America for some fun in the sun.

Acapulco is still known for its nonstop night life where revelers can party from dusk till dawn. Daytime diversions for families, other than the beach, are easily found too, such as an aquarium with marine animal shows, an old Spanish fort, and an amusement park with rides. But Acapulco's most famous tourist site is a breathtaking display of daring and timing when the divers at La Quebrada gracefully swan-dive off of cliffs 130 feet high into the crashing surf below.

Check the condition of the bay (some days it can be polluted) and the swimming conditions. There is occasionally a dangerous undertow, which will be indicated by a red flag. Warm balmy breezes keep the temperature a comfortable 79 to 85 degrees for most of the year. The older center of town is very different from the tourist areas, with its pollution and poverty a sharp contrast to the glitzy hotels just a few miles away. The zócalo, or town square has been recently renovated, though, and is worth a stop to sit at a sidewalk café and sip a drink, or listen to a strolling guitar player.

Visitor Information Secretaria de Fomento Turistico del Estado de Guerrero, La Costera 187, telephone 86-91-67.

Best sweet Treat: Look for mangos on a stick, peeled and cut into flower shapes.

WHERE TO STAY
Expensive

Westin Las Brisas Hotel
Address: Apdo. Postal 281, Carretera Esénica, Las Brisas, 39868 Acapulco, Guerrero, Mexico
Telephone: 800-228-3000, (52) 74-84-1580, fax (52) 74-84-2269
Website: www.westin.com

One of the most romantic hotels in the world, Las Brisas is also a delightful upscale family destination thanks to the private swimming pools that front your *casita*. These "little houses" are situated on five different levels of a hillside and offer complete privacy. Young guests may feel a little like Barbie and Ken while riding the hotel's trademark pink jeeps, which are available to guests to explore the town or to head to the resort's beach club with swimming pools a ten-minute ride away. Guests are pampered with discreet hand-painted signs personalizing their villas for the duration of their stay. A breakfast of hot coffee, sweet rolls, and fresh fruit is brought each morning and left in a box, to be consumed at your leisure. The property is on a steep incline, so expect to get some exercise as you explore, or call the front desk to request for personal ride service in a four-wheel vehicle.

Accommodations: 300 casitas have either a king size bed or two double beds, air-conditioning, ceiling fans, telephone, minibar, but no TV or radio. Junior and full suites are more spacious.

Special Features: 250 swimming pools, fresh flowers delivered daily, four restaurants, five tennis courts, transportation provided on grounds, jeeps for rent, travel agency, gas station, beauty and barber shops, laundry and room service.

$$$: One child under eighteen free in parents' room. Shared-pool *casitas* $150–$215, private-pool *casitas* $210–$315, private-pool junior suites $350–$499, private-pool one- to three-bedroom suites $495–$1,034.

Acapulco Princess
Address: Carretera Excénica (at Playa Revolcadero Beach) 39868 Acapulco, Guerrero, Mexico

Telephone: 800-223-1818, (52) 74-69-1000, fax (57) 74-69-1017

This luxury hotel property is a twenty-minute drive from Acapulco and quite removed from the activity of the Costera strip—a plus for anyone looking for greater peace and quiet far from the nightlife for which Acapulco is known. Its location on a wide expanse of Revolcadero Beach makes it seem ideal for swimming, but the open ocean here can be rather rough, and on many days you're better off enjoying the five free-form swimming pools, the saltwater lagoon complete with water slide, or sunbathing on the sand. There are three towering buildings on the 480-acre property, the main one designed to resemble an Aztec pyramid, all surrounded by two manicured and palm-flecked eighteen-hole golf courses. The gardens and grounds are lavish with waterfalls, fountains, tropical flowers and trees, and swans, peacocks, and flamingoes wander and float about. The Princess is used to having children on the premises, and you'll find cribs, high chairs and baby-sitting very easy to arrange. All nine outdoor tennis courts are lit for night play, and the two indoor tennis courts are air-conditioned for daytime play no matter what the weather. In-season rates include breakfast and dinner.

Accommodations: 1,019 rooms and suites all have floor-to-ceiling sliding glass doors, that lead to private terraces, and air-conditioning.

Special Features: Five swimming pools, saltwater lagoon with a slide, thirty-six holes of golf, nine outdoor lit tennis courts, two indoor courts, seven restaurants, swim-up bar, disco, barber and beauty shop, massage, health club, aerobics, shops, laundry, room service, wheelchairs upon request.

$$$: During high season, rates include two meals per day. In the low season, children under a certain age stay free with parents. $305–$450 per night for a double, $415–$675 per night for a suite.

Moderate

Camino Real Acapulco Diamante
Address: km 14 Carretera Escénica, Calle Baja Catita, Pichilingue, 39887 Acapulco, Guerrero, Mexico
Telephone: 800-7-CAMINO, (52) 74-66-1010, fax (52) 74-66-1111
Website: www.caminoreal.com/acapulco

A winding brick road leads you to the Camino Real, a luxurious hideaway perched on a gentle slope overlooking the sapphire waters of Puerto Marquez Bay. It's a relative newcomer in the Acapulco resort scene and a hotel that warmly welcomes families and makes their stay comfortable with a children's program offered during peak season and part of the summer. Though the Camino Real is only a short taxi ride away from all the excitement Acapulco has to offer, you would never know it listening to the undisturbed sounds of waves lapping against the shore and waterfalls splashing into the courtyard pools. The watersports center arranges all kinds of water fun. Rooms are spacious and all have some sort of ocean view.

Accommodations: 156 rooms and suites. Rooms have two double beds or a king-size bed, private balcony, air-conditioning, ceiling fans, minibar, and an in-room safe-deposit box. Junior and master suites, and Royal Beach Club rooms all provide upgraded amenities and services.

For Kids: The Little Rascal's Club, for kids ages four through twelve, provides activities daily during the high season, and on weekends at all other times of the year. Baby-sitting can be arranged after hours or for younger kids.

Special Features: beach, tri-level pool, tennis courts, restaurants, a lobby bar, fitness center, beauty and barber shop, room service, travel agency, car rental, sailing, fishing, waterskiing, and scuba diving.

$$$: Kids under twelve are free in parents' room. Daily rates, double occupancy: rooms $135–$230, suites $350–$800.

Budget

Acapulco Ritz
Address: Apartado Postal 259, Acapulco, Guerrero, Mexico
Telephone: 800-237-7487, (52) 74-85-7544, fax (52) 74-85-7076

Surprisingly enough, the Ritz is one of the best deals in Acapulco. The good old-fashioned hospitality and amenities in the rooms and suites surpass many other hotels that charge twice as much for a nightly stay. It's located on a quieter section of beach at the opposite end of the strip from the Hyatt. The spacious white-sand beach is surrounded by palm trees and dotted with umbrellas and lounges, and a free-form swimming pool is just steps from the beach.

Accommodations: 252 rooms and junior suites. Rooms have TVs, telephones, and air-conditioning. Suites have a balcony, king-size bed, and sitting area with couch.

Special Features: beach, oceanfront swimming pool surrounded by a garden, three restaurants, bar.

$$$: Kids under twelve can stay free with parents. Rooms are $77–$90 per night, junior suites $88–$105.

WHAT TO SEE AND DO

Papagayo Park—Located along the Costera, just after the underpass at the end of The Strip, the park is fifty-two acres of fun activities. The entire family can enjoy a lake with paddle boats, a children's train, rides, a life-size Spanish ship, a race track with tiny cars, a rollerskating rink, and an aviary containing hundreds of birds flying overhead as you walk through the shaded paths. Costera Miguel Aleman. Open daily from 10 A.M. to 8 P.M.; rides open 4 P.M. to 10 P.M.

CiCi, or the International Center for Coexistence of Children, bills itself as a family water park, but it's got more to offer than the kind of water parks we're used to. There are dolphin and seal shows, and a mini-aquarium plus a water slide and a pool with artificial waves. Open daily 10 A.M.–6 P.M.

La Quebrada Divers have been amazing tourists with their feats of daring and precision ever since 1934 when the first divers leaped off the steep cliffs high above town and glided 130 feet down into the deep blue Pacific waters below. Arrive early to get a good spot to view the dives, which take place at 1:00 P.M., 7:30 P.M., 8:30 P.M., 9:30 P.M., and 10:00 P.M. Divers sometimes take off in tandem and often carry torches. You can view from an observation deck next to the Mirador Hotel or from the restaurant bar of the hotel's La Perla restaurant and linger over a drink and enjoy the show at the same time. You'll pay a fee to get into the bar that entitles you to two drinks.

El Fuerte de San Diego—was built in 1616 to protect the harbor from English and Dutch pirates, and the five-sided fort remains the same as it was years ago. It was largely destroyed after a 1776 earthquake but was rebuilt and has been beautifully restored over the years. It houses a small museum with historical exhibits. Open Tuesday through Sunday 10:30 A.M.–4:30 P.M. Calle Hornitos and Morelos.

Magico Mundo Marino—Swimming pools, slides, and all kinds of rental watersports equipment such as jet skis, kayaks, and banana boats plus an aquarium and sea lion show make this a popular family stop.

IXTAPA/ZIHUATENEJO

Four hours north of Acapulco, this resort area consists of two winning sections: Zihuatenejo is a charming fishing village, with fishermen unloading their catch on the shorefront, school children bouncing balls along the sidewalk, and all the vibrancy of an attractive Mexican town. Just next door over the hill, Ixtapa is all tourist resort, with a line of large hotels flanking a broad swath of white sand and the blue Pacific Ocean. Independent and budget travelers like to stay in Zihuatenejo to enjoy all that a typical Mexican town has to offer, while other vacationers wanting the services and activities of a resort prefer Ixtapa. Staying in this area gives visitors the best of both worlds.

Designed by the government as a planned tourist destination, Ixtapa's development started in 1975. Its hotel zone is situated along a spectacular beach, and there is no real town center but there are several small shopping plazas and a small crafts market. It's a beautiful place to escape to a white sand beach paradise, but make sure you visit Zihuatenejo to get the feel of the real Mexico.

WHERE TO STAY—IXTAPA
Expensive

Club Med

Address: Playa Quieta, Ixtapa, Mexico
Telephone: 800-CLUBMED, (52) 755-200-06, fax (52) 755-200-40
Website: www.clubmed.com

Club Med is for people who like to be with people, and since most kids like to be with others their own age, they love this place. If they're old enough, they can have the run of the resort safely, choosing whatever activity they wish whenever they want. The food is surprisingly good for an inclusive resort—since the resort caters to Americans, Canadians, Mexicans and French, you're likely to find dishes that will please an international group of palates all in one seating. One price covers your accommodations, three meals a day including beer and wine at dinner, and most activities on site. If you want drinks and snacks between meals you pay; excursions cost an additional fee, as do extras such as ceramics painting, and hair braiding. The place is a three-ring circus of activities that includes a well-known circus program where kids and adult get to use a real circus trapeze. The beach is gorgeous—a long strip of ecru sand shaded by plenty of palm trees—and the resort is constructed in a low-rise form, so from the ocean it blends in beautifully with the shore. Nearly all guests bring children, and the ones who seem the happiest are the parents of the youngest ones, who leave their kids to play in the children's program or with one of the sweet and very inexpensive baby-sitters so that parents can actually finish a sentence or read a complete book.

Accommodations: 375 rooms have one king bed or two twin beds and a window seat that can double as a third single-size bed. There are no TVs or telephones, but air-conditioning (no fans or window screens) and private baths with showers. Nearly all rooms connect. There's no guarantee that couples receive king beds rather than twin beds; check your room out before you move your luggage in.

For Kids: Kids programs operate for toddlers through teens. Babies younger than two will need to have a baby-sitter. Petite club is for two to four year olds (extra cost); Mini-club is for four to twelve year olds, and Junior club for teens operates during French school holidays for ages thirteen and over

Special Features: beach, pools, circus program, sailing, kayaking, tennis, archery, basketball, soccer, two restaurants, bar, disco, evening entertainment, baby-sitting, laundry facilities.

$$$: Nightly rates based on double occupancy, per adult $116–$140; children two to three $12; children four to eleven $46–$60. Club Med has many land/air packages; be sure to inquire.

Moderate

Krystal Ixtapa
Address: Boulevard Ixtapa, Ixtapa, Mexico
Telephone: 800-231-9860, (52) 755-30333
Another giant along the Ixtapa strip, the Krystal is shaped like a long narrow triangle with the pointed end aimed at the beach. That allows most of the rooms to take advantage of breezy ocean views. Off to one side, vast shaded grassy grounds contain two immense playgrounds and a hammock pavilion that guests can use when they need to get away from the sea and sun. Closer to the beach and the hotel, a free-form winding pool has a volleyball net at one end and curves around under a couple of bridges past a swim-up bar to a waterfall and slide. Kids jump off the top of the man-made waterfall into the eight-foot deep pool—something that would never be allowed in the United States but is immensely enjoyed by all children here. An adjacent wading pool for toddlers is shaded by palm trees and edged by lounge chairs and a small

snack bar. A larger poolside restaurant serves drinks and snacks. The extra acreage this resort has gives it an open and airy feeling with plenty of places to explore and escape to.

Accommodations: 260 rooms have a king or two double beds, air-conditioning, mini-bars. Suites are also available.

For Kids: The Krystalistos Club de Adventures is open from 10 A.M. to 5 P.M. for children ages four to twelve. They meet outside under a shady *palapa* and enjoy a charming fenced-in yard full of toys.

Special Features: beach, pools restaurants, playgrounds, bars, tennis, raquet ball, car rental, shops, beauty salon, fitness center, baby-sitting.

$$$: Daily rates, double occupancy: $125–$175. Children under thirteen free in their parents' room.

Westin Brisas Resort Ixtapa
Address: Playa Vista Hermosa 40880, Ixtapa, Mexico
Telephone: 800-228-3000, (52) 755-32121 fax (52) 755-30751
Website: www.westin.com

Off by itself at the very far end of the Ixtapa strip, the Westin sits on a rocky ledge above crashing Pacific waves. An elevator takes guests up and down to the beach, which is remote enough from the rest of the Ixtapa hotels that it remains very private and uncrowded. The hotel was designed by a prominent Mexican architect who built it to look like a Mexican pyramid, and the shape allows each room to have a spacious terrace overlooking the ocean, big enough to use as living quarters. The terrace contains a table and chairs, hammocks and a chaise lounge, and is partially shaded. Both the terraces and rooms have Mexican tile floors. There are four pools, all tiled in small, square, sapphire blue mosaics. One is for adults only, while another long lap pool is used for swimming and activities such as volleyball. A shallow wading pool is reserved for babies and toddlers. The pools are a short walk away from the main hotel along a breezy garden path beneath palms and blooming tropical shrubs. There are no watersports at the Westin—guests can arrange sports through the recreation desk but will need to go to the Sheraton. There's a beach bar with light snacks such as hamburgers and hot dogs, and during daylight hours the beach has lifeguards keeping an eye on the guests. The stark and harsh lobby is somewhat uninviting but several shops and an ice cream parlor and candy store help liven the place up.

Accommodations: 423 rooms have one king bed or two twin beds and many connect. All rooms have ceiling fans, air-conditioning, a minibar, a coffee machine, room safe, and hair dryers.

For Kids: The kids club is in the pool area. It's a colorful air-conditioned room decorated with large Disney characters where arts and crafts projects take place and games are played. The program operates daily year-round, even if just one child is in the hotel.

Special Features: beach, three pools, restaurants, bars, fitness center, car rental, shops, ice cream parlor.

$$$: Daily rates, double occupancy: $135–$250

Sheraton Ixtapa Resort
Address: Boulevard Ixtapa (near Paseo del Palmar) Ixtapa 40880, Mexico
Telephone: 800-325-3535, (52) 755-31858, fax (52) 755-32438
Website: www.sheraton.com

The Sheraton's enormous and colorful lobby is atrium style, filled with light and somewhat open on both sides. Out the back side are three swimming pools—one for wading, one accommodating a small pool bar, and the third for volleyball games and general horsing around. There are *palapas* and lounge chairs on the beach and around the pools. A small old-fashioned playground for the kids includes swings, a dramatically slanted teeter-totter, merry-go-round, slides, and a jungle gym. This resort has a very casual and comfortable feel, and because it has the most watersports along the Ixtapa strip, it's a good choice for active families.

Accommodations: 331 rooms. Standards rooms all have air-conditioning and safes. Connecting rooms are available and have two double beds in one room and a king bed in the other. Rooms have colorful striped bedspreads in red, blue, green, and yellow, a TV, and very tiny balconies plus a minibar. Cribs are available.

Special Features: beach, swimming pools, scuba, fishing, snorkeling, gym, playground, gym, medical services, shops, restaurants, bars.

$$$: Daily rates, double occupancy: $140–$290.

WHERE TO STAY IN ZIHUATENEJO
Budget

Bungalows Pacificos
Address: Cerro de la Madera, Zihuatenejo, Mexico
Telephone: (52) 755-42112

The best part about this budget property high above Playa Madera is the terrace fronting each unit. Each terrace is enormous, allowing for indoor and outdoor living, with a shady portion and a portion completely open to the sun. The terrace can comfortably serve as your living room, as it contains tables and chairs, a hammock, and lounge chairs. Views extend to the village of Zihuatenejo off to the right and the broad sapphire blue Pacific directly in front. Accommodations are simple and quite plain. The beach is accessible via stairs down to a rocky beach area if the tide is in, but a sandy beach is close by. A seaside path leads to the main part of Zihuatenejo village, perhaps the equivalent of five or six blocks away. Views are all spectacular, especially from the top. The proprietor of the small hotel is a charming woman who speaks English and makes guests feel like family.

Accommodations: Six one-bedroom suites are all exactly the same. The bedroom has a king-size bed while the main room has two twins. The kitchen allows you to cook on a small range with an oven; there is a small refrigerator and a shelf full of pots, pans, and dishes. The bedroom is cooled by a ceiling fan while the living room has a portable fan and sea breezes off the terrace take care of the rest.

$$$: Daily rates: $55–$125

Bungalows Ley

Address: Apdo Postal # 466, Playa Madera, Zihuatenejo, Guerrero, Mexico
Telephone: (52) 755-44563

Also above Playa Madera, this budget property has rooms and small apartments of varying sizes, two of which are especially well suited for families. Most elegant and well outfitted is number 8, the Club Montara Suite, which has its own private terrace atop the building, complete with grill, tables and chairs, bathroom, and *palapa*-style roof covering, if you want some shade. Below is the living space, which contains two bedrooms, a small living room, a full kitchen, and two bathrooms. It's cooled by both a ceiling fan and air-conditioning and has a TV. One bedroom has a king bed and the other has a double and a small daybed. Number six also has two bedrooms, each with two twin beds and a couch in the small living room that can sleep several more. There's a kitchen with a stove and refrigerator and cooking utensils, and it's cooled by ceiling fans and has no air-conditioning. There's a path along the beach to Zihuatanejo.

$$$: Daily rates: unit #8 $70–$100; unit #6 $55–$95.

Los Urracas

Address: Playa la Ropa Box 141, Zihutenejo 40880, Mexico
Telephone: (52) 755-4-20-53

Located on Playa la Ropa, the area's most beautiful beach, is this attractive shady property exploding with lush tropical vegetation. Private bungalows are scattered throughout the lovely gardens along meandering paths. Most of the rooms are set up for couples, but some of them have a small extra bed in a small alcove. Most bungalows look out onto the gardens rather than the beach; the two that look out onto the beach are the most modern and consequently the least charming. The place is a find and books up early in high season.

Accommodations: 16 bungalows. Each bungalow has a kitchen and a large porch. Most rooms have a double bed, and a few have a tiny second alcove bedroom.

$$$: Daily rates, double occupancy: $75–$125.

WHAT TO SEE AND DO

The staff at the NAUI-certified **Zihuatenejo Scuba Center** (Cuauhtémoc 3 near Alvarez, tel. 755-4-21-47) speak English.

MANZANILLO

Two sparkling bays, Manzanillo Bay and Santiago Bay, divided by Santiago Peninsula, are home to a variety of pleasant seaside resorts. The small coastal city of Manzanillo was once a railhead where cargo was transferred between ships and trains, and it's still an important Pacific port with a bustling seafront. The area is relatively undeveloped compared with the other Pacific coast resorts.

The tourism boom started with the opening of glitzy Las Hadas in the mid-seventies, and the region continues to add both luxury and moderate tourist accommodations along its bay and coastline, but at a much slower pace than neighboring resort towns. Its prices and selection of all-inclusive resorts, and its friendly low-key atmosphere, make it a popular family vacation destination. Downtown Manzanillo is worth visiting, especially in the evening when locals visit around the plaza.

Visitor Information: State tourism office: Costera Miguel de la Madrid 4960, km 8.5, 333/3-2277 is open Monday through Friday from 9 A.M.–3 P.M. and 6 P.M.–8 P.M.

Best Sweet Treat: The fresh-squeezed orange juice is some of the sweetest you'll ever taste.

WHERE TO STAY
Expensive

Grand Bay Hotel
Address: Isla Navidad, Puerto de la Navidad, Colima 28200, Mexico
Telephone: 888-80-GRAND, (52) 335-5-6390, fax (52) 335-5-6071.
Website: www.grandbay.com

Just across the yacht channel from Barra de Navidad, about twenty minutes north of the Manzanillo airport, this fancy luxury hotel on 1,200 acres overlooks the Pacific Ocean, the Navidad lagoon, and the village and bay. A twenty-seven-hole golf course and active marina is what attracts many of its guests, and those with children in tow enjoy the use of a *Club de Niños* (children's program) in its own brightly colored room. Nongolfing adults in the family can use the extensive spa facilities or take all types of excursions arranged by the hotel. The hotel's beach is on the lagoon and a better beach is opposite the hotel on the bay. High chairs and cribs are available for guests' use. The hotel's architecture has a traditional Mexican charm, with arches, fountains, patios, and lavish gardens.

Accommodations: 191 units. Rooms have a king bed or two doubles, in-room safe, hair dryer, cable TV, ceiling fans, air-conditioning, and balcony. Suites have extra space plus a sound system and a team sauna.

For Kids: The children's program operates from 9 A.M. to 6 P.M. with crafts, games, and all kinds of other activities for children up to age eleven.

Special Features: beach, pool, swim-up bar, fitness center, twenty-seven-hole golf course, pro shop, driving range, three lit grass tennis courts, restaurants, spa, 24-hour room service, shops, beauty salon.

$$$: Daily rates, double occupancy: $250 and up.

Camino Real Las Hadas
Address: Av. de Los Riscos s/n, Santiago Peninsula, 28200 Manzanillo, Colima, Mexico

Telephone: 800-722-6466, (52) 33-34-0000, fax (52) 33-34-1370
Website: www.caminoreal.com

This landmark property in Manzanillo is best known for its exotic, domed, Moorish fairy-tale architecture and its role as the setting in the movie 10 with Bo Derek. Bolivian tin magnate Antenor Patino built the resort in 1974 to lure the rich and famous to this part of Mexico, and for over a decade it was one of the most luxurious resorts in the country. Its shimmer began to fade in the late 1980s when service and accommodations slipped, but it has recently been revived and upgraded to close to its former splendor by the Camino Real chain. Its gorgeous free-form pool is one place to stop and sun and swim, as is its modest 500-yard stretch of sandy beach. Golfers appreciate the excellent La Mantarraya golf course, and tennis fiends can play to their heart's content on ten tennis courts. There are a number of restaurants (and a complimentary continental breakfast is served to all guests), but best is Legazpi, the hotel's fine dining establishment that is well worth a visit with or without the kids. Despite the resort's size, it maintains a feeling of seclusion, with lush foliage and fifteen acres of gently sloping hillsides.

Accommodations: 236 units. Rooms are spacious with white marble floors, sitting areas, and furnished balconies, air-conditioning, minibar, TV, telephone, robes, in-room safes. Camino Real club rooms have beautiful bay views and private pools.

For Kids: Kids activities are available during the high season.

Special Features: beach, two pools, eighteen-hole golf course, ten tennis courts, marina, scuba diving, snorkeling, sailing and trimaran cruises, four restaurants, five lounges with live entertainment, disco, room service, shopping arcade, travel agency, beauty salon, barber shop.

$$$: Daily rates, double occupancy: rooms $252–$386, suites $360–$927.

Hotel Sierra Manzanillo

Address: Av. La Audiencia 1, Los Riscos, 28200 Manzanillo, Colima, Mexico
Telephone: 800-448-5028, (52) 33-33-2000, fax (52) 33-33-2272
E-mail: sierra@bay.net

An attractive inclusive hotel with a dawn-to-dusk (and then some) assortment of activities is for those who like their fun to be organized. Its twenty-one floors (with elevator) of rooms overlook La Audencia beach on one side and a pleasant hillside on the other. There's a large free-form pool practically on the beach, and a children's pool, watersports concessionaire, kids club, and free drinks that are part of the package.

Accommodations: 350 rooms and suites, most have balconies overlooking the beach or the hillside. All rooms have air-conditioning and minibar. Rooms have either a king bed or two doubles, plus a table, chairs, and a desk.

For Kids: A kids program is available for ages two to ten.

Special Features: beach, pool, four tennis courts, seven restaurants and bars with nightly entertainment, health club, aerobics classes, scuba diving lessons, room service, beauty salon, and a 24-hour currency exchange.

$$$: Daily rates, double occupancy all inclusive: $240–$375. Children six and under are free, seven to twelve $25 per day.

Moderate

Club Maeva
Address: Santiago-Manzanillo Road at Playa Miramar, Manzanillo, Colima 28200, Mexico
Telephone: 800-466-2382, (52) 33-35-0593, fax (52) 33-35-0395

A monster of an inclusive with nonstop action for all ages, this resort thankfully has a pool restricted to those eighteen and over, so the few guests who didn't bring their kids can get away from the noise and laughter. Special fun for kids includes crawl-through railroad cars, a small puppet theater, a video game room, and a pool with a long curving water slide. A children's program is available for toddlers. Family-oriented entertainment is offered each night in the Tropical Hut while a disco attracts singles and couples for evening fun. The property is across the street from the beach, but there is a pedestrian bridge across the highway that leads to the pleasant beach lined with umbrellas, snack stands, and a few artisans' stalls. Singles and couples stay in hotel rooms, families of three or four people are assigned a one-bedroom villa, and families of five or six people stay in a two-bedroom villa.

Accommodations: 514 units: rooms have one king or two double beds; one and two-bedroom villas have kitchenettes and terraces.

For Kids: Two- to twelve-year-olds are divided into age-appropriate groups. Children age eight and up can go to the beach; younger children stay and enjoy activities in the playrooms, kiddy pool, and playground.

Special Features: beach, twelve tennis courts, four swimming pools, four restaurants, bars, small theater, dance club, scuba, snorkeling, windsurfing, kayaking, volleyball, basketball.

$$$: Inclusive daily rates, double occupancy: per adult age thirteen and over $75–$125; children seven to twelve $43–$60; two children under seven are free, third child pays regular kids' rate.

PUERTA VALLARTA

A combination of spectacular beaches—twenty-six miles of superb coves, secluded shorelines, and busy downtown beaches—combined with a true feeling of colonial Mexico makes this town of 300,000 one of Mexico's most popular vacation destinations. Once a sleepy seaside village, tourism first got started in the 1950s, but it wasn't until 1964 when John Huston filmed *The Night of the Iguana* on a deserted cove that the town was catapulted into the international eye. Richard Burton was the star, and cinema queen Liz Taylor arrived soon after filming began to keep her *amore* company despite the fact that they were both married to other people—all providing fodder for the gossip mills and showering the tiny and quaint village with international attention. Now, 2.5

million people visit each year, but despite the crowds, the town is still pictur-esque, with cobblestone streets and whitewashed red-tile-roofed houses and a crafts market that has one of the best selections of native crafts and beautiful goods anywhere in Mexico.

Playa de Oro, just north of town, is the main hotel hotel beach, and was the original resort strip built up in the sixties and seventies. You'll find an assortment of high-rise hotels and shopping malls with little natural beauty other than the beach, but you can stay here (or in a few other areas in the region) and head into the beautiful downtown to enjoy the restaurants and quaint cafés. To get a glimpse of unspoiled Mexico, visit the villages of Yelapa and Quimixgo of Las Animas, both accessible by boat.

WHERE TO STAY
Expensive

Four Seasons Resort Punta Mita
Address: Punta Mita, Bahia de Banderas, Nayarit 63734, Mexico
Telephone: 800-332-3442, (52) 39-16000, fax (52) 329-16060
Website: www.fourseasons.com

This sparkling new Four Seasons Resort just north of Puerto Vallarta is a winner for golfers, beachcombers, and any family with young kids. Situated on 1,000 acres that contains four different ecosystems—seaside, desert, jungle, and mountains—the resort has worked hard to maintain its surrounding nat-ural environment's native flora and fauna. Its excellent and well-planned chil-dren's program, one of the best in the industry, is offered on a complimentary basis.

Rooms are housed in thirteen quaint, low-rise, clay-tile roofed Mexican-style *casitas*. All guest rooms feature full ocean views from their terrace. The resort has a private Jack Nicklaus–designed championship golf course with seven ocean-side holes and several hundred acres of lush, rolling hills and flowering landscapes. The dramatic (and optional) 19th hole features a 199-yard carry over water to a natural island on a rock outcropping called the Tail of the Whale.

Guests can enjoy the white sand beaches of Bahia of Banderas, which is also a natural sanctuary for four types of marine turtles. During the summer, guests can observe the turtles' nesting and hatching phases and if they're lucky, may spot baby turtles scurrying into the ocean after hatching. Each winter, migra-tory gray whales can be seen from several on-site vantage points.

Accommodations: 113 guest rooms and 27 suites. All rooms have a private balcony, safe, minibar, coffeemaker, air-conditioning, and ceiling fan. Many suites have their own private plunge pool.

For Kids: The Four Seasons trademark "Kids for All Seasons" program runs year-round in the spa area with indoor and outdoor activities, plus a wading pool adjacent to the patio.

Special Features: beach, pool, fitness center, full-service spa, whale and dolphin watching, snorkeling, sailing, deep-sea fishing, scuba diving, non-motorized water vehicles, tennis (four night-lit), eighteen-hole golf course, pro-shop, restaurants, 24-hour room service, beauty salon.

$$$: Daily rates, double occupancy: $350–$800. Children under age eighteen free in their parents' room.

Presidente Inter-Continental

Address: Carr. Barra de Navidad, km 8.5, Puerto Vallarta, C.P. 48300, Mexico
Telephone: 800-327-0200, (52) 322-80-508, fax (52) 322-80-146
Website: www.interconti.com

Small for the Inter-Continental chain at only 139 spacious suites, this hotel sits on an almost private beach on a sheltered sandy cove that is protected by rocky points on both ends. It shares the beach with just two condominium complexes, ensuring great privacy on the shore for years to come. Higher-end rooms have furnished balconies, tile floors, and white wood furniture. Bathrooms are spacious with marble bathtubs/showers.

Accommodations: 139 units are all suites, with air-conditioning, furnished balconies, and telephones.

For Kids: Kids Club activities year-round.

Special Features: beach, pool, watersports equipment rentals, lit tennis courts, fitness room, sauna, activities program, game room, three restaurants, two bars, travel agency, shops, car rental.

$$$: Kids under eighteen free in parents' room. Daily rates: $250–$360 per night for a double, $320–$650 per night for a suite.

La Jolla de Mismaloya

Address: Off Hwy. 200 at Mismaloya Bay, 48300, Puerto Vallarta, Jalisco, Mexico
Telephone: 800-322-2344, (52) 322-80-660, fax (52) 322-80-500
Website: www.puerto-vallarta.com/jolla

This massive hotel dominates Mismaloya Bay, allowing its guests to really spread out on the beach. The other half of the beach is home to numerous thatched-roof restaurants and boat launches. Plan to wander the beach and grab a bite of lunch while your kids dig in the sand. This area was once the set of *The Night of the Iguana* and is now a major tourist attraction. Its location is a fair distance from town, but the hotel offers plenty of distractions to keep guests entertained. From the hotel, visitors have a view of the rock formations rising from the sea.

Accommodations: 303 one- and two-bedroom suites with kitchens.

For Kids: The Kids Club entertains kids with piñatas, treasure hunts, and beach activities.

Special Features: beach, four pools with waterfalls, Jacuzzis, fitness center, shops, five restaurants, bar, two tennis courts.

$$$: Daily rates: $293 per night for a one-bedroom suite

Moderate

Westin Regina Resort

Address: Paseo de la Marina Sur 205, Puerto Vallarta, Jalisco, Mexico
Telephone: 800-228-3000, (52) 322-11-100, fax (52) 322-11-141
Website: www.westin.com

The Westin Regina is notable not only for its striking architecture, but for its excellent service as well, and its daily kids program makes it a good match for parents looking for vacation time both with and without their kids. The resort is large, spread over twenty-one acres of grounds and 850 feet of beachfront, yet it remains intimate by secluding each of the four swimming pools from each other with tropical vegetation. There's a playground right next to the beach, and many of the resort's restaurants have children's menus. The design of the hotel rooms combines classic Mexican comfort such as large windows open to ocean breezes, smooth concrete floors to cool hot feet, and charming cultural details such as the creative display of wood-carved animals. The hotel's floors are scaled back from the ones below, allowing for private balconies. Views are better from higher rooms, but rooms on the lower floors have easier access to the pool and the beach.

Accommodations: 280 rooms and suites, all with tile floors, wood furnishings, in-room safes, air-conditioning, minibar, TV, telephone, bathtubs, and showers.

For Kids: A Kids Club and a playground on the beach.

Special Features: beach, playground, four swimming pools, (one of which is oceanfront), health club, three lit grass tennis courts, two restaurants, two poolside bars, massage services, salon, Marina Vallarta Golf Club, 24-hour room service, travel agency, car rental, shopping area.

$$$: Daily rates, double occupancy: rooms $115–$195; suites $245–$495.

Camino Real Puerta Vallarta

Address: Carreterra de Navidad, km 3.5, Playa Las Estacas, Puerto Vallarta Jalisco, C.P. 48300, Mexico
Telephone: 800-722-6466, (52) 322-15-000, fax (52) 322-16-000
Website: www.caminoreal.com/puertovallarta

Nestled between a dramatic mountain range and a beautiful white-sand beach, one of Puerto Vallarta's first hotels can still claim a secluded atmosphere despite the nearby infiltration of condos and time-shares. Tropical gardens act as a cushion to keep the resort comfortable and private. A natural waterfall cascades down the mountain through blooms of white jasmine only to trickle out to sea. Rooms have marble floors and white stucco walls. Private terraces are equipped with large hammocks, perfect for long, relaxing siestas. Estacas beach offers calm waters for swimming and water sports. Camino Real has one of the best restaurants around, the award-winning La Perla.

Accommodations: 387 spacious rooms and suites, all with air-conditioning, minibar, TV, telephones, bathrobes, and in-room safes.

For Kids: Kids program operating in December, July, and August.

Special Features: beach, two swimming pools, beach *palapas*, two lit grass tennis courts, watersports center, health club, three restaurants, shopping arcade, 24-hour room service, travel agency, and car rental.

$$$: Kids under eighteen free in parents' room. Daily rates, double occupancy: room $130–$250, suites $400–$1,050.

Budget

Hotel Playa Los Arcos

Address: Olas Altas 380, 48380 Puerto Vallarta, Jal.
Telephone: 800-221-6509, (52) 322-21-583, fax (57) 322-16-000
Website: www.playalosarcos.com

The Playa Los Arcos Hotel is located seven blocks south of the Rio Cuale, in the heart of Los Muertos beach, but the atmosphere is far from dead. Lining the streets to either side of the hotel are the quaint sidewalk cafés common to Olas Altas, and downtown is just a short walk away. The rooms are divided among three separate buildings, each with a unique feel. The main building is where all the action is, with 180 small and simple rooms, some with balconies, surrounding a beachfront pool. Around the corner is another, more tranquil building containing forty suites with kitchenettes; a third complex houses thirty-five apartments with semiprivate pools. Breakfast is included in the rates.

Accommodations: 185 units with air-conditioning, TV, telephones, and carved wooden furniture.

Special Features: A *palapa* beach side bar, coffee shop, gourmet restaurant, pool, and central courtyard.

$$$: Daily rates, double occupancy: $48–$82; suites $76–$105.

MAZATLÁN

Mazatlán is Mexico's largest Pacific Ocean seaport and a vacation resort city that claims the longest stretch of uninterrupted beach in Mexico. Directly east of the southern tip of Baja California, the city has some of the best sport fishing in Mexico, where the meeting of the Sea of Cortez and the Pacific Ocean creates a natural fish trap. Sportfishers find bill fish and bass fishing just offshore and sailfish and marlin a bit farther out.

Known as "the pearl of the Pacific" because of its gorgeous beaches, it's also a busy commercial center with a lively port and fertile surrounding country that produces tons of produce that is shipped to the United States. It's the closest resort area to the United States and the price of high-end accommodations can be quite reasonable—almost half that of Cancún.

In addition to enjoying the beach and the fertile fishing grounds, families should visit downtown Mazatlán—with its central market, plaza, and cathedral—to experience a real Mexican city. Your children will enjoy a climb up El Faro, the world's second highest lighthouse, where they'll be dazzled by the magnificent 360-degree view at the top. Avoid the town during Easter week and carnival, when students by the thousands turn the town into one big party. **Tourist Information** Coordination General de Turismo, Avenida Camaron Sabalo, Tel. 16-51-60/65.

Best Sweet Treat: Sidewalk stands sell popsicles in funny shapes: my kids liked the Pink Panther pop and the dracula with a chocolate outside and a bright red center.

WHERE TO STAY
Moderate

Hotel Camino Real
Address: Punta de Sabalo s/n, 82100 Mazatlan, Mexico
Telephone: 800-722-6466, (52) 69-13-1111 fax (52) 69-14-0311
Website: www.caminoreal.com

Resident iguanas are regular visitors and you'll find them dozing in the sun on the grassy lawns or seawall of this resort. Set on a rocky cliff overlooking the sea on the quieter west end of town, the hotel's beach is protected on both sides by rocks that break the waves and calm the water. The property is secluded and landscaped with lush gardens. Although it's not one of the Camino Real chain's poshest resorts, it's a good value for a secluded getaway on a pretty cove.

Accommodations: 169 rooms, half with balconies. All have air-conditioning, minibar, TV, telephones, and marble floors. Junior suites come with king-size beds and sofas.

For Kids: A children's program operates during July, August, the Christmas holiday, and Easter week.

Special Features: A small heated pool, watersports, two tennis courts, two restaurants, two bars, a travel agency, a boutique, and room service. The front desk will arrange deep-sea fishing and golf excursions.

$$$: Children under twelve free in their parents' room. Daily rates: rooms $130–$150; suites $190.

El Cid Mega Resort
Address: Camaron Sabalo, 82100 Mazatlan, Mexico
Telephone: 800-525-1925, (52) 69-13-3333, fax (52) 69-14-1311
Website: www.elcid.com

El Cid is a huge resort offering every service and amenity imaginable—a 100-slip marina, a full-service spa and fitness center, a school of golf, its own deep-sea fishing fleet, cultural tours, all the watersports, and a half mile of beach. Its 1,320 rooms are spread over nine hundred acres in three large buildings—Castilla, El Moro Tower, and Granada—that share a common reception area. Room choices are vast, from time-share-style condos to hotel rooms and suites with kitchenettes. To fill all the rooms, the hotel regularly offers package deals to independent travelers and also has a convention and wholesale business, so be sure to ask when you inquire about a stay. In addition to the endless array of sports, there's a large shopping arcade, a fancy disco, and all kinds of restaurants. The lengthy stretch of beach in front of the hotel is partially roped off, discouraging vendors and providing guests with lounges and *palapas* for shade.

Accommodations: 1,320 units; all have air-conditioning, TV, minibar, telephones, and balconies.

For Kids: The Mega Kids Club operates during vacation periods and summer vacation and offers a wide variety of activities for children.

Special Features: beach, eight fresh- and saltwater swimming pools with bridges and waterfalls, watersports center, sailing school, marina, twenty-seven-hole golf course, fourteen tennis courts, spa, disco, fitness room, fishing, shopping arcade, fifteen restaurants and lounges, baby-sitting.

$$$: Children under twelve free in parents' room. Daily rates, double occupancy: $80–$700.

Holiday Inn Sunspree
Address: Av. Camaron Sabalo 696, Mazatlan, Mexico
Telephone: 800-465-4329, (52) 69-13-2222, fax (52) 69-14-1287

The Holiday Inn chain serves up plain and simple rooms that are reliably clean and comfortable. Their Sunspree properties operate in warm vacation areas and offer special activities and programs to lure families. A Kids Club operates daily, and a small playground amuses the children when they're not playing in the pool or on the small beach. The pool is so close to the beach, at some angles it looks like the pool and ocean meet.

Accommodations: 183 rooms with TV, refrigerator, coffeemaker, and hair dryer.

For Kids: Kids Spree program provides activities for kids ages six to fifteen, and there is a playground.

Special Features: beach, two restaurants, two bars, pool, tennis courts, fitness room, and beach volleyball courts.

$$$: Kids under eighteen free in their parents' room. Daily rates, double occupancy: $94.

Pueblo Bonito
Address: Av. Camaron Sabalo 2121, Mazatlan, Mexico
Telephone: 800-442-5300, (52) 69-14-3700, fax (52) 69-14-1723

The all-suite nature of this pleasant hotel makes it an excellent value for families wanting to cook their own meals while enjoying all the advantages of a first-class resort. There's a full-service watersports center and a fitness center with a gym, massage, and sauna, plus restaurants, when you need a break from cooking. It's attractively Mexican in style, with a multihued exterior, domed ceilings, colorful tiles, arched windows, and antique art. Peacocks and flamingos stroll the beautifully landscaped grounds and large koi swim in small ponds. The swimming pool is divided by a bridge into two sections—one more adult oriented, and the other the center of splashing fun. A long row of *palapas* line the beachfront, offering shade when your little ones have exhausted themselves in the sun.

Accommodations: 247 suites with either two double beds or one king-sized bed with hand painted headboards, carved wood furnishings, balcony, kitchenette, and air-conditioning,

Special Features: beach, fitness center, two swimming pools with a swim-up bar, watersports center, restaurants and bars, shops, beauty salon.

$$$: Kids under eighteen free in parents' rooms. Daily rates, double occupancy: $110–$150.

Budget

La Casa Contenta
Address: Av. Rodolfo T. Loaiza 224, 82110 Mazatlan, Mexico
Telephone: (52) 69-13-4976, fax (52) 69-13-9986

La Casa Contenta is one of the most popular of Mazatlan's budget properties, and for good reason: its seven one-bedroom apartments and a large three-bedroom house right on the beach all have fully equipped kitchens at a very reasonable price. Even though you're right in the heart of the tourist area, the resort has a secluded atmosphere. The furnishings are simple and there are no TVs or phones in the rooms, but all units have attractive decks or terraces. An excellent find—book far in advance.

Accommodations: Seven one-bedroom apartments that sleep four, one three-bedroom beachfront house that sleeps eight with three baths, a living and a dining room, and even servant quarters. All units have kitchens, decks, and air-conditioning, but no TVs or telephones.

Special Features: beach, swimming pool.

$$$: Daily rates: $62–$146.

Days Inn Suites Don Pelayo
Address: Av. del Mar 1111, 82000 Mazatlan, Mexico
Telephone: 800-325-2525, (52) 69-83-2221, fax (52) 69-84-0799

Located on the North Beach at the edge of the *malecon*, the Days Inn is a newly refurbished budget resort that is an excellent buy for families. Suites come with kitchenettes though the rooms do not, but all units have air-conditioning and satellite TV. There are two pleasant swimming pools plus a wading pool for little ones and a reasonably priced coffee shop.

Accommodations: 168 units, with air-conditioning, a king bed or two double beds. Waterfront rooms have small balconies. Suites have minibars and kitchenettes.

Special Features: Restaurant, bar, two pools, and tennis courts.

$$$: Daily rates, double occupancy: $55.

WHAT TO SEE AND DO
Mazagua is a family aquatic park with a water slide, a wave pool, and other attractions. Open daily 9 A.M. to dark.

Baja California/Los Cabos

The long, skinny Baja peninsula, bordered on one side by the Pacific Ocean and on the other by the Sea of Cortez, is a land of dazzling contrasts where sharp, arid, and craggy desert terrain is bordered by the intense and brilliant blue of the sea. Longer than Italy, a road now links both ends of the peninsula, from the American border to Los Cabos at its southern tip. The Los Cabos area is the heart of the peninsula's tourism, although you'll find beach resorts near the border and quaint Mexican villages sprinkled throughout the region.

Before the developers turned Los Cabos into a world-class resort filled with luxury hotels, time-shares, marinas, and golf courses, wealthy sportsmen visited to partake of some of the best sportfishing in the world. The confluence of the Pacific Ocean and the Sea of Cortez create one of the world's most productive fish traps, and early visitors endured a drive over hundreds of miles of rutted rocky road or a terrifying plane ride into a tiny airport. Now hotels and condominiums crowd the villages and a two-lane paved highway and a modern airport make traveling easier, but sportfishing fanatics still come for big game, especially marlin. Excellent surfing and windsurfing is found along this coast, and there are golf, tennis, and horseback riding, too, for action-oriented families.

Two separate towns constitute Los Cabos: San José del Cabo, and Cabo San Lucas with an eighteen-mile-long road connecting them, called the Corridor. San José del Cabo is the most Mexican of the two towns, but families may want to visit rather than headquarter here because the Pacific Ocean waters are too rough for swimming. Cabo San Lucas is the central tourist zone that was once a fishing and canning village and now is a lively tourist playground that overflows with college students at spring break time.

Whales come each winter, just as they have for centuries, to feed and raise their young in the warm waters of the Sea of Cortez. Whale-watching expeditions are easily arranged and are well worth the expense.

Listed here are a selection of resorts that are particularly well-suited for families, along with more moderately priced properties and a few real budget finds, two of which are in quiet little Pueblo la Playa, which has a particularly calm and lovely swimming beach.

WHERE TO STAY
Moderate

Hacienda del Mar
Address: Corriedor Turistico km 10, Lote D, Cabo del Sol, Mexico
Telephone: 800-537-8483, (52) 1145-8000, fax (52) 1145-8002
Situated on one of Cabo's safest and most beautiful beaches and surrounded on three sides by the Cabo del Sol Golf Course, this luxury resort, reminiscent of a Spanish colonial inn, debuted in 1997 and has been expanding ever since.

The property is located in a secluded area yet is only minutes from the town of Cabo San Lucas—either a long walk or a short cab ride away. Families are comfortable in the deluxe studios or colonial rooms, but can really spread out in the suites and town houses if budget permits. The watersports center has jet skis, kayaks, snorkeling gear, and anything else you might need, and fishing charters are easily arranged.

Accommodations: 169 rooms and suites. Rooms have two twin, a king, or two double beds, suites have a variety of bed configurations, some have kitchens.

Special Features: beach, swimming pool, tennis court, scuba diving, sailing, windsurfing, snorkeling, kayaks, jet skis, restaurant, bar, paddle tennis.

$$$ Daily rates, double occupancy: rooms: $139–$279, suites $340–$1,600. Children under five free in their parents' room.

Hotel Presidente Inter-Continental

Address: Bulevar Mijares s/n, 23400 San José del Cabo, B.C.S., Mexico
Telephone: 800-327-0200, (52) 11-42-0211, fax (52) 11-42-0232
Website: www.interconti.com

The Inter-Continental Hotel in San José del Cabo is an unobtrusive set of three-story adobe buildings rising from the sand next to the estuary Estero San José right at the end of the hotel zone. It offers accommodations on the inclusive plan, and if your is an action-oriented family, you can satisfy your family with nonstop fun at a decent price as two children under twelve can stay free in their parents' room. The resort is home to the largest swimming pool in San José and offers horseback riding along a gorgeous beach, tennis, bicycling, snorkeling, watersports, beach and pool volleyball, a PADI dive center, shopping tours, and much more. If you crave solitude, try to get one of the rooms overlooking the estuary where your can observe herons, egrets, and other wildlife right from your terrace.

Accommodations: 250 rooms and suites have air-conditioning, shaded terraces, and king-size beds.

For Kids: An all-day kids club has activities designed for ages five to twelve. Baby-sitting service is also available.

Special Features: beach, two pools, swim-up bar, kiddy pool, four restaurants, two tennis courts, disco, golf, bicycling, fishing, horseback riding, room service, and a shuttle to Cabo San Lucas making two trips a day.

$$$: Daily rates, double occupancy: $155–$195, suites $210. Room rates include meals, drinks, and all activities except for motorized watersports and scuba diving.

Melia San Lucas

Address: Playa Medano, 23410 Cabo San Lucas, B.C.S., Mexico
Telephone: 800-336-3542, (52) 11-43-4444, fax (52) 11-43-0420

The Melia is a popular hotel set in the middle of all the excitement Cabo has to offer, right on long Medano Beach with its calm and glassy waters. Downtown Cabo is minutes away on foot. Rooms are huddled around the oceanfront courtyard giving the whole complex a village feel. In the center of the courtyard is a two-level pool—one has a lively volleyball court set up, and the other pool features a swim-up bar covered by a *palapa*—and best of all (for your kids, anyway), the two are connected by a water slide. While sipping on cold drinks in the lobby, guests look out to see the stunning Los Arcos granite rock configuration holding its own against the forces of the sea at Land's End where the Pacific meets the Sea of Cortez. You'll find a full selection of watersports including parasailing and windsurfing.

Accommodations: 150 units. Rooms contain wicker furniture and are accented with colorful Mexican artwork. All rooms have terraces with ocean/pool views, air-conditioning, minibar, coffeemaker, safe, and a king bed or two double beds.

Special Features: beach, two heated pools, large hot tub, watersports equipment rentals, bicycles, two lit tennis courts, three restaurants, live nightly entertainment, two bars, room service, hair salon, gift shop, car and motor scooter rentals.

$$$: Kids under twelve are free in parents' room. Daily rates, double occupancy: $167–$232, suites $325–$375.

Palmilla

Address: Apartado Postal 52, 23400 San José del Cabo, B.C.S., Mexico
Telephone: 800-637-2226, (52) 11-44-5000, fax (52) 11-44-5100
Website: www.palmillaresort.com

Cloaked in swaying palms and adorned with bougainvillea, the Palmilla sits atop a rugged cliff overlooking the Sea or Cortez. The hotel was originally built in 1956 and accommodated mainly sportfishermen, but is now a home away from home for vacationers looking for a relaxing getaway on one of the sweetest beaches on the Sea of Cortez. The architecture is traditional Spanish style, with white-stucco walls and red-tile roofs, and guest rooms have handcrafted furniture and walls dressed with traditional Mexican folk art. Though none of the rooms are directly on the two-mile-long the beach, they meander along the shore in a series of *casas*. Families may prefer the two-bedroom suites or five-bedroom casa. Snorkeling is spectacular in the resort's protected snorkeling cove, and a second beach is overlooked by a tiled swimming pool. The resort's safe swimming beach is a two-minute walk from the hotel. Rates include a continental breakfast that is delivered to your door, and the lunch and dinner menus feature some of the best food in Cabo. A watersports center can arrange sportfishing or scuba diving, and a twenty-seven-hole Jack Nicklaus golf course wraps around the property.

Accommodations: 114 rooms and suites have a king bed or two double beds; all have air-conditioning and ceiling fans, and a complete bar that is restocked daily. Most rooms have ocean views.

Special Features: beach, oceanside pool with a swim-up bar, book and video library, fitness center, tennis courts, croquet lawn, watersports center offering scuba diving and deep-sea fishing, kayaking, horseback riding, sunset cruises, whale-watching trips, two Jack Nicklaus signature golf courses, room service.

$$$: Children under fourteen free in their parents' room. Daily rates, double occupancy: $175–$2,500.

Budget

Hotel Mar de Cortez

Address: Lazaro Cardenas s/n at Guerrero, 30032 San José de Cabo, B.C.S., Mexico

Telephone: 800-347-8821 or (52) 114/3-0032, fax (52) 30232

Website: www.mardecortez.com

This well-priced hotel about two blocks off the main square is made up of two sections of rooms: the older, built in the 1960s, has more charm but smaller rooms, while the newer section is more spacious but its rooms are reminiscent of a standard motel. Families should select one of the suites that has accommodations for four people. There's a large pool under the shade of palm and banana trees, and a restaurant plus a freezer for your catch if you manage to land some big fish. The bar closes at 10 P.M. to ensure that all guests enjoy a good night's sleep. Reserve early, as word is out that this family-run establishment is a good buy. The beach is one mile away, about a twenty-minute walk and the marina is fifteen minutes away.

Accommodations: Seventy-two rooms have air-conditioning and screened windows, and some have small patios facing the swimming pool. Rooms in the older section can accommodate up to two people in one queen bed or two twins, while the newer rooms have two double beds. Suites have a king bed and two twins or two doubles and two twins. Rooms and suites do not have TVs or telephones

Special Features: pool, restaurant.

$$$: Daily rates: double $56, triple $62, quad suite $66. Note that credit cards are not accepted.

La Playita

Address: Pueblo la Playa, Apdo. Postal 175, 23400 San José del Cabo, B.C.S., Mexico

Telephone: 888-288-8137, phone/fax (52) 11-42-4166

Website: www.mexonline.com/playita/sqq

For those looking to play hermit for a week, La Playita is the spot to do it. Located down a long and bumpy dirt road, La Playita is isolated from the action in San José del Cabo, yet just two miles away when you feel like venturing out. Every single room in this resort is only steps away from the deserted beach, which is the only swimmable beach in the San José area. The pool is roomy enough for lap swimming, and visitors often enjoy taking fishing trips on one of the small boats available for rent on the beach. Rooms are simple yet comfortable, and two penthouses have kitchenettes. A restaurant is a two-minute walk away.

Accommodations: 24 rooms and two penthouse suites all with screened windows, air-conditioning, ceiling fans, satellite TV, two queen beds, and ample closet space. Telephones are available at the front desk. The penthouse suites have one or two separate bedrooms and kitchenettes.

Special Features: Restaurant, bar, pool, beach, and fishing.

$$$: Daily rates, double occupancy: $62–$80.

El Delphin Blanco Cabanas and Casitas

Address: P.O. Box. 147, San José del Cabo, B.C.S. 23400, Mexico
Telephone: (52) 114-2-12-12, fax (52) 114-11-99
Website: www.art-and-soul.com

Just a little more than a mile from Cabo San Lucas is this charming bungalow-style resort not far from an unspoiled beach on the Sea of Cortez. It's about twenty minutes from the airport in the little village of Pueblo Las Playa, which has three restaurants. There are three types of simple accommodations available: cabañas, casitas, and campsites, and an outdoor community kitchen with a barbecue. A sandy beach is just a few hundred yards away. Fishing is out the door. In winter, whales frolic in the waters just offshore. Owner Mrs. Asa Franzen de Lopez speaks English and will tell you about the interesting sites in the area, such as the hot springs and the best diving and snorkeling areas.

Accommodations: Cabanas have a double bed and a single bed and share community bathrooms; casitas have private baths and coffeemakers, and either a queen bed or a double and a bunk bed. All units have refrigerators. Campsites allow you to pitch your own tent or rent a tent from El Delphin.

Special Features: outdoor communal kitchen.

$$$: Daily rates: cabanas $36–$50; casitas $45–$65; campsites w/o tents $10, with tents $15.

Index